Building Your Own Home

Building Your Own Home

Murray Armor and David Snell

Sixteenth edition

EBURY PRESS

London

3   5   7   9   10   8   6   4   2

First published in the United Kingdom in 1978 by Prism Press

Updated editions 1980, 1981, 1982, 1984, 1985, 1986, 1987.
Revised editions 1983, 1988, 1989, 1990, 1991, 1993, 1996.

This sixteenth revised edition published in 1999 by Ebury Press
Random House
20 Vauxhall Bridge Road
London SW1V 2SA

Random House Australia (Pty) Limited
20 Alfred Street, Milsons Point, Sydney
New South Wales 2061, Australia

Random House New Zealand Limited
18 Poland Road, Glenfield
Auckland 10, New Zealand

Random House South Africa (Pty) Limited
Endulini, 5a Jubilee Road, Parktown 2193, South Africa

Random House UK Limited Reg. No. 954009

www.randomhouse.co.uk

A CIP catalogue record for this book is available from the British Library.

ISBN: 0 09 186943 9

This book contains only general advice, and neither the author nor the publishers will accept responsibility of any sort for
the consequence of the application of this advice to specific situations. In particular, planning and other legislation is
described in outline only, and professional help should always be obtained when dealing with these matters.

Produced and designed by Colin Spooner and Myra Giles.
Printed in Singapore by Tien Wah Press.

Foreword

This is the 16th edition of *Building Your Own Home* and the first one following the untimely death of Murray Armor. As I write this foreword, I am conscious of the importance of this book to many people and the part it has played in helping so many fulfill their dreams of building their own home over the more than two decades since its first publication. I first met, and then worked for and with, Murray in 1976, and when his family asked me if I was interested in preparing and rewriting this new edition it took me about three nanoseconds to say yes.

Without turning this into an obituary, the story of how this book first came into being and the story of Murray's first entry into the selfbuild field runs parallel with the creation and expansion of the selfbuild movement into the homogenous industry that exists today. It was always there of course but, apart from a brief revival following the end of the war, those that did it ploughed an extremely lonely furrow, their efforts consigned to the eccentric end of the social spectrum. So it was that when Murray and Jeanne Armor returned to England in the mid sixties, after a distinguished career in the Colonial Services, they found a seller's market where builders would build what they wanted to build and still, when they released a phase, there would be queues around the block. Where choice was limited to whether a bathroom would have a pink or a primrose suite and where design was something that decent people left to those who knew better.

It wasn't good enough for Murray and Jeanne but, try as they might, they still couldn't find what they wanted. They had one stoke of luck though, in that during their honeymoon in America they had appeared on a coast to coast quiz show and they had won enough money to be able to buy a large walled garden in a Nottinghamshire village close to where Murray had got a job managing a block manufacturing company. That was it really; they had enough for the land and they had the income from Murray's new job and a bit of cash left over but certainly not enough to be able to employ a builder to build them any sort of a house that would even be remotely suitable. From this came the idea of selfbuilding and from

that came the whole string of events and achievements that have led to the selfbuild industry in its modern form.

There were no books available on selfbuilding, no advice on how to deal with the vast bureaucracy, no package deal companies. Builders merchants positively discriminated against selfbuilders, to the point where sometimes, purchases had to be made by friendly builders who would, nevertheless, often want a cut and almost always wanted the money up front, long before they would have to part with it. Architects couldn't get their heads around the concept of a person telling them what they wanted rather than accepting what they, as professionals, had designed for them. There were a few plan books but all they did was sell a set of plans and licence to reproduce or build the plans, as drawn. Happily one plan fitted almost exactly what Murray and Jeanne wanted and, without going through the whole story of their selfbuild, they managed to get through it whilst, at the same time, making every mistake you could possibly imagine. "Why isn't there any help?" was their constant refrain, even as they moved into their new home and realised that despite all the things they had done wrong, they had still managed to build at under half the cost that any of the local builders had wanted to charge. "If there was more help, would more people do this?" they asked themselves.

They gave themselves the answer when they formed their first package deal company, the descendants of which trade to this day, although long since cut loose by Murray as he moved on to other things. The idea was simple. A book of standard plans with a package deal price for the basic structural materials and help in getting planning permission and Building Regulations approval. It was an instant success and its development was followed, emulated and expanded upon to the point where now there are a wealth of differing companies offering a whole host of different services, most of which are discussed in later chapters of this book.

Through all of this Murray became more and more aware of the dearth of information that was available to the prospective selfbuilder. People came to him for advice on so many different aspects of selfbuild and, over the years, the pigeon holes of pamphlets that he prepared to answer their problems, grew and grew in number to the point where he decided that the only course of action was to put them all together in book form. The first edition of *Building Your Own Home* hit the shelves in 1978. It was what the industry had been waiting for and it found a market with all of those who wanted to selfbuild, even those who had studiously turned their back on involvement with any of the recognised professional bodies or commercially available assistance and advice. Some idea of the importance of this first edition was that Colin Spooner, the original publisher, is still involved in the production of the book, and used the book as inspiration to build his own home in the early '90s.

Now the industry was growing up and, from these simple beginnings, and due in large part to the influence of this one man, the modern version that we see today took form and became a cogent movement within society. Soon there were monthly magazines, their development actively encouraged by Murray, and within a few short years those magazines transformed the industry once more as they expanded into, firstly annual exhibitions and then regular road shows that toured the country, exciting and promoting the concept of selfbuilding. So successful is the promulgation of the ideas and the ideals of selfbuilding, that now, as is chronicled in the selfbuild stories at the back of this book, people who would, in previous years, never even have come across the idea of selfbuilding, successfully complete their own projects without ever questioning their motives. Such is the move from periphery to mainstream that has occurred within my working lifetime.

In 1983 *Building Your Own Home* was joined by a plans sales book, written by Murray, called *Home Plans*, and in 1986, he added a further, larger, book of plans, *Plans For A Dream Home*, both of which made an undoubtedly important contribution to the available help and advice for selfbuilders. *Plans For A Dream Home* is still available and a new companion book, with exciting plans drawn from across the industry, *The Home Plans Book*, now joins this distinguished stable.

I have maintained much of the format and content of the previous editions and I do hope that, for those purchasing this updated version, the changes that I have made are helpful and that this book can sit comfortably alongside your treasured earlier editions. Tens of thousands of selfbuilders have realised their dreams as a direct result of reading *Building Your Own Home*, and for those buying the book for the first time, I do hope that this edition proves just as instrumental in helping you achieve your goal of a new selfbuilt home.

I do feel I have to repeat a comment made by Murray in all of the earlier editions. In conversational and colloquial language it is exceedingly difficult to weed out single gender terms and to change them, at all times, to either a neutral gender or a direct reference to both sexes. For example, a granny flat is a term used for self contained living accommodation that could just as easily suit grandad and my use of its common name is not, in any way, meant to be mutually exclusive. I would, therefore, ask that you to imply this in any reference or passage.

Likewise we still suffer from a mix of metric and imperial measurements.

Contents

1 Introduction

Selfbuilding isn't a modern phenomenon and in early civilisations it was, of course, the norm rather than the exception. At some time, however, society in general, turned its back on it and, with the move to the cities, the general skills within the populace at large, began to be lost in favour of living in 'homes' that were provided by or built by others. But not lost entirely, I'm pleased to say, and I can well recall buying a book, for 20p at a jumble sale, with the very same title of this book, that was published in 1894. It was a very different book. It didn't, of course, have to bother about planning laws or any rules and regulations apart from a reference to the approval of the local Squire. It gave details of how to slake lime, how to cut lathes from willow trees and how to ram mud and hair to form a wall. In short it was a detailed technical manual, listing just how to perform the various tasks involved in building your own home and, as such, even its modern repetition would not, on its own, serve to guide the prospective selfbuilder through the minefield of conflicting advice and legislation that one now needs to get through.

Building Your Own Home, in this and in previous editions, explains what is involved in building for yourself and describes exactly how it can be done in this age of regulations and restraint. It does not attempt to be a technical manual and instead, concentrates on leading you along the paths of discovery, exploring the options available and evaluating them without fear or favour.

It's estimated that at least eighteen thousand families per year move into new homes that they have either built themselves or had built to their own specifications. Most of them get exactly what they want in terms of accommodation and most of them can demonstrate significant increases in equity, with the market values of their complete homes far outweighing the costs of both building and land purchase. All of them were involved in a great deal of decision making, most of them managed the building work themselves, some did some of the work with their own hands, and a few, a very few, did everything themselves. On average the whole process took them between a year and eighteen months, with six to nine months spent finding a site and setting everything up, and the same amount of time spent doing the actual building work. They built homes that were well constructed and finished, and, whether they had an architect to handle everything for them or whether they managed the whole project themselves, they invariably found it immensely satisfying.

There are many differing terms in use to differentiate between the various ways of building for oneself and the situation is confused by inventive journalists who constantly try to coin new phrases, the latest of which I've noticed is BIY (Build it yourself), destined for a short life due to its phonetic similarity to the well known DIY. Of the eighteen thousand families who move into a new home that they have not simply bought from a builder of developer, about 11,000 are true *selfbuilders* in that they are involved in a degree of self management on site. These are the ones who do not place a single contract with a builder, and who make use, in whole or in part, of subcontract labour, that they employ and directly manage on site. They are easily identified by the arrangements they make to reclaim the VAT at the end of the project, which, without

---

Selfbuilders and individual builders annual statistics
18,000 individual builders build on their own land

of which

over 11,000 build as selfbuilders.
* They use sub-contractors without formal contracts.
* They provide all the management.
* They reclaim their VAT.

and

approximately 7,000 are *not* selfbuilders.
* They have formal contracts with builders.
* They make all the choices but do not provide site management.
* They do not pay VAT.

H M CUSTOMS & EXCISE
VAT POLICY DIRECTORATE
Commercial Division, Construction and Utilities Branch
4th Floor West, New King's Beam House
22 Upper Ground, London SE1 9PJ

Tel 0171-865-4885   Fax 0171-865-4824

Dear Mr. Snell,

Listed below are the numbers of DIY claims from selfbuilders
under Customs and Excise Notice 719 that this Department has
processed during the financial year 1997/98.

A total of 10915 claims were processed.

Your sincerely,

for VAT Policy Directorate

STATISTICS FOR SELFBUILD

The VAT figures quoted in the letter above enable the total of selfbuild homes completed to be estimated as follows:

10,915 families reclaimed the VAT which they paid in building their new homes in the financial year 1997/8.

1000 homes are estimated as built by the 10% of all individual selfbuilders who reclaim their VAT through their business accounts (mainly rural enterprises).

200 families are estimated to have moved into new homes built by members of selfbuild groups during the year.

This gives a total of 11,115 selfbuilt homes completed during the financial year 1997/8.

No figures are available for Individual Homebuilders who place a single contract with a builder, and who do not pay VAT on their builders invoices as they are zero rated. However, experience from the large selfbuild developments and other sources suggests that they total at least 60% of the number of selfbuilders. This gives another 8000 homes completed, which brings the total of individually built homes to at least 20,000, or 11.5% of all private sector homes built in the UK in that period.

stealing the thunder from the later chapter on VAT, may need some explanation here, as the fact of it being recoverable, is both an incentive towards selfbuilding as well as the means by which we can calculate and arrive at the numbers who actually do it.

New housing and the conversion of non residential buildings into dwellings, is zero rated under the VAT regulations. That means that, although VAT has to be paid for materials at source, and in subsequent sales, this VAT is then recoverable. If a builder builds a new house for a client, then he will recover the VAT on any purchases he makes and he will not, therefore, pass its costs on to his client. If a selfbuilder elects to buy his own materials, then the VAT that is paid out in their purchase is recoverable from the Customs & Excise, at the end of the project under a special scheme that is outlined in the chapter dedicated to VAT.

Those 11,000 *selfbuilders* are the hard and fast figures, reproduced and verified by the letter, printed above, from the VAT Policy Directorate, inflated just a little by the numbers who build as members of selfbuild groups, of which you may read more later in the chapter dealing with group and community selfbuild. What about the other 7000? Well, these are the people who are, probably, more properly called *individual builders* and they are the ones who place a single contract with a builder to construct their new home. They still buy their own land. They still have a huge amount of input into the choice of everything from design right though to the intimate details of the specification, but they don't make a VAT reclaim, as their builders do not charge the VAT to them that they themselves can recover. Their numbers are estimated as being anywhere between 60% and 150% of the VAT total, but common perception, and the gut feelings of the package companies, tends towards the 60% being certainly demonstrated.

Whichever way you cut it, these numbers are big and if you compare them to the numbers of houses built by each of the major house builders they are huge. One in ten new homes are owner built and when you relate those figures to detached houses and bungalows the proportion

rises to one in four. Small wonder therefore, that those sections of the building industry who, for so long, ignored the selfbuild industry have now woken up to its existence and clamour for a place at the feeding trough. Small wonder that, even as they struggle to come to terms with this 'new' breed of potential client, they trumpet their new found support and invent a history which includes their contribution. Consumer choice in new housing has well and truly arrived and selfbuild is its vanguard but, before you go off thinking that we are unique in this, you might like to consider that we, in Britain, have a lot of catching up to do. In Austria selfbuild accounts for 80% of owner occupiers, in France and Germany 60% and in Australia and America it approaches 25%.

For most people, it has to be said, the purchase of a ready made home remains a primary objective, with the decision to buy being part of the accepted transition to maturity and independence. Almost all of the publicity, promoted by builders, estate agents and building societies is consistently designed to lead the average person to this fulfilling, safe and socially desirable decision. So what makes people take the decision to step outside this cosy norm to spend up to eighteen months of their life concentrating all of their efforts, finances and thoughts on selfbuilding and are those that do it so very different to their fellow countrymen and women?

Is it all down to money? Well, money comes into it of course and building for yourself does offer considerable savings to those involved. This often leads to the assumption that it is these cost savings that motivate the selfbuilder in the first place and that they build cut price homes.

Nothing could really be further from the truth and, although there are smaller and cheaper homes built by selfbuilders, by far the largest number of them are four bedroomed, double garaged properties built, and fitted out, to a very high standard indeed. Yet in well over two decades of involvement with selfbuilders, I could probably count on the fingers of one hand, those people whose sole motivation was financial and, when I think of them, there is no doubt in my mind that this small group form the least

Right - Typifying an Essex cottage, with its simple lines belying the accommodation available, this lovely house designed by D&M Ltd., looks truly authentic right down to the choice of materials and the exposed rafter feet.

Below - A really grand looking house from the Potton stable. Elegant simple lines, echoing more graceful days, display a character that crosses county boundaries and, with a simple change of external materials, would fit in almost anywhere.

successful of selfbuilders, at least in terms of the satisfaction achieved.

By far the greatest motivation for selfbuilding is, and always has been, the desire to achieve and create one's own individual living environment from within one's own resources, and the fact that increases in equity of between 15% and 30% are often demonstrated seems almost incidental. We were cave men for many thousands of years before estate agents arrived, and the urge to find one's own cave is deep rooted. In a world where opportunities for self-expression are diminishing, building one's own home both satisfies primaeval urges and exorcizes modern frustrations, with enough obstacles to be overcome to provide a sense of achievement. The rationale may be economic - the motivation is more basic. The new home is an expression of the individual himself, and it will be built to the highest standard to which he can aspire. At the very least the standard will be several levels above the property developer's lowest common denominator. Selfbuilders come from all walks of life from manual labourers through to highly paid professionals, from soldiers through to vicars. Some are more successful than others but any measure of success has to be related to an almost complete lack of failure. Some have advantages in that, either the pattern of their work allows them to spend more time on site or the nature of their employment means that they can take advantage of accommodation during the build period. Some of them have skills that are directly attributable and included in their selfbuild, whilst others possess little or no knowledge of building. What the most successful, undoubtedly, have in common, is a capacity to get things done, to see beyond the immediate problem and to seek out the solution.

It starts and it ends with management and the critical paths of that management are set down in the following chapters of this book. Whether you are intending to get out there with a shovel and a trowel to do everything yourself, or whether you are planning to go to the Bahamas until a builder gives you a shout and tells you that it's all over and it's alright to come home and move in, management is still the key. Management of your

ideals, tailoring them to your needs and your resources. Management of your own skills and the husbandry of other people's skills. All of this needs to be carefully evaluated and thought through before ever site is bought and before ever pen is put to paper or sod first turned.

"Does one have to have a lot of technical knowledge to selfbuild?" is an almost constant refrain from would be selfbuilders. Not at all. Of course, if you've got a good grounding in the general sequence of events then that's all to the good but the facts are that, in the main, you're going to be employing people for the skills they possess and your job is going to be the management and co-ordination of those trades and of all of their ancillary requirements. No lay person can, in the short time frame between deciding to selfbuild and its execution, learn all that there is to know about all or any of the trades and sequences involved. All selfbuilders can learn enough to know what questions they should be asking the experts they have employed and to understand the answers. All selfbuilders should learn that, if they're not happy with the answers or, if they feel that they are heading in a direction that they're not happy with, they should stop and seek another opinion or another choice. All selfbuilders should temper any knowledge that they might gain with, what is the ultimate skill in selfbuilding, the ability to manage people and situations. Learning about bricklaying to the point where you can chat with your bricklayers about the type of sand they would prefer, or the additives they want you to get for them, is fine, but if that knowledge leads to you standing behind them in a white coat barking instructions, don't be surprised if the relationship very quickly breaks down.

So, how do you increase your knowledge? Well, you're at the very beginning of a book that will, by its end, have given you much of what you need to know about selfbuilding. Nevertheless, there's a lot more that you can do and what follows is a short list of suggestions. What I would warn against is taking single interest or narrow perspective advice too much to heart. Always keep the bigger picture in mind and remember that what the successful selfbuilder

The selfbuilder's savings — a comparison with developers' costs

Developers' costs	Selfbuilders' costs
1. Land cost	1. Land cost
2. Interest on land cost over a long period	2. Interest on land cost over a very short period
3. Design and planning fees	3. Design and planning fees
4. Site labour costs	4. Site labour costs, which may be as low as the developers' or could be at premium rates
5. Labour overheads — cost of labour between profitable jobs, in periods of bad weather, holidays, Training Board levy, N.I. etc.	5. No labour overheads
6. Materials at trade prices	6. Materials probably at trade prices
7. Up to 10% of materials damaged/ wasted/stolen on site	7. No site losses
8. Office overheads	8. No office overheads
9 Staff costs and staff overheads	9. No staff
10. Expensive general contractor's insurance, NHBC warranties, Trade Association levies	10. Cheap simple site insurance and the premiums for your chosen warranty scheme
11. Sales costs	11. Nil
12. Provision for bad debts	12. Nil
13. Interest on building finance assuming worst sales situation	13. Interest on building finance kept to a minimum
14. Corporation Tax or other revenue involvement	14. Nil
15. Return required on capital	15. Nil

has to do is balance out all of the advice, some of which may be conflicting, most of which is probably true and all of which needs weighing up with just one objective in mind – your new home.

Books

I wouldn't want to pretend for one moment that this is the only book on the market that is worth reading on the subject of selfbuilding. There are literally hundreds of technical books on single subjects like bricklaying, plumbing or laying drains, and they vary from DIY manuals for the layman to text books for students. It is unlikely that the ones that suit you will be in your local bookshop, and the only place to find all of them is in the Building Bookshop at the London Building Centre. If you cannot get there in person send for their catalogue.

If you are using a library to obtain books of this sort, look at the publication date of any book that you find there and ignore anything written more than five years ago. Also ignore American books unless you propose to build in America.

Useful books in a different category are the Building Regulations and the NHBC and Zurich Custom Build handbooks, both of which are

considered invaluable by some selfbuilders and ignored by others. The Building Regulations are published in sections, so you can buy only those which are of interest to you. You may find the various illustrated commentaries on them easier to read than the regulations themselves. All are on display at the Building Bookshop (see below).

The NHBC have a catalogue listing a wide range of publications concerning every aspect of their services, and the building standards which they promote. They are a good buy.

Magazines

There are two major monthly publications, *Homebuilding & Renovating* (formally *Individual Homes)* and *Build It,* both available at most newsagents or by subscription. In addition there are a further two, *Selfbuild* and *Selfbuild South West,* with the former being relatively new and the latter fulfilling a regional role with plans to expand a similar model into different regions. They are essential reading and, as well as

detailed case histories about other selfbuilders, they contain a whole host of information and features. Most importantly they also carry a great deal of advertising and from this, and the brochures you can send for, you can keep yourselves up to date with what's available and what's going on in the selfbuild scene.

Exhibitions

Without doubt, it is the exhibitions, both national and regional, that have done the most to transform the selfbuild industry over the last decade. They are not to be missed by the serious selfbuilder as they feature hundreds of firms providing all sorts of services, from manufacturers and package deal companies through to architects and financial agencies. In addition there is rolling programme of seminars, with advice centres on hand to help with any queries that you may have. *Build It* magazine runs two major national exhibitions, one at Alexandra Palace in London, every September and another in Scotland. In addition they hold at least five large regional shows throughout the year, advertised in the magazine. *Homebuilding & Renovating* magazine runs the Individual Homes show at the NEC every spring and, in addition, a southern regional show in the summer and, again, details and dates are available within the magazine itself.

In preparing the selfbuild stories for this book, and for other articles I've written, it is remarkable just how many of the projects really got off the ground, either as a direct result of a visit to the shows or through the information gained at them. Sometimes the visits were almost accidental, sometimes they were planned long in advance but, in so many instances, the shows seem to have been the catalyst for the eventual selfbuild and they certainly were the means by which many selfbuilders made their choices.

Show houses

Some of the package deal companies have show houses and many that don't can arrange for you to visit the finished homes of some their clients. Potton has a show village of three houses available for inspection, by appointment, with regular seminars. Scandia-Hus have a group of fully furnished showrooms at their offices, again available for inspection by appointment.

The Building Centre

The Building Centre at 26 Store Street, London, a minute's walk from the Goodge Street tube station, has six floors of displays of everything to do with house building. Leaflets on the materials on display are available at a special counter, and there is both a general advisory service available and various agencies dispensing advice to enquirers. All of this is aimed at the architect and builder, but enquiries from the public are welcome.

Selfbuild clubs

Some of the smaller independent builders' merchants and in particular, Elliots of Southampton, run selfbuild clubs where you can go along to meet other selfbuilders and listen to guest speakers. They also have a regular newsletter giving product and pricing information, together with a constantly updated land list. There is also an Association of Self Builders, as well as the Marley Self Build Club and Grahams Builders Merchants, who provide selfbuild information packs.

BUILDING ON YOUR OWN:

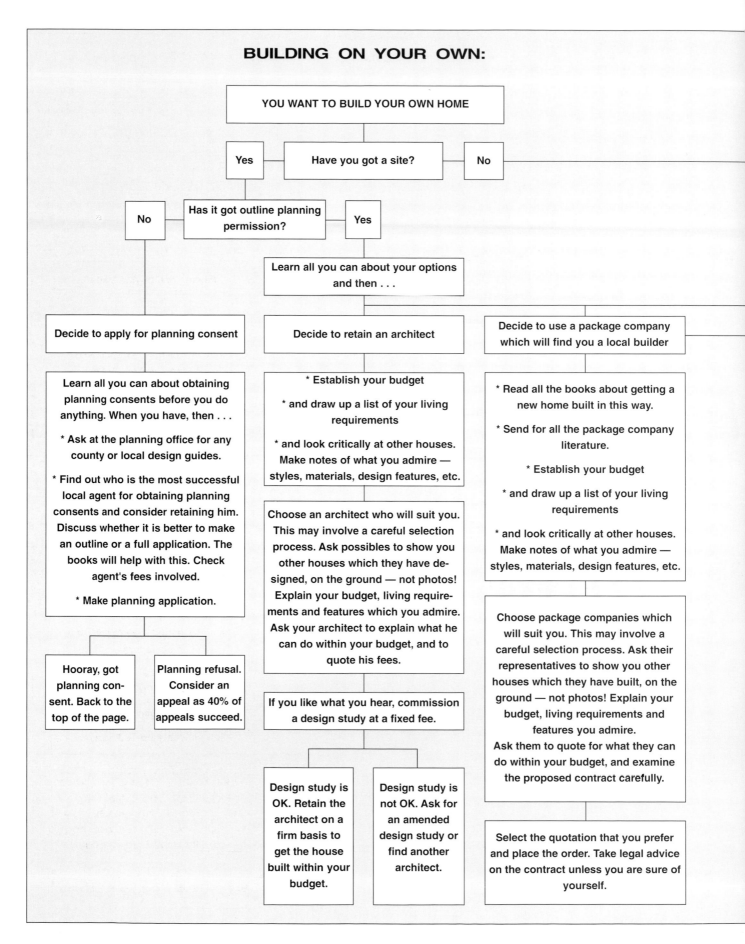

YOU WANT TO BUILD YOUR OWN HOME

Yes — **Have you got a site?** — No

No — **Has it got outline planning permission?** — Yes

Learn all you can about your options and then . . .

Decide to apply for planning consent

Decide to retain an architect

Decide to use a package company which will find you a local builder

---

Learn all you can about obtaining planning consents before you do anything. When you have, then . . .

* Ask at the planning office for any county or local design guides.

* Find out who is the most successful local agent for obtaining planning consents and consider retaining him. Discuss whether it is better to make an outline or a full application. The books will help with this. Check agent's fees involved.

* Make planning application.

---

* Establish your budget

* and draw up a list of your living requirements

* and look critically at other houses. Make notes of what you admire — styles, materials, design features, etc.

---

* Read all the books about getting a new home built in this way.

* Send for all the package company literature.

* Establish your budget

* and draw up a list of your living requirements

* and look critically at other houses. Make notes of what you admire — styles, materials, design features, etc.

Hooray, got planning consent. Back to the top of the page.

Planning refusal. Consider an appeal as 40% of appeals succeed.

Choose an architect who will suit you. This may involve a careful selection process. Ask possibles to show you other houses which they have designed, on the ground — not photos! Explain your budget, living requirements and features which you admire. Ask your architect to explain what he can do within your budget, and to quote his fees.

If you like what you hear, commission a design study at a fixed fee.

Choose package companies which will suit you. This may involve a careful selection process. Ask their representatives to show you other houses which they have built, on the ground — not photos! Explain your budget, living requirements and features you admire. Ask them to quote for what they can do within your budget, and examine the proposed contract carefully.

Design study is OK. Retain the architect on a firm basis to get the house built within your budget.

Design study is not OK. Ask for an amended design study or find another architect.

Select the quotation that you prefer and place the order. Take legal advice on the contract unless you are sure of yourself.

THE CRITICAL PATHS TO MAKING A START

Choose between

Joining a selfbuild group

Finding and buying a site

Become an individual selfbuilder

Learn all you can about selfbuilding on your own.

Choose whether to build entirely on your own or to use a package company that provides a special service to selfbuilders.

Building entirely on your own

Learn all that you can:

* Read all the books.

* Find other selfbuilders and learn from their experiences.

* Go to conferences and exhibitions.

Turn to the end of the chapter called 'Selfbuilding with sub-contractors' and follow the relevant flow charts and programmes.

Learn all that you can about group selfbuild:

* Read books and contact all the relevant agencies listed in this book.

* Attend selfbuild conferences.

* Send for brochures from Selfbuild Management Consultants operating in your area.

* establish a budget for the new home and how much you can spend on the site (books will tell you this).

* Assess whether you are likely to be able to build on it within your budget, and draw up a checklist of things to consider when looking at possibilities.

* explain to your solicitor that you are land hunting and that you will want some fast legal action when you find what you are looking for.

Start looking for a site:

* Contact estate agents in the area and consider appointing an estate agent as a buying agent to find you a site.

* Place 'Building Plot Wanted' ads in local papers.

* Cultivate personal contacts. Most selfbuilders buy plots this way.

* Study magazines with relevant adverts.

* Join a national land-finding agency

Found your plot? Don't commit yourself without legal advice. While your solicitor is making his searches you investigate any snags over building on the plot. Read and follow the books.

Bought it! Back to the top of the page!

2 Finance

There are some people who will wonder at the first substantive chapter being about finance, when for most people thinking about selfbuilding it seems as if it is the availability of land that is the most important first hurdle. Well, important as that may be, finance is where it all starts, and setting the budget, working out how much you can pay for the land and just how much the project, as a whole, is going to cost is where it should start. In some cases, if the budgets do not work out, it can also be where the whole thing finishes or, at the very least, is put on the back burner until the time and the finances are right and available.

Building for yourself is about spending money. It's also about spending huge amounts of money in comparison to the average person's normal expenditure. It's about spending that money so that you get exactly what you want and it's also about spending it so effectively that you end up with a bigger or better house than the money would buy on the open market. How you manage this money is as important as the management of the whole of the building work, and far more hazardous. The Building Inspector, the warranty inspector, your architect – all and any of these will be concerned to see that nothing untoward goes wrong with the construction but far fewer checks are in place to prevent a financial incompetent from wilfully steering their selfbuild ship onto the rocks. Having said that, most of the reputable package deal companies and architects specialising in the selfbuild market will ask the relevant questions at an early stage and, as long as they're told the truth, will try to steer you in the right direction. This has every bit as much to do with their interests, of course, as it has with yours, as they will want to be assured that they are going to get paid. No selfbuild venture can be entirely risk free but if you follow the paths laid down in this book and use and listen to common sense and professional advice, rather than ill informed pub talk, you are most unlikely to have any major problems. It is a fact that selfbuild disaster stories are, happily, few and far between.

When planning the finances for your new home, start off with the following questions and carefully evaluate all of the answers before moving onto the next stages:

1. If a mortgage is going to be involved, how much can be borrowed and how much is it going to cost?

2. Where is the money coming from to pay for the site before a start is made?

3. Where is the money coming from to pay for the materials, sub-contract labour and services as work progresses?

4. How can this be managed so that I pay as little interest as possible?

5. What warranties will be required by those who are providing the mortgage?

6. How can insurances cushion the major risks?

7. How can all this be done without placing an unacceptable strain on the family's pattern of living?

First of all, not all those who build an individual home require a mortgage. If you read the magazines for individual home builders, or attend the exhibitions, the very high profile of the building societies may lead you to assume that all selfbuilders take out the largest possible mortgages. The experience of the package companies is quite different, and suggests that up to 50% of those who build for themselves do so using family funds and the proceeds of selling an existing house. The figures given by some building societies for the number of selfbuild mortgages which they approve compared with the known number of selfbuilders tends to confirm this. Let us look at the position of these fortunate people, most of whom had parents who bought modest homes in the 1950s for perhaps £1,500 and who have now inherited properties which may be worth £150,000. Families inheriting two such homes are dealing with serious money, although they may think of themselves as ordinary people.

People with the problem of how to best deploy family wealth have an interesting situation when planning to build a new home, and if it is a new situation for them, it may not be easy to handle.

Wealthy families that have guarded inherited money down the generations have their own attitude to it. They tend to consider their funds as family assets, and use trusts and other devices to ensure that it passes smoothly down the generations with the minimum interference from inheritance tax. Often this is their favourite topic of conversation, and very boring they can be too! In contrast, those whose modest capital has always been kept in the Post Office until they inherited a couple of houses with telephone number values, tend to keep their affairs very much to themselves. They may refuse to face up to the fact that they cannot take it with them and that the taxman is lurking.

Inheritance tax is often described as a voluntary tax, because if someone makes appropriate arrangements at the right time, nothing at all needs to be paid. However, this involves giving money away in one way or the other, and just try discussing this with Aunt Lucy who, after a lifetime of being careful with money, is now worth a cool £500,000. If she is able to take a realistic view of things, she should be able to continue to enjoy her present standard of living indefinitely and ensure that her favourite niece and nephew use her money for a new house so as to avoid inheritance tax. This all depends on her seeing her capital as a family asset. If she does, there are various ways of going about it. If very large sums are involved, it is appropriate to make specialist arrangements and consider setting up a trust which will cost money but which is cheap at the price. Finding the right professionals to handle this may not be easy, since they should be totally independent and not people who are wanting to sell you some sort of financial service. A large firm of accountants is probably best.

If the funds involved are more modest, there are a number of straightforward approaches. The simple way of obtaining help with the cost of your new home from, say, an elderly relative, is for them to just give you the money that they intend will be yours someday, so long as they can then manage to live for at least another 7 years. After that the gift escapes inheritance tax, as do gifts from one individual to another so long as they do not exceed £3000 in any one year, although if Aunt Lucy didn't give you anything the year before, she can backdate her gift and give you £6000. In addition, outright gifts, which can be classed as normal expenditure 'out of income',

A realistic appraisal of your finances and careful financial planning is the first stage in building the home of your dreams.

are also allowable, as are some gifts made on the occasion of a marriage. Here, parents can each give a further £5000, grandparents £2500 and anybody else can give up to £1000, all of which could make a very useful contribution to anybody's budget for a new home. These figures haven't changed for donkey's years but they are a movable feast and could come to the attention of the Chancellor at any budget.

A more complicated way of going about this, but one that may appeal to an elderly person who has capital invested to earn interest, is for them to give you a mortgage. Anyone can provide a mortgage, not just a bank or building society, and tax relief is available for the mortgage in the ordinary way providing that the paperwork has been done properly. Any solicitor should be able to arrange this.

This really is a most useful approach. Suppose Aunt Lucy has £30,000 invested, currently earning her interest on which she pays tax. If she uses it to give you a £30,000 mortgage at 1% under the current mortgage rate she will get a better return (on which she will still pay tax), you will have a cheap mortgage on which you will get tax relief, and the money stays in the family. Aunt Lucy's will may have to be rewritten to avoid complications in the future, but this is not a complicated undertaking. If both parties are interested in Aunt Lucy living in a granny flat in the new home, a whole new range of possibilities is opened up and I shall discuss this in the chapter 'Designing a New Home - to suit your lifestyle'.

Turning now to bank or building society finance, it is first essential to understand what happened to various building society schemes to finance selfbuilders when the housing boom ended in 1989, as this affects the current attitude which the financial institutions take towards individual home builders.

Prior to 1987, banks and building societies normally required anyone building for themselves to find their own money to buy the site, following which they would lend the money for a house to be built on it, with the land itself as the security. When the house was built this loan was repaid by taking out a mortgage in the usual way.

It was very common for a bank to lend the building finance, and for a building society to issue the mortgage on the finished property, with the two of them working closely together. This meant that a very high proportion of borrowers had to sell their existing house in order to buy the site for a new one, moving into temporary accommodation until the new home could be occupied.

In 1987, when it seemed that the rise in property values would go on for ever, the National & Provincial Building Society launched a '100% finance' scheme for selfbuilders who had an existing home. This involved transfering their current mortgage to the N & P, who after a careful assessment of their proposals, would lend them a further sum to cover the entire cost of both buying the site and building a home on it. The interest on this further loan was rolled up with the capital, so that no additional repayments were required until the new house was occupied, the old house was sold, and the special selfbuilder's mortgage could be converted to a standard mortgage. This scheme attracted a four figure total of borrowers in a very short while, and everything went well until the housing market collapsed in 1989, when borrowers who completed their new homes found that they could not sell their old properties.

This caused serious problems for both the society and its borrowers and the situation attracted widespread publicity. The National & Provincial withdrew its scheme, much to the disappointment and near despair of the large number of people who were proposing to take advantage of it to finance their new homes. Other building societies, and in particular the Birmingham Midshires, had similar schemes up and running at the time and they too pulled out, although they were not as heavily committed and avoided large losses. Selfbuild lending began to curry bad favour with financial institutions and the situation went from bad to worse as selfbuild group after selfbuild group failed in the wake of the housing market crash leaving even more lenders with serious bad debts.

The memory of this lingers on and it is now virtually, and justifiably, impossible to borrow

100% of both the cost of the site and the costs of building on it, from a mainstream financial institution.

Building Societies still promote themselves within the selfbuild market. In any given year there is a different main player and they all tend to dip in and out like reluctant bridegrooms, afraid to leave this huge pool of business alone and equally afraid to fully commit themselves to it. Some of the larger building societies prefer to state that they deal with all applications for finance on their own merits, others have leaflets which describe their arrangements for financing those who are building on their own. The offers that they make are frequently changed, but in general they are crystallising down to the requirement that the borrower should sell their existing house and repay the old mortgage, following which they will then lend a proportion of the cost of the land, plus a further proportion of the building finance required. One current player in the market has ingeniously got around the problem of seeming to require its potential customers to sell up and move into temporary accommodation by saying that it has no objection to the provision of a selfbuild mortgage for the new house in tandem with the mortgage on the existing house, so long as the potential borrowers can demonstrate their ability to service both mortgages. In practice this means that only the seriously rich, those with an extremely small existing mortgage or those with an enormous income relative to their borrowing requirement can benefit, as the way it works is to deduct from the applicant's income the cost of the existing mortgage and then to treat the remainder as the total gross income. Now, all of this may seem unfair at first glance, but remember, it wasn't just the building societies who got their fingers burnt when everything changed so very quickly in 1988/89, it was ordinary people, just like you, and all of these new precautions and hurdles are there to prevent you coming a cropper just as much as they are there to protect the financial institutions.

Other building societies which do not advertise a special service for those building on their own, and almost all of the banks, will always discuss making appropriate arrangements with established customers, and often these are marginally more advantageous than those offered by the building societies which have formal arrangements for selfbuilders. Their enthusiasm for this and the terms which can be arranged will usually depend on an applicant's standing as an existing customer.

All lending which eventually leads to a conventional mortgage on the finished property is limited by normal building society considerations of maximum overall loans, income multipliers, valuation fees and administration fees. The only unusual feature is that some lenders charge a premium or surcharge on top of the standard rate of interest during the time that the house which they are financing is actually being built. This is supposed to cover the cost of their 'management' of your scheme. Most selfbuilders are under the impression that they are providing the management themselves but it will not help you to point this out to the branch manager.

Another issue here is the choice that has to be made between endowment and repayment mortgages, the early redemption arrangements and of course the interest rates. The pros and cons are always changing, and there are magazines available on the bookstalls which provide useful up-to-date information. If your finances are complicated because you are self-employed, work abroad, or have a significant investment income then you may decide to use the services of a mortgage broker. A number of these specialise in finding finance for selfbuilders, and advertise in selfbuild magazines. They can be very useful, although if the arrangements that they suggest are in any way unusual it is important to have them checked out by a solicitor or accountant.

Two cautions. First of all, do not be tempted to borrow further from any other source without disclosing it to the principal lender. Secondly, do not be tempted to exaggerate the cost of the land so as to gain an advantage. In other words, if you are buying a plot for £60,000, do not tell the bank it is costing £80,000 in the hope that you will get a 75% loan which will be equal to the whole of the real cost. This is sometimes advocated by those who should know better or who will even offer to arrange it for you. It is dishonest, and a potential recipe for disaster.

Whichever route you decide to take when arranging finance for an individual home, it is important to give careful consideration to how to make your approach to the lender in the best possible way. Imagine yourself in the chair of the branch manager concerned. He or she earns their reputation with their head office by arranging mortgages that are simple, straightforward, and generate no problems of any sort at all. Normally these are ordinary mortgages on ordinary homes bought on the open market. A proposal linked to a house which is yet to be built, and which may be being built on what they regard as a DIY basis is not in the category that they really like. You have to persuade them that your proposals carry no risk of any sort, and that you are very well able to handle everything in a completely risk free way. How do you do this?

Do not casually drop into a building society office and start asking about how they would help you if you decided to build for yourself. Instead, it is better to write and ask if they have any leaflets regarding the services that they offer to those who are having a house built on their own land. Study these leaflets carefully. At the right time, when you think you have learned all that is necessary to make it obvious that you know what you are talking about, make an appointment to call on the manager and go along equipped to demonstrate how well-organised a person you are. If you are married, or building with a partner, it is better that both of you should go along. Take with you a concise note of your budget for your lifestyle, your income and your outgoings, and also your rough budget for the project. If you know that you will only be able to borrow 75% of the project cost, explain where the other 25% is coming from. Produce a tentative programme for the work, and above all, make sure that you have allowed in your costings for the interest which you will have to pay on the loan – remember, as far as the manager is concerned, this is what it is all about!

One of the most important aspects of your loan will be the arrangements that are made in respect of stage payments and it really is essential that, right at the outset, you establish some sort of cashflow relating to income from these stage payments set against the outgoings to suppliers and labour. Banks and building societies normally offer stage payments in five stages - at completion of the foundations, at wall plate, at roofed in, at plastered out and on completion. They won't normally release monies until the relevant stage has been reached and they will then require that the building is inspected, usually by a surveyor appointed by the lender, and that his certificate is received before any funds are actually authorised for release. Even if they agree to accept the Stage Completion Certificates given by the warranty company or the Architects Progress Certificates, this can take an inordinately long time which can seem even longer if you're being hassled every day for money by a large bricklayer or you have an intransigent package deal company which will not release materials until such time as they have the money in their hands. However hard you try to jump the gun and prearrange the surveyor's visit this never seems to go to plan and the 'stop/start' that this creates is often a feature of those selfbuilds where stage payments are being used up to the hilt and there isn't a cushion of money to carry things forward. Try to make sure that your lender knows just how critical the timing of the receipt of monies is to you and, above all, make your builders and subcontractors aware of your particular problems before they crop up rather than afterwards; you'd be surprised just how helpful a tradesman can be if he knows that the money is going to be there and, on top of that, he knows that its getting there is reliant on his reaching a stage in the construction of the building.

Many of the package deal companies and, in particular, those where there is a bespoke or manufacturing element, require their monies up front or in stages in advance of any deliveries. In addition, stage payments are often front loaded to the point where the company can take their margin and leave a 'cost to complete' in their books. None of this needs to cause too much of a problem just as long as you've allowed for it all in your cashflow and, if you're making large payments in advance of deliveries, you try and make sure that the payments are made into a client's deposit account, of which more later. Certain of the larger and more reputable companies have long recognised that the selfbuilder does, sometimes, need a bit of help over the financial hurdles and they have recognised, too, that it's a question of *when* the monies will arrive rather than *if*. These companies have various schemes on offer, which can help you and, at the same time, guarantee their payment when the money finally comes through.

Building warranties

All lenders will want you to prove that you have arrangements for building warranties. This is an important subject. It is usual for all new homes to have warranties of some sort to guarantee that they are properly built and to provide for the cost of putting right damage due to structural failures. Such warranties are required by banks and building societies as a condition of mortgages, and also by a bank or building society providing a mortgage for any future purchaser of the house. If houses do not have such cover, special surveys are usually required when they are sold, and the properties are not such a good resale proposition as those with appropriate warranties.

The principal arrangements for this are: -

*   The NHBC 'Buildmark' warranty offered by the National House Building Council, which is a building industry organisation.

*   The NHBC 'Solo' warranty offered by the same organisation to accepted selfbuilders.

*   The 'Custom Build' guarantee offered to selfbuilders by the Zurich Municipal Insurance Company.

*   The 'Trenwick Willis Corroon' scheme which operates through the local authority Building Control Department.

*   Project Builder devised by F. E. Wright with the backing of Commercial Union and Sorema (UK) Ltd..

*   Architects Certification.

THE NHBC 'BUILDMARK' WARRANTY

This is the 'lighthouse' guarantee that everybody knows about, although it's ages since they dropped that particular icon. It's available to those selfbuilders who are using an NHBC registered builder in just the same way as any developer or house builder offers it to his purchasers. At one time the NHBC tried to enforce the fact that all of their registered builders had to offer this warranty to the exclusion of all others but that was held to be an unlawful restriction of trade so that, now, an NHBC builder may choose to offer one of the other schemes and, in particular, one from Zurich Municipal. Nevertheless, it is the NHBC that is the one that is undoubtedly recognised throughout the broad spectrum of the population, both lay and professional, and if we ever get back to the position of having a sticky housing market, it is this name which will achieve instant recognition with a prospective purchaser, or his advisors – a point that could well make the difference between having a sale or not. A builder who is registered with the NHBC has to pass certain basic tests of financial probity and building knowledge and, until he can demonstrate a clean track record, he is only allowed on the register as a probationer and is prohibited from advertising himself as a member. Before any work commences on site, and in cases where there is bad ground or where there are trees on site, at least 21 days in advance of a start, the builder must apply to register the proposed dwelling and send in the appropriate fee. The NHBC will check out the drawings with care, particularly in relation to any peculiar circumstances and then, in due course, they will allocate a registration number, which the builder's customer is advised of. The selfbuilder will usually have to tell his bank or building society of this registration and separate documentation is issued for the attention of the 'purchaser's' solicitor (They insist on referring to you as purchaser). As the work progresses but, in particular, at certain crucial stages before the work is irrevocably covered up, the inspector will come along to site and check the work for compliance with the regulations and accepted standards of workmanship. This is his total concern at this stage; your arrangements or relationships with the builder are not his responsibility - unless the builder dies or becomes bankrupt, in which case the NHBC will step in with limited and defined assistance. The only other time that the inspector becomes involved in the nature of your contract with a builder is when an agreement has been reached whereby the builder is only responsible for construction of the weathertight shell of the building. This is something which, up to now, has not been heavily advertised in the NHBC literature but can be easily arranged and authorised, as long as there is written evidence and understanding of the limitations of the work and responsibilities.

It is not generally understood, but the NHBC is principally an insurance company which undertakes to take on responsibility for the warranty for the structural shell and integrity of the building and, in so doing, requires that its registered members, the builders, take on responsibility for the other areas of the building and that they stick to those obligations on pain of being struck off the register. Even the structural warranty requires that the builder takes on full liability for the first two years so, in effect, with 'Buildmark', the NHBC is only exposed for the last 8 years of its 10 year warranty, so long as the builder remains in viable business.

Brief mention should also be made here of the fact that the NHBC is an Approved Inspector, authorised to approve and inspect under the Building Regulations. This means that a registered builder can opt to have all of his Building Regulations approval and inspections carried out under the auspices of the NHBC, negating the need for a separate application to the Building Control section of the local authority.

THE NHBC 'SOLO' WARRANTY

Prior to the 1998 exhibition at the Birmingham NEC, the NHBC had consistently stood clear from offering any scheme directly aimed at selfbuilders, apart from a pilot scheme which they had run in Northern Ireland which they emphatically and repeatedly denied would ever be brought to the mainland. All the while,

however, they must have been carefully evaluating the strength and nature of the selfbuild market and having, presumably, reached the conclusion that it was a viable market and that most selfbuilt houses are better built than many 'off the shelf' houses, they have entered the selfbuild scene with a vengeance. 'Solo' is specifically designed for the individual building their own home on their own land, using either subcontract labour or doing all or part of the work themselves. It notably excludes anybody who is not intending the home for their own or their immediate family's occupation, requiring a declaration to that effect within the original proposal form.

On application the NHBC inspector will arrange a meeting, on site, at which he will make a full appraisal of your proposals, explain the scheme to you and discuss the complimentary copy of the NHBC Standards which will have been sent to you. There is no requirement for technical qualifications or specific knowledge of the building industry or process, but there is no doubt that the inspector will be making an assessment of your ability to carry through what you're planning. If it is decided at that meeting, or as a result of it, that you aren't going to go ahead and that you won't be proceeding further with the NHBC, then your initial payment will be refunded in full.

Essentially the core cover that is provided is the same as for the 'Buildmark' scheme with the obvious exception that, with no builder being involved, the cover for the structural shell and integrity of the building is the sole responsibility of the NHBC for the full 10 year period. Under the 'Buildmark' scheme the builder would also have been responsible for the finishing trades for a period of 2 years and, therefore, under the 'Solo' scheme there is an optional Damage Limitation Period Cover available which will insure you for minor damage caused by latent defects for a period of 6 months. There is an additional premium for this extra cover and there is also a requirement that the work is carried out by bona fide subcontractors and that you enter into a formal contract with them requiring them to put right any faulty work within, at least, the 6 month period. Once again, therefore, the NHBC are only really at risk if the subcontractor fails to honour his obligations or goes out of business.

The NHBC divide their description of their 'product', for that is what it is, into two phases. *Phase 1* covers the period during the actual building works. The inspector will come along at various stages, which are, for a brick and block house: excavations, substructure, ground floor preparation, visual drainage, walls to 1st floor, walls to plate height, roof framing & masonry complete, first fix complete and, finally, completion and drains tested. For a timber framed house the stages are: excavations, substructure, ground floor preparation, visual drainage, timber frame erected, external leaf to 1st floor, first fix complete and finally, again, completion and drains tested. At each stage he will either, approve the work and issue a Stage Completion Certificate or, if the work is not up to scratch, he will require that any faulty workmanship is remedied and then, when it's done to his satisfaction, he'll issue the certificate. The important and exclusive thing is, that once a Certificate is issued then all of the work up to and including that stage is covered by the NHBC and you can go ahead and use the certificate as a tool to obtain any draw down of finance.

Phase 2 is when the building is finished and the full 10 year warranty is issued covering the main structure of the building, any defect or damage to flues and chimneys, defects to the drains and damage to the roof and tiling. It's worthwhile mentioning that the NHBC also offer a service giving help with SAP ratings (of which more later) and, in the same way as they do under the 'Buildmark' scheme, they can also take on the responsibility for the Building Regulations approval and inspection, on payment of extra fees as required. This last service is not available in Scotland, the Isle of Man and Northern Ireland and the entire 'Solo' scheme is not available for conversions, although I understand that this is under review.

At the time of writing the scheme is in its infancy and there is no doubt that there will be a few teething troubles. As it gets into its stride, changes will be made but there is no doubting that 'Solo' will be anything other than hugely successful, given the NHBC's vast experience of building and the housing market in general.

THE ZURICH 'CUSTOM BUILD' WARRANTY

This is the company that pioneered the idea and the actuality of selfbuild warranties, helping so many selfbuilders to achieve their dreams of a new home. In no small way, it is this scheme that enabled the selfbuild industry to change up a gear and it stood alone in the market for many years. I remember the buzz that went around the exhibition hall, at the NEC, in the spring of 1998, when the NHBC finally entered the field, and the speculation about why they had stayed away for so long and what had prompted them to finally devise their scheme. In fact, it turns out that the NHBC scheme owes much of its existence to the movement of staff between the two companies and the natural cross pollination of ideas.

Having said that, there are several major differences between the two schemes. First and foremost, the Zurich Municipal is not authorised by the government to perform the work or undertake the role of Statutory Building Control and Inspections. In practice that's not a drawback because, in any case, the 'Custom Build' scheme works by a tie up with the Building Control Department of the local authority. This means that the Building Inspector always visits their sites and that the 'Custom Build' inspections are timed to coincide with the statutory inspections made by the Building Inspector. In addition quality control inspections are made by 'Custom Build's' own surveyors as the work progresses. A strong argument can be made for the separation of these responsibilities and, for some, the very fact that two or more sets of inspections are being made by differing bodies can give added reassurance, especially when linked to the perception that the local authority Building Inspector has little or no commercial axe to grind.

The track record built up by 'Custom Build' over the years is enviable and bears fruit in the many testaments by selfbuilders to the help and assistance given by their staff and inspectors. Although not possessing the instant recognition

that the NHBC are favoured with, the Zurich 'Custom Build' warranty is equally as acceptable to most building societies and banks; so much so, that many house builders and developers now offer a variation on the scheme, known as Zurich 'Newbuild'.

As with any scheme, 'Custom Build' starts with the application form and its sending off with, in their case, a non returnable deposit after which you'll receive their Technical Manual & Builders Guidance Notes, which is, undoubtedly, an excellent reference book in its own right. They do insist on a few more things than the NHBC currently appear to require in that they demand that the house is designed by a qualified architect (or other professional), that the work is carried out by professional contractors or tradesmen and that full Building Regulations consent is sought and obtained. There is also an additional expectation that the selfbuilder should have a source of technical advice, a 'professional friend'. This would obviously come in the form of the architect or the package deal company, if they were using one, but, equally, the role could be filled by a suitable friend or somebody with the relevant knowledge of building. Whilst all of these requirements may, at first, seem a trifle pedantic, they are born out of years of experience and there is no reason to suppose that, as the 'Solo' scheme progresses, they too will not adopt similar requirements.

As with any warranty scheme, if bad ground or unusual ground conditions are suspected or known, then they will require a copy of a site investigation, soil report and/or foundation design. At the completion of the project a 10 year structural warranty will be issued with the option, on payment of an additional fee, of extending this to 15 years. There is also a scheme up and running for conversions and rebuilds called 'Custombuild Conversions Solutions' where the offer of insurance is subject to an initial survey report and the cover offered is for 6 or 10 years.

TRENWICK WILLIS CORROON

A bit of a mouthful of a name I'll agree, especially as it's also referred to as the Forest of Dean scheme after the local authority that originated it. Names apart, though, it's the simplest of all of the schemes in that it works through the local Building Control department and relies on their approval and inspection of the building as it progresses. It came about through the foresight of one man, Joe Chetcuti who is the chief Building Control officer at the Forest of Dean District Council. He built his own home after reading an earlier version of this book and very quickly realised that there was a vast duplication of responsibility with, on some sites, each stage being inspected by up to four different surveyors or inspectors, all of whom had to be paid for in some way. He also realised that with the privatisation of the Building Control function to the NHBC, the local authorities were increasingly at a disadvantage in that builders who required a warranty would be persuaded to leave all in their hands. He felt that the Building Control departments of the local authorities had unrivalled experience and he was sure that a warranty scheme which directly utilised their inspections and powers would be successful. He got nowhere with any of the established bodies in this country and it was only when he approached a French insurance company Sorema that he managed to get people to listen to what he had to say. Sorema recognised that the local authorities exercised their control under Statutory powers, with the full force of the law behind them and that, in consequence, if a warranty scheme could be tied around their inspections, such a scheme could also be offered at a very competitive rate. The French company then merged into an even larger conglomeration with an American company and the scheme was initiated. Full cover attachment is given from day one and provides for any defects in the design, workmanship or components of the structure of a new domestic dwelling that affects or causes physical loss, destruction or damage and/or affects or causes imminent instability to such a dwelling. Coverage automatically extends to include common parts, retaining or boundary walls and the drainage system within the perimeter of the building together with any garage or permanent outbuildings. The cover offered is 10 years, with an option to extend this to 12 years on payment of a slightly higher premium, and confidence in it is so high that it is applicable to any valid construction method and applies equally to new build, renovations and extensions. Anyone can apply, be they a builder, developer or selfbuilder and the rates at the time of writing appear to be significantly better than their competitors. Not every local authority has yet signed up to the scheme but, as time goes by, more and more are doing so. In any event there is nothing to prevent it being run without the direct participation of the local authority, so long as local authority Building Control and Inspections are made. Joe Chetcuti of the Forest of Dean District Council is the chap to talk to about regarding how you can take advantage of this scheme which I have a feeling will develop and may, very soon, end up with a brand name and a higher marketing profile.

PROJECT BUILDER

F. E. Wright, a medium sized Lloyds broker with extensive insurance experience, are offering, under the name of Project Builder, a structural warranty scheme, backed by Sorema (UK) Ltd. The scheme covers the whole of the UK and is available to selfbuilders whether they use a builder or subcontractors or even if they undertake the entire project on a DIY basis. You still need to have Building Regulations approval with the normal inspections carried out by the Building Inspector but, in addition, Project Builder will arrange for their own inspections to be carried out on their behalf by a specialist company, Tarmac Professional Services (TPS), once the government Public Services Agency and now privatised under the Tarmac group. The inspection stages are, footings prior to any concrete being poured, followed by one at plastered out but, if they deem it necessary and on difficult or special sites, they will come out and inspect at other times.

Cover is given for ten or twelve years, depending on premium and runs from the date that the certificate is issued following the final inspection.

ARCHITECT'S CERTIFICATION

In the years before the advent of the Zurich Municipal 'Custom Build' scheme, if a selfbuilder wanted to build with subcontractors or his own labour then, unless they could persuade a friendly NHBC builder to take them under his wing and almost pretend to be building the house for them, the only other way of achieving the necessary certification to satisfy the bank or building society, was to go for what is known as Architect's Progress Certificates.

This was an entirely different procedure to Architectural Supervision but there was, and still is, endless confusion between the two, exacerbated by what appears to be a deliberate blurring of the distinctions by some of the building societies. *Architect's Progress Certificates* are where an architect comes out to the site, at recognised, agreed and specified times, for an agreed fee of anywhere between £50 and £250 and certifies that, at the time of his visit, the building has reached a particular stage in its construction and that the work appears to have been carried out in accordance with the plans and specification. It is not necessary for the architect carrying out the certification to be the same architect who was responsible for the design. Differing architects will place different emphasis on their responsibilities under this arrangement. Some will want to make as certain as they can that the work has been carried out satisfactorily and some will merely be concerned that the correct stage in the construction of the building has been reached. Some building societies and banks leave the question of the architects actual responsibilities and obligations open for the architect to define, whilst others try and tie down the architect to a warranty which he clearly cannot give under this scheme and which would override, completely, any legal limitation by reference to reasonable skill and care. For this reason the current advise to architects is that they do not accept the wording or documentation provided by these institutions and that they confine their responsibilities and legal obligations to certifying that they have visited the property to inspect the progress and quality of the work to check, as far as they are reasonably able to do so on a visual inspection, that the works are being executed generally in accordance with the approved drawings and contract documents.

Architect's Supervision, on the other hand, involves the architect being responsible for every detail of the work, necessitating his visiting the site frequently and being involved in every aspect of the construction. It is relatively expensive and it is usually carried out by the same architect who has formulated the design, probably as part and parcel of his original arrangement with you.

Building societies and banks will accept Architect's Progress Certificates. They do not carry any warranty, as such, and the only way a claim can be established is for the selfbuilder to sue the architect who will then fall back on his Professional Indemnity Insurance. So, if you do go along this route it's a good idea to make absolutely certain that the architect carries such a policy and that the amount of cover under that policy is sufficient for your needs. The interesting fact is that these Progress Certificates and the liability of the architect extend only to the original party to the contract - that is the selfbuilder. The burden of the contract is not passed to any successor in title, so that anybody buying the house from the original selfbuilder would not be able to pursue a claim against the architect. Perhaps the banks and building societies have drawn a blind eye to this point in the past – it has always been open for them to insist on a collateral contract but, the instances where this has been the case are few and far between.

The same, of course, goes for Architect's Supervision but it can be argued that, with this service, the chances of anything going wrong are lessened to the point of slim. If an architect has designed a property and he is also supervising its construction then he knows, 'to the last nut screw and bolt', just what goes into that house and he can, not only watch out for potential problems but, head them off before they even occur. It is also likely that the architect will be responsible for the total construction and will therefore be just as involved in the second fix and finishing trades as he is for the structural parts of the building.

Recognition of these truths is given by the fact that the Zurich Municipal offer a discount if their warranty scheme is used in conjunction with an *ASBA (Associated Selfbuild Architects)* architect's supervision and inspection. I've no doubt at all, in my own mind, that before long, maybe before this book hits the shelves, they will have beaten a path to the NHBC door and tried to arrange a similar concession.

Before I leave this subject, just a word of warning about your choice of architect, should you decide to opt for Architect's Progress Certificates using a different architect from your original designer. Architects who work consistently in the selfbuild field, or are members of *Associated Selfbuild Architects*, are more likely to be amenable to your requirements and your aims. Others of, let's say, the more crusty persuasion might not be quite so sympathetic to your needs, might show distinct signs of sour grapes at the fact that you didn't go to them for their services in the first place and might, if you've used a package deal company, have a marked aversion to the whole concept of everything you're trying to achieve.

The Budget

So, how much can you afford to spend in total on building your new home and what can you hope to get for your money? Of course, everything depends on finding the right plot and on the design of the house but you have to start somewhere and the best place to start is by adding up all of the monies that are available to you, to find out just exactly what you can afford to go to.

For most people the money available to them will be:

* The money that you will have after you have sold your existing home and have repaid your existing mortgage.

* Plus the finance that you can hope to borrow to fund the new project, which will eventually become your new mortgage. At this stage take this as two and a half times the family income.

* Plus any other capital which you intend to spend on the new home.

This will give you your total budget, and it has then to be split between the various component costs of your new home such as land cost, building costs, fees of various sorts and, the one which is most often forgotten, costs relating to borrowing the money during the period of your selfbuild. So, what proportions should be allocated to each of these categories? Well how long is a piece of string? (A useless phrase if ever there was one and one, which is, used as many a get out – but not here). The land cost is likely to be the least movable object. Finding a plot is the first hurdle in the race and it's the one at which most selfbuilders fall, which is why the next chapters are devoted to its finding and acquisition. In parts of the country the land cost can account for as little as 25% of the total cost of the project whilst in others the very scarcity of any suitable land for building can mean that it can rise to as high a proportion as 60%! You'll know what it's likely to be in your area and by rough calculation of the type and size of plot you're going to be looking for you'll soon get to know what sort of prices you're going to have to pay. In this book it would not make sense to state definitive figures on land costs, which can vary hugely from area to area, as we obviously hope to cover the whole Kingdom and the shelf life of a book such as this means that you could be reading these words some time after they have been written. On the next pages I have made some assumptions on land cost but one of the easiest ways you have of quickly checking their appropriateness to your circumstances, is to quickly flick through the back pages of the major magazines catering for the selfbuild market such as *Homebuilding & Renovating* and *Build It*, where plots are often advertised.

Building costs, too, are likely to vary but here it's more the style of the building and the choice of the materials that are likely to create that variation, rather than geographical considerations. With this element of the costs, therefore, we can, at this early stage in the assessment of your budget, generalise and start off with figures of £45 per square foot if you're going to be building with subcontractors and £55 per square foot if you're going to be using a builder. These assume a fairly standard design with a fairly ordinary choice of external materials but, as I've

---

Areas of houses and bungalows

Up to 700sq. ft.
Holiday chalets and one or two bedroom old people's bungalows only.

700 to 800 sq. ft.
Smallest possible three bedroom semi-detached houses. Small two bedroom bungalows.

800 to 900 sq. ft.
Small three bedroom bungalows with integral lounge/dining rooms and a compact kitchen.
Most estate-built three bedroom semi-detached houses.

Around 1000 sq. ft.
Large three bedroom semi-detached houses.
Three bedroom detached houses.
Small four bedroom houses.

Four bedroom bungalows with integral lounge/dining rooms.
Three bedroom bungalows with separate dining room or large kitchen.
Luxury two bedroom bungalows.

Around 1300 sq. ft.
Three or four bedroom detached houses or bungalows with the possibility of a small study, or second bathroom, or a utility room, or a very large lounge.

Around 1600 sq. ft.
Four bedroom houses or bungalows with two bathrooms, large lounges, small studies, utility rooms.

Around 2000 sq. ft.
Large four to five bedroom houses and bungalows.

Initial Budget

Total funds available £115,000
Land cost £50,000
Allow legal costs and interest £5000
Available for building £60,000
Anticipated costs per sq.ft. = £45
Max size of new house = 1333 sq.ft.

Amended Budget

Total funds available £115,000
Land cost £40,000
Allow legal costs and interest £5000
Extra cost of special foundations £7000
Available for building £63,000
Anticipated costs per sq.ft. = £45
Max size of new house = 1400 sq.ft.

---

said before, you've got to start somewhere and we'll build up on the possible variations as we go through these sections. Next, you've got to make some assumptions on the probable, or hoped for, size of your new home and here you can use the information in the box entitled, 'Areas of houses and bungalows' or else you can flick through books of plans, such as *The Home Plans Book* which give the areas of the designs featured. Supposing you're interested in a house of 1500 square feet. If you elect to build this with subcontractors then your guideline budget cost is £67,500 and if you decide that you want to get it built by a single builder then that will rise to £82,500. To keep things simple let's stay with the selfbuilder using subcontract labour.

Let's also assume that this selfbuilder's budget is £115,000. He's added up the money that he thinks he'll have left when his house is sold. He's added up the savings that he and his wife have decided to invest in their new home and he's added up the amount of the mortgage he expects to receive, to come up with this figure. The house he's hoping to build of 1500 sq.ft. is going to cost him roughly £67,500 to build but, at this stage, he needs to add a contingency of

about £5000 for interest and legal costs so if those two figures are added together and taken from his total budget figure he's left with £42,500 to go out and spend on the land. Off he goes on what is probably the biggest shopping trip of a lifetime and, lo and behold, the only plots he can find are on the market at £50,000. Something's got to give. If the vendor of the land won't come down in price then our selfbuilder has got to trim his ideas on the size of his new house and, if we work the figures backwards that means that he's only got £60,000 to spend on the actual construction and, if we divide that figure by the £45 per square foot that means that his new home has got to be 1333 square feet instead of the 1500 he was hoping for.

In similar vein let's assume that our selfbuilder is 'luckier' on his second shopping trip and he finds a plot which is for sale at £40,000. He goes to visit it and finds that, whilst it's a lovely plot it was once the site of the village pond and that the foundations will have to be piled at an extra cost of roughly £7000. Again we work the figures backwards and we end up with a total left for building of £63,000. Now that's better than with the more expensive plot but it still means that our selfbuilder has got to trim his sails and think in terms of a house of 1400 square feet.

Does this all seem complicated? Well, it probably is at first but it is absolutely essential that everyone buying a building plot gets to learn how to juggle the figures like this and I've shown the same figures in the box. Now, I don't know when you'll be reading this but, even if the figures change, the principle will remain and, therefore, the first thing you need to do is to find out the probable costs which you should apply to the formula which will lead you to your budget figures and there are several ways you can go about establishing these.

Firstly disregard any analysis of figures based on the costs of houses for sale by speculative housebuilders and developers. These have no bearing on your costs and in any event the costs which a developer would experience will have little or no relationship to your costs. A developer may buy the land very cheaply; he may also have huge overheads, which he can partially offset by being able to purchase both labour and materials in bulk. You will have to pay more for your land, you may pay a little more for your materials but need not pay too much more for the labour and you certainly don't have any overheads.

Some architects are reluctant to quote costs in terms of £'s per sq.ft and, indeed some package deal companies are just as hesitant, although, without doubt, the representative sitting in your lounge telling you that it's not a very reliable way of arriving at costs is working things out in his own head in just those terms. Builders, too, think in terms of £'s per sq.ft. but will tend to go along with whatever figure a first time enquirer talks of. This is not because they are devious but more because they have to survive in a harsh commercial environment and, without proper plans, a site and money in your pocket, they regard you as wishing to make conversation rather than seeking definitive advice.

Really first class and constantly updated information is always available in the national monthly magazines, which specialise in the selfbuild market. The 'Case Histories' they publish, pack a whole load of information on costs that you can use to compare and arrive at your budget projections. Information of this sort is invaluable as is information gained at first hand from other selfbuilders who are well down the road on their projects and are probably more than happy to share their experiences with a like minded individual and his family. Bear in mind that these costs only reflect that one job and that you need to take extraneous costs and peculiar circumstances into account but bear in mind also that it all adds up to your essential store of information

In 1998/99 national average costs for average sized houses and bungalows, built on single sites by individual selfbuilders, on normal strip foundations, including fittings and fixtures appropriate to the size of dwelling, central heating, double glazing, connections to drains or septic tank, short length of drive and no landscaping were:

When built by a well established NHBC builder, *working from his offices, following a formal invitation to tender and a formal contract- £55 per sq.ft. and over.*

When built by a reputable small builder, *NHBC registered, working from home, usually a tradesman himself, following an informal approach and contract established by offer and acceptance - £50 to £55 per sq.ft.*

When built by a reliable small builder to erect the shell *with subcontractors on a supply and fix basis finishing off the building - £46 to £50 per sq.ft.*

When built on a direct labour basis by a private individual *using subcontract labour without providing any of the labour himself - £42 to £45 per sq.ft.*

The square footage of a building is arrived at by measurement of the internal dimensions of the building on each habitable floor.

Obviously, these figures are average but, peculiar circumstances apart, they do remain remarkably consistent irrespective of whether it's a house or a bungalow. For either very small dwellings or extremely large ones the figures won't work at all. For properties within the normal ranges, however, the economies of scale that are undoubtedly gained by the larger dwellings are then matched by a corresponding increase brought about by the natural use of more expensive fittings and fixtures.

Tax and the selfbuilder

Any consideration of financing a new home involves looking at your tax situation, and there are a number of factors which you need to take into consideration.

Stamp Duty
Buying a property, including land at any

figure over £60,000 will involve you in the payment of stamp duty at the rate of 1% on the total sum paid and you will find this tacked on to your solicitor's bill as part of the conveyancing cost. The cut off point is absolutely precise which means that a plot sold at £60,000 won't attract any tax whilst a plot sold at £60,001 will attract a tax bill of £600.01! - surely a spur for negotiation. Above £250,000 the rate rises to 2% and it rises again at half a million to 3%, but I don't expect that will affect too many selfbuilders. Stamp duty is paid on the land purchase only and whatever you then spend on the house construction does not come into it.

Income Tax Relief

If you are borrowing money to buy a plot, then as long as you borrow on the basis of an intention to build yourself a new home, and not as an investment, you will be able to reclaim interest on the first £30,000 of the loan against income tax. This mortgage tax relief is the subject of many a debate in political circles and has even involved the House of Windsor in a discussion of its merits. The relief is done through MIRAS and it would seem that successive Chancellors have set their faces against its perpetuation and at each Budget the rate of actual relief is either reduced or its total demise is trailed. At the time of writing, though greatly diminished in value, the relief still applies and if you are borrowing from a bank or building society and the loan takes the form of a mortgage which is paid to you in stages, then you will not actually have to make a claim for a refund but, instead, on taking out the mortgage, you will fill out a MIRAS application form enabling the tax relief to be deducted from your mortgage payments at the appropriate rate. If you borrow from a bank in the form of a bridging loan then although short-term bridging loans are not usually included in the scheme you may be able to claim relief by writing to the tax office. Those who are self employed may make their tax claim at the end of the year when they make their tax returns and this is something that they should discuss with the lender and/or their accountant.

Claiming MIRAS on your selfbuild project will in no way affect any claim which you are making against the interest payments on your existing home. Even that dwindling band of couples who still live, unmarried, in the same home they occupied in August 1988 with the same mortgage, who are still enjoying MIRAS relief on two lots of £30,000, can go on to claim allowances on a third £30,000 for a selfbuild project. When their new home is finished, however, and they sell their old house, they will revert to interest relief on a single lot of £30,000.

Although MIRAS is only generally described as being available on your 'principal private residence', which is your main home and not a holiday or second home, double MIRAS for that existing home and your new selfbuilt home can go on simultaneously for at least one year. However, if there are delays and it goes beyond the 12 months period do consult your local tax office who will usually be sympathetic. This also applies to selfbuilders who are unable to sell their old home when the new one is complete provided that they do eventually move into the new one. If a selfbuilder decides against moving into the new home and sells it on instead, then they will have to repay the extra relief they have claimed.

If you are building your home with the intention that it shall also be part of a business activity, and financing part of it from the business, then the situation regarding tax relief will be very different. This is a matter about which you must consult your accountant, as the way in which you do things, and the way in which you describe the building can be critical. It may be important to describe a farmhouse with a study, an outside lavatory, and an outside outhouse store as a 'farmworker's dwelling with integral farm office, including provision of lavatory facilities for employees and separate store for hazardous chemicals as required under EEC regulations'. This sort of matter is often important if part of the cost is to be reflected in the farm accounts.

Capital Gains Tax

Many selfbuilders achieve a 20% cost value differential by building their own home, and some do even better. Providing that the new property is your principal private residence, and that you live in it for at least 12 months, then you are normally at no risk of having to pay capital gains tax if it is simply a way in which you have moved from one home to another. Even if you are left with two properties because you are unable to sell your existing home, or if you are forced for some genuine reason to move on from the selfbuilt home in less than twelve months you will usually find that the tax inspector will exercise his discretion on your behalf.

However, for some this is a tricky area. There are some selfbuilders who go on to build again and again, each time living in the latest home for a year while they are building the next one. The tax inspector will only tolerate this for a limited period, after which he will claim that you are in business as a developer and will ask for a tax return to be submitted on this basis. When you meet other selfbuilders at exhibitions and conferences you will hear many anecdotes of those who have built ten homes in ten years, often changing wives every three or four homes, and who have avoided paying tax on these activities. I suggest that you take some of their boasts with a large pinch of salt.

Value Added Tax (VAT)

New homes, unless built for letting, are zero rated for VAT. This means that if you have your new home built by a builder, he is not required to charge you VAT on any of the goods or services he is providing and that he will go on to reclaim any VAT that he pays. A selfbuilder choosing to build with subcontract or his own labour, buying his materials from various sources, will have to pay VAT on his material purchases but will then be able to reclaim that VAT at the end of the project. VAT has a chapter, all of its own later, in this book.

3 Finding a site

What makes a piece of land into a building plot? Well, it's Planning Permission, either the actuality or the certainty of it. Without planning consent it is simply part of someone's garden, a corner of a field or a parcel of waste ground valued in the hundreds. With planning permission that same piece of land becomes worth tens of thousands of pounds. But should you try to cash in that bonanza? Well if you already own the land then it might be worth a try but if you don't, you have to decide whether you're a self builder or a property speculator.

Planning permission first of all. The phrase is used all the time but it does need some explanation and expansion here, although I'll go into it in more detail in a later chapter. Planning Permission, is necessary before any building or development can take place on land. You hear, every year, of people who have built without planning permission and, although the stories are not always followed through to their end by the media, unless of course someone gets out the shotgun and barricades themselves in, they always end in the same way - with the demolition of the illegal structure. The written authority of the local council grants planning and it is normally given in two parts. The first part is known as *Outline Planning Consent* and this is the mechanism that confers the value on the plot. It runs for 5 years and establishes the fact that the land can be built on or developed, subject to various conditions the most important of which is that, within a period of 3 years, Approval of Reserved Matters is sought. This second part of the planning permission is more commonly referred to as *Detailed Planning Permission* and this deals with things like the design, access, siting and choice of external materials. Detailed consent does not usually confer any extra cash value to the land although, as a self builder who probably goes on to buy a plot with Outline Consent, it is the part which will, in the end, be of the most personal importance to you and in which you will invest most of your hopes. There can be a number of applications for Approval of Reserved Matters pursuant to a single outline consent some of which will be successful, some of which may fail, but all of which will have no

bearing on the validity of the original Outline Consent. In the past some building societies dipping into the selfbuild market, failed to appreciate this distinction and demanded the almost impossible in that they required their potential customers to demonstrate a Detailed Consent before any offer of mortgage was forthcoming – it merely served to highlight their lack of understanding.

Mention should be made of Full Planning Permission. This is not a third form of planning as such – it serves to roll the Outline Consent and the Detailed Consent into one document. It is a useful tool in certain circumstances and I'll discuss why and how in the chapter devoted to planning but first of all let's stay on the subject of plot finding.

If you imagine for one moment that you're just going to pick up the telephone and ring up the local agents, that you're going to wait until the details arrive and that, if it's a nice day, you'll jump in the car and drive out to look at the plots and then select the one of your choice, you're in for a rude awakening. It doesn't happen like that at all. Finding land is, as I've said, the first hurdle at which most self builders fall in the race to build their own home. It takes perseverance of the utmost kind and it takes luck. Perseverance in that you have to be prepared to follow all of the avenues that could lead to a possible plot, and luck that it's you and not somebody else who's there when one comes up.

So what do you need to start off the search? What do you have to consider even before you even pick up that phone, don the walking shoes or get in the car? Well, an idea of the type and nature of the plot would help. In the previous chapter we've discussed how to get to the amount you've got to spend on your plot but in reality that's only part of the question. What can you get for that kind of money and what sort of property can you hope to build on any of the plots within your price range. Now, as I've said, the price is going to be different in each area of the land but there are some rules and basic guidelines you can follow and they can usually be reached by observation. You will hear the words, 'carrying capacity' used in respect of land. It's got nothing whatsoever to do with the ground's ability to withstand loads. It's about avoiding over developing or, indeed, under developing a plot. Most self builders are concerned that their new home should represent the best possible investment but there are times when this gets distorted by either inflated accommodation requirements or lack of finance. For example, a plot comes up in a suburban street mainly comprised of 3 bedroomed and small 4 bedroomed houses built in the late seventies valued for Council Tax purposes in bands 'B' or 'C'. You, however, want to build a 'Tudorbethan' house with 5 ground floor reception rooms, 5 bedrooms and 3 bathrooms. Even if you get planning for such a house in that street scene, the area as a whole will have a ceiling value on houses and although you may be building a house which could well be considered for Band 'G', the likelihood is that you would never achieve those kind of values - you would have overdeveloped the plot. Anybody with the kind of money that you would be hoping to eventually sell for would not be looking in your area in the first place. In the same way if a plot came up in a street full of large 5 bedroomed Victorian houses and you wanted to build a small 2 bedroomed bungalow, then, not only would it look lost and incongruous, but you would never be achieving the potential of the plot which would, almost certainly, have been indicated by its high price in the first place.

Obviously you want to get the best and the most out of your self build but you do need to think carefully about what you build. Let's suppose that the most any property could possibly sell for in your area is around £150,000. If selfbuilder 'A' builds a 1600 sq.ft. house with a 400 sq.ft. garage, all of which is valued at that £150,000 but then selfbuilder 'B' comes along and builds a house 500 sq.ft. bigger with a triple garage, he might then be very disappointed that although he's spent 30% more than Mr 'A', his increased value might not be greater than 3%! That is, unless that's what he planned for in the first place and he's made the decision, the choice, that that's what he wants and to hell with the values! After all that's what selfbuilding is all about – informed choice. In

reality much of this can be academic as nowadays the planners will be very concerned to see that just what you're proposing fits in, in proper planning terms, but there are times when it breaks down and the controls are a little lax. You can see this clearly on the self build sites where councils like Chesterfield sold plots off in the late seventies and selfbuilders, for all the right emotional reasons, tried to get as much as they could into their plots by overdeveloping and building right up to both boundaries, in some cases to the point where looking along the street it's difficult to see where one house ends and another begins, even though they're all detached.

Evaluating the plot and the actual process of buying it will be dealt with in the next chapter, so now let's move on to finding one. Of course there are a happy band of people who don't have to find a plot because they already own one and if you're one of them then you can skip the next section and move on to evaluating your plot and how to go about getting planning on it. For the rest of you the really hard bit is about to begin and even the later stages of actual construction may pale into insignificance when set beside this task. So where do you start?

Estate agents sell land. Most of the land that is sold goes through an agent, sometimes because the agent was instrumental in getting the Outline Consent in the first place. In any town there are two distinct types of estate agent. Firstly there are the long established traditional agents who sell houses as part and parcel of their general business which can include activities as diverse as furniture sales and livestock auctions. These are the types of agent who are also more likely to have a professional department and it is this department which is often used by prospective vendors to obtain planning on their land. They will be cagey about what they've got coming up, preferring to maintain the anonymity of their clients and the potential plots until such time as they have a consent and specific instructions, but once they have those instructions they will act in the way that is best suited to their client, the vendor. The other sort of estate agent is fairly familiar to us all. They very rarely get involved in actual applications for planning and instead simply take on properties and land as it comes on to their books. They have a much more brash way of dealing with things and they won't always see the full potential in any particular property, existing, as they do, through high turnover, rather than long term investment. They're much more likely to discuss what's up and coming and you'll come out of their offices, even if empty handed, with a feeling of greater hope – a feeling which may dissipate quite quickly when nothing further happens. You see, estate agents sell land, yes, but given half the chance they'd rather not sell it to a self builder just the same. Why not - surely your money's as good as anybody else's? Well, no, it isn't actually, because if an estate agent sells that piece of land to you and you build your new home on it then in the short to medium term all the agent is going to get out of it is a commission fee which barely scrapes over four figures. Whereas, if he sells it to a builder or a developer he'll, first of all get the same commission fee for selling the land, and then in a very short time he'll get the very much larger commission fee for selling the new house that the builder constructs. As if that's not enough he'll have his board up at that site for a much longer time to bring in more customers and get more noticed than his rivals. Of course he's got to balance that wish with a duty to his vendor but in normal times that isn't too much of a problem for him and even if it's not normal times, the time lag between his recognition of that duty and his view of the plot as a key to other things takes a long while to sink in. So, just putting your name on the books of an estate agent isn't going to produce too many plots. Visit them weekly. Get to know them almost on a person to person basis and, even if you suspect that when they see you coming they're inwardly groaning that it's you again, greet them with a cheery "Hi it's me again – anything fresh in on the plot front". Sooner or later you'll be recognised as a bona fide purchaser and if your name's the one at the forefront of their minds on the day a plot comes in then, chances are you'll get to hear of it. Of course if you suspect that no matter what you do and no matter how many times you go in they're always going to want to sell it to their builder chums then you're really up against it but

there are things you can do. Try going in at the weekend, possibly on a Sunday when temporary staff are on duty. Tell them you're on the books – even confirm it with them by checking your details with them whilst you're there. Ask if there's any land that's come in during the week and if they go across to the relevant cabinet and get you out some details then, even if they get told off on the Monday for showing them to you, you'll have got to hear of that plot and above all, you'll have done nothing wrong. They were instructed to sell that land for the best price. Their duty is to the vendor and if you buy the land what's wrong with that?

Auctions. The more traditional agents will often want to sell land by auction and whilst that can be a benefit to the self builder insofar as it brings the land onto the open market there are several drawbacks. Auctions are distinctly uneasy places for lay people, who sit there nervously trying not to scratch that itch that inescapably comes up on their eyebrow whilst at the same time trying to keep track of the stream of indecipherable words coming from the rostrum. They do however, firmly establish a true value for the plot and a self builder, who doesn't have to think in terms of an immediate profit margin, may possibly have the edge on a developer who's got to think in terms of a return on his money in the short term. When the hammer falls the last bidder is the successful bidder and there's no getting out of it. In effect, if it's you, you've exchanged contracts at that moment and you are committed to paying the full deposit right there and then in the room and completing within the timescale laid down in the contract. You can see, therefore, that you really need to have everything in place before you even think of making a bid. Your house sale has to be organised and/or bridging finance or mortgage funds have to be in place and your solicitor will have had to have already made all of the necessary enquiries and searches to enable you to buy. And if you aren't the last bidder? Well, you've missed that plot and you've probably got a hefty bill as the only thing to show for it.

Newspapers, national, local and classified and some well known sales magazines are a good source of land. If there's land advertised in any of them and it's what you're looking for, at the price you're thinking of and in the area you're interested in then don't delay, get right onto it – if it's any good at all it won't hang about until you just roll up at the weekend. And of course newspapers work both ways in that you can advertise for a plot. You may get time wasters, you may get a string of no hope plots which never would get planning consent. You may get the chap who's just fed up with mowing his large lawn. But, you may get the humdinger of a plot. You may even get someone who's been trying to sell his plot through, would you believe it, your friendly local estate agent who hasn't been able to interest any of his builder chums but still didn't tell you about it.

Self build magazines recognised long ago that if their readers were going to be able to move from the stage of thinking about self building to actually doing it, then many of them had to have some help in finding land. For a long while they just took in advertisements from all and sundry and gradually their back pages began to fill up with plots for sale. At the same time various land finding agencies sprang up and some of them were particularly successful, so much so that both of the major magazines saw this format as

the way forward. In truth, they also saw this as a way of cashing in on the service, either in the form of being able to attract sponsorship or by direct subscription, and whilst both of them went about things in a slightly different way from the potential self builders point of view, their approaches do tend to tidy up and simplify the mass of information. *Build It* magazine now have a tie up with Landbank Services, a family run company that has specialised for a long time in providing lists, available by subscription, of land for sale throughout the country and abroad. In addition they also fill several pages of each issue of the magazine with lists of land for sale, county by county, that is either on their records or is being directly advertised by estate agents and others. Any advertiser approaching the magazine with land for sale does not have to pay for their land being listed and, instead, the details are entered onto those appearing in the magazine. At the major self build exhibition held at Alexandra Palace in London every September, and at the rolling programme of self build shows held around the country throughout the year their stands are extremely well attended and for those without a plot, they are, and should be, a magnet.

Homebuilding & Renovating magazine did things slightly differently in that they formed their own division, 'Plotfinder' that advertises its subscription services in the magazine and also takes a large stand at the big self build exhibition held every spring at the Birmingham NEC. Although listings of particular plots do sometimes appear in the magazine, their system differs in that a single premium rate call will elicit a free list of all the plots for sale in three counties of your choice with an invitation to increase that, by subscription, to receipt of a listing every three weeks. Talking to them and seeing them all in action at the hive of activity, which is their offices, I can see the reasoning behind this approach. One of the failings of some of the companies that first jumped onto this bandwagon was that, by the fact that decent plots do not stay on the market for very long, many of the listings were out of date by the time they reached the subscribers. If you couple this with the fact that, say, an August edition of a magazine

Plotfinder's busy office.

goes to print at the end of May, beginning of June, then you can see that it's awfully difficult to maintain any currency. To escape this trap, Plotfinder staff update their lists on a daily basis, maintaining Nationwide coverage with both their advertisers and their subscribers through a comprehensive computer database that can be accessed on a faxback number.

Both of these services provide, not only an invaluable product to the prospective self builder in terms of being able to find plots but, perhaps just as importantly, for those in the early stages of planning, a guide to plot prices and availability and to who's selling what. If you're having difficulty in deciding which of the estate agents you should concentrate on then, a quick cross reference to the land finding lists should give you the answers.

Local Authorities sell land. Some of them are well known for doing so and have a regular supply of plots, which they put on the market specifically aimed at the self builder. Ring your local authority and ask what plots they've got for sale and what plots they've got coming up. Those that do sell plots have become pretty efficient at doing so and the plots they sell are highly valuable and desirable plots, which normally

have most of the roads and infrastructure taken care of. Of course land doesn't grow on trees, so to speak, and as many authorities get to the end of the landbank and have sold off land that they would previously have built council housing on, the supply can begin to dry up. But, that doesn't mean that it's not worthwhile getting on to them because things do change and at any one time either a complete site can be in the offing or the odd spare parcel of land can be identified as suitable. In Wales, the Welsh Land Agency has been selling serviced plots but more as an effort in social engineering as, many times, the requirements are that the land is sold to local people and that it is developed for a certain type of housing.

The Commission for New Towns (CNT) is an agency that sells fully serviced plots in the new towns up and down the land. In some areas, as their land holdings diminish the supply of self build plots is rapidly drying up but in other towns such as Milton Keynes there is still a ready supply. There is no doubt that this is a diminishing resource and the CNT itself shrinks into smaller and smaller offices each year with the possibility that, as the millennium approaches they might centralise for one last gasp around

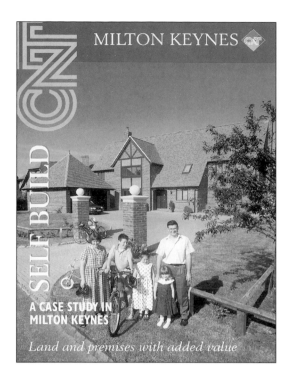

MILTON KEYNES CNT

SELF BUILD

A CASE STUDY IN MILTON KEYNES

Land and premises with added value

Milton Keynes. Nevertheless, as I write there are plots available in the other new towns and they expect a small supply of them onto the market over the next few years.

Asking around can produce results. Try having a haircut or just chatting in the local pub and when you've cut out all the horror stories which invariably happened to someone who knew someone, and got over trying to explain that you're not completely mad, you may come out with a few pointers which could lead you to a plot.

Looking around villages or areas of your choice to see if there are any obvious plots on the ground is well worth a try. In all the dire warnings about not buying land without the benefit of some sort of planning consent, there are circumstances where a piece of land which does not have an express consent can, nevertheless, be considered as a plot. It's difficult to describe in absolute terms just how or why this can occur but in general I am referring to those obvious plots of land where history has, for some reason or another, left them undeveloped whilst, all around them, similar plots have long since been built on. Now, you have to distinguish in your own mind the difference here between, say, a street scene of large houses where each property

has 30 metres to each boundary and another street scene where similar houses have long since had the land at the side developed but one, for some reason or another, has been left undisturbed. It's not a certainty that it's a plot but it's a pretty good bet – one that could make it worth your while making enquiries at the Planning Department and one that could, if you can track down a willing vendor, make it worth your while making an offer subject to contract and subject to receipt of satisfactory planning permission.

Infill plots don't just occur in towns and it's a good idea to look out for an unexplained gap in a village street. It could well have once been the village duck pond, clay or sand pit that's since been filled in. Just as equally it could also have been left as a gap to give access to fields at the rear when the farmer originally sold off the land on the road frontage for development. Now that machinery has brought about the enlargement of his fields the access is no longer useful or possibly even the fields themselves are now developed and this tongue of land remains, unused and unwanted, until either you happen along or someone thinks to make proper use of it.

The public utilities often have parcels of land which, with the advance of technology, they no longer require. The Gas Board often used to have buildings the size of small bungalows set in urban or village streets to house their equipment, all of which can now go into a plastic box the size of a chest of drawers. Telephone relay stations were often situated in a large plot of land as were water pumping stations. Try writing to the Estates Departments of the various undertakers in your area and, failing that, get out and about and look around for these anachronisms and, when you've found them, write off and register your interest.

H.M.Land Registry. Not all land in England and Wales is registered with the Land Registry but quite a bit of it is, especially if it's changed hands in the recent past. Prior to December 1990, only registered owners or persons with their consent could inspect the register but now it is open for anyone to do so. A registered title is the legal evidence of ownership, or title, of land that has been registered and it includes, details of the address and location of the land, the owners of that land and any charges, covenants and easements affecting the land. The information supplied is in the form of a Property Register containing all the details in three succinct sections together with a plan upon which the land is outlined. If you find a piece of land and you want to trace its ownership then you need to apply to the Land Registry with full details of the address and, if at all possible, a map or copy of the OS sheet, to identify it. If you cannot identify the land in this way then you can send off for, or inspect, the Index maps held by the Registry. These Index maps have all registered land marked and numbered and, if the plot you're interested in appears on them then you should be able to find out just who owns it. I repeat, not all land is registered, and it is the empty parcel of land that has lain fallow and unused for donkey's years that is the most likely not to have been. Nevertheless, if you're unsure of the ownership of a piece of land that's caught your eye and local enquiries will either, stir up a hornets nest, or have been unsuccessful, you could do no better than to apply. A modest scale of fees is payable and I would suggest that, in the first instance, you write to H.M.Land Registry at Lincolns Inn Fields, London, WC2A 3PH, or telephone them on 0171-917-8888, asking them for their Explanatory leaflet 15.

Planning offices. It is not generally understood, but the Planning Register is open for inspection by the general public and if you go to the planning office at your local authority, you can ask to see it. You may have to wait in turn for it, as many company representatives also use this source of information, but when you do get to it you will find listed all of the recent and current applications for planning permission. It's the Outline ones that are most likely to be of interest to you. Some may be under the name of your local estate agent but the chances are that he's listed as the applicant's agent and you can glean the applicant's name from the application. A short letter to the owner, in the first instance, can elicit a positive response. At the very least it will let the owner know that you're out there, and when the agent takes a long time to interest his builder chums and tries to tell his vendor that the market's a little slow, the vendor will either be able to correct him or may contact you direct – I've known that to happen in quite a few cases. Of course it may well be that the vendor doesn't want to sell and that's, of course, more likely if it's a 'Detailed' application, but not always. For the sake of a first class stamp it's well worth a try. On the other hand, many people who get planning on parts of their gardens are awfully keen to get the money for the plot but are equally apprehensive about what happens to the land, what gets built on it, who'll be their neighbours, and what effect it'll have on their existing house. The thought of some faceless and uncaring builder sticking up something as huge as he can get it and selling it on to God knows who will keep them awake at night. A letter from you telling them that you are a private family, telling them that you're very keen to live and build somewhere where you're all welcome and stressing that you would wish that whatever you built fitted in properly, could allay some well founded fears and bring you a plot.

New for old. Quite a large number of self-build/newbuilds are carried out on the site of an old dwelling that is demolished. Sometimes local

---

IR   15 • Explanatory Leaflet •

The Open Register ~
A guide to information held by the Land Registry and how to obtain it

Since 3 December 1990 the register of title in England and Wales has been open for inspection by the Public.

This 'Question and Answer' guide gives advice on the kinds of information held by the Land Registry and how to obtain such information.

The guide aims to do no more than give brief straightforward answers to the general questions that follow. For a better understanding of information provided by the Land Registry and its legal or business implications it may well be in your interest to seek legal advice. Although members of the Registry staff seek to assist the public in every possible way, it must be emphasised that they themselves are not able to act as legal advisers.

1. Why is land registered with the Land Registry?

The object of registering title to land is to create and maintain a register of land owners whose title is guaranteed by the State and thus simplify the sale (transfer) and mortgage of such land.

2. What does 'Open Register' mean?

Anybody can now obtain information which is held on the register of a registered title. Prior to December 1990 only registered owners and persons with the owner's consent could inspect the register.

3. Is all land registered?

Not yet. Although the Land Registry has details of more than 16 million registered properties in England and Wales, a number that increases daily, there are still many millions of properties not yet registered, for which the Registry holds no information.

4. What is a registered title?

A registered title is the legal evidence of title to land which has been registered at HM Land Registry. When a title is registered the register provides an up-to-date official record of the legal ownership and certain other matters relating to the property or piece of land in question.

5. How do I find out if land is registered?

The Registry holds a series of large scale Ordnance Survey maps covering the whole of England and Wales on which is shown the extent of land in every registered title. These maps are called Index Maps and each single map is called a 'Section'. Index Maps will indicate whether or not a particular piece of land is registered and, if it is, the registered title number and whether the registration is of freehold or leasehold land.

An application for an official search (inspection) of the Index Map should preferably be made by post and must be on Land Registry Form 96. In

Right: A lovely house with a great deal of living space on a tight site.

Left: A house which looks really impressive on a large site.

Right: What was formerly a building site ends up with this grand building with its surrounds close to completion.

Left: A rural design that complements a rural site.

estate agents will try for ages to sell a substandard bungalow or house, with mortgage application after mortgage application going in, only to be rejected time after time. Nobody seems to realise that this is a building plot rather than a viable building in its current form, especially the poor young couples who keep on trying to buy this cheap home. Sometimes the demolition costs can add up to a few thousand pounds, sometimes they cost a bit more, especially if the existing building is asbestos. Sometimes, however, the demolition costs can be offset completely by the salvage value of the materials, especially if the roof tiles are local clay peg or pantiles which are no longer available and therefore in high demand for extensions and renovations. All times, however, there are savings over a green field plot. In all probability the driveway and entrance are already in. The drains and services may well be connected and the garden will probably already be laid out and established, if a little overgrown. Be careful not to alert the estate agent to the possibility of this being a plot. You'd be surprised, but they still won't click if you ask for plots and then, as an aside, just in case there aren't any, you ask for old properties to do up. I know 'cause I've done it myself. The last benefit is that the new building doesn't always have to go in the same position as the old one and that could solve your accommodation problems for the duration of the building.

Multiple sites. What do you do if you find a large site, which you want to share with other self builders? In previous issues of this book the advice could have included that you consider the forming of a Private Self Build Group. The 1998/99 crash brought an end to all that and group selfbuild, in many of the forms it existed in before those dates, is no longer around. That's not to say that it won't be back, but, certainly as this book is being written, it is not a cogent force other than where it fulfils a specific social need and comes under the auspices of community self build, of which more in a later and dedicated chapter.

But still, there's that multiple site that's where you want it and if only you could team up with some other like minded individuals, surely you could then buy the plots between you and you'd get what you wanted? Well, yes you can, but there are several things you need to think about and quite a few different ways of achieving your aims. The idea of being involved with others, perhaps developing a site together, sharing work on common services and co-operating in hiring plant and employing tradesmen, can seem attractive. But, in order to do so you would have to become one body, either in the form of a limited company or a selfbuild group, and the financial institutions don't want to know about private self build groups, tending to think of them in the same light as the Pharaohs considered the plagues.

So, it's better that if a larger site comes up, you devise some way of building on it with others, *with you all acting as individuals*. The ease or difficulty of doing this will depend on the nature of any road or drainage works and therefore the smaller the number of actual plots, the simpler the task of sorting it all out will be.

In most local authority areas three or four houses can be built with access off a private drive. The drive will not be adopted by the local authority and the home owners will have to maintain it themselves. This makes it simple for each of them to buy a plot with the usual reciprocal liabilities to be responsible for the drive and drains, which are either built by the vendor of the land, or by one of the purchasers who buys it from the vendor more cheaply than the other purchasers in consideration of his entering into a bond to do this. Sometimes all the purchasers get together to share the common costs. If they adopt this course they will be wise to look at safeguards, explained later, but the cost of a joint drive is unlikely to be a major proportion of the development costs of any one plot, unlike the cost of a road.

If there are to be four or more homes requiring a new access it is likely that the authorities will require the short length of road and the drains under it to be constructed to highway standards, with a road bond to lead to formal adoption of the road by the authority. This costs a great deal more money and is complicated, as either a single person or a formal body of some sort has to take legal responsibility for the bond. This is not always easy to arrange, but it is far safer for individuals to buy the land that they are going to build on, and to make complicated arrangements for the road, than to let anyone else have an interest in their own plot.

All this supposes that a vendor of a site for two or more homes is willing to sell it to multiple purchasers. Ignoring situations where someone has set out to sell serviced plots, what happens when Joe Selfbuilder sees a site for three units and thinks how nice it would be to build one of them himself, with two other guys building the other two? He has two options: either he buys the whole of the site himself and immediately sells off two plots to people he has found to buy them, or else he and his two friends persuade the vendor to sell the site in three parts. In either case all the contracts will be signed at once, either with everyone using the same solicitor or else with a gaggle of solicitors sitting round the same table. The contracts should either include appropriate arrangements for any shared drive or services, or take into account any requirement for an adoptable road, or else a separate agreement for this should be signed by all the purchasers at the same time.

Either way, the first selfbuilder who takes the initiative in this will probably have to obtain an option of some sort to 'hold' the land while he finds his fellow purchasers and sorts out the details with them. Sometimes this may take the form of conditional contract. Invariably he will either have some experience of this sort of thing or he will retain an estate agent to handle it. Occasionally a solicitor who is particularly interested in land may help set up the arrangements, (which is distinct from simply giving legal effect to arrangements). However, whoever helps with the details, it is Joe Selfbuilder who will have to provide the enthusiasm to make it all happen.

The actual arrangements to build any common drive, road or drains have to be made very carefully. Avoid any joint responsibility for this work: it is far preferable that it should be the responsibility of one person, who may be one of the selfbuilders or more often will be a contractor or civil engineer. This person or firm should provide a guarantee that the work will be done, preferably as a bank bond so that if he defaults the bank will step in and get the work done. In return he will look for a guarantee of payment from all of the plot owners, often with the money deposited with a solicitor, or with a second charge over their plots. In this way there are mutual obligations all round that will ensure the work is done, without any one participant's special circumstances threatening the whole job.

4 Evaluating a site

Before you get into your car to go to look at a building plot, there are some things you must be sure about: such as how much you can afford to pay for the plot that you want, the size and character of the home that you want to build on it, and all the other factors that you must consider when you are looking at a potential site for the first time.

The sum that you can afford to pay for a suitable piece of land, and the probable size of the house that you will be able to afford to build, have been discussed in an earlier chapter. The whole business of design, and what the planners are likely to let you build, have chapters of their own later in this book. It is important that you have read them before you start plot hunting.

There are many other things to consider. Some of them, such as the slope of the land, the view, the orientation, drainage arrangements etc., will effect the design of any new home that you build, and these factors are dealt with in the chapter on designing a home to suit your site. They may, or may not, have a significant effect on building costs. The considerations which are dealt with in this chapter are those which may affect whether or not the site can really be developed at all, or which may detract from the value of the finished property. Remember that the fact that a piece of land is described as a building plot does not mean that it is a practicable place to build a house: it merely means that the vendor has used the words to attract prospective purchasers. Remember also that outline planning consent, or even detailed planning permission, is merely consent for a house to be built there by someone if they can. There is a legal term 'caveat emptor' – which means let the buyer beware. What follows is about what you must be aware of.

Start by wondering just why no-one has built there before. Really first class individual building plots have been in very short supply for the last thirty years. Why is this still a building plot? Why did no one build there twenty years ago?

There may be a simple answer. The site may have been part of the garden of a large house and only split off from it recently, or planning consent may have been granted very recently following a change in the local structure plan, which has hitherto prevented any development. Or it may have been covered by old buildings which have recently been demolished. If this is so, all well and good. If not, try to find out why no one has built on it. The reason may not preclude you building on it, but it is something that you have to establish at an early stage.

Planning

In the normal course of events the advice must be to only buy plots that have an express planning consent, either Outline, Detailed or Full. To every rule there must be an exception, and I have discussed this partially in the preceding chapter and will discuss it further, under the chapter dedicated to planning. However, for the purposes of this section of the book we will assume, in the main, that you are buying a plot with planning permission. The first thing to say about Planning Permission is that it normally 'runs to the benefit of the land'. That means that whoever the applicant was, the consent relates to the plot and not to the applicant or the previous owner. The exceptions to this are rare and relate more to things like the siting of mobile homes for prospective farm enterprises and the occupation of an annexe. In these cases the exclusivity is normally achieved by the wording on a condition on the consent, of which more later.

It's surprising to some, but the number of times a plot is offered on the market on the basis of it having planning consent when the reverse is in fact true, are manifest. This situation doesn't usually occur through any deliberate attempt to mislead but oftimes happens through the naivety of the people selling the plot. The first thing you need to check when buying a plot with planning permission is whether that consent is still in time. Planning consent lasts for a period of five years from the date of the permission. If it's a Full permission then it will simply state this fact but, if it's an Outline consent, it will usually say that the consent is for a period of five years and that within a period of three years an application for Approval of Reserved Matters must be made. In effect, therefore, if your prospective plot has Outline consent and you are being offered the land more than 3 years after that consent was given, with no Detailed application ever having been made, then the outline consent is out of time. What normally happens here is that either a fresh Outline application has to be made or else your prospective Detailed application has to, instead, revert to being a Full application. Either way you are at risk in that, if the policy of the local authority has changed in the intervening time, your application could fail, leaving that parcel of land with no valid consent. You can see, therefore, that it's vital that, in these circumstances, you very quickly identify the problem and only agree to purchase the plot 'subject to receipt of satisfactory planning consent'.

Again land will often be offered with either a Full consent which has expired or else with the benefit of a Detailed consent which has itself expired when related back to the original outline permission – *check the dates on all planning documents.* If the expiry date is fast approaching then the choice could be for the vendors to apply for an extension of time on the consent, but the chances are that they will fail to see your concern. In their minds the land has got planning and it won't occur to them that the piece of land they've thought of for so long as money in the bank could be anything other than that. Your only option is to again insist on buying 'subject to receipt of satisfactory planning approval' and if they won't play ball on that, then really you have three other options: you take an enormous gamble and buy the land anyway, you pull away altogether or, you consider getting an option on the land and make your own application.

It may seem strange to some people but you don't have to own a plot of land in order to make a planning application on it. In fact you don't even really need the consent of the owner and all you must do is inform them, by means of a form in the planning application documents, that you are making the application. This means that if you come across a plot where the planning is suspect, it is open for you, preferably by agreement, to make your own application in order to clarify matters. In similar vein if the plot you're interested in has no consent, but you feel that it stands a good chance of getting it, then it's open for you to make an application before you

actually buy the land. Beware though – the owner could very well let you get on with all this and then when you've sorted it all out and enhanced the value of his land a thousandfold he could turn around and sell it to somebody else. To avoid this, either tie things up beforehand with a formal legally binding option or else, as I've said above, buy the land subject to receipt of satisfactory planning permission in which case, if it fails, the contract is voided.

Does the consent relate to the plot being offered? What a silly question I hear you say. Well, not so silly really. Many's the time a vendor gets planning permission for a part of their garden and then when it comes to selling decides that they really can't stomach the thought of the loss of a particular tree or area of garden and that they just don't want the new house so close to theirs. The plot which was outlined in red on the plan, which got planning permission and which was shown as being 60 feet wide and stopping 6 feet from their house wall, suddenly becomes 40 feet wide and a long way from their wall. The area of land is still contained within the original outlined site, but it palpably is not the same site and it is open for the planners to consider that the Outline consent is, therefore, invalid on this smaller plot. A way around this, if the smaller site is acceptable to you, is for the detailed planning applications to go in on the basis of the larger plot whilst at the same time you proceed to purchase the smaller plot. But be very careful. Although there's nothing to stop this happening, the planners won't necessarily go along with your new home being situated to one side of the plot, as they see it, and any explanation that you're only buying a portion of the original consent will have no influence on their opinions. In like manner, vendors can often simply move the original sized plot to one side so that it either partially or wholly slips out of the original area shown on the Outline consent. They won't see that they've done anything wrong but, planners don't see it that way. To them the area which is outside the original red line does not have the benefit of any planning consent and whilst they may be amenable to this 'new' plot being developed it, nevertheless, doesn't have consent and your application will have to be a Full one rather than an Approval of Reserved Matters. Once more in any and all of these instances you need to be buying 'subject to receipt of satisfactory planning permission'.

Sometimes planning is granted conditional upon something else happening. An example of this would be where planning consent is granted on a plot, or plots, conditional upon, say, an old building being demolished. You're only buying the plot and the condemned building is outside your jurisdiction. If that part of the site is sold to another party who fails to demolish the old building then, although your vendor, and/or the other purchaser, is technically in breach of contract, you might find it very difficult to strictly satisfy the conditions on your consent. It probably won't come to the point of totally invalidating your planning but it could well lead to some sticky moments and more than a few letters exchanged. So, it's best to point this all out to your solicitor at an early stage, unless of course he's already picked up on it, and to make sure that some sort of timetable and undertaking is given for the work to be done. Multi plot sites are often given planning on the condition that certain works will be undertaken to improve or create an access and it needs to be established, right at the outset, that this work will be undertaken and that it is capable of being carried out - I shall touch on this subject again under access, roads and visibility splays.

And that brings us to the numbered *conditions* on the planning document. They're not there just to fill out the paper and they are part and parcel of the consent. Any breach of those conditions or failure to abide by them has an effect on the planning consent as a whole and can lead to its negation. Many of the conditions are standard and appear on every consent. They are, nonetheless important and must be adhered to. Special conditions can also have an effect on whether or not the plot is suitable for your purposes in the first place. It has become common for local authorities to stipulate the maximum, and very occasionally the minimum, size that a dwelling can be on the consent. They mean what they say. If it says that the dwelling

must not exceed 1900 sq.ft. plus a garage then that's what you're going to get and no more. If it says the building must be single storey then a bungalow is what you're going to be able to build there, under that consent. In some cases it may even go on to limit what is known as 'Permitted Development' thus disallowing the future extension of the dwelling or the occupation or conversion of the garage, without express planning consent. Before I move on I'd better, therefore, explain briefly just what this 'Permitted Development' is, although I will be covering it in greater detail later in the book.

Within the Planning Acts there are certain classes of development that can be carried out without the need for express or specific planning consent. You may still need Building Regulations approval but you don't have to apply for Planning Permission to carry out certain classes of development, including extensions up to a certain size, garages where none exists, and development within the curtilage of the building. It can be varied or negated within a consent and is usually excluded in Conservation areas and in sensitive planning situations.

A condition that crops up quite often on rural plots may require that the property is 'occupied by a person wholly or mainly or last employed in agriculture, or the widow or widower thereof'. It may vary slightly in the wording and it may relate the consent to a particular operation, to forestry or to a rural industry such as horses (Horses are most definitely not agriculture in the eyes of the planners). Whatever the wording, the import is the same; the property can only be legally occupied by someone involved in those occupations. Many is the time, however, when parcels of land come onto the market with such a consent, sometimes with a few acres attached, sometimes not, and many's the time that someone tries to pretend that they're farming when all they've got is a goat, a pony and a few chickens. Just occasionally they get away with it but more often than not, it all goes very sadly wrong. The probability is that, if you're borrowing money, most banks or building societies wouldn't be interested in giving a loan on that project anyway and those few that do will want to be assured that you fit the criteria and that the price you're paying for the land reflects its encumbered status.

Other areas where conditions can affect the suitability of the plot concern access, roads and visibility splays and these deserve sub chapters of their own.

Access first of all. Unless you can gain access to the plot then it's of no use to man nor beast. Does a road serve it and if so what sort of road is it? Read on to find more about roads but first back to the access itself. Whatever sort of road there is, does it directly abut that access or is there a strip of land in between and, if so does the plot owner have the clear right to join the two - is there a *Ransom strip*?

Ransom strips are pieces of land, narrow strips, as little as 6" wide in some cases, between your plot and the access, which prevent the site being developed. They are not there by accident: someone has arranged for them, and the purpose is either to stop anyone building on the plot at all, or to make him pay a huge sum to buy the strip. This may sound like some sort of sharp practice, but in fact it is rarely anything of the sort. What has happened is best understood by looking at the background history to the situation.

The usual situation is that the ransom strip is in place to stop anyone building on the site at all, and the story probably starts when all the land, including both the strip and the plot, were part of the garden of a house or possibly a smallholding or farm. This may well have been a hundred years ago. The land owner was probably approached by someone who wanted to buy part of the land for some purpose or other, but who did not intend to build on it. The buyer probably knew the owner did not want anyone building there anyway, perhaps because he wanted to preserve his privacy or the view from the house.

Now, the land could have been sold with a covenant to the title to prevent anyone ever building there. However, to make it even more certain that no one could do so, it was sold with just a pedestrian access and no way of getting a vehicle to it at all. As the purchaser did not want to build on it anyway, everyone was happy with this arrangement.

A hundred years later the big house has been demolished and the site where it stood is covered with modern homes at ten to an acre. At the time when they were built, it would have been sensible for our plot to have been developed as part of the same estate, but, maybe because the owner could not be traced, the plot lay dormant. Perhaps for many years.

Then, possibly by inheritance, the plot passes to someone who bothers to go to look at it. It is a gap in a built up area and as such likely to get planning consent. The new owner applies for outline planning permission, not knowing or not bothering to mention that his boundary does not go quite to the road. Consent is granted.

What does our plot owner do now? He can trace the owner of the ransom strip, who will probably now be the hard hearted builder who developed the site of the big house, and ask him to sell the strip. Alternatively he can build anyway and hope that no one else remembers about the ransom strip.

If he does the former, the owner of the ransom strip may ask him for a sum just below the value of the whole plot as a building site, reasoning that it is worth nothing at all to the owner unless he can buy the strip. If the owner takes the other course and simply annexes the strip and builds a house, he then runs the risk of being detected and ending up with a house without an access.

One way out of this problem is to sell the plot, now with planning permission, as a building plot and to let the purchaser deal with this situation. The vendor can claim that he knew nothing about the ransom strip. In every sense of the words, the unsuspecting purchaser will then have 'bought it'. You must make sure you are not such a purchaser. There are thousands and thousands of plots like this in Britain, and architects and surveyors who deal regularly with one-off houses for private individuals come across them quite frequently.

A similar situation arises when land without planning permission is sold and the vendor wants to ensure that he will receive a share of the increased value if it ever gets planning permission. To do this he creates a ransom strip. Both parties will agree to this, but a subsequent purchaser may not be told about it.

So what can you do to guard against finding you have a ransom strip situation? First of all, your solicitor will make sure you have a good title, but as far as access is concerned he can only rely on the vendors' solicitor's reply to a standard question in his enquiries. If the vendors' solicitor has not been told of the ransom strip, he may not be able to detect it from an old deed plan to an unregistered title. The planners may also simply not know it exists.

Does this frighten you? No need. If you follow a few simple rules you can spot a ransom strip very easily.

Rule one is that whenever you buy an isolated building plot you must first ask yourself 'why has no one built here before?'. The vendor may give you a good reason, which you should treat with suspicion until it is confirmed. By following this simple rule you can avoid buying plots which are village duck ponds that have been filled in, or have a war time air raid shelter below the ground, or suffer a horrid smell from a tannery across the valley whenever the wind is in the east, - or which have a ransom strip.

Rule two is to measure every part of the boundary on the ground and compare it with the plan on the title deeds – and this means the title deeds and NOT the plan in the estate agents particulars! Why is the plot the shape that it is? If there seems to be a mystery go to the public library and look at the nineteenth century ordnance survey maps of the area. They often provide clues as to what has happened.

Rule three is to drop in at the local pub, strike up an acquaintance with the local busybody and ask his opinion of your prospective purchase. You may get told the soil is full of eelworm and won't grow brassicas, or that it was once the scene of a horrible murder, or that 'it has a funny title you know'.

Finally, if you do find a ransom strip situation remember that it may be possible to sort it all out at a practicable cost if you go about things in the right way. Do not tell the owner of the strip that he is a despicable rogue. It is unlikely that

he is. He did not create the ransom strip. It is often better not to approach him at all, but to employ an estate agent or intermediary. And certainly do nothing at all until you have taken professional advice.

A similar problem can arise when the access is off a private road. The title to the land may include the right to use the private road, but some other user of the road may have made a practice of blocking the end of it by parking his family cars there for many years. He may be advised by his solicitor that he has now established a right to do so. Again, you have a special situation, and resolving it may cost you a lot of money. The usual answer to the problem, which is not uncommon, is to build a garage for the car owners on your own land and give it to them! This may cost a great deal, but it may be worth it in the long run.

In some situations insurance is available to deal with an old ransom strip or an access title problem and this is covered a little later on in this chapter.

But, back to the question of access and the planning. It's no good assuming that if the access is shown in one way on your planning, that you can simply change it. If the entrance to your plot is shown on the right hand side of the road frontage then you cannot automatically assume that it can be moved to the middle or the left hand side of the plot without exciting attention from the planners. In equal measure, if the planning has been granted on the basis of a shared access and driveway but you don't like the idea and, anyway, the man in the pub has told you that the property value would be lessened by such an arrangement, then you can't simply ignore things and go on to create a new access to the highway without the express consent of the planners. Even if they do agree that a fresh access to the road is acceptable, then they're going to insist on that access conforming to laid down requirements and they may not be achievable, particularly in respect of visibility splays but also in respect of requirements for gates, turning and parking areas.

Gates first. Although many modern houses don't seem to employ gates and the drive is usually open to the road, in rural and forest areas a gate is essential, if only to keep sheep and other animals from consuming your garden (The sheep in the Forest of Dean have long since learned to roll over cattle grids). Where gates are employed, there will usually be a requirement for a 45 degree splay from each side of the gate and for the gates to be set back at least 5.5 metres from the edge of the carriageway, so as to enable a motor car to pull off the road completely whilst the gates are opened. In addition the gates must then open inwards and if the slope of the land makes this impossible then your gates will have to move even further back.

Parking and turning. In some cases there is a requirement for all cars to be able to enter the site completely and then to be able to turn and leave the site in a forward gear. This is not universal. It will obviously be necessary if the access is off a busy road but might not be required at all if the access is from a side or estate road. If the requirement does appear on the planning document then you need to make a note of it because such a requirement can take up a large amount of land and will undoubtedly affect the positioning and indeed the size of your proposed new home. Parking is also usually stipulated on most consents both in the form of

Visibility splays

The local authority will want an access like this . . .

. . . which would look like this . . .

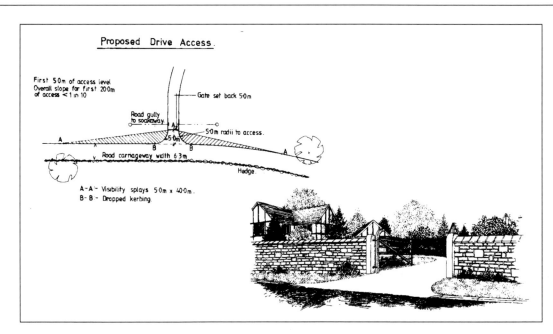

. . . but if your plot is field no. O.S.372 and this is how you want to site your new house, you will have to negotiate with the owner of field no. O.S.371 to provide your visibility splay.

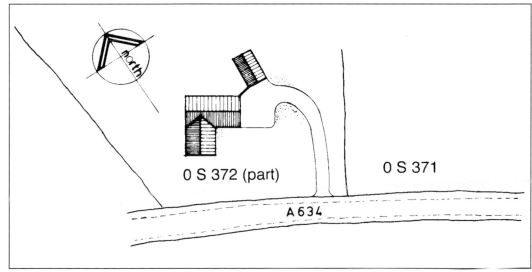

garaging and outside parking spaces. These can often be the parts of the driveway created and taken up in the formation of the turning areas, but check the planning documents and requirements to make sure that what is being asked for is achievable.

Visibility splays. These cause endless problems, which probably start with a simple condition on the planning consent that says, 'the access onto Acacia Avenue shall be formed in accordance with the County Highways requirements'. All perfectly innocuous, you may think. That is, until you realise and read on that their requirements involve a visibility splay and when you get out and measure that visibility splay it crosses your neighbour's land. A word, first about what a visibility splay is so that you can understand the full implications. The wording might ask for visibility splays 5.5 metres by 120 metres east and 5.5 metres by 90 metres west. Almost certainly that means that your plot is on the southern side of an east west road with the frontage facing roughly north. The longer visibility splay will relate to the traffic approaching on your side of the road and is calculated by measuring to a point 5.5m back from the carriageway edge along the centre line of your proposed driveway. From that point you then take a line eastwards 120m until it meets the carriageway and a similar line from the same point but to the west this time, and for only 90m, until it strikes the carriageway edge. These are your visibility splays. Now, if everything within those two triangles is within your plot then you've nothing to worry about except for the fact that at all times you'll have to keep those areas clear of any obstruction higher than 1005mm, and that includes shrubs and trees. But what if the triangles you arrive at go outside your boundaries and cross the neighbour's land? The planners aren't particularly concerned about the legalities of this. Planning permission says that you *may* build on the land, it does not say that you *can*. In their eyes it's up to the developer of the land to sort out any necessary easements and all they're concerned with is that the requirements are demonstrated. So, if you're offered a plot with such a requirement and the vendor

can't demonstrate that he has secured such easements from his neighbours, the planning is inoperable and until such time as suitable legally binding arrangements are in place you need to steer clear of that plot. You could, of course, try negotiating directly with the neighbours yourself, but be prepared for a chap who either sees this an opportunity to afford a holiday home in Spain, or is equally determined that the plot next door will never be developed, even to the point of deliberately planting tress and shrubs within the visibility splays. It all sounds pretty hopeless, docsn't it? Well it's not always that bad. In many cases the requirements are limited or even nonexistent and in others you'll find that the visibility splays cross the grass verge of the highway, which is fine. The thing is to check it both on site and on plan before you move on to buying a site.

Roads

Let us start by considering the road, which leads up to, your new front gate. It will fall into one of the following categories and if there is any doubt, your solicitor will establish exactly which one it's in:

A private road on land owners land.
If you are fortunate enough to be building in the country on a site reached by a road in this category, then you are involved with special circumstances. You should make sure that you are getting the best advice on the arrangements which the land owner will have suggested when he offered you the land. If your solicitor has a local rural practice then he should be an expert. If he is not, discuss with him where he is going to get you the best local advice.

A private unadopted road.
Access onto a private unadopted road is a different matter, and again you need a solicitor who has, or will get, relevant local experience. There are many sorts of unadopted roads, but the ones most usually found by selfbuilders were built in the first forty years of the century. At that time developers often sold plots leading off a private road with no intention that it would ever

be taken over – or adopted – by the local authority. This was considered to be a way of guaranteeing that the development would always be suitably exclusive in the days before the planning acts. The plots and houses built on them were often very large, although sometimes this way of doing things was used in low cost 'bungalow towns' like some of those on the Sussex coast and in Essex.

Fifty years later these unadopted roads are often in a sorry condition. Planning restraints have now largely removed the fear of unacceptable further development, and the residents owning the road would usually dearly like the authority to take it over and put it in good order. The council will not do this unless all the residents pay 'road charges' which may amount to tens of thousands of pounds for each property. As it is most unlikely that they all can (or want to) do this, the road remains unadopted with only the most urgent repair work paid for by some form of residents' association, usually only when they find the cost of filling the potholes is less than the cost of replacing the exhausts scraped off their cars.

Houses on these developments have large gardens, and high land values means that they will be subdivided and sold as building plots if planning consent to do this can be obtained. Plots like this are very popular with those wanting to build an individual home, who should consider certain aspects of such opportunities very carefully.

What are the arrangements for the ownership and maintenance of the road? What road charges are likely to be levied if it is ever adopted? Above all, what is the long term future for property values when the 1930 vintage road in terminal decay deteriorates further? Local solicitors and estate agents will be well aware of the local politics in such a situation, which is why a vendor may be hoping for a prospective purchaser from a distance. Also consider that road charges are levied at a rate per yard of road frontage, so that residents may wish to sell off a plot with a disproportionately long road frontage. You have been warned.

There are instances where no legal ownership can be established yet clearly several houses enjoy joint and uninterrupted access from a road, which they all maintain to one standard or another. These situations exist in Kent, for example, where developments sprang up in the immediate aftermath of the Second World War with bombed out people moving to the countryside to construct wooden and asbestos bungalows on plots of land sold off by local farmers. The bungalows are now fast disappearing, demolished to make way for modern country homes but the roadway still remains in its old state, both legally and physically. Nobody thought when whole communities originally bought their individual parcels of land that the access would be anything other than just used by them all. Nobody thought that in 50 years time each house would have 2 to 4 cars coming and going daily and, above all, nobody thought that, one day, people would need to demonstrate legal rights of way to get to their houses. Your solicitor will want to, nonetheless, and he may face an uphill struggle with no party having exclusive ownership and all parties unable to show collective responsibility. It doesn't mean that you can't buy the land. Quite clearly the other residents are enjoying their access and it would be in none of their interests to block up or frustrate the use of the road. The older residents probably won't see what the fuss is all about with these newcomers wanting all this legal mumbo jumbo. The simple solution, if you can't just accept things as they are, is a *single premium indemnity policy* guarding against the extremely unlikely event of a chap arriving back from Australia and claiming the road as his own, and that can be arranged quite easily by *DMS Services Ltd.* who can be reached on (01909) 591652.

Adopted roads.
Adopted roads, looked after lovingly by the council, would appear to present far less trouble. However, councils make rules about anything and everything, and their roads are no exception. Their rules for roads on new housing developments are demanding and precise, with thought given to the shape of cul de sacs to enable a fire engine to turn around easily, etc., Arrangements

for the junctions between new estate roads and highways are very carefully considered, and this is all very right and proper. However, unfortunately for those who buy infill plots fronting a highway, the same careful consideration is given to their own modest drive access.

In general terms, the higher the category of the road – A, B, unclassified, etc. – the stricter the requirements, and whatever the classification there will be a concern for road safety. At the very least this will involve an absolute ban on vehicles joining or leaving the road at a sharp corner or at a blind spot. More usually the requirements will also involve setting back any gate a fixed distance from the carriageway, and providing a visibility splay. The actual junction may be required to be level or at a gentle gradient for a certain distance inside your property, with a further maximum stipulated gradient for the next few yards of your drive. It is no use saying that you and your friends have Landrovers: the councils concern is the brakes on their dustcart. You will be expected to make sure that surface water from your drive cannot spill onto the road, and you will also have to meet specific standards for turning radii, which themselves may depend on the width of the highway at your proposed entrance.

None of this is relevant to the selfbuilder who is taking access off an existing private drive to another house, and whose planning consent shows this arrangement, or to the individual who is buying a serviced plot in a residential development where the road is not a highway.

Highway Department requirements for access to an infill plot in a village where the road is also a highway are absolutely crucial to every aspect of the project, and must be given very careful consideration. The fact that there is a planning consent is not enough: the writer has seen planning consents on such plots with a standard condition that 'the access shall be formed to the requirements of the Highways Authority', where these requirements involve 60% of the plot having to be excavated to achieve required levels.

Highway requirements vary in different parts of the country, and the rules in Suffolk are obviously very different from those in Powys or Cumbria. If you are considering a plot with

access from a highway, you must get hold of the local highway department requirements at a very early stage and consider whether the development that you propose for the plot will be practicable. You will be able to get details at the Town Hall, and bear in mind that it is most unlikely that you will be able to negotiate any relaxation of the requirements.

Shared drives

Because selfbuilders are often concerned with plots that have been carved out of a large garden, they are often involved with arrangements for shared drives. If planning consent has been given on this basis, then the existing access can continue to be used. However, if you alter it in any way, the local authority may take the view that you are forming a new access, and will insist that it meets all of their requirements. This requires careful thought. Equally careful consideration has to be given to the arrangements which you make with the established owner of the drive for its future maintenance, for its use by vehicles delivering materials to build your new home, and for parking on it. Local authorities will usually permit up to four houses to share one private drive, beyond which they are likely to consider it to be a road and subject to all sorts of regulations. The basis on which you may be sharing a drive with three other people requires very careful consideration. A very basic requirement is an arrangement that there is no parking of any sort under any circumstances on the shared part of the drive. It is also very desirable that the shared length should be constructed to a very high standard, and should be properly kerbed, so that it is as indestructible as possible to avoid difficulties over sharing the cost of rebuilding it at some time in the future. And when that time arrives, are you going to be able to insist that it is rebuilt, and that your neighbours pay their share of the cost?

Shared drives have short term advantages and long term problems, and if there is a shared drive some building societies will restrict the percentage of the value of the property on which they will grant a mortgage. Solicitors will elaborate on their disadvantages to prospective purchasers. However, this is frequently the only way in which some individual plots can be developed, and they are a necessary evil.

Unknown owners

Sometimes you'll come across a dream site and it's nigh on impossible to develop because no one knows who owns the land. Now, you could try the Land Registry but not all land is registered and the details and title deeds may be lying, gathering dust, in some solicitor's basement. Sometimes an owner may live close by but simply doesn't want anyone to know that he owns the land. Sometimes it's because an owner went abroad or was killed in the war. Other times it's because an elderly person has simply forgotten all about it. What can you do about it? Well, very little really except ask around, take out adverts and possibly put a notice on the site, all of which may alert all the other prospective selfbuilders in the area to the existence of the plot, meaning that, when an owner does surface, you could find yourself in a long queue. If you live next door or are prepared to risk all, you could simply occupy the land and squat on it until you can claim squatters' rights which is more properly known as *Adverse Possession*. If you occupy land, 'without let or hindrance' (in plain English that means without any permission from an owner, without paying any rent for the land and without an owner telling

you to clear off) for a period of 12 years or more you can then register a possessory title and take out an insurance indemnity policy to cover you for the eventuality of an owner finally turning up. After a further 3 years you can register an absolute title and the land is irrevocably yours.

It sounds fantastic but it often happens and it also happens the other way around. If you buy a plot where the neighbour seems to have extended his garden to within your boundaries and you arrive one day to tell him to clear off, and thank him very much for mowing your grass, but in future he needn't bother, you might be disappointed to hear that he considers that he has established squatters' rights over your land and that he's just returned from his solicitors where he's registered a possessory title. It doesn't immediately establish his claim but it could mean that the whole thing goes to court and he could well win, especially if he's got photographs of his children, now aged 20 but then aged 8 playing joyfully on the neatly mown lawn of your plot whilst he and his young wife sit, beaming happily, on carefully laid out garden furniture. If you visit a prospective plot and there appear to be signs of occupation, you need to move fast and inform your solicitors and/or the vendors. Any let or hindrance within the twelve years negates the adverse possession and if the owner tells him to clear off his land, preferably in writing, then for the squatter, the clock goes back to zero.

Footpaths

First of all, there may be legal problems. In rural areas a common difficulty is that there is a public footpath running over the land, possibly coming over fields from the village and joining the village street through the land where you would like to build your new home. It does not matter that the footpath is disused: if it has been gazetted and appears on the local authority's footpaths map, then it is as firmly there as if it was a public road.

Now it is possible to have a footpath moved, but usually only if the realignment is going to be more convenient, in every way, for those using the path. This usually means that the new alignment has to be shorter, less muddy, more

All is peace now with this house from D&M, but I can remember when the ground shook as piling rigs sought firm ground deep beneath the peat on this plot.

easily maintained and provide a nicer view and a more pleasant walk. It is absolutely no use thinking that the footpath can be shifted to run round the edge of your site, which will not bother anyone because hardly anyone uses the path anyway. Not only are footpaths protected in law and jealously guarded by local authorities, but there are also footpath preservation associations with members who make it their business to try to make sure that they are never, ever moved. Probably the best advice on moving a particular footpath will be obtained from a local solicitor, who may know what applications to do so have been made in the past, and why they failed.

Ground conditions

The purpose of this chapter is to evaluate your potential plot and ground conditions, and the foundation type you will need to employ is obviously an important part of that evaluation. I'll go into greater detail about the differing systems of foundations in the chapter on 'Designing a new home - to suit your site' but, here, let us consider whether or not any of this needs to concern you at this stage. Ideally you are hoping to build on good bearing ground, which will support the weight of your new house using simple and cost effective foundations. Sadly, this is not always possible and you must be conversant with other options. Incidentally, the cost of dealing with difficult foundation situations as a proportion of the total cost of the whole house has dropped dramatically in recent years as a result of new building techniques. It is unusual to find a site with foundation problems that cannot be overcome at an acceptable cost.

The first potential problem is that there may have been mining activities in the area and that there is consequently some danger of ground subsidence. This is normally detailed in a mining report attached to the planning consent, and at the very worst it means that you will be building on a reinforced raft instead of on orthodox strip footings. The additional cost is unlikely to be more than 5% of the total cost of the new home.

Geological problems are more complicated, and more difficult to detect. The principal hazards are that there is a spring on the land or a slip plane between two types of rock which outcrop on the land, or that you have a pocket of greensand under the turf. Fortunately all of these hazards are normally easily detected by someone with a practised eye, and in areas where they are likely to occur you will find plenty of people to point them out to you. The usual warning is an area of grass that is unnaturally green in the summer and marshy in the winter, perhaps with indicator sedge grasses. At the worst, this can involve you building on piled foundations at an additional cost of up to 20% of the building cost, but it is more likely that you will have to install a few hundred pounds worth of land drains.

A serious foundation problem can exist if you are building on filled land. This is not always readily detectable, but if there was an old building on the site you should check whether there are cellars below the ground. Again, for hundreds of years there were brickpits in villages where the locals fired their own bricks for their homes. When this ended the pits became rubbish tips, and now they are gaps between homes which appear to make ideal building plots. So they are - provided that you understand the need for special care in designing foundations.

Should you immediately rush to employ the services of a soil investigation engineer? Well, not immediately, although it may well come to that in the end. First off, try having a chat with the local Building Inspector and tell him what you're planning to do and where. He'll have seen and inspected nearly everything in the area and, even if he wasn't directly involved with the site next door to your plot, he's probably still just as aware of what went on. He won't only have had dealings with new properties being built, he'll also have inspected any extensions that have gone on and, especially if he's from the old school, I bet there's very little he doesn't know about ground conditions generally in your area. If he thinks that there's a possibility of bad ground then he'll say so and in that case you really need to get hold of a soil investigation company who will come along and dig or bore some trial holes to establish just what you've got. Another thing to do is to ignore my usual advice about listening to pub talk and to make a beeline for the oldest inhabitant and ask him about the history of the plot. He may remember that the village duck pond was there or that the butcher used to use the hole in the middle to chuck the old bones in.

Now, this soil investigation, should it prove to be advisable or necessary. Normally everything's fine and dandy but there are a few things you need to understand about this survey. The engineer will dig or bore holes in three, possibly four, positions on the site and he will evaluate the contents of each bore and come to his conclusions and recommendations based on those trial holes. What he is telling you is what he's discovered from those holes. He's not telling you what would have been in a hole a few metres away although from the holes he's dug he may well extrapolate and assume certain conditions. What you've got to remember is that this report, useful as it is, important as it is, is nevertheless, a report based on four trial holes and the only real survey that is 100% accurate is, in the end, your actual construction work. That makes it all the more important that you get out and about and ask around, because that's the only way you're going to find out that there was an old air raid shelter in the centre of where you're going to build and in the middle of all these trial holes. And if all this fails to turn up a problem and you go on to buy the plot? Well, chances are that it's not going to be that serious anyway and you'll know you did all you could but the rest was in the lap of the Gods. In the end, that's what your contingency fund is there for.

Trees

Almost everyone's ideal dream site visualises their new house nestling into a plot surrounded by leafy trees whispering quietly in the breeze as the sun filters down to a dapple shaded lawn. But cut to reality. Trees may complicate your plans, may limit the size, the shape and the siting of your new house and, they may make it considerably more expensive to build. There are many angles to this and they are best considered under four separate headings.

Trees and planners

This is where the trouble starts. Planners can place a Tree Preservation Order on any tree or group of trees that they think worth protecting, except for fruit trees, even if they are obviously dying or not worth keeping, just so they can have a say in what happens to them. An application for planning consent that involves felling TPO trees always receives special consideration, although a planning consent showing that trees have to be removed overrides the TPO.

The first problem is knowing whether the trees on the plot have a TPO on them, and if you write or ask in a direct way at the Town Hall you may trigger a TPO being issued. You will have to make general enquiries - 'can I look at the TPO map for the village?' and proceed with caution. If there is not a TPO you may decide to fell any tree which is in the way straight away. If this is likely to upset anyone, do it very quickly to that a TPO is not issued in a hurry while you are sharpening your chain saw. It does happen. Local advice is useful in this sort of thing.

If there is a TPO, you will have to consider the situation very carefully. If there is outline planning consent, then a condition of the consent will probably be that the tree has to be retained, even if this seriously limits the size of the property that can be built on the plot. You will have to show the protected trees on your site plan for the detailed application.

At this stage it is probably worthwhile getting a tree specialist to make an inspection, and to provide you with a report. Hopefully he or she will write 'the specimen is over mature and should be replaced' or at least 'an unremarkable specimen which can be replaced without affecting the character of the local arboreal environment'. For every tree that you show on your plan to be removed you should show at least three replacement trees elsewhere in the garden, and make sure that the species are from any recommended list in the local design guide.

This will usually do the trick, especially if there is already outline planning. However, you may find that you get involved in negotiating about it with the planners, often with the suspicion that they care far more for trees than they do for people. As a last resort you can of course, as is your right, appeal.

Whatever you do, this is one area where the guidance of someone with local experience is invaluable.

Trees and foundations

Trees can affect the foundations of houses in three ways: by the roots simply pushing into the foundation brickwork and cracking it, or by roots rotting and leaving voids under the foundations when the tree is felled, or, in clay soils, when a tree is felled and no longer takes hundreds of gallons of water out of the subsoil, the ground may heave and rise by two or three inches. All these potential difficulties are dealt with by a combination of special foundation design and a limit on the distance that a new building can be constructed from a tree.

Foundation design to meet problems due to trees is a matter for your architect, and your plans will not receive Building Regulation approval unless they are satisfactory. One thing to watch for is a bad ground situation due to a tree having been felled before you bought the plot, often because the vendor wanted it out of the way before he advertised the land for sale. Sometimes he will have carefully filled in the hole. If the subsoil is clay the work involved in dealing with this can be considerable.

The minimum distance which a house can be built from a tree depends on the species, its potential height and the nature of the ground. There are strict rules for this and they are, most conveniently, set out in the NHBC handbook. Whoever is designing your house and its foundations will deal with these problems, probably on the basis of, and as a result of, the soil investigation survey that you have almost certainly had carried out if there are mature trees present on your site. As a rule of thumb, though, it is unwise to build closer to a tree than four metres or one third of its mature height, whichever is the greater. On some soils this distance may be increased and with some species, which are particularly harmful to buildings such as poplar, elm and willow, the distances may be quite considerable. I will deal with special foundations in the chapter, 'Designing a new home - to suit your site'.

Tree roots can also cause problems with driveways, which will be a nuisance but not specifically expensive to deal with. What is more likely is that the planners will be concerned that any driveway should not adversely affect the tree by compaction of the ground beneath them or by interference with the soil's access to air and water. Tree roots can also quite dramatically affect drains. The small young and beautiful weeping willow that you plant when you first move in may grow into a very large tree indeed – a joy to behold. But one day, the toilet may refuse to flush and you might find out that your prized tree's sustenance and vigour was gained from its roots complete invasion of your drains!

Trees and your design

A large tree or a group of trees within a hundred feet of any house or bungalow is going to enhance

Trees form the framework to the picture of this Scandia-Hus house and were obviously an important consideration with the design. Perhaps too, they had a profound effect on the design of the foundations.

the appearance of the property, but must be taken into consideration at the design stage. Will part of the building be in shade at certain times of the day? What about views from key rooms? Should rooms be arranged to suit this? Above all, remember that an attractive green woodland scene in June can be a dank, dark miserable outlook in January. Big trees need their own sort of garden, bearing in mind that they affect everything growing beneath them, produce huge quantities of leaves, and usually rule out having a swimming pool. Living with trees means letting them dominate your garden: most people like that very much indeed, but do not let it come as a surprise.

If you are planting trees, possibly to replace those cleared to make way for a house, keep in mind that they will be there for a century at least. If your garden is big enough to split off a building plot in the future, do not cause problems by putting a tree in the middle of the potential plot. If you are planting a tree at the corner of your vegetable garden, make sure that it is on the north corner so that it does not shade your vegetables in the years to come. Choose a species carefully, and consider whether you want to make a modest investment in something really worthwhile. A ten foot Catalpa, the Indian bean tree, or a similarly sized Tulip tree, may cost about £100. This may be more than you intended to spend, but what other present for your partner will grow to 80 feet tall!

Trees and neighbours

If your neighbour has a tree which overhangs your boundary and which will interfere with the house that you want to build, you must clear the situation with your solicitor before you commit yourself to buy the plot. In most circumstances you can cut the branches which overhang your fence, and you can cut roots that will affect the foundations of the house that you want to build, but this can be a complex issue. It is particularly difficult if the result of your activities would result in the tree becoming unsafe. Perhaps it is already unsafe? If it falls onto your house, you hope that your neighbour is properly insured or else very rich. He may be neither, and almost

certainly he is unlikely to tell you, which is why you have to take out a selfbuilder's policy to cover you until the house is built and your domestic insurance takes over. Also remember that a neighbour may choose to fell his own trees and seriously affect your view. There is little you can do about this but it is something you should consider.

Everything is simpler if the trees are on the land that you want to buy, but you must still consider the implications at an early stage. First of all, your tree may fall across the boundary and damage your neighbour's property. This risk is covered by your selfbuilder's insurance policy while you are building and by your householder's insurance when you have finished, but the policies will require that you exercise normal prudence in this matter. This definitely includes being aware of dangerous trees and trees that present a special hazard, and doing something about it. If there is a potential problem here, you should get the tree inspected by a qualified tree surgeon who can either give you a report saying that there is no hazard, or can advise on sorting things out. If you are buying a plot with potentially dangerous trees you might be able to negotiate for such a report to be a condition of your purchase.

Drainage

Any consideration of a plot must include drainage from three points of view. The first and most important is, of course, *foul drainage*, the drains which will take and dispose of the waste water from kitchens, bathrooms and toilets. Is mains drainage available and, if so, is it at the right level in the ground to enable you to connect to it by a normal gravity connection or will you have to employ a pump? Is the connection available within your plot or on the highway directly adjoining your plot and, if not, do you have the necessary easements and consents, to cross other people's land in order to make the connection? If mains drainage is not available will you be able to use a septic tank or a mini treatment system? If the ground is capable of accepting percolation, will the Environment Agency and/or the local authority delegated to act on their behalf accept such a system in that location or will they insist on a cesspool? Septic tanks are not normally acceptable in urban or built up locations. I will discuss the various methods of foul drainage in more detail in the chapter called 'Designing a new home – to suit your site' but for the purposes of this chapter these are questions you need to know when evaluating your plot.

Surface water drainage is the other form of drainage, which you will have to evaluate. This is the water that is collected by the rainwater guttering systems on your house, from its outbuildings, driveways and pathways. It all still has to be got rid of and except in a few, ever diminishing locations where there are combined drains, most local authorities will not allow it to discharge through the foul drains. In some areas the local authority will insist on surface water being connected to their surface water drainage system. In others they prohibit any private connections, even from driveways directly abutting the highway. Usually surface water drainage is discharged through gullies and pipework to a series of soakaways on the plot. These soakaways can in acceptable ground be quite simple rubble filled holes, but in other areas where the ground is less amenable to accepting water you might be required to construct quite elaborate soakaways from perforated concrete rings or purpose built brickwork. It may be necessary to conduct a percolation test for both foul and surface water drainage systems, of which more anon.

Land drainage is the one aspect of drainage that everybody forgets. If a site is waterlogged then it's an absolute certainty that your construction work will exacerbate the problem unless specific measures are taken to get the water away. Sometimes it's necessary to lay land drains in the foundation trenches of the new home, before they're backfilled, in order to conduct the water around the house and away. At other times it may even be necessary to lay individual land drains across the site to take water coming onto it from the surrounding land. What you don't want, is to live in a swamp. When looking at the plot for the first time, make a note of the kinds of vegetation. Crack willow and alder prefer damp conditions

and sedge and rush growing on the land is an indicator of bad drainage.

One way of draining land quite well can be the foul drains themselves. You can't, as I've said above, directly connect any surface water or land drains to the foul drains. But the drains are, nonetheless, surrounded by clean pea shingle and the lie of that medium will follow the drains away from your site creating a form of 'French drain'.

Easements

Easements grant a legal entitlement to the benefit of one party or owner of land, over land belonging to another party. Statutory Undertakers take out easements to enable them to cross land with, say, electricity cables or gas mains. Such services can benefit the land but they can also blight it. A high pressure water main or sewer can sterilise land up to 6M either side of the run. Easements can also give others access or the right to pass over your land for the purposes of access to another parcel of land and their import needs to be properly examined when you are evaluating your possible purchase. That's the negative side of things but, easements can also run to the benefit of your land in granting you, say, the right to use a driveway or access or in giving you the right to connect drains or services over an adjoining piece of land. In general they are very similar to covenants although they tend to grant specific rights of passage and use, rather than attempt to modify, the way in which a particular piece of land may be used. Just as with covenants, they can be altered or modified and there are the same rights of application to the Lands Tribunal and the same warnings.

Diverting drains and services.

This book repeatedly urges anyone considering buying a building plot to find out why it has not been built on in the past. One reason can be that there is a sewer, gas line or electricity cable across the site, and that the authority which installed it bought an easement to do so from the previous owner of the land, and the easement prohibits anything being built on top of the drain or service, or within a certain distance of it.

Unless the drain or service can be diverted, the plot cannot be developed.

This is a situation which is regularly exploited by selfbuilders, because unlike builders and developers, they often have time to arrange the diversion, and the patience to cope with the huge correspondence that is likely to be involved.

If you meet such a situation it is important to arrange an option or conditional contract on the land before you research the problem, as otherwise you may get everything sorted out only to find that the vendor puts up the price or decides to build on the land himself! The price should reflect the cost of the diversion, which can be significant, and so you have to establish this before committing yourself in any way.

Make a start with obtaining a photostat of the actual easement granted to the service authority, which should be with the title deeds. If it is not in intelligible language you will have to seek the help of an expert to work out exactly what it says. If it is a very old easement, particularly a 19th century one, you may find that there is a clause which requires the authority to move their service at their own expense if the land owner wants to build his dwelling on top of it. This is often a feature of old electricity cable easements. Do not celebrate too soon: in the 1950's the electricity boards offered sums to all the land owners who owned such rights to extinguish this part of the easement, and many of them accepted. If they did, the documentation involved may never have been with the title deeds. However, the board will not have lost their copy!

Usually you can expect to be quoted a most unreasonable sum for moving a service, and it may take a lot of patience to get a quotation at all. However, once you have a quotation it is an admission that it is technically possible to move the service, and you can then start to negotiate. Try to reach the engineers concerned, rather than the legal department of the services authority. The engineer may permit you to seek tenders for this work to be done from a list of approved contractors, which will probably be cheaper. It may also be possible for you to open the trench involved, lay the gravel bed and back fill after the drains, pipe or cable have been laid by the contractor. This will probably save a lot of money.

If you are successful in negotiating some arrangement for the diversion, and the arrangement to buy the land reflects the cost of the diversion, make sure that the legal arrangement with the authority refers to you *or your successor in title*, so that if you buy the land but have to sell it on for any reason a potential purchaser does not have to re-negotiate the whole business.

If a private drain or sewer crosses your land, probably linked to the houses on either side, then this can often be a cause for celebration rather than dismay, even if it crosses your plot in the position you envisage your new home going. You're not going to have to go to the expense of having to create a new road connection for a start. In all probability the drains are laid at 1 in 40 when modern drains can run at 1 in 60, or at a pinch 1 in 100, so levels aren't usually going to be a problem. Your designer will probably show the drains diverted around your house with you connecting your drains to them, but the reality is that you would've had to build the drains anyway and what actually happens is that you build your drains and then the other drains are diverted into yours. Usually the existing drains are allowed to continue running through the site until the last moment with your foundations built around them and then, when the diversion is made, they then become redundant and can either be removed or left in the ground.

A word of warning on this point, one which does not crop up very often but is not unknown. Sometimes on a private estate the deeds allow for the use of a private drain by named houses with no provision made for the splitting off of plots and the creation of extra houses. In these cases it is often necessary to get the agreement of the other houses on the estate for the fresh connection and this is something that your solicitor needs to check out and which is really the responsibility of the vendor in the first place. On the other hand, as I've said repeatedly, vendors have a habit of failing to understand your concerns and you might find yourself having to make the running on this one. Make sure, therefore, that you do have things tied up by some sort of option or contract before you go about enhancing the vendor's land and if ransoms are payable to the other occupiers then this really should come off the asking price of the plot.

Services

Most estate agents' details state that as far as they're aware all mains services are available but then go on to say that any prospective purchaser should satisfy themselves as to their availability. Chances are that the agents haven't even bothered to really investigate. We've already discussed drains so what we're talking about here is gas, water, telephone and electricity. You may not wish to make formal applications for all of these before you have actually bought the land, if only because you wish to avoid paying the application fees, but you should satisfy yourself that they are readily available at a reasonable charge. If the gas main is close by and you intend to use gas for your principal form of heating and hot water then they don't usually make a charge. The electricity boards always make a charge and the water boards achieved notoriety with their high charges in the aftermath of privatisation but, of late, these have come down to more reasonable proportions. If mains gas isn't available it's not the end of the world as there's always the option of Lpg or oil as the firing source. If mains electricity isn't available then things get a little more tricky although modern small generators have made huge efficiency strides in recent years. The non-availability of mains water can be a problem but in some areas even that can be got around by the use of bore holes. If you're in any of these situations then you're probably thinking of building in an extremely rural location; in which case you're either a farmer or a seeker of things from another age and much of this will be old or welcome news for you.

Covenants

Another legal problem which can prevent the development of a site is the existence of a covenant on the land. Covenants are clauses in an earlier contract for the sale of the land which are binding on all future purchasers, and either require that something shall be done, or dictate that something shall not be done when the land is developed. Such covenants may be very old indeed, and may have passed with the title to the land since the middle of the last century. The reason for them is often lost in the mists of time. Quite often one comes across covenants preventing any development on a piece of land in case it should spoil the view from a manor house which has long since been demolished. The manor house may be no more, but the covenant marches on.

Positive covenants typically require that any property to be constructed shall be of only one storey or shall be set back a certain distance from one of the boundaries, often to preserve a distant view. Another common covenant gives a right to an adjacent landowner to pass through any part of the plot to gain access to a distant field, or, in urban areas, gives a neighbour who once owned the land access through it to his own back garden. In these cases the land was probably sold off as a paddock and the covenants are appropriate to that use. Although it may now have planning permission as a building site, the covenants remain.

Negative covenants are more usual, and often preclude any building at all. Sometimes they forbid any development unless the plans are submitted to the original vendor, who can approve them or disallow them as he or she wishes. However, it has been held that the words "such consent not to be unreasonably withheld" are implied, even if they are not expressed in any covenant reserving such a right of approval by a vendor. This goes back to and demonstrates the original intention of land laws to maintain the proper use of land.

It is sometimes possible to have restrictive covenants removed but this is, undoubtedly, a job for a suitably experienced solicitor. It is an extremely lengthy business involving application to the Lands Tribunal who have discretionary powers to modify or remove covenants if they see fit. The outcome is never certain and, as with all lengthy legal procedures, the costs can escalate quite alarmingly. It is usually quicker and easier to take out indemnity insurance against the possibility of anyone claiming rights under the covenant.

Looking at a building plot

What are the questions you ask yourself when you get out of your car and walk over to a hedge with a 'For Sale' board planted in it?

1. Is it where you want to live? (Surroundings, outlook, travel to work, shops, schools, etc.). Do not let your enthusiasm for selfbuild override a critical consideration of whether an ideal plot for an individual home is really where you want to live.

2. Is it in an area where property values can be expected to appreciate ahead of the market, or at least keep in step with it?

3. Is the price appropriate to the total budget?

4. Has it got planning consent? Are you likely to get approval for the sort of house that you hope to build? This is likely to be so if there are other similar new homes in the area.

5. Is it in an area where the planners are likely to require expensive traditional materials like natural stone, handmade bricks or clay tiles? If so, the budget will have to be adjusted.

6. Will the dimensions at the building line permit you to build a house of the size and style that you want without it appearing cramped or out of place?

7. Does the shape of the plot and its boundaries match up with the plans in the estate agent's particulars? It is surprising how often they do not, and this is the time to investigate discrepancies.

8. Are there any signs of anyone else, other than the vendor, occupying or using the land? Do they have consent for this or could this be an Adverse Possession? If so, you need to establish just how long this has been going on for and you may need to go back to the vendor and ask him to sort the matter out.

9. Is the access off an adopted road without any obvious requirements for visibility splays or expensive earth moving? If not, then consideration has to be given to the legal position regarding access and any effect that this problem will have on the budget.

10. What about drains? Is there a sewer in the road to which access can be gained at a reasonable cost? If not, there is a special situation to be evaluated and costed which may affect the budget.

11. What about surface water drainage? Does the soil look well drained enough for soakaways? If not, are there surface water drains in the road - look for road drainage grids.

12. Do the ground conditions look normal? Is there any sign of wet ground as evidenced by unusual vegetation? If so the cost of special foundations will have to be allowed for in the budget.

13. Are there any signs of old buildings or of the site being a filled quarry or clay pit? Either might involve special foundations.

14. Are there any mature trees on the site? Might you ever want to cut them down? If so, might they be subject to Tree Preservation Orders? Are they within 30 feet of the house site, thus requiring root barriers?

15. Are there any signs of trees being recently removed — often done by a vendor to make a site appear larger? This may involve special foundations.

16. Services. Do water, gas, electricity and telephone services appear to be available? If they are not close at hand, then their provision, and the cost involved, become major factors.

17. Easements, etc. Are there any signs of underground services running through the plot or of overhead power lines? This may be a reason why the plot has never been developed.

18. Public footpaths and rights of way. Are there any signs of others using the land, especially any gates or stiles which give access to land beyond the boundary?

19. Is access adequate for deliveries of building materials? Many infill sites with access along an existing drive cannot be reached by a lorry, thus adding difficulty and expense to a building operation.

20. Why has no one built on this site before? There has to be a reason in these days when building plots are in short supply. Make sure that you find out, and that it is not because of a hidden problem.

21. Finally, what can the locals tell you about the site in the local pub? Is it worth having a word with the village builder before taking things further? Remember the estate agent is working for the vendor, not for you. It is up to you to find out all that you can about it. Your solicitor will only concern himself with the title. Everything else is up to you.

Legal contingency insurance

Defects in titles can take many forms, and many can be dealt with through special single insurance policies. As far as restrictive covenants are concerned, the policy protects the insured and their successors in title against enforcement or attempted enforcement of the covenant. It includes the costs, expenses and any damages in connection with a court action or lands tribunal action, the cost of alteration or demolition following an injunction, the loss of market value of land as a result of development being prevented and abortive capital expenditure.

Legal contingency insurance can also cover situations where title deeds are lost, problems over uncertain rights of way, services indemnities where the rights to use drains or other services is uncertain or unknown, and even the validity of possessory titles.

The premiums payable are assessed and evaluated according to the risk factors determined by the underwriters. They are usually payable as single premium and are sometimes referred to as 'single premium indemnity policies'. It is surprising, but many solicitors seem either not to have heard of them or to have forgotten about their existence. I can recall many a time when a solicitor very nearly persuaded a prospective selfbuilder to withdraw from a plot where the title was mildly defective or ownership could not be proven over an access. In nearly all of these cases, when the suggestion of a single premium indemnity insurance was put back to the solicitor it was very speedily arranged and the purchase was able to proceed, usually with the premium being paid by the vendor!

This is a very technical area of insurance, and each proposal is evaluated separately. DMS Services Limited, who handle the standard selfbuilder's policies are able to help. Ring them on 01909 591652.

To some extent the actual process of buying the plot will have overlapped the evaluation process which was described in the previous chapter, and as each consideration in the evaluation process is made then, hopefully, the buying of the land moves one more notch forward.

Buying land is not the same as buying other goods or services. By long established law the purchase of land has to be evidenced in writing, and by long established practice the legal profession has gone out of its way to make that evidencing as complicated and as obscure as possible, with its own unique vocabulary and sets of procedures. Solicitors, land agents and estate agents make their living by operating within this system and they make very little effort to explain it in any sort of plain English to their clients. If you are going to buy land then it is important that you familiarise yourself with the terminology and the procedures and you prepare yourself to have the professionals to make sure that they look out for any of the pitfalls. When you buy a property in England, you in effect buy the land with whatever's on it at the time. The concept of land ownership goes right back to William the Conqueror who, when he stepped onto the beach at Hastings, threw his arms out wide and claimed the Kingdom for his own and for his successors and heirs. He got his feet wet, which is why the title of any coastal land extends to the medium high water mark! As time went by the Crown then parcelled out the land under various forms of tenure, which normally required payment or favours of some kind. This payment could vary from provision of goods and foodstuffs right through to the supply of soldiers for the army and wenches for . . . well, for whatever they used wenches for at that time.

The basic tenet of land occupation stems from that early appropriation, in that all land law endeavours to ensure that land is used and that it serves some useful function. Great pains were always taken to make sure that land could not, in the natural course of its division and subdivision, become landlocked, for instance. As time went by the crafty got around that by the use of ransom strips and covenants as I have already discussed, but they were always against the driving spirit of land serving a useful function. Easements of necessity are established in law, where an owner can be prevented from selling off land that has been in a common ownership, in a manner that would prejudice or prevent part of it being used for its natural purpose.

The most important form of tenure which has come down to us through the ages is that of 'Freehold', and when you own land in this way it basically means that you hold the land free of any payment. Most land outside that still retained by the Crown is now freehold and in turn it is open for the freeholder to consider letting off all or part of their land on leasehold. There are still areas in the country where there are anachronisms such as 'Chief rents' payable to institutionalised landlords and it is still possible that land may be offered on the basis of a long leasehold or ground rent in perpetuity. Such things are now rare and in the areas where they occur, Manchester for one, the solicitors are quite au fait with them and they shouldn't cause any problems.

Of course it's open for the private individual to do the conveyancing on their own sale or purchase of land and, so long as it is properly evidenced in writing and the title is then suitably registered that's fine. Easements, access rights and other matters can be dealt with by those who are not solicitors. But why? Oh sure, there are savings to be made but, for the individual selfbuilder, with all the other things they've got to do and worry about, those savings are simply not cost effective. The time and effort needed to properly transfer land ownership is simply disproportionate and, when all is said and done, your title will be looked at with suspicion. If you're hoping to borrow money then you're stacking the odds against yourself with a home made title and when, and if, you ever sell, the purchaser's solicitor, and/or his building society's solicitor will go out of their way to make your life difficult.

Solicitors

If you already have, or know, a solicitor who you wish to act for you, that is fine. Otherwise you will probably entrust your affairs to the man whose office you first contact. If you are buying a plot of land with planning consent, it is unlikely that there will be anything to choose between the competence with which different firms of solicitors will deal with the purchase, but there may be a big difference in the speed with which they will do the job and the advice which they will give to you as someone building on your own. If time is important, it can speed things up to use a local solicitor as he will be familiar with local titles.

The best way to find the right solicitor is by a personal recommendation from another self-builder who tells you what a super legal service they had, but you may have to start from scratch with the yellow pages. Always have a word with your solicitor once you've decided on a piece of land and try to make sure that, if at all possible, your proposed purchase is handled by someone in the office who's fairly senior or at least has experience of plot buying and the particular pitfalls and problems that need to be guarded against. Sometimes a busy office will allocate files to different staff by order of value and your plot could well be handed over to a junior member with little or no experience of plot purchase. Your solicitor will be concerned to advise you on just how to make your offer and he will want to make sure that you are not irrevocably committed before he's had a chance to properly examine the title. This normally means that you should never sign any papers or make any written offer unless it is qualified by the words 'subject to contract'. If you pay a deposit on the land then you must also make sure that your payment is made subject to contract and that the deposit is fully returnable in the event of you not proceeding. As I've said before, if you've bought at auction, then the fact that you were the last person bidding means that you have to sign and effectively exchange contracts at that point and, in turn, that means that your solicitor must have been given the chance to do all of his work before you enter that auction room.

Your solicitor will be concerned with the title to your land. It is his job to see that it is transferred to you together with any advantages, and that you also know of all the disadvantages of the title. He will see that it is registered in your name when you finally complete the purchase. You can

expect that he will be very punctilious in this, and that he or she will make sure that everything is explained carefully to you. So far so good, but beware. A solicitor will deal with the situation regarding your land on paper and only on paper. He is unlikely ever to see the plot, and will certainly not get involved in peering down manholes or wondering why part of the ground looks so green in dry weather. It is your job to relate everything that he finds out about the title to the actual situation on the ground, and it is not really part of his job to make sure that you do this. You have to get cracking on it yourself, and

Before any work was started on this site, arrangements would have been made about access, ownership of the wall and the availability of services.

by and large, it is something that only you can do unless you are engaging an architect to handle the whole project for you.

In considering this matter, let us first look at exactly what your solicitor is going to do for you. First of all, he is going to make sure that there is a clear title. This means that the land is really owned by the fellow who is selling it, and that if he has mortgaged it or offered it as a security in some other way, the mortgagee has agreed to release his rights over it.

Your solicitor will also examine any covenants that are attached to the land together with any rights or easements that you may have over the land of adjoining owners, or which owners may have over the plot you want to buy. Easements are legal rights giving one party, owner or occupier of land the right to do something on or over another owner's land. The most common example would be where a statutory authority such as the water board, gas board or electricity board have legal rights to pass under or over a piece of land with their services. The easement giving them rights for this will probably also give them the right to enter upon the land for the purposes of maintenance and, in some cases, it may also 'sterilise' an area of land. An example of this is where a high pressure main crosses land and the easement prevents any building over or for a distance either side of the centre line of the service. In some cases this can be as much as 6M on either side so it's important that you know about this as, in anybody's book, that's a heck of chunk to take out of a plot. All of these things will

be found in the papers, which will accompany and form part of your title. Remember too, that easements can exist in your favour and that it's up to you to check their operation. An easement may give you the right to cross someone else's land to connect to a drain and your solicitor will confirm this to you. What he cannot confirm, however, is whether that connection you're entitled to is physically possible and that's something you'll have to check out or get checked out.

Both covenants and easements can, some-times, be altered or extinguished but this is a long winded and expensive business and it's unlikely that you'll have the time to get involved with this, unless it's absolutely necessary. Most selfbuilders are on a fixed budget with a fairly fixed timetable and it's often easier to consider the Legal Contingency Insurance we talked about in the previous chapter. In some cases the covenant can be so obscure and unlikely that it's as well to leave it there. A prohibition against the salting of pork on the land is unlikely to inconvenience too many people and the interest it will confer on the title means that it will be remembered and that those dealing with it will pay it a little more attention.

What a wonderful site for a new home, but this type of plot might come with severe restrictions.

Your solicitor will also be concerned to evaluate and verify the planning situation on the land and we have discussed that in the previous chapter.

Title deed plans

Along with all the documents which the solicitor receives there will of course be the title deed plans and these may well be the first time that you have anything to compare with the badly copied fragment of the local Ordinance Survey which was reproduced on the estate agent's details. The title deed plans will, in effect, form a record of plans down through time and will show the history of the plot and how it was arrived at by subdivision of larger segments of land or by addition of others. As I've warned before, there is a chance that none of them necessarily represents the site that has been pointed out to you and that possibly none of them represent the plan that the planning authorities have. Your solicitor can notice and point out any apparent discrepancies in the plans but what he can't do is verify them on the ground. You need to be able to get out there with a 30M tape and measure up your plot to make certain that what you're buying is the same as that which is being offered on paper. If you can't do it, or there's any doubt at all in your mind, then engage a surveyor for the purpose. Oftimes the discrepancies are immaterial but there are times when it's vital, such as with visibility splays and accesses. These things need to be sorted before, and not, after you've signed the contract. If you go ahead and buy and then, when you're clearing the land that you think and need to be 60 feet wide at the building line, you find out it's only 55 feet, you're stuck with it. You can't just go to the next door neighbour and demand that he moves the fence and it's your plans that will have to change, not the boundary.

Undisclosed problems

All vendors have to answer, through their solicitors, a list of what are known as preliminary enquiries. These ask questions like, "Do you know of anything adversely affecting the property?" The honest vendor will answer just as honestly but the less than honest one may answer, "No", even though he knows of something. And proving that he gave the wrong answer at a later date might be frightfully difficult. If you do come across an undisclosed problem then hopefully, having read this book, you've found out about it long before you've signed the contract. And if not? Well, you'll know that you did all you could and, unless it's a blatant fraud, in which case you probably have got a legal remedy, it's probably not that serious and you'll get around it one way or another in ways which are, almost certainly, explained in other sections of this book.

Final checks

If you make all the checks and you go back to the last chapter and go through it all again, then you should avoid any unpleasant surprises. However just to make sure, ask yourself one more time, "Why hasn't this plot been built on before?" Maybe there's a good reason. Maybe the vendor is right when he says that he's just inherited the land. Maybe the previous owner really did want to preserve it as garden. Maybe the planner's attitudes have changed or they've been changed after a long fight, which went to Appeal. All of that is perfectly possible and perfectly reasonable. But maybe, just maybe, it was the site of the village duck pond, which was filled in a few years ago, and then grassed over. Maybe it's open because there's a high pressure pumped sewer running through it and the land is sterile. If you've done your homework on the plot, if you've chatted up the oldest resident in the pub and asked around you'll probably know the answer. And if not? Well, ask around just one more time, just to make sure.

Signing the contract

Eventually you'll get to that all important and long hoped for stage of signing the contract on your land. Your solicitor has satisfied himself that all's well and he'll have given you a report on title and explained to you exactly what rights and obligations are involved. You in turn will have discussed with him just what you've found out during your own investigations and the two of you will have pooled your respective knowledge to arrive at the decision that this is the right thing to do and that all eventualities have been covered as far as is humanly possible.

If you're buying a plot with outline planning consent then the chances are that, at this stage, your detailed application is still going through the planning office. It's not possible to be absolutely sure about planning but it goes without saying that when you sign the contract you need to be as sure as you can be that you're going to get planning for what you want to build – at the very least you need to know that you're going to get planning for something that makes economic sense on the plot you're buying even if, during the planning process, things get changed. If the land has Full, or even Detailed, consent already then, if the plans suit your purposes, that's fine but at the very least you'll know just what can be achieved on the plot. We'll discuss planning in greater detail in a following chapter.

Each party to the contract separately signs their copy of the document and gives it to their solicitor. You, as the buyer, also have to give your solicitor a cheque for the deposit. You haven't, at this stage, exchanged. In the old days the opposing solicitors would actually meet somewhere public, like under the town clock and exchange contracts, with the buyer's solicitor handing over the signed contract together with the money and the vendor's solicitor handing over the signed contract together with a clod of earth, supposedly from the plot. Nowadays they just contact each other on the telephone and agree when the exchange shall be deemed to have taken place. Once that point has been reached, you're committed. The land isn't yet yours but you are contracted to buy it and more importantly, perhaps, the vendor is committed to sell it to you. Within a period, usually 28 days, the completion will take place and the balance of the purchase price will have to be paid so, when you sign the contract, you do need to know that the finance is there. Your solicitor will have covered that point with you and he will want to have made sure that the money is in place. A promise that granny will be sending it on in the next few weeks probably won't cut much ice and he's unlikely to let things proceed to contract.

Technically you can't use the land until after completion but many a vendor will allow you to make a start, assuming, of course, that you've already got detailed planning for your new home. His solicitors will either want to receive the full monies or at the very least they'll want to know that the money is held by your solicitor.

Insurances

Even though you're only contracted on the land, and you technically still don't own it, you do now have a beneficial interest in the land. It is possible that you could find yourself with shared liability for any mishaps that occur on the land and, on exchange, therefore, you will need to take out the necessary insurances, even if you don't intend to start work immediately. A selfbuilder's policy will cover you for all eventualities such as a child wandering onto the land and falling down a hole or a tree falling over onto next door's house in a gale. The cover lasts for two years or until the new home is finished, whichever is the sooner, so it's not a question of having to pay extra money out as you've going to need the cover anyway. Full details appear later in this book but for now make a note to contact DMS Services Ltd. on (01909) 591652 and they'll tell you all about how you can arrange the necessary cover.

Completion

Exchange of contracts means that you have to complete within the time frame set out in the contract, usually 28 days but it can be varied by agreement, prior to exchange. Failure to complete means that you are in breach of contract. Your deposit can be forfeit and you may be liable for extremely heavy damages, which is why your solicitor will want to be absolutely sure that the monies for completion are in place. The conveyance itself is a long legal document, which will list all the terms and conditions and refer to schedules and appendices setting out the obligations of each party to the contract and the covenants and easements attached to it. You may see this - usually it's signed by the vendor and, equally as usually, it's joined onto all the other conveyances that have come down through time to form the title deeds, which are then spirited away to the vaults of your lender.

Buying a building plot: checklist

Checks to be made on site before signing a contract. These are essentially the same as those made when appraising a site which you made to alert yourself to possible problems. This time you are making the checks to be sure you know all that you need to know before you sign the contract.

1. Boundary dimensions to be compared with the title plan, planning consent plan, etc.
2. Access to be compared with the access shown on the various plans.
3. Any visibility splays required to be checked on the ground, and especially if there is any risk that they cross the plot boundary.
4. Check access for building materials.
5. Foul drains – where is the existing sewer? What is the size, depth etc?
6. Surface water drains – any existing surface water drains, agricultural land drains ditches? Is the land suitable for soakaways?
7. Ground conditions. Any sign of wet ground or unusual vegetation? Any sign of demolished buildings? Any sign of quarrying or spoil pits?
8. Trees. Tree preservation order situation. Species and heights of trees (which affect permissible distances from new buildings). Any sign of trees recently removed which will involve special foundations.
9. Services. Are water, gas, electricity, phone services really available? Are the costs of the services going to be acceptable?
10. Easements. Are any cables or pipes where they are supposed to be? At the correct depth?
11. Are the easments and covenants in favour of the plot operable? Are the owners of the adjoining land aware of your plans? It is sometimes possible that they aren't and they will, after all is said and done, become your neighbours so you need to get off on the right foot with them.
12. Is there any sign of adverse possession. If so how long has it been going on for and is the vendor aware of the situation – if so what has he done about it and when?
13. Planning. Do you know exactly where you stand?

6 Designing a new home – the basics

Among many popular illusions concerning an individually built home is the idea that those building for themselves are able to express their own personalities by building homes which are uniquely their own, and in which they can indulge their wildest dreams. In fact all of them suffer many of the same constraints as the developer, and if they succeed in avoiding standardised features it will only be with considerable effort. All influences in modern society urge towards conformity. Many features of this conformity are desirable, and reflect the best in modern living standards, but others are imposed, directly or indirectly, by the planners, the dictates of finance, and fashion. This situation ensures that a new home is the best possible investment.

For most selfbuilders the making or saving of money, whilst important, is not the issue that has brought them to the selfbuild table. Nevertheless, most will be concerned to achieve the most they can for the money that they can either afford, or it is deemed suitable to spend on the project, and to understand how this can be achieved requires a basic understanding of what makes buildings cost more or less.

To a large extent many of the factors that influence the costs of your new home are beyond the selfbuilder's control but the purpose of this book is to lead the enquiring mind along the paths of understanding so that, in the first place, you're probably aware of the problems when you buy the site and, if not, then you have an appreciation of their effects when, and if, they crop up. Quite apart from the cost of the plot in the first place, the land itself is probably one of the most

Border Oak demonstrate their true inheritance of the traditional oak beamed house with this lovely property.

important factors in determining the costs of your new home. The location of the plot will be the first major design influence. Planners are concerned, nowadays, to retain what they consider to be the local characteristics of their areas as a whole, and individual parts of it in particular. You will hear them talking of the 'local vernacular'. What they mean is the local style of building, the regional materials used, particularly on the outside and on the roof, and the features which are peculiar to their area. This book isn't a book on design, there are companion books from the same stable that deal with those aspects of selfbuilding, but it is a book which wants to make you aware of the implications. The cheapest structure to build is a simple rectangle with gable ends. Take that simple shape and change the rendered blockwork exterior walling to natural stone and you've increased the walling costs by up to 400% and the overall costs by 10%! Take the same structure and change the roof tiles from concrete interlocking to hand made plain clay tiles and you've added yet another 10% to the originally envisaged costs. Making the shape more complex will again add to the costs but the chances are that in today's planning environment that's exactly what the planning authorities will want you to do. Chances are though that that's what you want anyway, as the features and characteristics of the area are probably what attracted you there in the first place. The challenge is to incorporate these desirable features in the most cost effective way. Dormer windows (windows with a small roof over them) which appear with their tops below the wallplate have considerably less impact on the costs than one's which appear above the wallplate and, in turn, these have less cost impact than those half way between which break through the wallplate. Hipped roofs are inherently more expensive than gabled roofs but, if the walling materials are particularly expensive, then the saving in external walling may wholly or partially offset the extra costs of the roof.

The nature of the ground and its topography will have an undoubted impact on the costs. We've already discussed ground conditions and the effects differing soils and the presence of

trees can have and I'll be discussing special foundations in a later chapter. For now, though, the very use of the word 'special' must, of itself, indicate the probability of extra costs. Levels of the land, as well as what's underneath the surface, also have an effect. The site like a bowling green, assuming nothing adverse below its turf, is obviously going to be cheaper to develop, even if less interesting. The hugely sloping site is always going to be more expensive to develop but that which is constructed on it will, in many ways, be more innovative. Having said that, if a design which was originally conceived for a sloping site is utilised on a site that's as flat as a pancake, then its construction costs may well exceed those which it would have experienced on a site more suited to its conception. In similar vein, a design formulated for a level site will sometimes be more expensive to construct on a sloping site than a more complicated design especially drawn up to suit the lay of the land. It's 'horses for courses' and we'll discuss and illustrate this more fully in the chapter devoted to 'Designing a new home - to suit your site'.

Size isn't everything, they say. Well, it certainly is as far as costs are concerned and the bigger your new home is, the more it's going to cost. Any logical thought which goes towards the making up of the design of your new home must start by finding out the likely size of the building that either your budget can stretch to or will be acceptable to the planners. We've already discussed how to arrive at the starting point for the size as far as your budget is concerned and whilst we've touched on the planners requirements, I'll go into them in more detail in a later chapter. However, if you are going to buy a plot and selfbuild, you must be able to visualise what can be built on it. It's no good thinking that, just because you want a large house on the plot and the rest of the street is made up with small bungalows, you're going to get your way. Quite apart from the visual blight that your proposals would place on the street scene, which the planners will be keen to avoid, the fact is that your completed project would probably not be cost effective.

Unless one has experience in designing houses with both Planning and Building Regulations in mind, it is certainly not a field for do-it-yourself. Virtually all who build for themselves use the services of architects, experienced designers or package deal companies. That is not to say that in many cases the original ideas and design conceptions cannot be arrived at by the selfbuilder and presented as the starting point for the eventual design. There's nothing wrong in giving the chap who's going to draw up your new home the pointers which will indeed make it your new home and not the product of some mass produced ideal. Take a trip around the area you're going to build in before you talk to the designer. Photograph houses or bungalows that you like. Photograph features and details that you like and see on dwellings, both old and new, and present them to the designer at the outset. Anybody worth their salt in the selfbuild world won't take offence – quite the opposite, they'll be pleased that you've given them a starting point and impressed that you've taken the trouble to elucidate your requirements.

It's likely that you, the planners and your architect or designer will want to build in the established local style, or at least in a style that doesn't conflict with the local vernacular. You, because as I've said before, were probably attracted to the area in the first place and the planners and architects because they, in concert with each other, are usually concerned, unlike in previous decades, to protect and enhance the local area. Perhaps a little history will help in your understanding of how we got to this point.

Most homes over 120 years old were constructed in local materials, and local designs styles reflected the best way of using local materials. Often these materials were relatively expensive. Then the railways made most of the country a single market for building materials, so that cheap Fletton bricks and cheap Welsh slates lowered the real cost of building. Design reflected social attitudes and conditions, so that in urban areas we had acres of back to back housing designed to house workers as cheaply as possible. The more affluent, who then lived in the town centres, were concerned about their relative

success in life, and this determined the appearance of Victorian town houses.

After the turn of the century the motor car and suburban commuter trains enabled the affluent to escape from the towns into the suburbs, where developers provided them with standardised housing that was designed to be affordable to buy and run. This housing was well promoted with image advertising. As a result, most houses reflected a supposed popular taste which had actually been established by the developers.

By the 1930s there was a marked distinction between the avant garde homes considered by architects as being the influential designs of that decade, and the design of popular housing generally. The homes admired by the architects had flat roofs, architectural use of glass, rounded corners and a German name – the Bauhaus style. Meanwhile, in this era of no planning constraints, builders and developers were building mock Tudor homes which were as different from the architects' homes as they could be. Then came the war, and after it the planning acts arrived, although as far as domestic architecture was concerned the new planners had little idea what they wanted.

The architects continued to experiment with what they thought was important, seeking to express the essentials of function in bricks and mortar, avoiding unnecessary decoration and contrived features. At the same time the developers were offering homes with simple (and cheap) shapes, and with low pitched roofs and picture windows (as in Hollywood films). Later in this period contrasting panels of timber and plastic became almost obligatory.

The next factor in all of this was the reorganisation of local government in 1974, which gave the new planning departments in the new local authorities an opportunity to spread their wings. County design guides were produced which set out clearly and unambiguously exactly what could be expected to be approved and what could not, and these had a far reaching effect on the design of low density housing.

The design guides were drawn up when there was no coherent establishment style for popular low density housing, and in the absence of anything better they looked back to the early nineteenth century and the essential elements of the local buildings of that era. In Nottinghamshire, farm houses used to have gable roofs with steep pitches, so hipped roofs and low pitched roofs were forbidden in Sherwood Forest. Essex cottages once had black boarded gables and dark stained joinery: these features became essential to speculators' developments in Basildon. In 1830 no builder had stuck panels of contrasting materials below windows, and so this 1960s fashion came to an abrupt halt. An even more far reaching innovation was the complex shaped and involved roof lines which were introduced to give interest to a design, in marked contrast to the simple shapes and functional structures of the previous decade.

Architects protested vigorously against the idea of design guides, but, facing commercial

A large house in the modern 'Tudor' style, from D&M that was built in the Midlands.

Victorian influences give this Potton cottage the truly authentic look of a schoolmaster's house.

A fine day in Scotland demonstrated this superb and well insulated home from Sandia-Hus.

Flint cladding gives this house from The Swedish House Co. a particularly English character.

pressures, they hastily became heavily involved in the minutiae of the regional styles. However, their dislike of aesthetic controls resulted in the planners' views on design issues being tested by

D&M were responsible for this pair of thatched cottages that look as if they really belong in their Devon village.

hundreds of planning appeal findings while ministerial directives established that the duty of the planners was to approve what was acceptable, and not what they considered desirable. The spirit of the county planning guides was to live on, but only as a guide, and not as a rule book as it had been when they were first published.

Meanwhile the public was delighted with the move to new homes that were prettier and more interesting than the stark homes of the 1960s and 1970s, and the building industry, which was by then facing a slump in house sales, was quick to give the public what they wanted. As a result we now have Tudor homes, Georgian homes, Victorian style homes, homes in regional styles and post-modernist homes. The variety and choice is in keeping with the spirit of the times, and it is hard to imagine that 'function' is ever likely to return as a key factor in house design. As long as we have a consumer market the popular view of what looks nice will determine what is built.

Surprisingly it's not the style that has the

greatest impact on costs, but the choice of materials, particularly external walling and roofing materials although, to be fair, many of these choices are part and parcel of the style in the first place. A roof which is made up with prefabricated trusses is always going to be cheaper to construct than one where the style dictates the use of a purlin and spar roof constructed on site. But either of those roof types are going to be cheaper to cover in flat profile concrete tiles than they are in natural slate which, in turn is going to be much cheaper than either natural or reformed stone slate, both of which have massive implications on the weight and loading on the roof.

House or bungalow?

At the risk of repeating the same example of the street scene that I've used before, the question of whether it's going to be a house or bungalow isn't always your choice. Nevertheless, there are many sites where the question of choice is open for the selfbuilder to decide and it's as well to explore the implications.

Bungalows are not indigenous to this Kingdom. The very word is Hindi and, indeed, India is where the original concept came from although single storey living accommodation was not unknown in the land, the traditional Essex or Welsh longhouse and the Scottish bothy, all having a long history. In the main, however, our tradition is for two storeys, even if the bottom half was sometimes occupied by the animals whose dung provided the heating for the living accommodation above.

The fact remains that the bungalow has been well and truly adopted to the extent that in some areas like Lincolnshire, Devon and Cornwall, one could almost be forgiven for thinking that it is indeed the vernacular. Its adoption continues in the public mind and, although out of favour with the planners in some areas, the number of bungalows built every year proves that the case for building them can be argued successfully. One major package deal company, Potton, have even gone so far as to set up a separate company division known as The Bungalow Company!

What makes bungalows so attractive? They need a lot more land than a house of identical size. Unless one's very careful it's all too easy for a bungalow to look crammed in on a plot and on the smaller plots there is the added disadvantage that, with all the major windows to habitable rooms being on the same floor, they can end up jostling for position with each other in respect of distances from boundaries. There's less waste of space, if you consider the staircase a waste of space but on the other hand, a badly designed bungalow can easily soak up at least that amount of space in long dark corridors. Equally as much of a danger are design faults which bring reception rooms into close proximity with sleeping quarters – there's not the natural division between these two sets of accommodation that one gets in a house.

All things being equal, the costs are pretty much the same, probably erring on the slightly more expensive for the bungalow. That is unless there's bad ground or the roof is of a particularly expensive construction or material. In these cases, as the bungalow has double the area of each of these components in comparison to a house, the cost increase is similarly multiplied.

What makes a bungalow so attractive in the market place is the very fact of it being single storey. Older people need and want single storey accommodation. Older people are at the end of the housing chain. They don't often need a mortgage and they can afford to pay more. Couple that with the fact that bungalows form a small proportion of the actual dwellings completed each year and that as land gets ever more scarce, a developer can get twice as many houses to the acreage than he can bungalows and you have all the ingredients of supply and demand which go to push up the value of bungalows. If the cost of the land is not the significant factor, an identical sized bungalow built beside a house, sharing all the same accommodation, amenities and fittings, may well command a price at least 10% higher.

Consideration of bungalows versus houses leads us on to the question of 'dormer bungalows' or 'chalet bungalows' as the estate agents love to call them. Many designs, which come under this heading, are nothing more than houses of a particular design with all their sleeping accommodation on the top floor and all their reception accommodation on the ground floor. Whether their naming had anything to do with the desire to cash in on the attractiveness and higher values of bungalows, is lost in the mists of time but in some respects their design concept may have been influenced by the post war rush to conversion of the roof space of many bungalows.

Whatever their origin, the chalet bungalow that evolved in the 1970's, with their hideous flat roofed dormers, still pretends to grace our streets as the answer to how to cram four bedrooms onto a narrow plot. Happily things have moved on and the dormer genre has now established itself as an attractive style of housing reflected in many of the design ideas illustrated throughout this book and its companion volume *The Home Plans Book*.

Which leads us on to consideration of the true dormer bungalow, as I see it; the dwelling with one or more bedrooms on the ground floor and additional sleeping and/or bathing accommodation on the first floor, within the slope of the roof. This doesn't have to be achieved in the same ugly way as it was in the seventies but consideration does have to be given to just how it can be achieved in an aesthetically pleasing way and, if it's something that will follow on at a later date, the practical and constructional difficulties. Dormer windows don't have to be flat roofed; neither do they have to be huge in terms of width. They look so much better, so much more balanced, as two lights rather than three or, worse, four. At times there isn't even the necessity to break the roof slope and a Velux window or rooflight can do the job. It's surprising, but a small rooflight of only 300mm x 450mm can flood more light into a room than a window 1200mm square and modern construction techniques mean that they are entirely weathertight. If occupation of the roof is going to happen at a later date, consideration also needs to be given to access to the upper part. There has to be space for a staircase, the provision of which may lose you vital existing ground floor accommodation. As long as the payback in extra accommodation exceeds or at least equals this

loss then presumably that's alright.

Of course it goes without saying that you can't just go up into the loft space and start hacking away at the roof structure in order to gain extra accommodation. It all has to be planned for in advance. A 'Fink' trussed roof (that's the one with all the struts forming a web within the triangle) is simply not suitable for any kind of loading or occupation and removal of even one of the timbers could jeopardise the integrity of the whole structure. On the other hand an 'attic' trussed roof is designed from the offset to be occupied within certain parameters and if you're building a bungalow with the thought that one day you just might want to occupy the roof space, then the relatively minor extra cost of these may well be a very good investment. Most cut and pitch roofs can be utilised as living space if they are designed for this in the first place. If not, then once again you can't just get up there with the bow saw and start taking out timber without checking with a suitably qualified architect or engineer that what you're doing is alright. Once more, attendance at the school of forward planning will pay off and, if you're building a bungalow with a cut and pitch roof, then the extra work involved in putting things in place for the eventuality of its occupation will involve you in relatively minor extra costs.

Garages

I shall now spend the next few pages discussing and describing one of the least used, most expensive and least necessary parts of your new home – the garage. Drive around any housing estate in the land and I bet you a pound to a penny that the majority of cars are on the driveway overnight rather than in the garage, which is probably too full up with other things anyway to allow the car in. Yet try and sell a house without a garage, even if it's got a large brick built shed or workroom, and you'll come unstuck. If it doesn't have a garage with a recognisable garage door then the value of the property will plummet. So, the chances are that, whatever I say and whatever you really think in your heart of hearts about the usefulness of a garage, you're still going to build one, so we might

House or Bungalow?

* A bungalow is likely to cost marginally more to build than a house of the same floor area.

* In most parts of the country a bungalow is usually worth rather more than a house of the same size. If this is an important factor, you should check it out with a local estate agent.

* A bungalow will take up more of a plot area than a house, and this can lead to it looking cramped between the boundaries. If your frontage is limited, a bungalow may not have the feel of gracious living that comes with a bigger garden around a house.

* Bungalows usually have less waste space than a house if you regard the staircase well and the landing as wasted space.

* Bungalows generally permit more flexible layouts as fewer walls have to be load bearing.

* Split level and multi level homes are more easily arranged as bungalows, and so are changes in ceiling height and sloping ceilings.

* If provision is to be made for a home to be extended at a later date, the ease with which this can be arranged, and how much room on the site is available for it, is often a key factor in deciding to build a house or bungalow.

* Routine maintenance work like painting and cleaning gutters is more easily dealt with by the average householder if he is working on a bungalow. This often appears to be a major consideration with those faced with making a choice.

* Finally the "no stairs" factor is enormously important to many elderly persons.

as well talk about them.

The first decision you will have to make is whether you want a detached garage, or one that is integral with your house. If you are building on a plot with a narrow frontage you may not have any option in this, but if you do have a choice it requires considerable thought. There is no doubt that in many ways an integral garage is more convenient, with a connecting door into the house which ensures that you do not get wet when it is raining. For many people, particularly the elderly, this is an important consideration and one which is often given priority.

On the other hand, there is no doubt that a detached garage has many advantages. To start with, the separate building gives complexity to the appearance of the whole homestead, and a house with a garage which is a subsidiary building, perhaps linked to it by a wall, looks much more imposing than a single building. This can often enable the drive to be kept well clear of the house, with a path through a lawn or flower beds leading to the front door. In addition to this, a detached garage is usually significantly cheaper that an integral garage, as it can be built on simple foundations with uninsulated solid walls, while an integral garage has generally to conform with the Building Regulations requirements for a dwelling.

If you decide to build a double garage or a larger than average garage then some interesting possibilities occur. You might like to consider whether in this case your garage couldn't perform some other function apart from housing a motor car, which is perfectly able and designed to stay outside. You might like to think about the inclusion of storage or workspace accommodation and you might also like to consider the possibilities of the upper part being used as accommodation or play space. Chances are that anyone thinking of building a double garage which, even in its simplest form, can amount to 15% of the cost of an average bungalow, is going to be taking light, power and water to that structure and it's not a giant leap to think in terms of heating and/or drainage. That opens up the possibility of the garage doubling up as guest or office accommodation and in that case the

building really does begin to earn its keep. Now, don't run away with the thought that I'm just anti garage per se. All I'm really trying to do is prompt the thought process, which might lead to the inclusion of the garage as a useful and integral part of your lifestyle rather than as an expensive junk store. Garages can undoubtedly add significantly to the visual appeal of a house if they are sympathetically designed. You only have to think about the larger country houses and chateaux with their sweeping arms of outbuildings, stabling and garaging to know that. You only have to see some of the designs, which appear in the companion books I have mentioned to know that the garaging can add considerably to the visual enhancement of a property. But, just as equally, you only have to look at some of the mistakes of the previous decades where the garage became, in some cases, the dominant architectural feature of many suburban facades, to know that it can all go horribly wrong.

Let us, for the moment, think of the design of the garage in terms of its usefulness for its original purpose. Even if you're not going to be using it for the storage of garden equipment and have no other intention other than to use it for the housing of your beloved motor car, there are important considerations. Most speculative builders really skimp on the garage. Its length is usually such that anything even slightly longer than a small family saloon will not fit in with the doors shut and the width makes no allowance for the fact that, having driven the vehicle into the garage, the driver has to get out of the thing without banging the door on the wall. As for passengers, well, they've usually already been dropped off in the rain, as their exit from the garaged vehicle would be next to nigh impossible. The selfbuilder, on the other hand, has the opportunity to think about these things and to make the garage more suitable for its intended purpose. An 8 foot garage door with reveals at either side of 450mm (I make no apology for the mixing of metric and imperial dimensions as this is commonplace in the industry, as indeed it is in life generally) means that your garage is going to be eighteen inches wider than the norm. But that eighteen inches is going to make all the difference to your enjoyment and the cost implications are fairly minimal when set against the overall cost of the project. If it's a double garage then instead of thinking in terms of a double garage door, something that is distinctly out of favour with the planners in any event, why not think in terms of two single doors? Not only will that afford you more room in the garage by the inclusion of the pillar between the doors but in bad weather it will mean that only the minimum area is opened to a gale of wind, water and fallen leaves each time you enter or leave the premises.

Garage doors themselves come in a range of styles, all of which can have a considerable impact on the appearance of your new home as a whole. Some of the better styles hark back to the late Victorian/early Edwardian age, when the motor car first came on the scene, with reflections of the coach house doors they replaced. Others laughably refer back to Georgian or even Tudor periods, expecting us to believe that Henry VIII kept his Jaguar in the garage next door to Anne Boleyn's Aston Martin! Many modern garages employ up and over doors in these varying styles but there is a refreshing trend back to the idea of side hung doors which, to my mind, seem to lend themselves so much more to the character we all try to include in our selfbuilt houses and bungalows. Having said that, if automatic garage door openers are to be employed, an up and over door is eminently more suitable, unless one is thinking of adapting or using some of the gate opening equipment on the market. Automatic garage door opening has been mooted as becoming universal for quite some time now. Whilst many houses do have it installed and many large suburban houses also employ electric gate openers, it is by no means living up to the earlier expectations of mass popularity. Nevertheless, even if you do decide that you don't really want to spend the £250 plus per door, it might be as well to think about their possible fitting in the future and to make provision for that eventuality.

Any joinery on the garage should always match that on the house and, if at all possible, try to include a window and a personnel door to the outside.

The garage on the left has an unusual and attractive appearance and is much more appropriate to a rural situation than the usual rectangular structure.

A double garage in an area where a steeply pitched roof is appropriate offers lots of opportunities. The upper floor of the design (left) is shown here fitted out as a study.

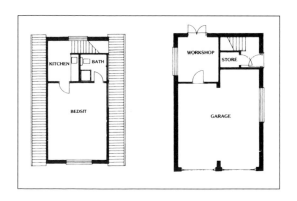

If it's an integral garage then the chances are that the ceilings will have to be insulated and finished with a double layer of plaster board which is then either set or artexed. It's open for you to do the same for the ceilings on a detached garage, of course, but unless you're thinking of utilising the roof space, as I've already talked about, you may consider that the open trusses and ceiling joists, possibly partially boarded only, will give you more scope for storage of those difficult items such as windsurfers and camping equipment. It's normal for the garage walls in brick and block type construction to be fair finished but it's open for you to consider whether or not to plaster the walls. Even if you're never going to convert the garage and occupy it as living space, there are obvious attractions in having smooth finished walls that won't scrape your knuckles every time you squeeze past the car. And once again, the option's there for its possible conversion at a later date. Of course, if you build a timber frame house with an integral garage then it'll have fully finished walls anyway and it doesn't take much to then decorate those walls.

Building a detached garage can, if the space on the plot allows, provide you with even more opportunities. The idea of an integral garage is really one that comes from suburban design requirements. In rural areas or on large country houses it was never even thought of. Oh yes, the coach house may well have been attached as a wing to the house but it was never integral, at least not to the main house as m'lud and m'lady didn't park or drive the coach. And think about just how the outbuildings and coach houses complemented the appearance and grandeur of those country homes. Well, their modern successor, the garage, with sympathetic and careful design can do the same for the more modest new home. Before I go on about how you can spend more money than you strictly need to on your garage there is one other consideration which also relates to money. If the garage is detached, and in certain circumstances where it's attached, it is open for you to consider whether or not you build the garage at the same time as the house. The most often plan of thought, is that the garage is actually built first but this plan often goes by

the wayside once work commences. Once machinery and men have moved onto site the imperative is continuity and you can't get that with a small building like a garage. Instead, quite the reverse of plan, the garage is usually used as the makeweight with work being done on it whilst bricklayers, for example, wait for scaffolding to be raised. If your budget is tight, then why not get planning for the garage and then concentrate all your efforts and monies on the house leaving the garage for another time? By building the house the planning will remain in perpetuity and, if there's enough money left over at the end then by all means go on and finish the garage, otherwise leave it until there's more money in the coffers or your next pay rise comes in. That way you won't find yourself skimping on the house for the sake of the garage. There are other permutations of this idea. You could do the footings only or bring it up to floor level to provide a suitable parking area until such time as you go on and finish it. You could also consider having the major materials delivered along with those of the house so that, not only would things like bricks match perfectly, but you could also reclaim the VAT. And, if you do decide to leave the construction of the garage until a much later date, then you'll probably miss out on the reclaim of VAT but it may well still make sense. After all, that VAT will only amount to less than 1% of the total costs of the project whereas to build the garage during the main construction could well be a bit of a financial struggle.

The garage doesn't have to be a huge boring rectangle with a vast open maw. It doesn't have to just have two roof planes. Instead it can vary in shape. Why not? Cars do, so why do both bays have to be the same length? Why can't the whole thing be a little bit longer or wider? Why can't it have a section on the side to house the work-bench or provide an office? The thoughts and ideas are endless and, once on this train of thought, the boring old garage takes on new dimensions. But before you get too carried away, it's worth reflecting that a large garden shed or summerhouse can often provide much of this for a fraction of the cost of providing the same area as part of your garage. Having said that, it'll never be quite the same and it'll never have that feeling of permanence and solidity. The choice is yours and as I've said before, and I'll say again, informed choice is what selfbuilding is all about.

Services are also important. There should be plenty of lights, both internally and externally, including at least one which ensures that the interior of the boot is well illuminated when you are unloading at night. Switches should be situated at both the main door, the pedestrian door, and, if appropriate, inside the house. If a security light with one of the new automatic switching systems is required, or is likely to be required in the near future, then provision should be made for it to be wired separately. Power points should be provided where they are going to be convenient for power tools, for a vacuum cleaner to clean the car, and also where they can be used for electric garden tools if there are no other external sockets. A garage is often a convenient place for an outside tap, sometimes with arrangements for the piping to run in the garage where there is some measure of frost protection, terminating at a position where there can be one tap inside the garage and another outside for a garden hose. Finally, when a trench

is open between a detached garage and the house, drop a length of multicore telephone cable in it: in the future it may be useful for an intercom, a burglar alarm or some other device that has not been invented yet!

Carports

The alternative to providing a garage is to think about a carport. These are very popular abroad, particularly in hot climates where it's obviously desirable that the car is shielded from the sun to prevent naked legs from being burnt on super heated seats. With global warming and hotter and hotter summers, or so it seems, every year, we may start to cultivate the same priorities. They can also have a use in this country in keeping the worst of the rain and snow off the motor car and in allowing people to get in and out under cover. The drawback is that they can look extremely ugly or give off an air of impermanence. That's not strictly necessary. If substantial pillars in either timber or brick are used rather than flimsy looking posts and if thought is given to the roofing, then it can be as attractive as any garden pergola or covered walkway, especially if plants are trained up and over it. Even if you do opt for

Here is a good example of where a detached garage complements the main dwelling.

Integral or detached garage?

* A detached garage can be positioned in relation to a house or bungalow so that the group of two buildings look better than a single building with an integral garage. A wall linking the two structures can add to this effect.
* A detached garage can be sited in the most logical position in relation to the drive, leaving the house to be sited in the most logical position relative to the view or other considerations.
* A detached garage is cheaper to build than an integral garage, as it does not need to meet the building regulations for a dwelling.
* A detached garage can be built after the house or bungalow is constructed, or when it is approaching completion. If it makes financial sense to build it at some time in the future, or if you simply want to be sure that the house is built within its budget before you start the garage, this may be useful.
* It is more expensive to put a water tap, electricity or an outside w.c. to a detached garage than it is into an integral garage.
* An integral garage provides somewhere to put the central heating boiler, or an extra freezer, and in many ways tends to be useful simply because it is part of the main building.
* An overwhelming advantage of an integral garage for the elderly or infirm is the opportunity to get in and out of the car "out of the weather".

translucent sheeting rather than a tiled or slated roof, this doesn't have to show and if screened by cover rafters and facias then, when the climbing plants have trailed over it, it can look an attractive and integral part of your landscaping.

Basic design considerations

Having decided whether you're thinking in terms of a house or a bungalow and having decided on where, whether and how you're going to provide garaging, you can now move on to consideration of what you want to achieve in accommodation terms. We've already explored design styles and I'll come back to that again at various points in the chapters on design and planning but for now let's consider what you want out of your new home – what you want it to give you. Very few selfbuilders are simply going to hand over the total responsibility for the design to another party, build their new home and then move in and complain that they wish it had all been different. The whole idea of selfbuilding in the first place is to get what *you* want rather than what someone else tells you you're getting. That's not to say that there aren't going to be some constraints and we've already discussed those earlier on in this chapter.

Whichever style is adopted, there are a number of considerations which require careful attention and evaluation. The first of these is the front entrance, which I'm assuming most people like to be at the front of the house. There are cases where it can be around the side but it's never popular and when you come to sell, people can get very sniffy about having to go around the side of the building to get in, even if it never bothers you. Do you want the front entrance to be the focal point of the front of your building or would you prefer to go for something a little more restrained? Do you like a large porch or would you prefer a simple canopy or nothing? If a porch then should it be open or a totally enclosed storm porch and if so should the main front door, the expensive door, be on the front of the porch or between that porch and the house? The front door itself. Should it be solid, glazed or partially glazed? Some people want total privacy in their front hallway whilst other prefer to let the light

in. The suburban answer that was in vogue through the previous two decades was to have a solid front door with obscure glazed full length sidelights, but how much better does it look with windows at either side of an impressive front door? I've already talked about garage doors in what some may think a slightly disparaging way. They don't have to look wrong. They don't even have to dominate their elevation and they can be integrated successfully into a traditional design. In similar vein patio windows are a wholly modern invention and have no historical counterpart except for the more appropriately proportioned french doors. That doesn't mean that they can't be successfully used in a design but it does mean that it's no use fooling yourself that your 'Tudorbethan' diamond leaded sliding patio doors do anything other than trace their history back to the very recent past and if it's authenticity you're after with a traditionally designed building, they do, perhaps, have no place.

Drawing up plans for a house or bungalow in the style which you prefer, incorporating all of the features that you want and doing it in a way that will enable your new home to be built within your budget is a job for your chosen architect or designer. Your task is to make yourself aware of all of the options and to decide on the design style and features you want. As I said above, the best way to do this is to take photographs, make notes and cut out features and pictures from magazines and the best way to collate all of these is to start a scrapbook.

At the end of the scrap book start pasting in pictures and photographs of houses which you particularly like which are about the size of the home that you intend to build. You can get illustrations from books, magazines, and estate agents' brochures. You can take photographs through your car windows, and however badly they come out, they will be clear enough to be seen and understood. Besides collecting illustrations of what you like, consider what you don't like. If you see a feature which you think spoils a house which you otherwise like, include it as well.

At the other end of the book start pasting in pictures of details: a front door, a way in which a garage is linked to a house with an interesting stone wall, a particular pattern of brickwork or the way in which roof tiles are kicked up at the eaves in the Spanish style. If you do this, you will both stimulate your own interest and also give yourself a good way of explaining exactly what you do and do not want to your architect or designer.

Books of house and bungalow plans can have a useful role in helping you make your design choices and perhaps you couldn't do better than to start off by buying the companion book to this book called *The Home Plan Book*. Maybe, just maybe, there's a design in there that completely fits the bill for you and, if so, then the best thing you can do is contact the company whose plan that is, to find out just how you proceed from there. What's more likely, is that you'll get design ideas from the various plans and that you then use the books to decide which company you will approach to get those ideas translated into your own individual home.

However useful the plans books are, and there's no denying their use, otherwise why would we be involved in their production, they are still no substitute for spending afternoons driving round the part of the country where you want to live, snatching photographs of houses which you admire. A lot of bother perhaps?

Certainly. And buying all the books of plans will cost a penny or two. But you are unlikely to build many homes, and you surely want to make sure that you know exactly what you want, you can be firmly in the driving seat when you are talking to your own architect or the council's planning officer.

Internal Design

Happily the planners will pay no part in the internal design. Here you have far wider opportunities to construct rooms to suit your own living pattern. For example, it will cost little more to have a family living room, dining room, and a small TV room than to have a large open living space, and this may be the way in which you want to live. The choice can be wholly yours. If you do want something unusual, perhaps a drawing room with a sunken floor and an island fireplace, it is simply a matter of being able to afford it, and you should be able to get a clear idea of the costs at an early stage.

Once again, make a scrap book or keep a note book with details of every idea you come across that might be right for you. It will definitely be worth your while. Some of the details that you should make up your mind about are overleaf.

Design details checklist

* Start with the hall. There is a refreshing modern trend to make this as large as possible after years of thinking of it as merely a waste of space. If guests enter into a room with a table in the centre with flowers on it, and doors off, it's much more impressive than having everybody crammed into a tiny space beside a staircase. On the continent the dining hall is very popular and as people spend more and more holidays over there the trend is coming this way. You either like it or you don't.

carefully proportioned one can make a room cosy. Fireplaces are important – they can't be changed very easily and some thought needs to be given to choosing a design that is appropriate to the style of home you're after.

* If you want patio or french doors leading out onto a terrace, give some thought as to how it will look from both inside and out and how you will arrange the furniture both in the room and outside on the terrace.

* Give some thought to the dining room. Is it going to be

This bungalow has a number of interesting design features. The carport is an integral part of the main building; there is a dining hall; the larger of the two bedrooms is en suite with a sunken bath; and there is a lot of storage accommodation.

Building for yourself provides an opportunity to have a home that suits your own personal living pattern. Make sure you take advantage of this.

* Staircases say an awful lot about your home and are probably one of the best ways to make an entrance area impressive. There are a myriad of styles and materials and even the most expensive won't cost as much as your kitchen units.

* Moving on to the living area. Do you want one single open space or would you prefer the rooms to be separated, even if only by archways? Do you want a sitting room with a separate dining room or would you prefer a lounge/dining room or even a kitchen/dining room? A house over 1800 sq.ft. can probably give you a TV room or a study and at over 2000 sq.ft., you can have both.

* What sort of atmosphere do you want from these rooms? Double doors and a higher than average ceiling height give a feeling of spaciousness. A large fireplace can look incongruous in a smaller room whilst a

just big enough to seat your immediate family or does it need to be big enough to entertain on a larger scale? Will it ever really get used or will it become the least used, most expensively furnished room in the house? Even if the plans of the house show the table in the room, is there going to be enough room for the chairs to be pulled back far enough for people to sit down?

* The kitchen. Probably the most important room in the house as far as making a statement of your own ideals is concerned. Do you want a smallish kitchen with a separate utility room? Does that utility room have to be very large? Do you even need it or would the space be better employed in creating a larger kitchen, especially now that washing machines and dishwashers don't sound like Concorde taking off. What sort of units do you want? Is there any need to spend a huge amount on these units or are there cheaper alternatives,

which, with flair and imagination, can still be as impressive? What sort of flooring do you want? Do you want to ever eat in the kitchen or do you always want to do so?

* Consider a projecting rear porch instead of a utility room. What do you use the utility room for? Is it connected in any way with the activities of the kitchen or is it really a laundry room? Is it even that or is it just somewhere to kick off the muddy boots, hang up the wet Barbour and park the dogs?

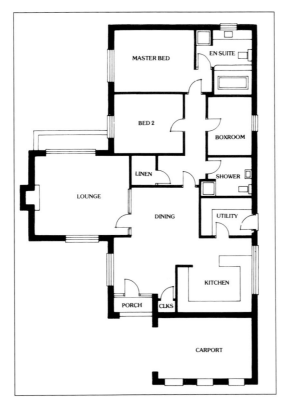

* Do you want a downstairs or separate WC? If so think about whether it's going to be of more use to your lifestyle by being positioned nearer the front or the back door. Perhaps you need both – perhaps you don't want strangers going beyond a certain point when they call and perhaps you don't want to traipse through the house to go to the loo when you're busy gardening.

* Are you going to be able to provide room to keep all those things that never seem to find a proper home like the vacuum cleaner and the brooms? Do you need to house a pram, pushchair or wheelchair?

* Would you like a coats cupboard or are you happy with hooks in the hall or the downstairs loo?

* Moving upstairs, do you want the master bedroom suite to be totally separated and private from all of the other bedrooms? Is sound transmission between these rooms, and the prevention of it, important to you?

* Staying with the master suite, how large do you want it to be in comparison with the other rooms? On some houses the master suite will take up well over a third and, sometimes, approaching a half of the entire upper floor. Is this what you want?

* How many bathrooms do you want? Does the main or communal bathroom have to be the biggest? Does it have to have things like a bidet or, will that only get used by the children for storing dirty socks. With children fighting to get ready for school each day would the provision of more than one wash basin be a good idea? Does the en-suite, assuming you want one, have to be big? Would you like it to have a bath in it or do you prefer a shower?

* If there are guest rooms, do they have to have en-suite facilities or could they or any of the other bedrooms do with a wash basin?

* With the bedrooms – do they all have to be of similar size or are there some that you would like bigger than others? Children start off in different sizes but, long before they leave home, they all assume roughly the same proportions.

* Going back to the master bedroom, or to any of the other bedrooms come to that, do they need dressing rooms?

* Built in furniture for bedrooms and dressing rooms is cost effective but if you already own free standing wardrobes and are happy with them then wouldn't it be better just to provide alcoves? Remember, when you move you can take your furniture but you can't take the fitted units.

* These days with insulated tanks, which lose less than one degree a day in heat, the cylinder cupboard might not double up as an airing cupboard. Do you need or want a large linen cupboard? Do you need a separate storage cupboard upstairs for household implements?

* Have you considered a built in vacuum?

* With increasingly hot summers have you thought about whether you should consider air conditioning?

* In similar vein and possibly in combination with the last point, have you considered whether you should install a heat recovery and ventilation system?

* What about a balcony? Planners have the vapours about them, thinking that all sorts of perversions are likely to go on. In reality, how often can you use them in this country – in the winter it's probably too cold or wet and in the summer you could probably fry eggs on the tiles.

7 Designing a new home – to suit your site

I have to admit to ambivalent feelings regarding the development of the countryside. On the one hand I have earned my living promoting and helping people build their own homes, more often than not, on rural plots and on the other hand, like everyone else, I bemoan the loss of our green and pleasant land. We are no longer even mildly surprised, when we revisit childhood haunts only to discover that the woods and fields we used to play in are now housing estates. I recently retraced my own past to a village outside Bedford. The house I grew up in was still there, the garage and the church, even the old police house were still as I remembered them. The snowberry hedge still grew where my brother and I had hidden as we fired our home made catapults, loaded with its white berries at the man who lived opposite, as he bent to his gardening. Everything rekindled a long forgotten dreamtime. But, the paddock that we played in, next door to our house, sported a brand new home. How long had it been there? Why had the site remained undeveloped for all those years before?

And then I remembered some more. I remembered how the two of us would hunt for frogs and newts in the rushes that surrounded the pond – how our burgeoning interests in wildlife, and in particular my brothers lifelong passion for herpetology were born in those muddy, smelly waters. I remembered the huge oak tree that grew on the hedgeline and the mushroom I picked, as big as a dinner plate, from beneath its base.

The tree was gone. The pond was gone and, in their stead was this fine new home with its carefully tended gardens and its sweeping shingled drive.

And the point of this story? The reminiscences of a middle aged man? No, not at all - well alright, maybe just a little. The practical point is that there is often a real reason for infill plots being there in the first place. Until fairly recently the costs involved in special foundations for a single house meant that it was often uneconomical to develop such plots. Now that almost any foundation problem can be solved for around £10,000, what was left alone before becomes a very desirable building plot. So too with the

curiously named 'brownfield sites', steeply sloping sites, sites with drainage and access problems and sites covered with trees that carry preservation orders. But if these sites are to be successfully developed then these special factors have to be taken into account, understood and evaluated fully, before pen is put to paper in the preparation of any design.

Brownfield sites

This is the name coined for sites, usually in urban areas, which have already been developed in the past but whose use has now lapsed, conjuring up visions of broken factories, contaminated land and disused waterways. In the years since the end of the 2nd World War, many of these sites have been left to decay in favour of the development of the greenfield site but now, however, political pressure is being applied in an attempt to stop the wholesale development of the countryside and attention is being focused back onto the redevelopment and regeneration of inner city and town areas. In the main these kinds of sites are more suitable for multiple development but there are sometimes, and they will increasingly become more common, single plots which come out of their redefinement as useful land. The problems experienced with their development are manifest but, of most interest to the individual selfbuilder, are probably those associated with existing foundations. That's not something that's entirely confined to an inner city site, as any who have developed an old farmyard will know, but what's more likely in the town is that these old footings may well be heavily reinforced, sometimes still having the steel girders protruding from them. New foundations may have to be constructed to go below previously disturbed ground and avoid 'hard spots'. Contaminated or previously consolidated subsoils and topsoils may well have to be removed and replaced entirely with fresh new earth if any kind of a garden is to grow around the new house. Almost certainly you will need a full soil investigation and survey followed by an engineer's report but, almost as certainly, there is no reason why your finished town house should not rival its country cousin.

Sloping sites

Consideration of the design of a house or bungalow on a sloping site depends largely on the part of the country in which it is situated. In parts of Wales, or in the West Riding of Yorkshire, homes are commonly built on sites with one in five slopes, and local styles and the local building practices are geared to this. In other parts of the country any slope at all is deemed to merit special consideration. Wherever you are going to build, the first thing to do is to have a careful look at how other people choose to build on slopes in the local area, and to try to analyse the basis for the regional practice.

This may depend on the ease with which excavations can be made. If there is rock just below the surface, it will probably determine that buildings are built out from the slope because of the high cost of quarrying into it. If the subsoil is easily excavated, there are many more options. It may be that local cottages nestle into the hillside because in earlier centuries they had to do so to escape strong winds which had an adverse effect on poor local building materials. This may have given local villages a particular style which the planners will expect you to accept.

Wherever you build, there are two approaches to be considered: should you arrange to remove the slope, or should you design a home to make use of the slope? If the site permits, it is invariably cheaper to excavate a level plinth for a new home, adjusting the levels and spreading the surplus soil as part of your landscaping. This involves either just digging into the slope, or else digging out part of the plinth and using the excavated material to raise the level of the other part.

This latter approach is called 'cut and fill' and the sketch entitled 'Building on a slope' more than adequately illustrates it.

Digging out a level plinth is not always possible, sometimes because the site is too steep or the ground too rocky, but usually because the plot is too small to allow for the necessary changes of level. Remember that you cannot excavate close up to your neighbour's fence: in law his land is entitled to support from your land. In this case you have to consider a design to make use of the slope, which will usually mean a multi level home.

A property of this sort is more expensive to construct than one which provides the same living accommodation on a level plinth, and changes of levels in a home are more attractive to the younger generation than to the elderly. This may affect the resale potential, and it is generally true that while split level homes are often exceptionally attractive and lend themselves to exciting décor, they often have a limited resale market.

New homes on sloping sites often involve special foundations. In simple terms, your designer has to make sure that the whole building will not slide down the slope. The cost of such foundations is one reason why many sloping sites have not been developed in the past, and are now coming onto the market now that property values make the cost acceptable.

One advantage of a sloping site is that it invariably comes with an interesting view. If you are deciding whether or not to buy a plot on a hillside, remember that the view that you have from your ground level is not going to be the same view that you will enjoy through the windows of the finished house. If the outlook is very important to you, do not hesitate to take a couple of step ladders to the site and make some sort of platform that will enable you to stand at a level from which you can see the view as it would be from the windows of a finished home. You may look rather ridiculous at the time, but if the view is a key factor in making your decisions, make sure that you see what you will really be getting!

Access

To a large degree, we've covered this point in the chapter dealing with the evaluation of your site. Nevertheless it's as well to stress, once more, the importance of the access arrangements and the effect that they can have on the design of your new home. If a plot has a large slope on it then this will affect the drive as much as it does the house and it may do so in a manner that is much more complicated than you would, at first, imagine. If your drive will join a class 1 or 2 road the Local Authority will probably want a visibility

Building on a slope

Option One. Build up above the slope. Involves suspended floors, some additional foundation costs, and the need for very careful landscaping to conceal the large area of brickwork below floor level. Will improve the view, especially from the balcony.

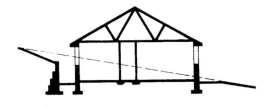

Option Two. Build into the slope. Permits a cost effective solid floor on natural ground, but may require a retaining wall or steep garden to the rear. Excavated material will have to be carted away unless it can be used for landscaping on stand.

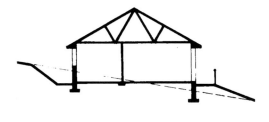

Option Three. 'Cut and Fill'. 'This is the usual approach, combining the minimum foundation costs with the look of being built into the hillside. Care required with land-scaping.

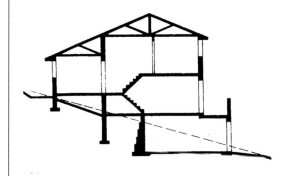

Option Four. Multi level. Garage below with living accommodation above, following the slope. Gives interesting layouts with opportunities for balconies to take advantage of views, but construction costs will be high. Inevitable steps outside and changes of level inside may limit resale potential.

A broad level plot adds grace to this Potton home but the trees may well have influenced the costs.

The slight slope on the plot has been cut and filled with this home from Scandia-Hus. The spoil has been placed to build up the ground to the front with a rockery and patio.

splay at the point where the drive joins the road, and in hilly country this can involve expensive excavations. The authority will probably insist that your gates are set back a car's length from the road, and they will impose maximum gradients on the drive. They will also insist that rainwater from your drive should not cascade across the pavement, which is often difficult to arrange. There is obviously a maximum slope which your car can negotiate, but long before you reach this limit, problems will arise in designing the drive so that your car does not "hang up" when making the change of gradients as it get onto the road, or into the garage.

The appearance of a drive is always particularly important with a sloping site. Any drive is almost always the largest feature in the front garden, and it has to be designed with the landscaping proposals in mind. If the site slopes, then the drive itself becomes even more prominent, and must be given even more careful attention. A requirement for a driveway allowing motor cars to enter and leave a site in forward gear, may mean that a dwelling has to be set back on the plot and, in turn, that may affect its eventual design, size and even viability. Every situation is different but the important thing to remember is that the arrangements for access determine the development of your site and are always a major factor in the design of your new home. Planning and Highway requirements are not specific to any individual and it makes no difference at all that you only ever intend to use a bicycle, the criteria will remain, and the assumption will always be, that your new home will also be home to at least one motor car, and probably more. Arrangements to actually carry out any work to the carriageway will need various consents and will almost certainly have to be carried out by an approved or accredited contractor. This is discussed in the chapter headed 'Building with subcontractors'.

Drainage

Just as important are the arrangements you need to make for drainage and here I'm talking, in the main, about foul drainage, having already broadly covered surface water drainage in the

chapter on evaluation of your site. If mains drainage is available and it's at the right place and at the right level for a gravity connection then that's obviously the best of all solutions and most local authorities will usually prefer that you utilise it. Having said that, there are circumstances where connection to mains drainage is not feasible by virtue of either the cost or the complexity and, in those cases it might be as well to look into the possibility of a different system as discussed below.

The best of all worlds is obviously a private foul sewer crossing your land to which you can make a gravity connection in the run of the drain. As easy, is the situation where the run of the drain is in the grass verge or on unmetalled land over which you have the right to pass for a connection. More usual is the fact of the sewer being in either the footpath or the highway and here, you're faced with an entirely different ball game. It's no use just thinking that you can gaily go along and dig holes in the Queen's highway. As with alterations to the carriageway and new access arrangements, any work in relation to new drainage connections will require various licences and consents being issued by both the highways authority and the relevant water board or sewage authority, although in most cases the local authority will act as their agents. This work can only be carried out by approved or accredited contractors and all of this is discussed in the chapter 'Building with subcontractors'.

If the mains drain is too far away to be reached by gravity or is at a higher level, in the first place, than the level of your proposed house then the answer is a pumped system. A pump can be used in two ways. It can either lift the effluent from the level of one run of drains to a run at a higher level after which it can then continue as a gravity drain to the connection with the main sewer, or else it can be employed to pump the effluent all the way to the sewer connection. It involves a small holding tank which is usually fitted with twin electrically powered pumps and macerators operated by a float control. These units break up the sewage and then pump it up and along a flexible pipe to its destination. If this is to be a drain at a higher level then it normally discharges into a manhole at the start of the next run of gravity drains. Alternatively the flexible pipe can be laid, possibly even by an agricultural contractor using mole drain equipment but, more usually, by a mini digger or the narrow bucket of an ordinary digger, to the discharge point. Some of these pumps can move the effluent for half a mile or raise the level by as much as 60 feet but the chances are that on a single dwelling or even on a small group of dwellings, nothing like this ability is needed. The pumps obviously cost money and they do need proper installation, maintenance and a power supply, but they are efficient and reliable nowadays and the costs can often be offset by the savings of having to lay a flexible pipe in soil rather than proper drains surrounded in pea shingle. In some cases where connection to a main drain is expensive by reason of it, say, being a very busy main road, the choice of a pump to take the sewage to a different discharge point, even if an easement has to be purchased, can prove cost effective. Incidentally, as a footnote to pumps, whilst we're not talking here about surface water drainage, there are specific cases where the levels may dictate that the only way to get surface water away is to utilise a pump. In these cases a similar system is employed only, firstly there is no need for the macerator and secondly the second, standby, pump isn't always necessary.

And then there is the plot where mains drainage is neither available or achievable. The person who is selling it tells you there will be no trouble, as everyone in the area has septic tanks. This may be so, but it will be a major consideration in your development of the land, and it is important to understand clearly what is going to be involved. First of all, the good news is that all the ways of dealing with the problem are now much cheaper as a percentage of the total cost of building a home than they were a few years ago, and the current solutions are also much more effective. This is because of the use of plastics and fibreglass for the underground tanks that are involved, which have replaced the old brick tanks. All the tanks arrive as prefabricated units which are simply dropped into place in a suitable

hole and connected up. On the other hand concern about pollution by the Environment Agency means that everything to do with the discharge of sewage effluent is extremely carefully controlled and monitored. Now you may think, therefore, that the best thing to do is to contact the Agency first of all to get their advice on what steps to take. Well, getting the various leaflets and guidelines may well be a good idea but contacting them about your specific problems at too early a stage, before you've taken the best advice and allowed the professionals working on your behalf to devise a system, may not be the best plan. Far better to 'keep your powder dry' until such time as you have the answers and can present these as an effective solution to your drainage problems as well as the Agency's concerns.

If there is an existing drainage arrangement on site, perhaps an old brick built septic tank, and it has been discharging the treated effluent for at least twenty years, and is still working, it may be that you have an implied right to the discharge and can continue to use the existing system. This may, at first sight, seem a very attractive option and certainly one that, on paper, could save you a considerable amount of money, time and effort. On the other hand, this is a very uncertain area in the law and with the advent of the Environment Agency they now have, in any case, the power to regulate and prevent any discharge that fails to conform to their requirements. Nevertheless you may well decide that, as there is an existing system you should use it and that your drawings should show the drainage going down a pipe which is marked on the drawings 'discharge to existing septic tank'.

Now at this point you may well stop to consider your motives as well as your morals. If the existing system is working well, and you know this for a fact, then you're doing nothing wrong. If, on the other hand, you know that, at times, the effluent flows across open ground or that there's a secret discharge to a nearby ditch or stream then it's open for you to question whether you really want to be responsible for a local typhoid outbreak at worst, or at best, a country stream flowing grey instead of clear. Don't imagine that such activity will remain forever undetected especially if attention is drawn to the system's existence by the presence of your new home. And don't imagine that the Environment Agency is a toothless organisation – far from it, it has tremendous powers and, once employed, the solution imposed could well prove to be far more costly that anything you would previously have envisaged.

There is one other thing that could make you re-evaluate your proposed use of an existing septic tank and that's a simple request from the Building Control Department for full details of the existing sewage arrangements including measurements and plans of the tank itself and its associated weeper drainage. At this point it's quite likely that each and every professional working on your behalf will tell you that they can't swim, are afraid of dark smelly places and that an internal inspection of the sewers, with or without a wetsuit, is quite beyond them.

If your plot and your proposals involve the creation of a completely new drainage system then it all comes down to three major options with a few variations on these themes and a couple of other interesting, more than practical, ideas. The Environment Agency, through the Building Control system will be the final arbiters of which system you do actually employ. They will take into account the type of soil and subsoil on both your plot and the surrounding land and whether you are in the catchment area of a water supply. Almost certainly a percolation test will be required, to establish exactly what sort of system is to be employed and once more, although we're talking principally here about foul drainage, some local authorities will also require a similar test to establish what type of surface water drainage is employed. A percolation test, which is usually carried out by the applicant or his agent with the details being given to the authorities, involves digging a hole in the ground, filling it with water and timing how long it takes for that water to go away. Obviously any old hole won't do and in general what is required is a 300mm cube with its bottom 600mm from the surface. This cube is then filled with water and allowed to soak away for 24 hours, after which it is refilled and the time taken for the water to disperse is noted.

A typical cesspool, the solution of last resort to a drainage problem.

Septic tanks are a much better proposition.

Conducting a percolation test - digging a standard size hole, filling it with water, and timing how long it takes to soak away.

Special foundations

Special foundations for problem sites need to be approved by the Local Authority, agreed by the NHBC or by your guarantor (if they are involved), be appropriate to your technical resources as a selfbuilder, and be cost effective. Make sure that the last two considerations are not forgotten by your architect or designer, and ask him to explain all your options. They may include some of these approaches.

Reinforced strips
A simple solution to minor problems. If you are pouring your concrete yourself take expert advice on how to keep the mesh in position.

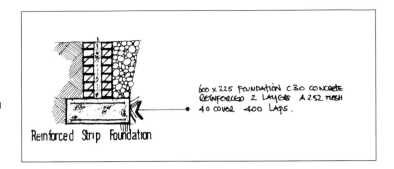

600 x 225 FOUNDATION C30 CONCRETE REINFORCED 2 LAYERS A 252 MESH 40 COVER 400 LAPS.

Reinforced Strip Foundation

Trench fill
Expensive in concrete but minimal labour costs. Popular with selfbuilders.

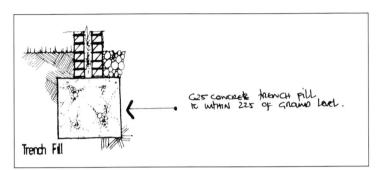

C25 CONCRETE TRENCH FILL TO WITHIN 225 OF GROUND LEVEL.

Trench Fill

Edge beam raft
Commonly used but a job for an experienced tradesman.

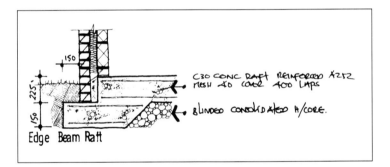

C30 CONC RAFT REINFORCED A252 MESH 40 COVER 400 LAPS

BLINDED CONSOLIDATED H/CORE.

Edge Beam Raft

Piled foundation
A specialist solution to difficult problems. Consultants and piling contractors will add significantly to your costs.

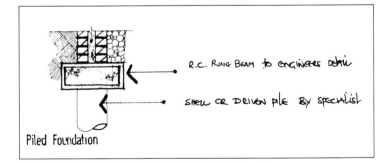

R.C. RING BEAM TO ENGINEERS DETAIL

SHELL OR DRIVEN PILE BY SPECIALIST

Piled Foundation

Subsidence raft
In coal mining areas the Local Authority will insist that you build on a raft like this, and if you still have subsidence problems you will have an automatic claim for compensation.

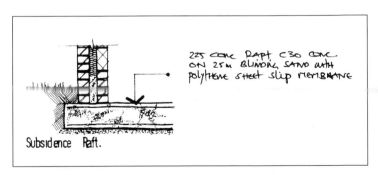

225 CONC RAFT C30 CONC ON 25m BLINDING SAND WITH POLYTHENE SHEET SLIP MEMBRANE

Subsidence Raft.

These figures are then used to calculate what system of drainage is applicable or workable on your land and the nature and quantity of any weeper drainage, which will be needed. The best possible solution and the one that is likely to prove the cheapest is to install is a septic tank.

A *septic tank* is a miniature sewage works that requires no external power, involves no pumps, and houses millions of friendly bacteria which break down the sewage into sterile effluent which is discharged into the ground. Septic tanks are quite small, requiring a hole about 8 feet across and 10 feet deep, and they can cost under £1,000. They are easily installed. They need to be pumped out by a small sludge tanker once a year, which will cost between £40 and £100, and all that you see of them, above ground, is the manhole, which gives access to the interior that you will very rarely have to open.

If the ground conditions are not quite right or there is a requirement for extra refinement of the effluent because of, say, proximity to a water-course, then the authorities may require that your septic tank discharges into a filter bed of some sort before the effluent is then passed on down the weeper drains. In some cases these extra requirements for land drainage may mean that a selfbuilder, building on a restricted plot, has to seek and obtain easements allowing the installation of drains on adjoining land. In other cases the requirements for the quality of the effluent discharge may mean that an entirely different system has to be employed, known as a mini treatment plant.

A *mini treatment plant* works like a septic tank insofar as it receives raw effluent and then processes it into a sterile effluent that can again be passed into the ground. Where it differs considerably is the fact that it is electrically powered and that the quality of the effluent is such that, whilst it's not exactly drinking water, it's often good enough to be discharged into a ditch, stream or other watercourse. In certain circumstances this can happen as a direct discharge but, more often, it is effected through either weeper drains or a filter bed of some sort. It works by a series of rotating, and sometimes contra rotating, turbines which lift the effluent

very slowly between immersion and exposure to the air, passing it, all the while, towards the unit's outlet. Whereas a septic tank utilises mainly anaerobic bacteria (those which live without air), the mini treatment plant utilises both these and the aerobic bacteria (those which live in air), to break down and neutralise the sewage. These plants are at least twice the cost of an ordinary septic tank and they may also have to have the sludge pumped out more often. In addition they do require a power source and they will require regular maintenance. That said, they are a significant advance on the sewage disposal systems of previous generations and as we all become more and more aware of the need to restrict contamination of our ground water, rivers and streams, they have an increasingly important role to play.

I mentioned at the head of this section that there were some interesting variations and these have much to do with the use of reeds. These can soak up and neutralise an extraordinary amount of effluent and, space permitting, a reed bed can often solve a problem with effluent quality. In some cases a septic tank can discharge, probably with the aid of a pump, onto a series of flat reed beds and in others an even more satisfactory system can be devised using floating beds of reeds growing on mats. With a series of baffles such a system can return perfectly good water to the environment and at the same time provide a magnificent habitat for all forms of waterlife. The drawback is that most selfbuild plots simply don't have the space for such enterprise.

And what if the authorities won't allow any of these solutions and all the tests in the world prove to you and everybody else that your ground just isn't suitable? What if the plot is in a built up area where mains drainage is either not available at all or is available but any further connections are banned until such time as either the drains themselves have been upgraded or the local sewage treatment plant has extra capacity? Well, then you're onto the third option, the one involving a cesspool. A cesspool is bad news in one sense but, if that's the option that you're left with, then it's no good dwelling on it and the best thing is to try and see it as the way forward in the development of the site of your new home. *Cesspools* are simply great big tanks which hold your sewage until a vehicle comes to pump it out and take it away. The normal size of a tank for a single dwelling is 18,000 litres, and it has be emptied once a month by either the local authority or a local contractor. The cost of each visit by the emptying vehicle can be anything from £40 to £100, and occasionally more. A modern cesspool will cost about £2,000 and the cost of the excavation and installation may be significant. It goes without saying that a cesspool is the solution of last choice. It also goes without saying that many of the factors which make the use of a cesspool necessary, such as waterlogged or rocky ground, are also the factors which tend to increase the cost of its installation. There may also be latent problems in that possible buyers may be put off by it and, where a cesspool is employed because the mains drains are not yet ready to accept additional burden, the planning consent may well require and demand that once the sewers have been upgraded, the house is then connected. That means that one day, maybe only a few years after the occupation of your new home, this large piece of expensive below ground equipment will become defunct. In that case perhaps the only thing you can do is to think about using it as some sort of aquifer so that you can water your garden when all about are having to watch theirs die. Once more, attendance at the school of forward planning is in order and the sensible selfbuilder in just such a situation will have already made the road connection and constructed the necessary bypass drains at the time of the original build.

One or two points about siting systems of this sort. First of all, access to them is very important. It is necessary for small tanker vehicles to be able to reach septic tanks and mini treatment tanks, and for very large tanker vehicles to be able to get to cesspools. This may seem to be an argument for putting your tank near to your gate, with manholes hidden behind the appropriate shrubbery. It is not as simple as this. The first Universal Law of Sewage Sludge Removal is that the tanker vehicle will always arrive just when the lady of the house has her guests arriving for a coffee morning. Bear in mind that this performance is going to be repeated at regular intervals forever, and you will see why siting the tank should be given very careful consideration. The system suppliers will be able to advise you on this, and in many ways it is the most important decision which has to be made in the whole business.

Probably the most convenient position to put the tank so that it will suit the visiting tankers which precludes natural land drainage to the herringbone dispersal system. In this case, it is worth considering whether you can put in additional pumping arrangements to move the sterile effluent to where the land drains can be more easily arranged. Again, the tank manufacturers will advise you and the expense of the extra pumps is certainly worthwhile. Another point is the importance of making sure that the hatches on top of tanks are absolutely secure. There should be no possibility of them being a hazard to small children, or providing and opportunity for horseplay by those who are older but have a warped sense of humour.

Do not be tempted to cut corners when installing any of this sort of equipment, and particularly do not skimp on or omit the concrete which should surround the tank. If you do, and the water table rises after a sudden downfall, the tank will pop out of the ground like a giant and very evil toadstool. This is all good fun if the tank is level, as all that will happen is that the contents will flow back into your bathroom. However, if the tank is installed on a steep slope it will have the potential to roll downhill like a runaway juggernaut. It sounds funny, but if you are responsible for several thousand litres of raw sewage approaching your neighbour's property in a huge plastic bottle at 90 miles an hour, you may find your popularity will suffer. The writer once saw the results of such an incident when a runaway septic tank from a farm on a Welsh hillside descended on the village below.

To continue with this fascinating subject, always give your new septic tank a good start. There is a great deal of folklore concerned with septic tanks, most of it because some strains of bugs are better at their job than others. The man in the pub, who is always such a splendid source of misleading advice for those building on their own will have very strong views on this. In some areas it is held that a dead sheep is second to none as a way of getting a septic tank working, and possibly this was true in the days of the old brick tanks. These days it is not to be recommended, but there is a lot to be said for collecting a bucket full of the contents of another local septic tank and transporting it very carefully to your own septic tank. The key word here is 'carefully'. Even better, borrow a car for the job from the man in the pub!

Finally some good news. When you install a septic tank, mini treatment plant or cesspool, you can apply for your water rates to be reduced and the savings can go a long way towards emptying and servicing costs.

Foundations

What can seem like a foundation problem to one party can, by dint of the fact that its solution has become common practice in an area, seem like the norm for another. In certain areas of north Nottinghamshire and South Yorkshire, to build without using an edge beam raft would almost be unthinkable. Yet, if the same system of foundation was suggested on a site in Essex, there would be much scratching of heads and the price would escalate way beyond its actual cost. In similar vein, the Essex builder is used to digging trenches 3M deep and lining their sides with compressible material surrounding amounts of concrete to rival the Berlin bunker, in what the Yorkshire builder would prefer to think of as Civil Engineering.

Presumably, having carefully gone through all the check lists set out earlier in this book, you know about any special foundation requirements long before work actually starts on site and you've made moves to ensure that they don't cost any more than they have to? If not, and it's still surprising just how many arrive at this point and then seem to discover that something different has got to happen, then you need an expert. Where do you find him? Well, free advice is available from piling contractors but they may be seen to have an axe to grind. You'll find them in Yellow Pages. Better still would be an independent view and this can be got from a soil engineer. Your architect will probably be the one to recommend him and the two of them will work in tandem to come up with the foundation solution that will suit both your site and the design

This is the exciting bit. The foundations are all done and this picture shows the first stages of a Potton aisle frame Heritage house going up.

proposed.

As a way of giving you some sort of understanding of the possible solutions and the reasons behind their employment perhaps a brief run through the main methods of providing a special foundation will help.

Reinforced strip – This is a simple solution to minor problems which can occur to a normal strip foundation where, say, there are a couple of soft spots or there are some minor differences in bearing capacity or depths. It really just involves putting either reinforcing bar or mesh, usually 50mm from the top and the same from the bottom, in the concrete, which is sometimes also thickened up a little. It's relatively easy but care has to be taken in the placing of the reinforcement and in keeping it in place during the pour. This should be done with little metal tripods but oftimes you'll see it wrongly done with bricks, blocks or even paving slabs.

Trenchfill – In certain cases where the ground is clay and there are trees present you may have to go for trenchfill foundations where the concrete, instead of just being at the bottom of the trench, is brought nearly all the way up to the top. It can also be used in wet or waterlogged ground or where the topsoil is unstable even though the bearing ground is fine. In these conditions it can often be the best choice as, by definition, one is out of the ground in a day and the need for bricklayers to work below ground or the possibility of a fall in is minimised. If these latter factors create this option then there can be a saving as the trench width can, sometimes be narrowed to 450mm instead of the more usual 600mm. Most often, however, the use of trenchfill is dictated by the presence of clay and trees and in these cases, as I've previewed above, they can go down to depths of around 3 metres. As we've talked about in a previous chapter, clay can heave and expand and in these cases an added refinement on the trenchfill principle is the employment of a compressible material down the sides of the trench, usually the inside edge but sometimes to both faces. This absorbs any sideways compression with any upward, frictional pressure being relieved by a slip membrane of sometimes one, but usually two layers of thick polythene. The problems are obvious in that if there is 50mm, and sometimes 100mm, of compressible material on each edge of the trench, then that trench has to be dug considerably wider to accommodate both this material and the concrete it will sandwich. Not only does that mean that there is all that much more spoil to dispose of but the deeper one goes the more unstable and the more dangerous the foundation itself becomes. Add to that the huge amounts of concrete (Sometimes up to 80 cubic metres for a single house) and the high cost of the compressible material and you can easily see that the employment of this as a solution has its limits and there comes a time when it's easier to go down another route.

Piled foundations – In the old days the very mention of the word would strike terror into the heart of any selfbuilder. But now, things have changed quite dramatically. No longer is the rig that comes like a mobile version of the Eiffel Tower and instead, a whole range of more user friendly mini pile rigs have been devised. It wouldn't make sense to try and describe all of the variants but essentially they boil down to either driven, bored or dug piles. Driven piles use either a shell of concrete or steel that is then filled with concrete. They are noisy and the vibration that they cause could well upset your neighbours and result in you having to replace an expensive set of antique plates that have fallen from their Welsh dresser. Bored piles are a little more friendly and mini pile boring rigs are often mounted on a small lorry or Landrover type vehicle which will of course need access on to the oversite area, something that needs to be considered before it arrives rather than afterwards. Dug piles are sometimes carried out by specialist contractors but they can just as easily be undertaken by your normal groundworker assuming he has the correct digger with the appropriate reach. Usually all sorts of piles have some sort of reinforcement built in within their concrete which is then left sticking out of the top for incorporation in the ringbeam. It is here, at this point, that the most recent and welcome advances have been made. One of the most difficult things after the completion of the piles, as far as the selfbuilder is concerned, is the ringbeam itself. If it is to be cast in situ, then not only might it need the compressible materials I have described but, almost certainly, the reinforcement these days is more likely to be in the form of cages rather than simple mesh top and bottom. These cages have to be fabricated by specialists to a bending schedule prepared by the Engineer and their installation is a daunting task. They need to be positioned perfectly within the eventual concrete and they need to be wired up and connected to a schedule. Now, along comes the great idea of having prefabricated pile caps with similarly prefabricated ringbeams that are simply lowered into place to span between the piles, thus achieving in hours what can take days if not weeks to realise.

A *raft foundation* – is employed where there is likely to be significant movement in the ground but the ground itself is inherently stable. In the coal mining areas of the Kingdom one can see a field with a depression of as much as 150mm running across it and as the days go by that depression will move across the land. It happens when the roof is allowed to fall in as the coalface moves forward half a mile or more below ground. Any structure which is to withstand that kind of movement has to be able to float over the 'wave' whilst, at the same time, maintaining its integrity and the solution is a reinforced raft. As I've said before, in the areas where these need to be used the builders are completely familiar with them and what looks suspiciously like a swimming pool in the course of construction turns out, in the end, to be a raft foundation which doesn't cost any more in real terms than those foundations which are considered standard in other parts of the country.

Remember, above all, when considering special foundation situations that you are unlikely to be alone and that others in the area will have experienced similar problems and invariably worked out the best and most cost effective solutions. As I've said before, perhaps the best place to start is at the council offices with a chat with your local Building Inspector. He'll have seen it all and I'm sure that he'll be pleased to point you in the right direction.

Radon

A special foundation situation in some parts of the country results from the presence of a naturally occurring radioactive gas called radon which seeps from the ground. Radon is present everywhere in the atmosphere, and accounts for 50% of natural background radiation. (Less than 1% of background radiation comes from Sellafield or Chernobyl or any other human activity.) Modern houses with good draught proofing can build up concentrations of radon which seep up through the foundations, and in some parts of the country this is now recognised as a health hazard, and makes a significant contribution to the statistics for deaths from lung cancer in those areas.

As a result there are special design requirements for houses built in areas where there is a high level of radon seepage, and Building Inspectors will advise on this as a matter of course. In England these are shown on the map, In Scotland these are mainly in Kilcardine, Deeside, Sutherland and Caithness, in Northern Ireland they are in the south east from Portaferry to Newry, while Wales is a natural nuclear free zone!

The precautions required involve making foundation slabs gas tight, and in some areas of high risk also providing ways for the radon to be discharged into the atmosphere. This is not complex, difficult or expensive but it has to be done. The government Radiological Protection Board has a range of free leaflets about this, and even offers test kits to indicate radon levels. You can contact them on 01235 831600 or fax 01235 833891.

Radon has been part of everyday living for the human race since the dawn of time, and until very recently our draughty houses meant only cave dwellers were at any risk from it. Modern houses built in certain areas without radon precautions would present a risk, but as current Building Regulations completely remove the risk, which is very small anyway, all this is really of interest only to those with enquiring minds. If you go to live in Devon there really is very little risk of ending up glowing in the dark.

Trees

Trees have been discussed at length in the preceding chapters and we have explored their effect on foundations, neighbours and planners, all of which can be quite profound. As well as the existing trees, some of which may well be the subject of Preservation Orders, there may also be a requirement that further trees are planted. If you are to plant new trees which will provide a back drop to the house, or just be a key feature in the garden, the choice of species is as important as your choice of bricks or tiles for the house itself, and should be made with just as much care. Trees have different shapes and grow to different heights, taking different lengths of time over growing to an appreciable size. Some are in leaf for all the year, some for seven months and some for only five months. Some prevent grass or shrubs growing underneath while others tolerate this. Make your choice an informed choice by reading the right books and in this respect you could do no better than to get the Royal Horticultural Society's *Gardeners Encyclopaedia of Plants and Flowers* and the very excellent *The Small Garden* by John Brookes published by Readers Digest. A further matter to consider if you are relating existing trees to the design of a new home, is that they change their character through the year. Dapple sunlight filtering through new leaves is very attractive in May. In December the same species may make a damp day look positively gloomy, with damp dripping from branches onto the sodden leaves below. As with everything the choice is yours.

River frontages

Plots with river frontages are always in demand, offering the prospect of interesting gardens and possibly fishing rights or even a boat house and river picnics. If you have a chance to build a riverside home you will have already considered flood levels and any special foundations requirements, but it is also important to know abut the rights and obligations of a riparian landowner, the name given to someone who owns a river bank. You may be obliged to leave an unobstructed route along the bank for River Board plant and vehicles, and the board may have the right to dump mud dredged from the river onto your land. You certainly cannot assume that you will be able to build a boat house or tidy up the banks without permission. On the other hand it may be a condition of your consent that the riverbank is shored up and that could involve you in some fairly expensive sheet piling. Nevertheless if you've managed to secure a river frontage plot then you're probably not short of a bob or two and, particularly in the Thames area, you'll not have flinched at paying as much for your plot as most would only dream of their finished house being worth.

8 Designing a new home – to suit your lifestyle

The whole reason for building your own home, rather than just nipping off and buying a house from a developer, is to get what you want, rather than something that somebody else thinks you should have. For those who have special requirements, such as those who work from home, extended families or chaps with hobbies, it is often the only answer to their particular or peculiar needs. Nevertheless great thought has to be given to these matters and, as I've said before, care needs to be taken to ensure that what you're planning isn't so peculiar to your own requirements that there's nobody else on the planet who'll ever want to buy it from you.

Perhaps the first thing you need to think about, when planning your new home, is how long you're going to be living in it. Are you planning to eventually go out of the door feet first in a wooden box or is this merely another step up the ladder on the way to your palatial Nirvana? You may think that it's going to be forever but the pattern of all our lifestyles suggests that, for many of us, 5-7 years in one house is the most we'll manage. If the answer is that you're going to be in that house for the foreseeable future then you need to think about how your lives will change over the years. If the answer is that you'll only be in it for the next five years then you need to keep a weather eye on the possibility of resale and think in terms of attractiveness in general market terms rather than any peculiar or individual requirements.

Children are the biggest consideration to take into account and most people forget to do so fully. If the new house is a step on your ladder and you're never going to have children, that doesn't mean that you can forget all about the needs and requirements for successfully housing the younger members of the species. When you come to sell, the chances are that the buyers coming around to see your home are thinking in terms of where little Willie and Rosie are going to sleep, play and study, and the accommodation you set aside for your beloved dog Fido, simply won't do. Even those who do have children make mistakes. What suits a ten year old is not right for a seventeen year old and what suits a seventeen year old will be redundant when the twenty four year old has long since left home. Children change. They grow physically, yes we all know that, but they also grow in their needs which grow and grow until, suddenly, they're not there any more. And then what happens? They come back, only this time they come back multiplied and you need room to house, firstly their university friends, then husbands and wives and finally, your grandchildren.

The answer to all these problems is of course flexibility and flexibility is something that can easily be designed into a house but is very difficult to properly achieve if it hasn't been carefully thought out in the first place. Small children will often want to play in their rooms but will also want to spend the evenings with mummy and daddy in the family lounge. As they grow they'll want to spend less time in their rooms, unless they're studying, and their tastes and choices in music and television will mean that there's a clash in the lounge. The answer? A separate family room. The problem? If the family room is so close to the main lounge that the noise affects you anyway. The solution? Try to get this family room closer to the kitchen, utility areas so that late at night your offspring and their hordes of hungry friends don't have to troop all through the house looking for fridges. Try, also, to arrange things so that your bedroom isn't directly above the family room, unless you find it easier to sleep to the rhythm of an extended base. You've now got to the stage in life where your existence has all the hallmarks of the owner of a guesthouse where the guests don't pay. Courage my friends, it won't last long and before you know it the house will be quiet again. What now for the family room? An office? Maybe, but just as possible is that you're also winding down at this stage. So here it is, that longed for room where you can do your writing, your painting, your planning of political campaigns,...in fact anything you want! Until? Until one comes back from a broken marriage with plans to make your long hoped for hobbies room into a bedsit where they, "won't disturb you...honestly daddy we'll be no trouble". How's that for flexibility? No wonder John Lennon said, "Life's what happens when you're busy making other plans".

Granny flats are very popular and social engineers would like them to become ever more so. For some it's the ideal solution to so many of the problems of modern life with its pooling of finances and the possibility of a built in friend, babysitter and house sitter. For others, the thought of their in-laws coming to live is as welcome as the onset of Bubonic Plague.

The problems are manifest. Culturally we've lost the natural progressions of family and social life, which lead up to the gentle inclusion of different generations. Personally we've lost the ability to exchange roles and inherit different hierarchies. For every mother-in-law joke that

they can tell in France, we have ten.

There are, undoubtedly, many advantages to having a granny flat and we shall discuss them. There are pitfalls and it's as well to think the whole thing through very thoroughly before any commitment is made and, possibly, before granny is over enthused about the prospect. As with the children, things change, granny won't always be the sprightly old lady she is now. One day she'll become infirm and may need nursing and attention on an almost constant basis. One day when she's gone to join the angels, the accommodation so carefully designed around her needs may lie empty and forlorn. Maybe, too, the

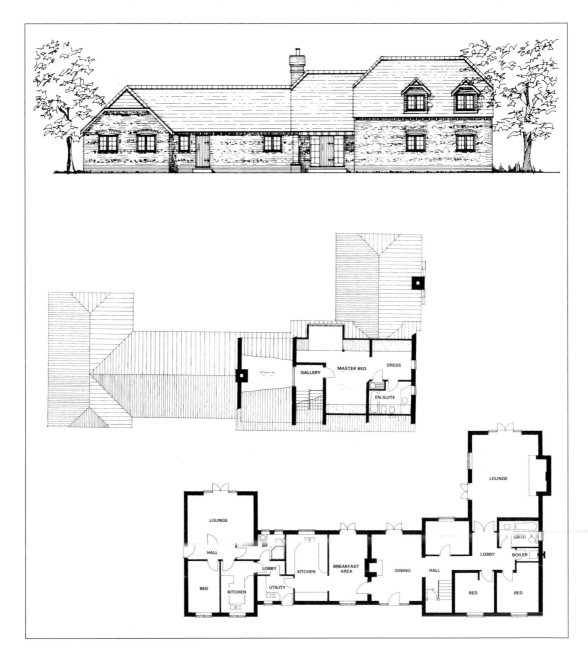

This large country home in Dorset has a large self-contained granny flat. As discussed in the main text, careful consideration must be given to handling a planning application for a design like this.

ideals and hopes that you all started off with will disappear in a welter of recriminations as living in close proximity exacerbates old rivalries and highlights generational differences.

But enough of this, let's look a little more on the positive side and consider the advantages and how the objective, once decided upon, can be achieved. First of all the financial side of things. The pooling of financial resources can often be the difference between the realisation or failure of the dream of building your own new home. Nevertheless if that's the only reason you're going along this particular path, then I suggest that you stop and think carefully about your motives and ask yourself whether you're really doing this for granny at all, or just for yourself, with granny being expendable once you've achieved your objectives. In a property owning democracy the very fact of the natural passing down of accumulated wealth from one generation to another is an established and desirable principle. If that can be done during, rather than after, the lifetime of the older generation, with all generations truly benefiting, then all to the good. If your dreams of selfbuilding are enabled or enhanced by the inclusion of the older generations financial resources and at the same time they get a home within the bosom of a loving and secure family environment then it's all worthwhile.

Inheritance tax comes into the equation, of course, but with the thresholds being, now, comfortably into six figures it shouldn't affect too many. If you feel that your situation may attract it then please consult an accountant with the relevant skills, before, rather than after, you've commenced the project. Possibly the older generation have the cash to put into the project. More likely is the fact that their contribution to the whole thing will come from the sale of their existing house in which case there are some extra things to consider. Will their house sell in time for everything to fit into place? Where will granny live between the sale of her house and the completion of the new one? Everybody knows that moving house can be a singularly stressful experience. Imagine that when you're older. Imagine having to do that twice within the space of a year. If there's room in your house and you're

able to put granny up then that's probably fine but expecting granny to camp out with you in a caravan on site might be going a bit far.

Will granny simply be passing over her share of the costs of the project as cash? Will granny be part owner of the completed establishment or will she just be coming to live in your house? What security of tenure will she have and, if it all goes wrong, how will she be able to recover her share in order to be able to house herself? All of these are questions which may seem unpalatable or intrusive, but they are questions, nonetheless, which need answers and they are questions which need answers before rather than afterwards. One way around things may be for granny to give you a private mortgage, negating or limiting your need to apply for outside finance. That way granny will retain a financial stake in the house and you will have security as long as you continue to meet the agreed repayments. Granny now has an income in addition to remaining a property owner and that is important if you project your thinking forward to the time when she is no longer able to live with you and needs to go into a nursing home. The going rate for care in a nursing home is almost as much as the average net wage. Help is available, of course, but, of late, that help has only been supplied by government upon realisation of the older person's assets down to a fairly paltry minimum. If the bulk of an older person's assets take the form of a share in jointly owned property, which is properly mortgaged, then that puts it beyond reach. The income from your repayments plus that from state and other pensions should then ensure a more comfortable placing for the latter stages of your parent's life.

The important thing with all of this is sound advice from solicitors and accountants. I keep stressing the importance of forward thinking and, unsavoury as it may seem, one has to think forward to death. On the death of the parent, with an arrangement such as I've described above, it's vital that any Will reflects the fact that you won't want to be turfed out of your home and that, if possible, the mortgage lapses and the deceased parents share of the home comes to you. What can complicate this, is the need to accommodate the aspirations of other siblings, who may well discount the loving care you've given your parents during the latter stages of their lives, and simply feel that you have purloined the bulk of their inheritance. Then again, what if you predecease your parents? Will they then be homeless and dispossessed or will there be provision for them to recover their equity in reasonable fashion with the minimum of upheaval? Nothing in life is forever and as much care needs to go into the possible future unravelling of any financial pooling of resources as it does with its original amalgamation.

So, you've carefully thought out the idea of having your parents living in self contained accommodation within your home and you've carefully gone through the finances and taken the right advice for your own particular circum-stances. The local authority is surely going to welcome your proposals with open arms, aren't they? Well not necessarily, and if you think that it's a certainty, then you may be sadly mistaken. Despite all the entreaties over care in the commu-nity and social responsibility, despite all the cries about shortages of care resources, the chances are that your proposals will be looked at askance. Planning departments seem to have an almost pathological suspicion of multi generational family occupation, viewing such applications in much the same light as an attempt to convert a family house into a block of flats. What they're afraid of, course, is that the planning which they accept as being for one dwelling, will be stretched into the provision of two separate dwellings, either from the start or by a simple conversion at a later date. They may have good cause to be suspicious. They may well have been caught out before. For everyone who manages to pull the wool over the planner's eyes and hoodwink them into granting consent for something that they didn't intend to give, there are a string of genuine applicants who will be forever blighted by that deception.

Of course there may be other reasons for the planners having reservations. Your proposals, inflated by the need to accommodate granny, may simply be too large for the plot. In which case the planner's objections have nothing to do with the proposed occupation and really have far more to do with their proper function of making sure that what is built fits in to its surroundings.

If you are in an area where the planners are cautious about granting consent for a building with self contained accommodation then there are things you can do to alleviate their fears. As I've said, one of the biggest of these is that one day the dwelling will be subdivided and part either sold or let off as completely separate accommodation. The single biggest test of this possibility seems to revolve around whether separate entrance facilities are provided. Taking the example of the large country home built in Dorset, which is illustrated in this chapter; if that was being developed in an area where such suspicions were raised then the simple omission of the hall and entrance door to the granny flat end could allay those fears. Using the same example, if the objections to the provision of separate accommodation within the dwelling were more fundamental, then it might be open to you to consider not denoting the second kitchen as such and calling it, either an office or a workroom. The second lounge could also change its name to a family room or bedroom. Doing it that way would then mean that the accommoda-tion is capable of being built and occupied as a single dwelling, with, say, the units for granny's kitchen being fitted later. In these cases there is no real need for any external alteration but, if it was felt necessary, then provision could be made for it to be carried out under Permitted Develop-ment rights, at a later date. A word of caution here. There are circumstances where it isn't possible to carry out any external alterations without express planning consent, of which more later.

Of course, I'm the first to admit that there is an element of trying to pull wool over people's eyes here, but you're not doing anything really wrong. In the end all you're trying to do is house your family and, if that is an extended family and you want to be able to exercise your legitimate rights to alter the internal layout of your home to suit those requirements, where's the harm?

The best of all worlds on this subject is, of course, the enthusiastic support of your planning

The swimming pool gives a sense of wellbeing but it does need maintenance and those trees might shed a few leaves into it in the autumn.

Everybody's dream of a new home finds its outlet in the kitchen.

office and despite what I've written above there are areas where that is forthcoming. Sometimes it has to do with a particular recognition of the benefits to society as whole from the care of the elderly within the family unit. At other times it can be further encouraged by a local policy which recognises a need for tourist accommodation and recognises too, that semi self contained accommodation within the home is eminently suitable for this purpose, once it has fulfilled its original requirement. A case in point, just in case you don't believe that could happen, is the example of the house in Dorset where just such a consideration was instigated by the planners.

Assuming the support of the planners, there are certain things that do need consideration when designing the granny flat accommodation. We have already talked about separate entrances. Is this really necessary or, in certain cases, even advisable.? Only you and your family can decide this fact but, if leaving it out is at all likely to tip the scales in your favour with the planners, then I would suggest that it is fairly expendable, especially if the lounge has either french or patio doors, or the kitchen has an outside door. And the kitchen itself? Will the granny flat need a full kitchen or will a kitchenette be all that's required? Living alone, granny might well want to cook for herself, but will she want to cook big meals and entertain?

It doesn't cost very much more to make the internal doors 2'9", or even 3' wide, to enable wheelchairs to get about and, whilst you're doing that, spare some thought about whether all or any of the doors within the main house should also be similarly treated. It doesn't cost any more to put the power points three feet up from the skirting where elderly people can reach them and similarly light switches can either be at this lower level or replaced by pull switches. Remember that granny won't always want to be cooped up in the house and that she'll want to be able to get out into the garden, walk around and get back into the house. Ramps, or at least shallow steps, at the external doors, pathways with a slight slope instead of steps, flat sitting areas and possibly even rails at certain points will help in this.

Of particular concern to granny may well be that the accommodation you're proposing for her is going to be very much smaller than her existing home. You may feel that it's all she needs and you may well be right, but remember, this is an older person who is undergoing some considerable upheaval and who may, in certain cases, have recently been bereaved. The furniture you think of as outdated, the ornaments you think of as a waste of space may well be familiar and beloved objects with memories and connections that far outweigh their face value. There won't be room for it all but care and loving diplomacy coupled with an invitation to share in the design process will go a long way to ensuring that you all start off on the right foot with each other. The bathroom facilities are one area where the enthusiastic support of the older person may be gained, as in many cases their existing accommodation is likely to be woefully inadequate. With a granny flat the opportunity is there to think about sanitary-ware which is designed for the elderly or infirm, about taps that can easily be turned on and off by someone with arthritic hands. Bath or shower? Older people can have developed almost a fear of baths yet they can still hanker after that long hot soak. What about a walk in bath? Showers too, can be made to accommodate a wheelchair entry or have seating facilities and here, try not to skimp on the size of the cubicle itself and think about the positioning of handrails which, while we're at it, can have applications in many other areas.

One feature advocated by architects who specialise in old peoples' housing is the provision of extra wide window sills, or window sills that continue over shelving beneath them. These are particularly valued by those who cultivate pot plants, and this is a major interest for many elderly person. Another feature often suggested for a room in which an elderly person is likely to spend a lot of time is making it L shaped or possibly five sided. This facilitates a number of windows which give different outlooks, and also permits interesting internal arrangements of the furniture. And then we're back to the issue of flexibility. I've already talked about the granny flat eventually becoming tourist accommodation but for some this isn't an option. Thought, therefore, needs to be given to an alternative use for the granny flat once granny has left it for good. Could it house another member of family in similar circumstances? Will it be suitable for a son or daughter to lead their lives under your roof with a measure of independence envied by most, including possibly you but nevertheless making your own life more comfortable in the remainder of the house? Could there even be a reversal of roles? Probably a little difficult to think about just now but in time it may become an attractive option.

For further advice on designing accommodation for the elderly, the bookshop attached to the Building Centre at Store Street in London always has a good selection or you might like to contact any of the well known charities concerned with the elderly, to obtain their various leaflets and information packs.

Home offices

The words can cover a multitude of applications right through from the company representative who sets aside a small space under the stairs, to plush suites with separate offices and toilet accommodation. What all of these reflect is, however, the growing trend towards working from home. In part that's due to the greater use of computers and the internet which obviate the need for a group of people working together to be in the same room and in part it's due to the fact that many working women with children now choose to do so at home. In addition companies find that they can expand into new geographical areas simply by employing representatives who are prepared to work from home, only meeting their colleagues in person at regular sales functions. It saves them the costs of office rentals and maintenance and it gives the employee a freedom and flexibility, previously only enjoyed by the self employed.

But before you go gaily marking out several rooms in your new home as offices, reception rooms and typists' rest rooms, there are a few facts to consider. Firstly the attitude of the planners which, while probably not as hostile as it can be towards granny flats, can be just as

suspicious. In all probability the planning that has been granted on your plot is for a single dwelling house. Dwelling house, not offices! Any hint that there's going to be a waiting room, that staff are going to be constantly present and that the road outside is going to be blocked with the cars transporting your customers to your door, is going to bring the planners out in a rash. Any thought that noisy machinery is going to disturb the tranquillity of the suburban idyll or that large vans are going to be parked in the driveway will upset not only the planners but Environmental Health and, of course, your neighbours. In any of these extremes, or in anything approaching them, the only course of action is to apply for formal planning for change of use and the reality is, that in many housing environments that's not going to be granted. No, what we're talking about here, in this section, is the genuine working from home, an activity that fits in with and complements the main purpose of the project as a whole.

That doesn't mean that it has to be a cramped little room where it's impossible for you to receive a client or your boss from time to time. It doesn't even mean that you can't for example, conduct a business of aromatherapy, from a room with a separate waiting area and dedicated toilet facilities for your clients. It's all a question of degrees and the situation and location of your proposed new home. The attitude of all and sundry will be entirely different if your new home and its ancillary office accommodation is self contained in an area where no neighbours are likely to be upset or where a range of outbuildings can be usefully utilised in conjunction with your house or bungalow.

There may well be covenants that prohibit the use of the property constructed on the plot being used for the carrying out of any trade or business. This is one of the more usual clauses that can find its way into any contract of sale for property and is put there specifically to safeguard the domestic nature of the environment. In normal circumstances it is held not to apply to the representative working from home, the writer or any person reasonably using a part of their home as a home office, but if things progress from that, then questions can be raised. Maybe nothing will happen, maybe the beneficiary of the covenant doesn't even live in the area any more or doesn't really care. But maybe, the covenants are mutually enforceable by your neighbours and maybe also, the planners have made similar stipulations in the various consents, which go to make up your planning permission. It may not get very far and all you may need to do is tone down your activities following a few threatening letters from solicitors but it's open for you to consider things from your neighbours' point of view and it's open for you to consider, also, the effect on the value of their properties, as well as your own. You might think that the conversion of the garage to an office is the right thing for you but will it affect the value of the house if it's done in such a way as to be difficult to reverse? Might not those people coming to look at the property consider that a house of its nature should have a garage and that, useful as the extra accommodation might be, it's not something that they particularly need. You are probably reading books on working from home, and most of them emphasise that you should be able to claim a

proportion of the running costs of the home as a business cost, and this is certainly possible in many cases. Beware! You may be able to persuade the tax man that 15% of your property is really an office, and he may permit you to charge up to 15% of the running costs of the house to your business. This may save a useful sum, but if you ever want to sell the property the Revenue will want Capital Gains Tax on 15% of the proceeds. This would be subject to indexing and the exemptions allowances, but it could easily outweigh many years of tax allowances.

For this, and other reasons, any proposal to use the word 'office' on design drawings that go to the planning office should be considered very critically. It can lead to business rates, problems with old covenants that restrict business use, planning considerations and even concern about workplace regulations. The word 'study' is fine: ladies and gentlemen have studies while only sordid business people have offices! Unless there is a positive reason why you really must use the word 'office' it is much more sensible to work from your study/family room instead: the same

D&M Kegworth design home altered to show a prestige office suite for a self employed consultant. Note the generous storage space which is something that is often overlooked when planning a home office.

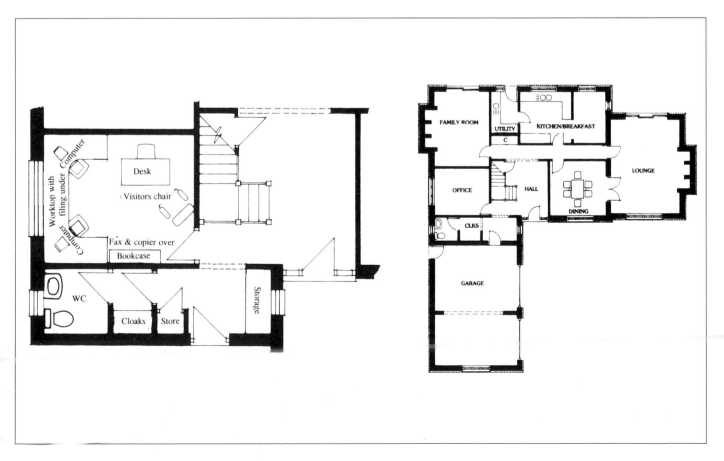

rooms with different names!

Whatever you call your workspace you should give a great deal of thought to how it fits into your overall design. The first consideration is whether you have business visitors who you will need to impress. These might be clients discussing a consultancy contract with you. You probably feel that you must project the right image, and your office suite will have to be adjacent to the front door so that your visitors will not be aware of the squalor of your domestic arrangements. There should be an adjacent loo, and the view from the office window should be as attractive as possible. Storage space will be important, with samples and old records properly out of sight instead of being piled in a corner.

On the other hand, if your freelance graphic design business will never involve visitors, you can locate your activities beyond the kitchen, where you can make all the mess you want. Or, if you edit a very intellectual magazine from home, you may want an office on the first floor where you can hope to enjoy the peace and quiet. You will know what you want your office for: locate it in a part of the house that suits this.

Next, make sure that the office space which you are creating is going to be adequate for the hoped expansion of your business. If you intend to employ a couple of people within a year or two, but will still be working from home, you will need working space for them, an appropriate cloakroom, and somewhere for them to hang wet raincoats or umbrellas. Do not assume that they will want to use the family facilities: this rarely works out.

In the same way, services should be planned for future levels of use, so you may decide to install four telephone lines although your short term requirements will be for one only. Next year you will want a dedicated fax line, the year after a dedicated computer link onto the super highway. Beyond that, who knows – but provide the infrastructure for it now. Remember lots of electrical outlets, lots of directional lights for the ceiling, and heating controls that are independent of those in the house.

The furniture layout is very important in an office, starting with making sure there will not be a reflection problem on computer screens. This is a major consideration. Built-in working surfaces along walls are space savers, while free standing desks are not. Two or three drawer filing cabinets can have fax machines or copiers on their tops, while a four drawer cabinet does

Children playing in the garden of this bungalow, but days aren't always fine and thought needs to be given to children when planning your new home.

not permit this. A computer printer on a low level trolley can be pushed away when not in use and does not take up any desk space. Computer screens on an arm projecting from a wall have same advantage. If visitors are going to be important to your business success you should make sure that a chair or chairs for guests are an integral part of your layout: seating a client on a chair carried through from the kitchen will not enhance your image! Remember that a well designed office layout will improve efficiency and even if the notional improvement is only 5%, the value of this over a few years will be very significant.

Animals

I've deliberately separated this heading from the one dealing with children but it's children and the having of them which may well bring about the involvement of animals with your house. For those of you whose daughters, and very occasionally sons, commence the long and expensive love affair with horses, there are some special considerations. Maybe it is the thing that has brought you to the selfbuild table in the first place. Maybe the livery costs, having to taxi offspring to remote fields at unearthly hours of

the morning and night and the fear of vandals have made it imperative that your home also includes a paddock and stabling. If so, is there room for tack rooms and feed rooms to be constructed as part and parcel of that stabling or will you have to make provision within the body of the main house? Will the horse transporter that's often the next 'essential' item on your child's shopping list have room to park and, if so, can that be arranged so that it doesn't become the dominant feature of your home?

Dogs come in various sizes, coat lengths and degrees of smelliness. The pampered pooch who only deigns to walk on the footpath doesn't really need any extra accommodation or consideration but the Springer spaniel just back from a walk down by the river, most certainly does. It's open for you to just think that he can be confined for a short while to the utility room but it's also open for you to consider that you don't really want him bedding down in your laundry. Why not design in a dog room with dog sized access to the outside and a floor that can be hosed down into a drain?

Cats too, can be specially accommodated. If you live on a busy road and you're fed up with coming home to find yet another pussy flattened to the carriageway like some old and discarded

Dry dogs are one thing, wet and dirty ones are another and as much thought needs to be given to your pets when designing your new home as to anythig else.

fur coat, then why not think about constructing some form of aviary against the house with a cat flap giving Tiddles access to the utility room. You can kit it out with benches, sandpits and climbing trees and pussy will live there happily and safely ever after. You might even witness an increase in the local population of wild birds as a result!

Extendability

Very careful thought has to go into the possibility of any future extension of a new house if the design is not to turn out 'neither fish, flesh nor fowl'. If you travel around the estates of the seventies and look at the extensions that have taken place, I bet you'll not find many that compliment the original - quite the reverse in fact. Inside can be even worse with rooms leading off though rooms and level changes that give full testament to their haphazard and piecemeal genesis. The reason is that, in all probability, the planners had no say in the design of the extension and the reason for that is that, in certain circumstances, planning consent is not required.

This is known as Permitted Development and it is given as part of the Planning Acts known as the General Development Orders. It gives consent for certain classes of development, of which an extension of, usually up to 15% of the volume of the original, is one. It's not a certainty and it can be varied or negated completely by the wording in a planning consent which may say something like, 'Notwithstanding the Permitted Development rights, granted by the General Development Orders, no extension or alteration of the building will be carried out without the express consent and approval of the local authority'. If you've got this clause or something similar in your planning consent then it's perhaps better to skip the rest of this mini section.

For those where there are still Permitted Development rights to be enjoyed, there are various conditions, stipulations and variations. Before going on, therefore, to consideration of just how you plan for an eventual extension, perhaps it's as well to run through just what you can do under these implied consents.

* You can build an extension to an existing dwelling so long as:

1. It is no bigger than 15% of the volume of the original dwelling or 70 cubic metres, whichever is the greater or:

2. If it is a terraced house or is in a Conservation Area, National Park, Area of Outstanding Natural Beauty or the Broads, the volume is no greater than 10% of the original dwelling or 50 cubic metres, whichever is the greater.

3. The extension does not protrude above the original ridge line or is more than 4 metres high or closer to the boundary than 2 metres.

4. The result of the extension does not mean that more than half of the area of land around the original house will be built upon.

5. The extension does not protrude in front of the original building line, unless that would still mean that it was at least 20 metres from the highway.

* You can carry out development within the curtilage of the building, which means that you can alter walls or rearrange rooms and occupy the roof void, subject to the limits below. However, if you do live in a Conservation Area, a National Park, an Area of Outstanding Natural Beauty or the Broads you will need to apply for express consent for any extension to the roof or any kind of addition which would materially alter the shape of the roof. This would include Velux lights or a dormer. In other areas loft conversions are allowed, so long as they do not add more than 40 cubic metres to the volume of a terraced house or 50 cubic metres to any other kind of house and the work does not increase the overall height of the roof.

* You can construct a garage for a dwelling where none exists so long as it does not go closer to the highway than the nearest point of the original house, unless there would be at least 20 metres between it and the highway, and as long as it does not exceed 3 metres in total height or 4 metres to the ridge if it's got a pitched roof.

* You can construct walls to the boundaries so

long as they do not exceed 2 metres in height or 1 metre adjoining the highway.

* In most cases you can also construct sheds, greenhouses, conservatories, accommodation for pets, summerhouses, ponds, swimming pools, and tennis courts.

There are other things but these are the ones that usually concern the selfbuilder and, in any event, it's better to check with the local planning office regarding any extension or further development that you're planning, just to make sure that you are within your rights. Building Regulation approval may also be necessary and any alterations that you make to the dwelling must not contravene the regulations or affect the stability or structural integrity of the dwelling. Incidentally the term, 'Original dwelling' is important. It means what it says and it harks back to the 1st July 1948 when the planning acts first came into force. For any dwelling constructed since that date, it refers to the original dwelling that was given planning permission. Any extensions undertaken since, either the 1st July 1948 or the original consent, have the effect of soaking up the permitted development rights. In some circumstances the volume of other buildings which belong to the house such as a garage or shed will count against the volume allowances, even if they were built at the same time as the house or before the 1st July 1948. These are where an extension comes within 5 metres of another building belonging to your house and where a building has been added to the property which is more than 10 cubic metres in volume and which, again, is closer than 5 metres from the house. In addition if you live in a Conservation Area, a National Park, an Area of Outstanding Natural Beauty or the Broads, all additional buildings which are more than 10 cubic metres in volume, wherever they are on the plot in relation to the house, are treated as extensions of the house and reduce the allowance for further extensions. In all these cases, the volume of the buildings concerned are deducted from the volume limits given for the extension of your house.

Phew! You can see why I suggest that before you contemplate an extension you should consult the planning officer and get a definitive ruling on whether or not you need express planning consent. And you can see why I urge that if you are planning to build a home with an eye for future extension you carefully think out the design and the strategy you employ. If you think that the size of the building, as you envisage it eventually becoming, will put the planners off your proposals and if you and your architect feel that Permitted Development rights are unlikely to be curtailed, then you may decide that the best course of action is to go in for the smaller dwelling with an intention to extend at a later date. If, on the other hand, you feel that the planners won't be particularly bothered about the size of the dwelling as you propose it will eventually be, but your finances dictate that you can only carry out the development in stages, then perhaps it's better to apply for the whole thing and then build in stages as finance permits.

Whichever option you adopt there are some important things that you can do to make the eventual extension easier and less intrusive. Building in the lintels for any future door or window openings and spacing the brickwork or blockwork to create straight joints ready for cutting out can save a lot of time and trouble as long as you take care to maintain the structural integrity of the walling with ties or reinforcing mesh. It's open for you to consider whether, as long as you've got the necessary consents, you put the foundations in for any future extension, thus limiting the amount of disturbance you will experience when you eventually get around to it. Foundations needn't be left open, they can be covered over and grassed or even be brought up to oversite where they can exist as a patio until such time as their true role can be realised. On a roof that is to be occupied it makes no sense at all to use fink trusses which can never be altered to create living space so, instead, think about either a purlin and spar roof or an attic trussed roof. If dormer windows or Velux windows are going to be used then you might not be able to put them in to start with but you can still 'cripple' the roof timbers for their eventual construction and, whilst we're on about the roof, get your tradesmen to consider your future plans when

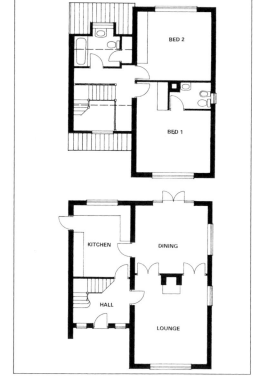
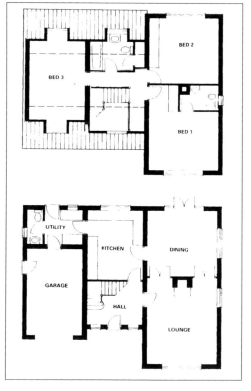

Building an extendable home. Two stages in building a three bedroomed house with an integral garage. Note that the foundations of stage two are used as a parking area for the stage one house.

installing any pipework, cable runs or insulation. Not only can they all then be positioned in the roof itself in such a way as to facilitate the eventual occupation but it's likely that the runs can also be constructed to accommodate their intended use and extension.

Designing for the disabled

Designing a new home for someone with a physical disability is an interesting challenge, and many people who are disabled, following an accident, move into a purpose built bungalow. They make excellent selfbuilders, possibly because the lengthy delays in receiving compensation payments give them plenty of time to become formidable experts on the subject, and they have an enormous enthusiasm for the job. The author has mixed memories of a selfbuilder client who used a wheelchair on the ground but could go up a ladder with ease, and who insisted on discussing progress on his bungalow with visitors while sitting aside his roof ridge. There are various bodies concerned with designing for the disabled, and they can be contacted through The Centre of Environment for the Handicapped, 35 Gt Smith St, London SW1P 3BJ. Details of the various relevant publications, addresses of suppliers, etc., can be obtained from them.

Larders and cold rooms

It's amazing that however many advances are made with kitchen appliances and kitchen units, the larder still retains its place of affection in the housewives mind. That's not to say that there's always space for it in the modern house and, indeed, with fitted kitchen units usually expected in a continuous run on most walls, there is a positive discrimination against there ever being room for the longed for larder. However, a 6ft x 6ft built in larder with 18" shelves all around from floor to ceiling will provide as much useable storage space as a lorry load of kitchen units so it is worth considering. If it can be positioned on a northern wall with fly proof ventilation in the traditional manner then it'll be so useful that it's likely to convert even the greatest sceptic to its worth. If it can't go on a suitable northern wall then there are electrical larder cooling units which will also require the installation of extra insulation to walls, floors, doors and ceilings.

Agas, Rayburns and their generic cousins

To many the epitome of kitchen design resides in the installation of a huge cast iron cooker fired by either gas, electricity or even solid fuel. Its solid presence has even moved a Poet Laureate to eulogise and wax lyrical. They are very expensive and some of the most expensive forms do not even do much more than cook. Others will run the domestic hot water and central heating as well but, even then, their cost is likely to be much more than the combined cost of a normal cooker and a domestic hot water boiler. What they give to a home cannot be evaluated totally in cost terms and their fans cannot often be dis-

suaded from their use. Care needs to be taken about their positioning both from the point of view of their weight and for the flue that they will require but, despite it all, once they are in, few can doubt the contribution they make to a home and a homely kitchen. If this is part and parcel of your dream of a new home of your own then go for it.

Hobbies

As far as the effect on the design of your new home is concerned it really depends on what your hobby is. If it's writing sexy novels then the study or office becomes, in effect, your hobbies room. If it's restoring old engines or turning things on lathes then perhaps you'd better turn back to the section where we talked about garages and think about whether such activities would be better confined to that area, albeit with some alteration. Most grown men won't admit to a yen for a train set but many harbour such a secret desire. I can well remember *my* train set when I was boy and I can remember, also, how my father wouldn't let me play with it unless he was there too! The roof is a perfect place for such an enterprise and if thought is given to the inclusion of attic trusses then the scope for this and other similar activities is practically limit-less. Sewing, needlework or knitting can often be carried out in any part of the house but, if such a hobby progresses beyond the occasional, thought might have to be given to a completely separate room. Some designs are able to utilise the otherwise 'wasted' space of the top landing and provide full length windows to a sitting area, which can double up as a sewing room or studio. Other hobbies or home sports such as billiards, table tennis etc. need more careful thought. The weight of a billiard table makes it unlikely that it can be housed in an upper part room unless, first of all the structure is beefed up to take it and, secondly thought is given as to how to get it up there when the room is ready for occupation. A mistake people can make when planning a room for such a hobby is in not realising just how much space they need, not only to get the table in, but also, to be able to move around and stretch to the full extent of a cue. Sometimes these activities can fit within the main body of the house but often, they have to be relegated to a completely separate structure. Thought also needs to be given to the proximity or provision of washing, changing and toilet facilities and the level of these requirements obviously reflects the level of your involvement with your chosen hobby or sport. One question that does need to be asked is whether a hobbies' room at this level should be of the same construction form as the house or whether thought should be given to it being some sort of purpose made or prefabricated building. A swimming pool is a case in point in that it often needs a fairly large structure with wide clear spans and it might, therefore, be better to consider one of the specialist manufacturers. Again, whilst the construction of a swimming pool, in itself, is not usually beyond the capabilities of the average builder working on a selfbuild site, it is open for you to consider whether or not, this too, shouldn't be carried out by a specialist company.

Security features

These days most windows that conform to the regulations and most doors too, have proper locks. Couple that with double glazing and as far as the structural components are concerned it's probably as much as most people will want. Nevertheless there are those for whom security is high on the agenda and for whom the building in of even greater security is an important incentive in the whole business of selfbuilding. Proximity alarms, sensors, floodlighting...there is a whole wealth of equipment to satisfy even the most insecure mind and there are plenty of companies out there who'll be only too happy to oblige your needs and supply you with what you require. A feature which can be built into a new home, is a secure cupboard which offers protection for valuables, shotguns and the like. If this is given consideration at the design stage, it is relatively easy for an ingenious carpenter to install a hidden door to a hidden cupboard which will escape the notice of a burglar! Those whose work involves keeping large sums of money in the house from time to time can arrange for an underfloor safe to be set in the foundation

concrete, to be reached by turning back a rug or carpet in one of the ground floor rooms. This may be a condition of their special insurance.

Services meter boxes

We seem to have a blind spot about the appearance of service boxes in this country, and one often sees an attractive new home disfigured by electricity and gas meter boxes prominently displayed on the front elevation. I have never understood why the planners do not take some sort of action that will lead to the electricity and gas authority's hideous plastic boxes not being so prominently on view.

The rules depend on the authority concerned, but generally the position is that the standard connection charge involves the services box being sited as close to the road as possible, and it is taken for granted that this is where everyone will find it most convenient and that this is the best place for it. Often those who are providing the supply will insist that this is where the self-builder 'has' to have his meter box. Needless to say you can challenge this, although you may be asked to pay a few pounds more for the extra length of cable. It may involve referring the matter to a senior manager, or even threatening to involve electricity and gas consumers' councils. This is very well worthwhile if it means that the boxes are installed where they are unobtrusive, or where they are easily shielded by appropriate planting.

Basements

In a situation where the slope of the land is going to dictate the design and that design ends up as a split or multi level design, there is the distinct possibility that you are also going to end up with one or more walls below ground level. In these cases the walls that find themselves in this position have to be treated in the same way as if they were basement walls and fully water proofed, something that is called 'tanking' in the building industry. That's still not the same thing as a full basement, which is normally thought of as having all four walls below ground. On the continent basements are very popular and the demand for them in this country often comes from those who have spent time living abroad, particularly in Germany. Older buildings in this country often have basements and their owners very quickly come to love and appreciate them, seeming to be perfectly happy to accept that at times they may even display patches of damp. But translate that to a new house and nobody would sleep at night with the worry of it.

Tanking has to be completely watertight and with a full basement, what one is seeking to create is, in effect, a swimming pool in reverse. But this empty swimming pool is having to contend with pressures of water from outside and, as well as that, it is having to cope with ground pressures. The purpose of this book is not to go into the technical detail of construction but to point the potential selfbuilder on to the right path of discovery. Suffice it to say that there are differing walling systems and that there are differing tanking systems and that the correct one for your own particular situation is the one that will be chosen by your architect working in conjunction with the engineer and with the approval of the Building and warranties inspector.

It takes a strong nerve to construct or commission a basement in this country especially in areas of heavy clay or where the ground water is high. It also takes a pretty deep pocket and, in the end, you may decide that it's not for you. A full basement requires a hole in the ground some 3 metres deep and once that's been excavated the foundation trenches themselves have to be further dug in. At this point nerves can begin to fray, especially as it's by no means a one day procedure and can drag on for weeks. Every mornings arrival at the site will start off with a quick check to make sure that next door's house hasn't taken up residence on your plot and even the fact that you've got insurance, to cover this awful eventuality, goes no way to calming nerves and does equally little to impress your terrified neighbours. If I haven't managed to dissuade you, and I'm writing here in the capacity of someone who has gone through this experience several times and vowed, each time, never to repeat it, then I earnestly advise you to take the very best advice and to make sure that your chosen contractors have specific experience of this sort of undertaking.

A basement is not naturally ventilated and the tanked walls cannot breathe: as a result it must have adequate artificial ventilation. If any activity is to take place in the basement which generates water vapour, as with a sauna or laundry room, special arrangements must be made to extract the water vapour. If the heating boiler is to situated in a cellar it is important that consideration is given to its specific ventilation requirements, and now that audible gas detectors are available cheaply they should be installed to detect any gas leak in the house which might lead to a build up of gas in the cellar.

Unusual features

I've said several times that the reason most people get into selfbuilding is so that they can have their houses just how they want them and not how anyone else thinks they should have them. That said, I have also stressed that an eye has to be kept on the probability that you will want to sell your new home some day. Think about peculiar or unusual features before you go ahead is all I'm saying and, if you can, think of ways to get what you want without compromising the value of your new home. For instance, if you want a small photographic dark room, do not omit a window. It will be a nuisance to have to make a screen to black it out, but with a window an estate agent can describe your dark room as either a box room or a fifth bedroom. All of this chapter has been about building what you want, but remember that your house must also be what a prospective purchaser will want some day.

9 Designing a new home – to be energy efficient

To most people this subject will revolve around the contrived argument between brick and block and timber framed construction. Given the fact that the most commonly used form of brick and block walling and the equally most commonly used system of timber framed walling share, to within a whisker, the same 'U' values, this is not a real issue and the question of which method to use, which I'll explore again in the chapter headed ' Making the choices', does not really interfere with the main considerations of this chapter. That is, apart from the illustration of choices within the two methods that seek to highlight just what can be achieved and just how a little prior thought can make the difference.

Much of the information for this chapter has been provided by Nick Jones of BRECSU which is the part of the Building Research Establishment that manages the Department of the Environment's Energy Efficiency Best Practice programme for buildings. Indeed, many of the words are mix and matches of Nick's writings and are reproduced with his kind permission.

Energy efficient features need not be expensive and they don't need to use advanced or wacky technology. Often the very best results can be gained by the use of simple tried and tested methods which need not add more that 50p per square foot to the overall cost of your new home. In the same way, however, as thinking about energy conservation and the saving of the environment is a forward thinking process, it is equally important that this forward thinking is applied at the earliest stages of the design process for your new home. If energy efficiency is high on your priority list, you need to make sure that your designer fully understands this, right from the word go. The maximum benefit from energy efficiency measures can only really be obtained by an integrated approach of combining a number of complimentary measures into a comprehensive package, rather than any piece-meal inclusion of single measures. An example of this would be the extra costs of insulation that could be offset against the savings in costs of being able to install a smaller heating system.

Standard Assessment Procedure (SAP) and the Building Regulations.

SAP is the Government's standard system for home energy rating and can be used to provide a simple but reliable indicator of the energy efficiency of a house. It estimates the space and hot water heating costs per square metre of floor area of a house (based upon such factors as its size, heating system, ventilation characteristics and standard assumptions such as occupancy and heating pattern) and converts it into a rating from 1 to 100. The higher the number, the lower the energy consumption. An SAP calculation is also a requirement under the section of the Building Regulations, dealing with Conservation of Fuel and Power, known as 'Part L', with which all new homes must comply. However, if it is your intention to build an energy efficient home, you should regard these Regulations as an absolute minimum.

There are three basic methods of demonstrating compliance with 'Part L' and all of them have to show a SAP rating. A high SAP rating will, therefore, save a lot of effort by providing most of the information that is needed to prove compliance. SAP calculations will be usually commissioned or undertaken by your architect, designer, timber frame manufacturer or package deal company but there are a number of commercial sources who will undertake them for you and many of the suppliers provide such a service.

The three methods are:

Elemental – This lays down maximum permissible 'U' values for walls, roofs, floors and windows. There are limits to the area of windows and doors of 22.5% of the floor area but there are options to increase this by the use of high performance glazing. The lower the 'U' value for each element, the better. Perhaps the best illustration of all of this is to think about walls. A standard timber framed open panel walling system, using 89mm x 39mm studs will have a 'U' value of around 0.39. If one increases the size of the studs and, by inference, the thickness of the insulation to 140mm then the 'U' value improves to 0.29. If one was to ratchet things up even further by using the closed panel Scandinavian systems then the 'U' values would be approaching 0.2 or slightly less. Set that against the target 'U' value for walling of 0.45, and you can see just how much can be achieved. If one's talking in terms of brick and block then a demonstration of just how the insulation, rather than the structure, affects 'U' value can be given by assuming a brick and block wall where the cavity is 50mm and the internal block is lightweight 125mm. If the cavity was left clear and hard plaster was used, then the 'U' value would be 0.6. If one changed the hard plaster to a lightweight plaster then the 'U' value would come down to 0.59 and, if one dry lined the wall, then it would come down to 0.54. Not a lot of difference and all outside the target 'U' value for the walling of 0.45. However, if one insulated the cavity with full fill insulation, then the 'U' value would come down to 0.32!

Target 'U' value – This allows you to calculate the average 'U' value for your design using a formula based on the outside area of your building and the floor area. So long as the average 'U' value achieves a target 'U' value, the building complies. There are also allowances that can be made for more efficient heating systems and for orientating the house and glazing southwards. This method is slightly more complicated than the elemental method but allows for greater flexibility in design. With both this and the elemental method, the requirements become more stringent if the SAP rating is less than 60 (a poor rating for new housing).

Energy rating – The principal requirement is that the design achieves a set SAP rating of between 80 and 85, depending on the floor area. So long as this score is met there are very few restrictions on the design.

SAP ratings can be a useful tool in setting

How much nicer is this scene when there's a warm and cosy home to go back to like this one from The Swedish House Company?

House 'A' (2500 sq. ft.) - built to meet the Building Regulations requirements	House 'B' (2500 sq.ft) – built to provide low running costs
* Basic wall insulation ('U' value of 0.45)	* South facing orientation
* 150mm loft insulation	* Good wall insulation providing a 'U' value of 0.3
* 30mm floor insulation	* 200mm loft insulation
* Standard double glazing (6mm air gap)	* 50mm floor insulation
* Gas wall mounted boiler serving radiators	* Double glazing with 12mm air gap and 'low 'e' glass
* Room thermostat, programmer and thermostatic radiator valves	* Gas condensing boiler serving radiators
* 30mm sprayed insulation on the hot water cylinder	* Room thermostat, programmer and thermostatic radiator valves
	* 70mm sprayed insulation on the hot water cylinder
SAP rating = 86	
Annual heating and hot water cost £476 (1998/9)	SAP rating = 100
	Annual heating and hot water cost £306 (1998/9)

targets for your design. You could, for example, set a target 10 points above the Building Regulations requirement for the Energy Rating Method. Alternatively you could set aside a fixed amount to spend on raising the initial design specification above the Building Regulations base line. If we take an example of two houses of a similar design of 2500 square feet we can compare the improved energy efficiency that is available.

The site

The orientation of the site is alluded to in the example of House 'B' and, if it is at all possible, choose a site that allows your house to face south, plus or minus 45 degrees, ideally with shelter from prevailing winds but without shading to the house. That said, plots are fairly hard to come by in the best of times and situations and whilst this is an ideal, don't go passing up a site just because this can't be achieved. Using the sun to heat your house saves energy and makes it more pleasant. You don't need to increase the window area as such but the more that can face south the better. You may need external blinds to prevent over heating in the summer months however and, of course, some windows may always have to face north to ensure good daylight in all rooms. Any gain from any of the above is known as passive solar heating and the most important thing about it is that it is free. More active forms of solar heating by the use of solar panels do tend to be expensive and have a sufficiently long payback time as to make them

impracticable for all but the enthusiast. The technology is, however, advancing and there may come a time when active solar heating for water or space may become mainstream – but not yet.

Insulation

I've already illustrated how the 'U' value can be improved as far as the walling goes. It needn't stop there and I would think that if you are going to specify anything about this subject to your designer you should, perhaps, think about asking that the 'U' value for the walling approaches as close to 0.3 as is possible. A loft with 200mm of insulation (100mm laid between the joists with 100mm laid across them) will have a 'U' value of 0.2. Rooms in the roof and dormer windows need careful attention to detail but can be insulated to a high standard. If you ever intend to occupy the roof void then you might like to consider the placing of the insulation so as to provide a warm roof instead of a cold roof. With a cold roof, the insulation follows the shape of the occupied rooms below, so leaving the loft outside the insulated area. The area between the insulation and the roof structure then needs to be adequately ventilated to avoid condensation. With a warm roof, the insulation is placed between and along the route of the rafters, under the tiles. Even though the loft is not heated it therefore finds itself within the insulated envelope. Condensation is therefore unlikely so there is not the need for ventilation. Neither is inherently more or less efficient than the other and if, therefore, you have no plans to occupy the roof then a cold roof will be perfectly suitable and will, by virtue of the fact that the area to cover is reduced, cost less to insulate. Ground floors are much more difficult as far as heat loss calculations are concerned, as there are so many different types of floors. All of them are, however, easy to insulate during the construction and a minimum of 50mm is suggested, with more if underfloor central heating is to be employed, so as to minimise heat loss to the ground. Whether using an oversite slab or floor beams, remember to draw the proposed use and thickness of the insulation to the contractors attention so that the floor levels and cill levels are set at the correct height to accommodate it.

House layout

A compact plan, without 'extensions' minimises the external wall area, reduces heat losses and reduces shading of other parts of the house. A bungalow will lose more heat than a three storey house of the same floor area. Rooms that are used most should be on the south side to take advantage of any solar gain. For rooms that are used mostly in the mornings, such as kitchens and breakfast rooms, a south-east orientation will get the best benefit from the sun. If possible halls, landings, staircases and less frequently occupied rooms such as bathrooms and utility rooms, can go on the north side. That's the ideal of course, when thinking about energy conservation, but all of this has to fit in with the street scene and what the planners will want and, in addition to that, there may be other factors that you may want to take into account such as the specific views from a window or windows. As ever, the conflicting requirements have to be brought into balance and that's the task facing you and your designers.

Windows

Double glazing is standard in most new homes. It reduces heat loss and offers sound insulation. Standard double glazing using a 6mm air gap gives a 'U' value of 3.3 (Remember the target for the wall was 0.3!). Increasing the air gap to 12mm and changing the glass to a low emissivity (Low 'e') glass will raise the insulation level to a 'U' value of 2.4. Changing the air gap need not cost very much extra at all but if larger air gaps are required then the cost of the window frames might rise considerably and they may have to be purpose made. Argon filled double glazing units and triple glazing, standard on some of the Scandinavian systems, may also be used, but all of these will undoubtedly cost more.

Conservatories

In certain areas the planners will have a lot to say about conservatories and in particular in Areas of Outstanding Natural Beauty, National Parks and Conservation Areas. In other areas they may be quite amenable but even then, may baulk at conservatories on the front of a house. Conservatories, however, can help to save energy by reducing heat losses through the adjoining walls and by trapping heat from the sun. The savings are small and to be effective they do need to be on the south side of the house without any overshadowing. Even high quality conservatories should not have any permanent heating as this could lead to very high fuel bills and there should be double glazed doors to shut them off from the house when they are not in use.

Heating your house and the hot water

Low energy houses require smaller and simpler heating systems than other houses of a similar size where little or no action has been taken to conserve heat loss. If one is retired or working from home and the house is occupied for most of the time, then an underfloor heating system, at least to the ground floor, with radiators and thermostatic radiator valves to the upper floor will be well worth considering. If, on the other hand, the pattern of your occupation means that the house is empty most of the day, then the lack of responsiveness inherent in underfloor systems may be a drawback. A warm air system or radiators with thermostatic radiator valves (TRVs) installed in a timber framed house which is occupied mornings and evenings would supply heat where and when it was needed but beware the resale potential of warm air heating systems due to its effect on asthma sufferers. Radiators with TRVs provide a very efficient system of delivering heat and they are inherently responsive. They cannot, however, provide such an even heat as underfloor systems, particularly in larger rooms. The pipework in underfloor heating systems is usually buried in a screed and it is this screed that then radiates the heat into the room and acts as a thermal store. Whilst pipes can be fixed to lightweight suspended floors, the system will not work as well. A popular compromise is therefore, the use of an underfloor heating system to the ground, and any solid upper floors, with the use of radiators with TRVs to timber upper floors. With underfloor central heating the system can operate at lower water temperatures and it goes without saying that increasing the insulation below the screed will also have a beneficial effect. A tiled solid screed floor works best with underfloor heating as do rugs instead of carpets.

Condensing boilers, with average efficiencies of 85%, are much better than conventional boilers, even though they do tend to cost quite a bit more. Essentially a condensing boiler works in just the same way as an ordinary fan-flued boiler, except that it has a larger heat exchanger which absorbs more of the heat from the burner and from the flue gases. Under certain conditions (when the return water temperature is low) the flue gases condense and release latent heat back into the boiler that would otherwise be wasted (It from this that the boiler gets its name). The gases coming out of a conventional boiler's flue are very hot (250 degrees centigrade) but with a condensing boiler they are around 50-60 degrees centigrade. The savings available from this kind of efficiency are obvious.

Hot water efficiency is governed largely by the efficiency of the boiler rather than the type of system, e.g. vented or sealed, but, the more insulation one has around the hot water store (cylinder) the better and 50mm plus is a good thickness to aim at providing. Good controls are essential to maximise the efficiency of any heating system and they are required by the Building Regulations. Individual room control is particularly important in rooms with large south facing windows and if your home is to have distinct

areas which will be used at differing times, such as an annexe or office, then zone controls may be worthwhile considering.

Electric showers have a fairly low flow rate and only heat the actual amount of water that is used. Nevertheless if there is a store of hot water only yards away, then the cost of their purchase and installation may not be worthwhile. If you want a powerful shower then either use a sealed hot water system, where the hot water is delivered at mains pressure, or think of a power shower where the water is pumped. Of course these do use a lot more water and energy and they are not inexpensive. Perhaps in today's ethos of saving they are an expensive and unnecessary luxury.

If you want a focal fire then multi-fuel stoves are a very good option if you also want to maximise energy efficiency, especially if you are able to take advantage of a free fuel such as wood. These are much more efficient than an open fire and won't give such high heat losses through the flue from increased ventilation when not in use. I repeat this information, knowing full well that the open fireplace is deeply embedded in the British psyche and that most of you will nod sagely and ignore it.

A truly superb conservatory reflecting the space and quality of a Scandia-Hus home.

Ventilation

Ventilation is important to provide both fresh air and prevent condensation. The Building Regulations require that there should be extractor fans or passive stack ventilation (PSV) in all kitchens and bathrooms. With PSV, air is drawn out of the house, without the need for electric fans, through a combination of the effect of the air flowing over the roof and by the natural buoyancy of the warm moist air. In order to prevent over ventilation, humidity controlled dampers can be fitted which need no electrical connection. Permanent ventilation must also be provided to all other rooms using trickle vents that are fitted to all windows.

Mechanical ventilation with or without heat recovery may offer benefits such as filtered air and reduced noise intrusion. The systems use fans to both supply fresh air and extract stale air in a very controlled manner. The heat recovery options recover much of the heat from the extracted air and add it to the returning air using a heat exchanger so that the two air streams do not mix. Filters can be fitted to the supply air to remove dust and pollen and they can, therefore, provide very good quality air. There is no need for trickle ventilation with such a system and this may be an important factor in reducing the noise from outside in certain locations. Mechanical ventilation will not work properly unless the house is well sealed and sealing of the house can only really be done at the construction stage, involving very close attention to detail and a close watch on workmanship. Unfortunately open fireplaces are incompatible with these systems. The running costs are also significant and may outweigh the energy saved, so, whilst they will provide good ventilation and good quality air, they should not generally be seen as an energy saving or efficient feature.

Lighting

Maximising daylighting with the design and good lighting design, combined with use of low energy compact or strip fluorescent lights will save considerable amounts on running costs. Fluorescent lamps have a much longer life than ordinary light bulbs. Amongst others, there are four in my house, as I write, that I purchased nearly ten years ago, and that have been in almost constant daily use ever since!

To sum up this chapter. Many architects and designers will be fully aware of all of the principles and all of the savings that are available and that can be usefully employed by the selfbuilder. That said, many of them will not design these features into your new home unless you pull the trigger and alert them to the fact that, for you, this is an issue. If the saving of energy, and by implication the environment, is important to you, then you do need to discuss and set targets and, when considering the employment of an architect, designer or package deal company, you should choose one that has knowledge of low energy design.

10 Designing a new home – the external works

Many will think that what follows in this chapter is 'jumping the gun', but I make no apology for trying to get you to think ahead and to consider all aspects of your finished home at the earliest stages of the design process. Look through the books of plans on the market, the company brochures and the sales leaflets and what do you see? You see the dream houses and bungalows illustrated as part of that dream, set in imaginary surroundings of trees, hedges, sweeping driveways and herbaceous borders. Look at the plans of your new home which have been drawn up especially for you and what do you see? You see plans drawn in strict elevational perspective with, perhaps the front elevation only, having an indication of trees or dark lines to signify planting of some sort. Nothing, however, will be drawn that could obscure the elevation as a whole. That's all perfectly understandable; the architect will be keen that you appreciate the fine lines of the house he has designed for you and the planners will want to see the building rather than some sketchy impression. Yet that wasn't your original idea – your dream wasn't of some stark and lonely building in isolation. Your dream, almost certainly, nestled into a backdrop of carefully laid out lawns and driveways with lovingly manicured flowerbeds and shrubberies.

So why is that so many selfbuilders seem to get to the point of moving in and then, just stop? Why do so many new selfbuilt homes spend their first years residing on a bombsite? Perhaps it's because the selfbuilder, having put all his efforts into getting in, just runs out of steam. Perhaps it's because, having moved in there's still a lot to do inside and that gets higher priority. That is until someone slips off the scaffold boards masquerading as the front path or the dog, having paddled through a sea of mud, ruins the new carpet. It doesn't have to be like this. Once again, attendance at the school of forward planning will pay off and pay off handsomely.

Planners will try to influence the garden design. They may even insist that no work is commenced on site without the prior approval of tree planting and/or landscaping schemes. But these requirements are one dimensional only and the plans that result from them can be wholly inadequate. It may look good on plan that a *Quercus robur*, English oak to you and me, is shown in the front lawn but what good is that if, when you come to sit in your favourite chair in the lounge, it obscures the view across the Downs that you'd so looked forward to. Consideration of external works and landscaping has to start by examining your living pattern. How much time are you going to want to give to looking after your garden? At one end of the scale you may think the less bother the garden is, the better it will suit you. Fine – carefully chosen shrubs, the right grass, no borders, no edges, paths set flush in the grass, and you will have a minimum maintenance garden which can look very attractive indeed. At the other extreme, you may intend that the garden will be a very important part of your life. If so, it is even more important that you analyse what you are going to be able to do, and plan accordingly. You should consider not only the gardening that you can currently undertake, but also the work load which you are likely to be able to enjoy in the years ahead, bearing in mind that keen gardeners who are unable to keep their gardens as they wish have many regrets. If you are fortunate enough to be able to pay someone to look after your garden for you, careful consideration of the labour requirement is just as important. You will want a perfect garden for your money, and an acre can be laid out either to need only half a day per week to maintain, or to occupy someone nearly full time.

The next thing to consider is your timetable. This is important, and is often overlooked. Do you look forward to watching the garden slowly taking shape, and hope to see your dreams come true in three or four years, or do you want visitors to be admiring it in six months' time? Remember a wisteria will take seven years before it makes a show but a container grown cherry will be in flower next spring. This can be an important issue if your lifestyle is such that you might move at any time, and need your home always to be a good resale prospect. An established garden may or may not add to the value of a property but it certainly always makes it more saleable.

This leads to the next consideration, which is that of cost. It used to be said that anyone building a house should be prepared to spend at least 10% of its value on its surroundings. The cost of building is now so high that this would require a large plot on which to spend the sum involved, but the principle that the garden deserves its place in the budget is important. This may be a cash budget if you intend to have a landscaping contractor do the work, or a budget for your own labour plus some cash if you intend to do all the work yourself. In this latter case, beware of overestimating your own capacity or the time that you will have available, particularly if you are going to do much earth moving by hand.

Finally, having made a realistic appraisal of the amount of time you wish to give to the garden, of how soon you want it to look established, and of the budget, you can think about what you hope it will look like, This involves a plan. Even if your garden is unimportant to you, it is worthwhile making sure that it is going to be as little trouble as possible, will show off your new home to the best advantage and will enhance its value.

One of the best books I have ever seen which deals with achievable plans for the smaller and average garden is one that I've mentioned before and one that is probably on quite a few peoples shelves anyway. This is *The Small Garden* by John Brookes, published by Readers Digest. I'm sure there are many others and I'm equally sure that, just like the plan books, what you'll end up with is an amalgamation, a fusing of the various ideas that you'll see in these books, leading up to your eventual garden design.

If you are building on an eighth of an acre in a built up area, your choices are limited, and you will almost certainly have a marvellous opportunity to look at all of your options by simply going for a walk to see what your neighbours have done with their own front and back gardens. Look over their hedges in winter as well as summer. Take local advice on what takes time and trouble, and what is easily looked after. Sort out your own master plan, and away you go.

Your garden can complement your house very well, but its size will impose a limit to what you can do. With anything over a quarter of an acre the challenge is much more complicated. At this size your garden can be given distinct character, and the house and garden can relate to each other in a very special way. If you have this opportunity, then you need to be a very experienced gardener to be confident that you can design the right garden.

Local landscaping contractors, nurserymen and garden centres usually offer to design gardens, but this is inevitably linked to their own services.

An alternative is to use the services of a garden designer. This makes the whole business more complicated but need not cost very much, and you will know that the advice that you are getting is free of commercial pressures. Plans and a list of plants from a garden designer can be used to obtain competing quotations from landscaping contractors, or can be your blue print for managing the job yourself.

Certainly you want to know exactly the shape and contours of your garden while the builder still has earth moving plant on site, so that you can ask him to dump soil where it will be required and to leave the site with ground at levels that will suit the landscaping work. If you have a large site it is a very good idea to fence off the builder's theatre of operations and to start making the garden on the rest of the land while the house is being built. In this way you will almost certainly be able to move one season ahead. Having one part of the garden finished will encourage you to make start on the area left by the builder as soon as you move in.

In similar vein if your plot is one where there was an old house that is to be demolished, then I'll bet that a lot of the garden and other works are already done. Why spoil them? Why allow the lawn to be used as a dumping ground for spoil or a storage area for bricks? Why let lorries break up that Yorkstone patio? Rope off as much as you can and make it clear to your contractors that no part of the building work is to go beyond that demarcation without your prior knowledge and consent. Give the contractors the whole site to play with and they'll use it, I assure you, whether

A fine drive, imposing gates and the sweep of the brick walls make an imposing entrance to this suburban house designed by D&M.

they need to or not.

To be realistic, if you are managing the building of a new home yourself, it is unlikely that you will have the time or energy to spare to give any of this the energy or attention it deserves, but even so it is important that you do have a landscaping scheme and that you try to give it consideration in spite of the overriding priority of making sure the roof it tiled on schedule. If you have placed a contract with a builder, then involvement with planning the garden will serve as an outlet for all your frustrations while the building work seems to proceed so slowly. You will have time for visits to garden exhibitions and garden centres, a great deal of reading, and you can even venture to plant trees amid the builders' confusion if you protect them properly. However much time you have for this, or however little, the important thing is to have a plan at an early stage, and to ensure that it is suited to the long term relationship between you and the garden which is going to be outside your window for as long as you live in the house.

Given the determination to make an effective plan for the new garden, and preferably before the builder moves his earth-moving equipment away from the site, what are the features to be considered? The landscaping itself is a matter for your expert, but all that he does will be framed by the way in which you have dealt with your boundaries, and will have to take into account all of your external works. Among the more important of these are the following.

Driveways

Unless you have a very big garden indeed, the drive is the largest single feature in your garden, and once it is built, it will be very difficult to move it. It is likely that your planning consent will require that the gates, if any, are set back a fixed distance from the road, that the slope for the first few yards does not exceed a certain gradient, and that there is provision for a car to be able to turn on the drive without backing out into the road. You will also be concerned that there is a large enough parking area for visitors and delivery vehicles. On most plots there will only be one practicable layout to meet these requirements, but if you do have alternative alignments for the drive, consider the feel they will give to your garden as well as thinking about them simply as a way of getting the car to the garage.

Consider whether, if there's room, the driveway can be curved or even have a double bend in it. A straight driveway does not afford any privacy but a curved one certainly can. Careful planting may be necessary but the effect

Right - Pavoirs from York Handmade Brick Company, lending their mellow air of permanence to this sweeping drive.

can be the realisation of a private front garden that can be of use to you instead of simply providing a visual amenity for passers by. Levels too, can come into this equation insofar as, where certain maximum gradients have to be achieved, lengthening the driveway by curving it around can bring you within the requirements. 'Horses for courses', the saying goes and nothing could more true than for the selection of the driveway surface. A pea shingle drive can look incongruous fronting a smartly tarmaced suburban road yet absolutely right in a rural setting. A tarmac drive with its neat edges and scattered marble chippings can look great in the town but how silly does it look carving its unyielding way through a field? As I've said above, the driveway is quite likely to be the single most important visual feature in your garden and your choices, in terms of both shape and finish, can dramatically affect your new home, so let's think about the various surfaces.

Pavoir bricks. Undoubtedly at the top of the range in cost terms and, if properly laid, in aesthetic terms as well. Please don't confuse these bricks with ordinary walling bricks as they are especially fired and shaped to provide the hardness and frost resistance necessary for their intended role. They should be laid by a specialist and a great deal of care should be given to the choice of colour and texture as well as to the pattern in which they are laid. The single most important thing that singles these out from imitations is their ability to mellow. The only drawback with that is that the very *verdigris* that serves to mellow them can, if allowed to flourish too much and in permanently damp conditions, become a trifle slippery.

Block pavers. The mass produced answer to the brick pavoir and one that, with sympathetic choice, can rival its relative. Badly chosen, however, it can do little more than imitate the petrol station forecourt it so often graces. Now available in a whole range of colours, its cost can start to rival that of the trusty tarmac drive and, if its foundations are properly prepared, it will prove almost maintenance free. They don't seem to mellow in quite the same way as the brick pavoirs but again this depends both on their surroundings and their owner. Some like it when the gaps between the blocks get mossy, some hate it and spend endless hours scrubbing and scraping – the choice, as with all things to do with selfbuilding, is yours.

Tarmac. If tarmac wasn't a good drive surface then God wouldn't have made a lake of it in Trinidad and a goodly proportion of the world's surface wouldn't be covered in it. That said, the real thing should never be confused with what you'll get if you employ the itinerant who knocks on your door telling you that, "he's doing a job around the corner and he can do you a good deal". What you'll get there is the heated up scrapings from the resurfacing work going on down the road, which will never bond properly and will very soon cease to be a homogenous surface. Carried out by a properly registered contractor, with premises, so that if there's any trouble you can find him again, a tarmac driveway can be every bit as serviceable as the Queen's highway. I question whether some of the colour choices that are available ever look right but, again, it's all down to informed choice. The edgings can be in either concrete, brick or timber but, whatever you choose, make sure that they properly contain the material. If wood is chosen make certain that it's treated with a preservative and make sure also that before the 'black' goes down the prepared subsurface is treated with a strong weedkiller.

Concrete. A short driveway in the town, with concrete laid in properly tamped bays with expansion joints of compressible material, can look quite alright. Similarly, in a rural area or farming situation, where long access drives are required which may, from time to time, be used by heavy vehicles, a properly formed and properly laid concrete driveway is often the best solution. Badly laid it can very quickly degenerate and remind one of the cracked and weed strewn surfaces between blocks of municipal garaging. Concrete can be imprinted with some sort of patterning, either freehand or with special moulds and it can also be coloured and given a shiny finish. I don't think printed driveways of mock cobbles, resembling some huge crocodile that's lain down and died will ever look right but, equally, I've met those who've made this choice and can attest to their delight. The thing that always strikes me about these particular driveways is the fact that when they crack, and concrete driveways always seem to crack in the end, they crack, not though the indentations but, across the patterning.

Grass blocks. Everybody's driven over these from time to time but, in spite of that, very few consider them for their driveway. Why not? If hardstanding, turning or parking areas are required, yet one doesn't want to spoil the lines of a main driveway of interfere with a sweep of lawn, they can be the perfect answer. Properly laid, properly seeded they can provide a perfectly adequate driving surface, which from most visual angles just blends into the lawn.

Gravel/pea shingle. Look in the front pages of 'Country Life' next time you're waiting to see the dentist. Go to the adverts for large country houses and look closely at the driveways. I bet you a pound to a penny that the poshest of them have a gravel driveway, as do many of the stately homes of our land. So why is the gravel driveway thought of as the 'cheap' option in such disparaging terms? Maybe it's because it can be the cheaper option in cash terms. Maybe it's because the pea shingle drive is often laid as the precursor to another form of surfacing, as and when it can be afforded. But don't let that distract from the very great worth of a gravel driveway which, properly laid and with careful maintenance can be an asset to grace many a new home. Of course there are situations where it's not really applicable and I've already mentioned one, and there are situations where it's not practicable. In a steeply sloping situation the gravel will always want to migrate downhill and no amount of baffles will prevent it doing so. In like manner, if a pea shingle driveway is to abut a tarmac driveway, precautions will have to be taken to prevent migration or the carrying over of stones onto and into the tarmac. This can often take the form of a band, or bands, of cobblestones. As with the tarmac driveway, the edgings have to be carefully thought out and planned and the prior application of weedkiller will pay off handsomely. The plus points of a gravel driveway most often

forgotten are, its ease of maintenance, if properly laid, its ease of repair and its value as a disincentive to thieves. You try creeping up a pea shingle driveway at night!

Lastly, although I've talked about each surfacing method in singular terms, it's open for you to think in terms of a combination of the various surfaces and textures. Whichever method or methods you choose, any driveway is only as good as its preparation. The specification for its foundations and its drainage arrangements need to be either drawn up or approved by your architect and the work needs to be carried out by a competent tradesman or company.

Pathways and patios

I've lumped them all together but there are three main considerations here. Firstly the path to the front door. Do you indeed need one or will your driveway double up as the hard access to the entrance? If you do use the driveway then remember to make it wide enough so that you can walk past any parked vehicles without having to step onto the grass. Your front door may not abut the driveway and you may need to have either a separate pathway orone leading from the driveway to it. Think about what width this will look best as. Think about whether the pathway should be straight or curved and whether it should invite people to walk up it or whether it should discourage casual entry and confine the postman to using a mailbox at its beginning. Some will want their front gardens open plan and some will want them to be fenced off with a gate at the end of the pathway. Maybe the planners have already stipulated what you're having and this kind of consideration is out of your hands.

If you're building on a sloping site then, in all probability, the architect has shown steps either up or down to the front door and presumably he has designed them in such a way as to be sympathetic with the type of house you're building and the area you're living in. Nothing looks worse than a large house with skimpy ill thought out steps leading precariously up to a front door and nothing looks sillier than huge ornate sweeping steps guarded by stone lions giving access to a small cottage. The right garden

A patio is an extension of your living space into the garden, and level and material changes can add to its interest and enjoyment as with this Scandia-Hus bungalow.

path gives a period feel to a garden, enables you and your guests to walk around it when the grass is wet, and will help your garden to look larger than it really is. On the other hand, all paths need maintenance to some extent or other, and if they are not made on properly laid foundations they will become uneven and dangerous. Some stone flags become very slippery in wet weather, particularly if they are in the shade, and if elderly people are likely to walk around your garden paths at all times of the year it is important to remember this.

The first consideration is whether or not you are going to build your path with a properly compacted foundation, possibly with a concrete base. If you do this, and have a proper path ending, there should be little risk of it becoming uneven and hazardous. However, this involves significant costs, and you may prefer simply to level flags that become uneven or replace gravel that has disappeared into the ground. However, a proper sub-base is essential if you are using paver bricks. In this case careful consideration of the finished level of the path is needed, and if it is set in a lawn, of whether or not you are going to mow over the top of the finished surface.

The patio or terrace is the means by which we project our living arrangements from within the confines of the house, into the open air. Often it directly adjoins the living area and access to it is gained from either french doors or patio doors leading from the house. At other times it can be divorced from the house and approached by the pathways we have spoken about above. At all times consideration must be given to its primary purposes. If it is principally a feature to be seen and admired, but not regularly walked on, then gaps between paving slabs can be filled with alpine plants, and dwarf walls can be of a height to suit the outlook, with everything arranged for visual effect. However, if your patio is to be used for sitting out, or for parties with lots of guests, it is important that there are no gaps in the surface to trap high heels, and it will help informal gatherings if any walls are at a convenient height for sitting on them. As with walls, materials for patios and terraces should complement the materials used for the main building, and cheap or inappropriate materials should be avoided at all costs. The norm used to be that patios and terraces were constructed with one material or another, but I invite you to consider whether a combination of different materials and textures might not give this important feature more interest. Why not have areas within a stone slabbed patio as large round pebbles set in concrete? What about mixing brick pavoirs or quarry tiles, or edging shingled areas and then planting them with specimen shrubs? And what about a raised timber deck?

Walls

Walls are a very special feature in a garden, and building a new one announces that you are seriously into landscaping. Walls also involve you in considerable expenditure. If you want to build a garden wall it is important that you make no attempt to cut corners, as a cheap looking wall will damage the appearance of the garden as much as an appropriate one will enhance it.

The material to be used has to be right. If you use the wrong bricks or stone your wall will look wrong and will get worse as it weathers, while the right materials will look even better as time goes by. Walls should give a feeling that they are part of the landscaping: they will not do this if they are inappropriate to the surroundings. In particular, this means concrete blocks of all sorts, particularly the ornamental pierced walling blocks, should only be used in the sort of urban or seaside situation which suits them, and never as part of a rural scene.

It is equally important that walls should also look massive and permanent, built in a local style, with an appropriate coping. They need a proper foundation, and there are tables which determine the minimum thickness for different heights of a wall if it is to be stable: 215mm solid walls can be built up to a height of 1.35M without piers, and 1.8M with piers at 3M intervals. This is largely irrelevant: to look right any wall has to be thicker than this, with 325mm (13in) as a minimum. To build to this standard, with the right coping, is expensive. If it is outside your budget, then plant a beech hedge instead!

If you have bought the site with existing old walls, or best of all have found a site in a walled garden, you are very lucky. It will give your home a very special character. Unfortunately the walls may also have a tendency to start to fall down the moment that you assume responsibility for them, especially if the ground is higher on one side than on the other. The worst potential problem is in the foundations. If a wall leans at all you should consider finding old bricks or stone to match the original material, and have a buttress or buttresses built to support the wall before it becomes unstable. This is cheaper than rebuilding, and if the buttress is really massive and in character, and quickly clothed with climbing shrubs, no-one will know that it is not an original.

The stone coping or coping brickwork of an old wall is another weak point: fortunately it is easily replaced and it is important to get this done before the rain gets into the masonry. Repointing is less essential than dealing with any water seeping in at the top, but if it needs to be done, make sure that the work is carried out in exactly the same style as the original, with mortar made from the same sand so that the colour matches. If the original wall was built with lime mortar, use lime mortar for the repairs.

Dry stone walls are indigenous to many upland areas and their construction, whilst following general principles, is equally regional in character. Do not imagine for one moment that it merely involves the placing of one stone upon another or you will be sadly disappointed when it all falls down. Rather it is the careful choice of stone and its placing which ensures the stability, usually by a slight inward slope to both faces with joining blocks and suitable rubble infill. If you inherit a broken down wall of this type then have a close look at how it's done before undertaking any repairs or ask around the village pub to find out the names of the surviving exponents of the trade.

Retaining walls are a different kettle of fish. It all depends on the height of the land that is to be retained and whether or not any buildings are to be supported, as to the type of construction but, as a rule of thumb, if you're retaining more than 1.2 metres, you need a specialist engineer to be involved in the design. As much care needs to be taken with the drainage of the retained land and the reduction of water pressure as it does with the actual strength of the wall itself. There are alternatives to building a wall, some of which, like the cages of stones one can see on British motorways, are singularly unattractive and some of which, like the cleverly designed interlocking planted blocks one sees on French motorways, are much more pleasing to the eye.

Fences

Previous editions of this book spoke in disparaging terms about fencing but the fact remains that, for many, it provides the ideal answer to the enclosure and privacy of the new home. A quick look out from my office window reveals several different sorts of fencing, all of which have their place in this world and all of which achieve differing purposes. The post and rail fencing with its solidity, its bold statement of enclosure, coupled with uninterrupted vision, serves, with the addition of mesh at the lower level, to keep the sheep out. The single rail fence serves to demarcate the boundary between public pathway and grass that should not be crossed. The 2 metre high close boarded fence serves to enclose a garden and give solid privacy at the same time whilst its cousin, the hit and miss slatted fence, gives a little of the privacy away yet provides an ideal backdrop for the climbing plants and shrubs that front it. If any of these were left in isolation and not combined with landscaping and planting then all would gradually fail in their role and that's where the problem lies with most fencing. Prefabricated interwoven fence panels are a flimsy and temporary solution to the immediate requirement for enclosure and privacy in a new garden. They are by no means even a medium, let alone a long term prospect but if they are used in the proper place, as the backdrop for a growing hedge or a system of climbing plants then they too can serve a purpose. Heaven preserve us, however, from the waving and unsteady lines of deteriorating timber that greet us on so many estates, purporting to represent permanent boundary definitions.

Hedges

If you have an existing field hedge on a boundary to your land, you are very lucky, but it may need a great deal of work to put it in good order. First of all, check with your solicitor whether it belongs to you or your neighbour. If it is your neighbour's, all you can do with it without his agreement is to keep it trimmed from your side 'in accordance with good practice'. If it is not regularly trimmed on the other side, it is worth considering whether you want to try to take on this work, because a hedge which is regularly cut on one side only, will soon become misshapen and unattractive. Again this is a matter on which to get expert advice, particularly if your hedge is of mixed species.

A properly laid hedge is a sight to behold and it's gratifying to see that the practice is coming back. The methods of carrying out the laying of a hedge vary slightly from county to county but in the main they involve the main uprights of the unlaid hedge being, almost completely, but not quite, cut through and then bent down and intertwined with uprights cut from the same hedge. Such a hedge becomes thicker with each season and can present a durable and stock proof enclosure, unlike its annually flailed compatriot, which becomes thinner and gappier year on year.

For those of you planting a new hedge, I can only join the howling chorus against the planting of the ubiquitous *leylandii*. Please let us confine this ghastly plant to the dustbin of history and return, once more, to the glorious mixed hedges that once graced our land. If you are going to be in your new home for a long time think of yew or beech. Otherwise hawthorn, wild rose, maple and privet in combination will soon provide a screen, one that will compliment your new home rather than surround it by a prison wall of impenetrable and poisonously dark, green.

Trees

If you are lucky enough to have mature trees on your site, you are probably determined to retain them and to make them a key element in your landscaping. There are lots of factors involved in this. Tree preservation orders have been mentioned on an earlier page, and it is also likely that steps will have to be taken to preserve the house from being damaged by the trees. Tree roots affect foundations in a number of ways, and precautions against damage can involve deepening the foundations or digging a deep trench between the building and the trees and filling it with concrete. Conversely, the building work may have an effect on the trees by altering the subsurface drainage as well as by interfering with the roots, and it may cause them to die. If this happens, then the voids left by the decaying roots will affect the foundations of the house. If a tree

is a key element in your landscaping, or is subject to a tree preservation order, it is a good idea to get it surveyed by a qualified tree surgeon. He should be able to advise on the size it will reach, its probable life and any work necessary to keep it healthy and safe.

When planting new trees it's important to relate the species to their eventual size, unless that is, you're of a mind to religiously cut them down and replace them whenever they outgrow their situation, something that most never even consider doing. Some trees are bad news for buildings. Some, like poplar and willow, can destroy foundations and block drains. Some, like elm, beech and oak, can lift and crack the heaviest load. Others, like most fruit and ornamental flowering trees, do little or no harm and don't usually reach sizes at which they can become over intrusive. Take advice on the clearances and precautions that need to be taken. Read the NHBC guidelines that I referred to on the section on 'trees and foundations' in an earlier chapter.

Water storage

Now that water shortages and hosepipe bans seem destined to be a normal part of our summers, building a new home, with excavators on the site, provides an opportunity for underground water storage arrangements to be made very cheaply. Tanks and pumps for this are already on the market, although they are very expensive. However, most people building for themselves are versatile enough to find a suitable tank and equip it with a pump for next to nothing. 2,000 square feet of roof receiving 18in of rain a year will discharge 30,000 gallons, and if you can catch and store only a tiny fraction of this it may enable your borders to be the envy of your neighbours at the end of a long dry summer.

Electricity

Electrical sockets in the garden can be very convenient for electrical garden tools, garden lighting and barbecue accessories, and if they are arranged when the contract is placed for wiring the house, and you use casual labour or a machine that is otherwise standing idle to dig the

With a plot like this how could this D&M home have failed to grace it? Nevertheless, those with children would have to take care.

trenches, the cost will be very reasonable. Special circuit breakers and weatherproof sockets will make everything safe. Garden lighting, and any lighting used with ornamental pools usually operate at a safe low voltage. All of this requires discussion with an electrician, and it is important to remember that the work involved is little trouble at the time the house is being built, but will be a nuisance to carry out afterwards.

Swimming pools

I've already talked about swimming pools as enclosed and covered areas either adjoining the house or in a separate purpose built building. On the other hand there are those for whom the outdoor pool, with or without heating, is a must. Whether or not it will always remain so I doubt, as is evidenced by the number of building plots I have known which contained a disused and dilapidated pool which in bygone years would have been someone's pride and joy. A swimming pool in a garden involves a maintenance commitment and if you intend to swim in it you can expect to spend as much time looking after the pool as you are likely to spend actually in the water. If you are an enthusiast you already know this, and will enjoy it. On the other hand, a pool

as a status symbol requires careful consideration of who is going to look after it, and of its effect on the value of the property. Except in a few areas, where high value properties are expected to have pools, they can make a house difficult to sell.

If this does not discourage you, then make your plans for your pool at an early stage. If it is to be built at the same time as your house, it is up to the pool contractor to arrange an effective liaison with your builder. If the pool is to be built later, then it is important to ensure that an excavator will be able to get round the site of the pool in due course You will probably want to retain the excavated soil in your garden, piling it up as a bank to be planted as a shrubbery, possibly to give some privacy to those using the pool. If so you should allow for this in your landscaping plan. If the pool is to be heated by the domestic boiler in the house then it's probably better to install the pipe runs from the outset, even if the pool is going to be constructed at a late date. On the other hand you might like to think of the heating of the pool as a separate item and as, in all probability, you'll be using it in better weather, why not think in terms of some sort of solar heating?

Ponds, raised beds and features

In any building site there will be large amounts of spoil to get rid of, something that can prove extremely costly these days. Why not, therefore, consider retaining some or all of the excavated material, assuming your site's big enough? Why not use it to change the contours of the land with, perhaps, a raised shrubbery or mounded up area giving either visual or sound privacy? Why not contain a heap of soil with a low brick wall to provide backache free gardening?

Whilst you've got an excavator on site you could dig out a pond and pile the excavated material around it to form an attractive rockery backdrop. I'll not go into the methods of pond lining in this book, as there are plenty of other tomes specific to that subject. Much of course depends on your idea of a pond. Should it be formal in shape or containment? Should it be informal and look as natural as possible. Is it intended to house expensive Koi or is it intended as a future residence for frogs and newts? If you're going to need lighting, either under or over the water or if you're going to need pumps and filters, then you're going to have to think about the supply of electricity and you may even have to think in terms of a small shed or building to house all the equipment. Might this be possible as a semi underground structure beneath the rockery?

The thing to do is think about all of this, if you can, when the machinery is on site and before you send away 'spoil' that you might need. Topsoil is very expensive to buy and extremely difficult to barrow around to a back garden. Stone for the rockery is horrendously expensive and having to pay for it would be all the more galling if you'd already sent loads away!

Summer houses, sheds, conservatories, tennis courts and greenhouses etc.

All of these, as well as a garage where there is none, can be constructed, at a later date, under Permitted Development rights, as indeed can the swimming pool we've just talked about. The main criteria is that you can erect such structures or carry out such works where they are incidental to the enjoyment of the dwelling. You will, however, need express planning consent if:

* You want to put up a building that is closer to the highway than the nearest part of the dwelling is, unless there would still be 20 metres between the new building and the highway.

* More than half the land would then be covered by buildings.

* The new building is not intended for a domestic purpose and instead, is used for parking a commercial vehicle, running a business or storing goods in connection with a business.

* The new building is more than 3 metres high or more than 4 metres high if it has a pitched roof

* If your house is a listed building and the new structure is more than 10 cubic metres in volume.

Interesting changes of texture and light turn construction towards art.

In addition, as explained in the chapter 'Designing a new home – to suit your lifestyle', some buildings constructed within the grounds of your property may have the effect of limiting or reducing your Permitted Development rights to extend your home. Of course this begs the question as to whether you should think ahead and include these ancillary structures within your original consent. I've covered the arguments for and against in the chapter dealing with 'Designing a new home – to suit your lifestyle', under the sub heading 'extendibility', and similar criteria apply here.

Fuel storage tanks

In all probability this will be dealt with by your architect as part and parcel of the application for the new dwelling but there are circumstances where consideration of these things comes at a later date. In that case you may need to apply for planning permission if:

* You need to install a domestic heating oil tank which has a capacity in excess of 3500 litres or is more than 3 metres in height.

* The tank is to be closer to the highway than any part of the original house unless there would still be 20 metres between it and the highway.

* You want to install a new tank to store liquefied petroleum gas (Lpg) or any liquid fuel other than oil.

To finish on this subject, huge advances have been made in the design and appearance of fuel oil tanks in recent years and it really isn't necessary to have those unsightly rusty green tanks of yesteryear. Lpg tanks too, have changed and, instead of the ugly white cylinder on your front lawn, they are now put underground where all one sees is a small green plastic manhole cover which happily merges into the lawn.

11 Making the choices – how to move forward

I do not flatter myself that this is the only book that you'll be reading about selfbuilding and, indeed, I sincerely hope that you are looking and asking around for as much information as you can get. Discounting the late night advice at the bar, over which one should be a trifle circumspect, there are a whole host of people out there ready and willing to give advice and perhaps, the best of these will be other selfbuilders. It's like a club and if, you come across another selfbuilder, then I'll lay you odds that you'll be welcomed within it and that you'll go home with sheaves of information and ears ringing with new found knowledge. The people who work within the industry know this and reputations and company successes are built upon its premiss. Read any brochure and you'll find that it spends as much, if not more time, relating how happy their clients were as it does explaining just what it is they do. Read any of the monthly magazines, such as *Build It* or *Homebuilding and Renovating* and you'll very quickly realise that, business as this is, industry as this is, it is predicated upon ordinary people realising their dreams.

So, the purpose of this chapter is to help you find your way through the minefield of conflicting advice, much of which, whilst true, has, nevertheless, a financial axe to grind. Who do you run with? Which company should you go to and should that be a package deal company or an architectural practice? Should you be building in timber frame or should you build in brick and block? Should you think about dumping all of the advice, all of the companies, to make your own way forward? These are the vital choices facing the selfbuilder who has already jumped the first hurdle of getting hold of a plot and they are choices, which have to be made. In many ways the choices you make at this stage will colour the whole outcome of your selfbuild project so it's important that you understand the range of options and that you feel your way though to the eventual decision with as much information as possible. When you've read this book, when you've read all the magazines and brochures, when you've met and talked to the people you think you might like to deal with, stand back for a moment and think. Don't be

rushed, don't be pushed into anything. Make sure that you're comfortable with what's on offer. Make sure that you're comfortable with the people who are offering it. Does it sit with what you're planning? Does it feel right? If you need more information or more time then take it – don't be hassled. Remember that to a successful company you're another client and that they don't stand or fall by your business alone. For you, however, this project is *the* project and it stands or falls by your decisions.

It is important that any professionals you engage should report back to you at specific intervals or stages. Planning a selfbuild project can be very worrying, and you will want to know how things are getting on. That doesn't mean that you should necessarily ring your architect or the package deal company representative every evening, but it certainly is appropriate for him to let you know just how things are progressing on a stage by stage basis. Keep in regular contact and don't be afraid to ask what's happening – after all you're the one paying for everything.

If one had just beamed down from the starship 'Enterprise' with the intention of reading and finding all one could about selfbuilding in Great Britain, Planet Earth, one could be forgiven for believing, in a very short time, that the *only* way forward was the timber framed option. In fact, as one got deeper into the subject one would then discover that timber frame is, and never has been more than, about 10% of the whole of the new housing market in England and Wales, although it gets to be over 50% in Scotland, where timber can truly be described as an indigenous material. How does one square this with the heavy promotion of the timber framed option in magazines, literature and at exhibitions? In part, it's because of the historical fact that it was, until relatively recently, quite difficult to build a timber framed house without using the services of a package deal company or timber frame manufacturer whilst at the same time there was, and is, nothing like the imperative to use a package deal company for brick and block construction. That said, that does not mean that there aren't package deal companies that either concentrate or specialise in brick and block forms of construction.

Despite the differing claims, it isn't really the package deal companies themselves that go out of their way to promote or denigrate either main method of construction. It's generally accepted amongst them that their clients can be put off by too much negative campaigning and in any event, most of the chaps who have been in the industry for some time know, full well, that, on the whole, the level of advice from all sides is good. Most of them meet their competitors at exhibitions and road shows on a regular basis, staying in the same hotels, eating and drinking, sometimes to excess, with each other. The successful ones are far too busy running their businesses to spend too much time running down their 'friends'. Conflict, however, makes good media copy and the blame for any contrived argument, if blame there is, rests more with the interests generated by the major block manufacturers and importers of timber, even if the package deal companies subscribe to their campaigns.

The fact is that there is no real argument about which method is best and the reality is that both methods are equally valid ways of achieving your new home. A recent survey of people living in modern homes asked, "Would you choose to live in a timber framed house?" Most didn't care one way or the other but, of those who said, "No", a significant number then had to be told that they already did! Now, before you all go off chuckling at the stupidity of these people, stop and think for a moment. The finished homes of either timber frame or brick and block construction can, and mostly do, look exactly the same as each other. A blurring of the distinctions, as far as the lay persons living experience is concerned, means that, for many it's not all that easy, if they didn't see the house built, to know. In days gone by the estate agent would knowingly tap the walls, nod and studiously write down something on his memo board. If he did the same thing nowadays, the chances are he'd probably get things wrong. In terms of time scales I can attest from the case histories I have written up, some of which appear in this book, that the pattern is that a remarkably similar time is taken from turning the first sod to moving in. That said, for

those for whom time is of the essence, there is no doubt at all that, if you want to save up to a couple of months, and you can get the organisation just right, then timber frame is the route to choose. Again, with costs it's the similarity that's the startling fact and any influence, either way, has much more to do with the level of fitting out and the expectations brought about by the design itself, than it does with the method of construction. Bad ground or difficult foundations have the same consequences with either main method of construction, as will any requirement for expensive roof coverings or walling materials. The levels of thermal and sound insulation can vary but, again, nothing very much is unattainable with either method if that is what your requirements are, and if they're thought out in advance – something that I have written about at length in previous chapters. As I've said many times, informed choice is what selfbuilding is all about and what I seek to do, in this chapter, is explore the options and point you on the road to discovery, rather than draw lines in the sand and form up on one side or the other.

So, let's look at some of the options that are put before you and evaluate each one. Forgive me if I leave out some of the more 'progressive' ways forward – I know they're out there and I know that they have a place in this world. If you want to live underground and take hormones to promote the growth of long ears and fluffy tails, then that's fine by me and I wish you every success, but the promotion of your ideas will have to find another forum.

Architects

When I first came into the selfbuild industry, many architects had virtually thrown away their right to have any place within it with their arrogant denial of the selfbuilder's right to their own expression. Indeed I can still tell the story of the time I timorously suggested to one architect that perhaps a few changes might be advisable to a plan he'd drawn - the setsquare embedded itself in the door behind which I had rapidly retreated! Happily architects like that are now slipping into a minority and the vision of the poor selfbuilder having to go in and see a crusty who demands as much respect and fear as the head master in his study used to, is fast receding. In no small way, this has to do with the advent of *Associated Selfbuild Architects (ASBA)* who entered upon the selfbuild stage like a breath of fresh air in 1992. Conceived and run to this day by chartered architects, Adrian Spawforth and Julian Owen, *ASBA* set out to show just how much the profession has to offer selfbuilders and to instill and promote, through a likeminded membership, the principles of architects working *for* and *with* their clients in order to realise their dreams. All *ASBA* architects are expected to fulfil certain basic conditions and, whilst this book is not a promotion vehicle for any one group or interest, those conditions do bear publication because their criteria could very well be applied to any architect, whether a member of *ASBA* or not, that you may be thinking of engaging.

1. All practices must have a registered architect taking responsibility for selfbuild projects. The title 'Architect' can only be used by someone who has undergone a thorough training course lasting seven years, and passed a tough set of exams that ensure a base level of knowledge and experience has been achieved.

2. The practices themselves must be members of the Royal Institute of British Architects (RIBA) or of the Scottish equivalent, the Royal Incorporation of Architects in Scotland (RIAS). Each of these organisations operates a strict code of conduct laying down rules regarding impartiality and the need to provide a professional service. Some manufacturers or suppliers do offer incentives for consultants or companies to use their services but architects must be independent in the advice they offer, or declare any vested interest. *ASBA* itself does carry sponsorship but the architects themselves do not receive any incentives or commissions and their practices are not under any obligation to those sponsors. All *ASBA* architects must offer truly independent advice to their clients.

3. *ASBA* architects must have no more than six professional staff. The idea behind this is that smaller practices are able to offer the flexible service that is applicable to the selfbuilder and to tailor their fees to suit the situation. Quite often clients will find themselves dealing directly with the partner or director who runs the business. The larger architectural practices do find it difficult to offer a personal service and, generally, are only really interested in expensive commissions that will cover their considerable overheads.

4. Architects must carry Professional Indemnity Insurance because of its great significance to the selfbuilder. Most banks and building societies will, in any case, insist on this before they will accept any payment or progress certificates.

5. *ASBA* architects also agree that they will provide an initial consultation free of charge and that they will provide as much free advice and assistance to selfbuilders, as possible, recognising that the earlier on advice is sought, the more likely the project is to succeed.

6. Finally, and perhaps most importantly, *ASBA* require their members to have appropriate design skills and a general commitment to one off house design as well as an approachable, unpretentious attitude to their work and to their clients.

Well, just a quick scan through those conditions shows that these guys are a long way away from my old setsquare chucking chum. Now, as I've said, whilst that all may sound like a promotion pack for *ASBA*, it isn't meant to be, however it comes across. What I do hope to promote is that these ideals are, perhaps the ones which should distinguish the sort of architects that you may wish to employ and I see nothing wrong in you taxing a prospective architect with questions of a similar nature to this list.

Fees are the biggest bugbear and the idea that architects are always expensive is deeply rooted in the public's mind. The key to a successful working relationship with your architect is to agree the level of services and the fees, methods and times of payment, at the start of your project. Very few of you will go out and buy bricks without inquiring what the price of them is so, why should you think that it's alright to engage the services of an architect without discussing his fee structure? If your request for this information receives either a stony reply, at best, or one so vague as to leave you still unaware of what you're in danger of letting yourself in for, then it's quite clear that this is just the sort of architect you shouldn't be playing with and it's, perhaps, time to move on to another. From personal experience, again, I do know that there are architects out there who would consider any move to negotiate their fees as an attempt at vulgarity. If you get stonewalled at all, or if you don't feel comfortable with what's on offer and at how much, then cut off the relationship as quickly as you can – and that advice refers to any trade, company or supplier that you come across.

Architect's fees vary according to how complicated your project is and the level of involvement you want your architect to have. Commissioning an architect to help you right through your project will, typically cost between 6% and 10% of your construction costs plus disbursement costs which can be £1-£2 per plan plus Quantity Surveyors costs of about £350 plus VAT. Some architects will quote a fee based on a price per square foot and again, depending on the level of service, this can vary between 90p, for plans only, right through to £4 per square foot for a more comprehensive level of service. Yet others may agree a lump sum fee which can be negotiated and, perhaps, spread over either monthly payments or in agreed stages.

The key stages of building an architect designed house using the full services right through the project from beginning to end can be described in the following list. Some of these points are exclusive to *ASBA* architects but, again, there is reason why they have to be and your search for a suitable architect could well start with an enquiry as to how much, or how little of this they can or will provide, and for how much.

1. Finding a plot. Technically this isn't part of most architect's brief but, nevertheless, try asking a prospective architect whether they know of any land for sale in your area. Don't expect them to tell you about plots where they are already involved with another client, but there is always the possibility that they know of a plot where a client has had to drop out. Certainly if you do identify a plot then the architect should be called upon at the earliest possible stage to advise on its suitability.

2. Making an offer on the plot. We've gone into this in a fairly detailed manner in previous chapters but, nevertheless, the input of your architect may well be beneficial. Hopefully the land has 'outline' planning consent and possibly your architect can help you negotiate the terms upon which you can buy, maybe subject to receipt of satisfactory detailed planning consent. If there isn't any kind of consent and you're weighing up the pros and cons of whether to do anything with the land or whether or not planning is at all likely, then your architect may be able to advise.

3. Site analysis. This involves an assessment of your plot to check it for hidden problems and to highlight its features. A professional can tell an awful lot about a plot just by looking at it, seeing what sort of vegetation grows on it and what sort of ground conditions are likely. If the architect feels that a more thorough site investigation is necessary, including a soil investigation, then they're almost certain to be able to put you onto the relevant people to carry out this work for you.

4. Developing your brief. The architect will want to talk to you in fairly intimate detail about what you hope to achieve and just what features you want your new home to have. The headings under which this discussion will probably progress may be, budget analysis, accommodation requirements, room by room analysis of your proposed occupation and construction and

materials preferences.

5. Sketch design. Using the brief prepared, the architect will draw up a sketch design showing the floor layouts together with elevations showing the external appearance of your new home, and any possible or suggested alternatives. This will be used to make sure that they are on the right lines to provide you with what you're looking for and at the same time make sure that the developing house designs are likely to find favour with the planners. At this stage you should also make sure that the architect feels that, and can verify that, your project is likely to be capable of being completed within your budget.

6. Purchasing the plot. Again this is not strictly within the province of the architect but they will want to be involved and will certainly want to assist with advice, in any way they can.

7. Detailed design. From the sketch design, the architect will move to the preparation of detailed plans that will be suitable for an application for planning permission. It is at this stage that the all important issues regarding window details, brick colours, roofing tiles, driveways and a myriad of other topics, many of which we've already explored in other chapters, are decided. For most selfbuilders this stage is, perhaps, the most exciting.

8. Planning permission. The architect will submit the planning application and prosecute it with the authorities. He will discuss any matters arising from the application with the planning officers, conservation officers and highways authorities. If any amendments are suggested or required following meetings and/or letters, then the architect will discuss these with you before agreeing to them.

9. Building regulations. The architect will prepare and submit plans for Building Regulations approval. These will include any necessary structural calculations and specifications describing the basic construction of your new home, a range of health and safety standards and energy conservation issues. If any special foundation details or designs are required as the result of either the soil investigation or in consequence of the application being made, then the architect will usually arrange for these to be carried out by other professionals, on your behalf. The fees for these additional professionals will normally be charged to you direct as they are outside the architect's normal scope of activities and you will be concerned that any warranties and liabilities given will devolve directly to you.

10. Drawings and specification for tender. The architect will draw up a detailed specification to accompany the plans, in order to obtain tenders from suitable builders or contractors. Quotations can vary quite considerably (Up to 100% in some cases!) so this is the stage at which an architect doing their job properly can save you considerable amounts of money. A properly drawn up specification can well make the difference and easily cover an architect's fees for the entire project.

11. Finding and appointing a contractor. The architect will suggest suitable contractors for the tender list and when the quotations are received, and the builder is chosen, he will assist in the preparation of the contract documents.

12. Monitoring the construction. The architect will visit the site and make spot checks to see that the construction is being carried out in accordance with the approved and contract drawings. If any form of 'certification' is required, as discussed in detail in the chapter headed 'Finance', then he will undertake this and liaise with the necessary lending institution.

13. Snagging. Once the building work is complete, you and your architect will inspect your new home together to check for defects. If there are any present or if work has not

been completed to a satisfactory standard, your builder will be required to put this right prior to you accepting the property.

14. Handing over and moving in. This is what it's all been about and once your new home is completed it will be handed over in return for the final stage payment. Normally a retention of 2.5% is made out of the total tender price. This is withheld for a period of six months to ensure that the builder will put right anything that may go wrong

I repeat that the list above details the full services that can be expected from an architect. You may or may not want to take advantage of all or any of this but the thing you must do is to make sure that, right from the off, you know what you are expecting the architect to be responsible for, they know the same thing and that you all know the fee structure involved. Above all make sure that you're comfortable with the people you engage for this, probably the most important project of your life. What you selfbuild should be, as far as is possible, what you want and not what somebody else wanted. Fortunately architects are becoming more accessible and approachable as market pressures force them out of their offices and into the real world where the client calls the shots. Their role should be of an enabler, transforming a series of wishes and aspirations into a set of working drawings and ultimately a finished new home. That doesn't mean that they shouldn't have a meaningful input of their own but it does mean that in the end it's their client's new home and it should reflect the decisions made by you, the selfbuilder.

Designers

It is easy to get the idea from publications that the great majority of individual homes are built either to architects' designs, or come from the package companies. If you go to the Town Hall and ask to see the planning register you will quickly discover that the overwhelming majority of applications are made by designers who are not architects, many of them working on a part-time basis in the evenings when they have

finished their other jobs. Many of them are council Building Inspectors and the like who will only design for the next door council's area, not the one that they work in. Some of them are listed in Yellow Pages, but all of them get most of their business by personal recommendation. If they have been providing this service for any length of time they are pretty good at it, although of course they do not have the professional indemnity insurances of the architects and the companies. What they are very good at is gaining the confidence of clients, who happily put their trust in them however well this may be deserved.

The problem comes when a person represents him/herself as an 'architect', either directly or indirectly. Only an architect who has passed all the relevant exams after a long training period is entitled to call themselves by that title and that is something that is protected by law. Inspections during the construction period by an unqualified person are not recognised by the banks or building societies and, if therefore, you do decide to use the services of an unqualified designer, you should make absolutely certain that you do have an approved warranty scheme in place, as outlined in the chapter headed 'Finance'. None of this is meant to denigrate the service these chaps provide but it is meant to make sure that you are aware of just what you're getting when you employ them and just how far their responsibilities and liabilities go. I have to tell you that during the writing of this book I met a couple who, having finished their new home, were awaiting the certificate from the 'architect' who had inspected their property as it was built. My quick scan of his letter heading revealed to me that no such certificate would be forthcoming and that even if it was it would have no validity!

Builders merchants

For years the builders merchants excluded themselves, almost by design, from the selfbuild industry. If one was able to set up an account, the credit limits were set so low as to make it almost worthless and there was little or no help for the lay person building their own home. Then, prompted, no doubt, by the constant boom to bust cycle of the building industry, the more progressive merchants started to look around to see just how they could iron out the peaks and troughs. To a few observant souls, not least Stuart Mason-Elliot of Elliot Brothers Builders Merchants, who have branches along the south coast of England, it became apparent that as the cycle in the building industry came to its bottom, the selfbuild market rose to its peak. What was the reason for this? The reason quite simply was that in times of recession in the industry, as a whole, the selfbuilder was able to obtain land that had hitherto been snapped up by the builders and developers. As time went on, the selfbuild industry grew ever bigger to the point where its combined numbers far outstripped any of the major developers, at times representing almost one third of detached houses and bunga-lows being built. This was major clout! But still some of the larger merchants failed to recognise the potential. Not so the smaller independents. Very quickly people like Stuart realised that if they were to attract the lay person selfbuilding, they had to provide a more user friendly environ-ment. No longer would it be acceptable for a chap to have to queue up at a counter, not sure of what it was he needed, only to be greeted at the end of his wait by obtuse staff making his ignorance the butt of their humour. No longer would the selfbuilder feel like the poor relation to the familiar builder client. Instead they would be welcomed as the high spenders they were and given all of the assistance and knowledge that was at the disposal of the company. Elliots set up their own 'Selfbuild club' with a dedicated club newsletter, evening meetings with guest speakers and training and product visits and displays. It went on from there. Not content with what they were doing for the selfbuilder, Stuart went out and actively campaigned, amongst the member-ship of the various trade organisations, for other builders merchants to adopt a similar line and his message was well received, especially amongst the more independent ones.

Of course what Stuart realised was that the merchants had always possessed the knowledge and the skills that would benefit the selfbuilder. What they hadn't done was apply that knowledge in the way in which it could be mutually benefi-cial. With a little bit of retraining here and a shifting of emphasis there, it was easy to reverse years of neglect. Now the headings of the services provided read like a manual of selfbuilding. Help in land finding. Help and specially negotiated rates for any valuation or survey of the land. Help in finding architects or designers, builders or subcontractors. And, of course, help, not only with the sourcing, obtaining and buying of materials but, most importantly, with their selection.

Before long the larger merchants jumped on the bandwagon and started to advertise and exhibit within the selfbuild industry. Now, most merchants will take in your plans, free of charge, and provide a quantity take off and costings. Some, but not all, have dedicated staff to deal with the selfbuilding client and most will actively assist you in the selection, evaluation and costing of materials. Whether you use a package deal company or not, at some stage you will also need to buy the materials that are not included in the package and it's important to establish just where you're going to go shopping for those, before you start work. The selection of the builders merchant, or merchants, you will use should take the same form as the selection of any other company or professional you are thinking of using. Make sure that you feel comfortable with them, make sure that they appreciate just what it is you're trying to achieve and, above all, make sure that they've got the user friendly service which you will need to rely on.

The package deal companies

In large part, the package deal companies evolved as a response to, and in consequence of, the lack of understanding previously given to selfbuilders by architects and builders merchants. In the early seventies there were no books such as this one, no *The Home Plans Book* and no monthly magazines devoted to the ideals and the concept of selfbuilding. If a selfbuilder was brave or lucky enough to get a design done for him by an architect or designer then when he went along to a builders merchants he was in for an even worse time. I can remember selfbuilders having to get proper printed headed paper, describing themselves as 'Private House Builders' before they could get any sort of an account and, even then, the credit limits were set so low as to make the account virtually cash on delivery.

The package deal companies moved to fill the gap in the market, many of them starting off life as poor brethren offshoots of either timber companies or major block manufacturers. In the early days their plans, published in the form of their brochures, showed houses and bungalows of mind boggling simplicity and an utter lack of imagination but, as the industry grew, so did the aspirations of the selfbuilder and, inevitably, the package deal companies shifted their positions to give the market what it wanted. For a while many companies held out and continued to run with the times by constantly updating their range of 'standard' designs but inevitably the more successful ones soon came to the conclusion that they would have to become completely flexible in their approach to design and that either the 'standards' would have to be capable of alteration or that they would have to be able to accommodate 'specials'.

Design is the key, of course, and the package deal companies recognised that this was the first hurdle that the potential selfbuilder had to jump, once he'd bought his plot. What the selfbuilder has to realise is that, although many of the package deal companies advertise and promote themselves through their designs, in truth, their real business revolves around the supply and /or manufacture of kits and materials. They do all of this in a very highly polished and effective way, as any recipient of their literature can see and as any visitor to the exhibitions will note. The expertise they have gained over the years is apparent within the breadth of their information and there is no doubt that most, if not all of them, successfully fulfil the role of specialist designers and builders merchants for the selfbuilder.

From all of this you may get the impression that the majority of selfbuilders now use the services of the various package deal companies. In fact nothing is further from the truth and there is still much scratching of heads in the boardrooms of these companies as they agonise over just why and how anything, can be done about it. Perhaps the reason lies with the mental makeup of the selfbuilders themselves. By opting not to conform, by choosing not to just go out and buy a developer's house, the selfbuilder steps, quite deliberately, outside the normal pattern of behaviour. Perhaps, for the vast majority, the desire to 'do their own thing' extends to not wanting to fit in with anyone else's concepts of how things should be done and, almost, a determination not to seek the help of others. Perhaps, also, a great many selfbuilders are people from within the building industry itself, with skills in one or more of the trades involved and opinions which lead them down the 'go it alone' path. Be that as it may, up to 20% of the people who do selfbuild, choose to do so using the services of a package deal company and for them there is no doubt that the comfort they get from having a 'friend' or mentor to guide them through the process is an important factor in getting them beyond the dream stage and onto to the realisation of their hopes. An interesting by-line on all of this is that whilst many selfbuilders actually go on to do it all again, only a relatively small proportion choose to use the package deal company the second and third time around, even if they have been completely happy with the service they got. Perhaps by then they fall into the same category and have the same opinions as the selfbuilder who originally disdained the use of a package deal company.

You cannot cherry pick the design ideas of the package deal companies and then run off and build the house without using the main part of their service. The plans in their brochures, the plans they publish in the companion book to this book, called *The Home Plans Book* and the plans they may prepare for you, are their copyright. That also extends to a design which a reasonable person would consider had been derived from one of their plans and is why you may see the words, 'or within the design concept', used in connection with their claim to copyright. If you commission a design study or feasibility study from a package deal company and then, for any reason, you do not proceed with that company, you are almost certainly going to have to think in terms of a different design.

Most of the larger package deal companies have an 'in house' drawing office with staff architects but others successfully employ a panel of outside architects or designers. There are arguments for and against both ways of working but, in truth, much of the competency of their drawing office service relies on the abilities of either their field staff or the sales staff that you actually deal with. If you're dealing with a sales force who are demonstrating a chosen product and making notes of your specific and individual requirements and alterations then, in many cases, and in particular in those cases where the product can be demonstrated in the form of a show home, it is easy to get across what you're trying to achieve. There may well be an element of shoehorning your requirements into a format but in most cases the compromise is well thought out and realises everybody's ambitions. If the product, for that indeed is what it is, didn't appeal to you, then you wouldn't be there in the first place and the companies are well aware that, for some, the idea of living in a particular design can be akin to a newfound religion.

Where a completely fresh design is proposed then, whether it is drawn 'in house' or by a panel architect, the translation of your requirements depends entirely on the representative you are dealing with. These individuals are a remarkable lot, with most of them having been in the industry for many years and many of them having either come into it as a result of building their own homes or having done so since they started. In many cases they will stand between you and the architect with the architect preparing the initial drawings on the basis of, and as a direct result of, a brief prepared by that representative. Architects and designers who work outside the package deal companies always express amazement that such a system can work. Clients of the package deal companies themselves are often sceptical at first and sometimes feel that they should be visiting the offices of the company or that the drawing office staff themselves should be visiting them, not realising that in the time taken for such a person to travel to and from them, their drawings could well be done. The amazing reality is that in the vast majority of cases the drawings that are produced from this arm's length way of doing things conform, almost exactly, to the client's wishes. In almost all cases this is due to the company representative's skill at interpreting what the client wants, his ability to balance that with what he knows is achievable in design terms, his knowledge of the planning criteria and his ability to translate all of that into a brief for his drawing office staff, with whom he is likely to have an uncanny rapport. If you add to that the fact that he, as much as you, will be concerned to make sure that the project remains on budget then you'll appreciate that he really has to draw a lot of strings together. Happily these guys usually do just that and, in most cases they do it jolly well.

The stages concerned with the planning and building regulations applications are also handled in two ways. Either the head office of the package deal company makes the application with the local representative progress chasing it, or else the local panel architect makes the application supported by the head office of the company. Once more the suspicion is that a company based in one part of the country will not be able to properly process an application in a different part of the land. Nothing could actually be further from the truth. The package deal companies have always set out to provide a service on a nationwide basis and their thought processes tend to consider the whole country in much the same terms as most think of their county. They are aware of regional variations in styles. They are aware of variations even within the larger regions and they have long since adapted to the provision of houses in styles that carry the local vernacular, even if, in some cases, the floor plans remain almost consistent. An example of this is demonstrated clearly in the series of Potton 'Granchester' houses illustrated, showing essentially the same house built in different parts of the country.

Perhaps then, to the chagrin of many local architects, it is this very ability of the package deal companies to look at architecture on a Nationwide basis, that enables them to be able to fully understand the local and regional variations

The Granchester design by Potton shown in six different finished forms.

that go to make up the delightful diversification of styles and detail. Perhaps, also, this is demonstrated in the remarkably high success rate that most companies have with planning applications, although to be fair, the more discerning and successful companies will always choose which applications they make and make sure that they control, as far as is possible, the quality of those applications.

Many of the package deal companies specialise in timber frame construction of some sort and their literature and advertising is concerned to extol the virtues of their own particular way of building. Not all of the companies, however, are concerned with timber frame. Some concentrate almost exclusively on brick and block construction, whilst others, recognising that the service element of their operation is of the foremost interest, do not really mind which method of construction is employed as long as there remains an element of supply. Historically the reasons why there is such a preponderance of timber frame companies, has been the fact that up until the fairly recent past, the contention was, that to build timber frame automatically meant that you would need to use a timber frame company. This idea, promoted in previous editions of this book, came about because of the very real problems that the average selfbuilder could have had in the provision of the necessary design calculations for the frames. What's changed here is, in fact, a spin off from the very success of the package deal companies, in that, they created a whole new genre of professionals working as timber engineers and designers and, inevitably, they found their way into the freelance market. Now, it is fairly easy for architects to either design a timber framed house themselves or else to design one and then get the relevant details and calculations checked or carried out by other professionals. This has given impetus to the 'go it aloners' who want to 'stickbuild', of which more later.

But back to the package deal companies. The services they offer, whether timber framed or brick and block, can be divided into yet more sub categories. Some offer a design service based on standard designs. Some offer a service based on the variation or modification of standard designs within carefully defined parameters. Some offer a bespoke design service, with each house or bungalow being individually tailored to the clients and the sites dictates. Some offer a planning service whilst others will want to provide you with the plans for you to prosecute your own application. Yet more do not have any design services beyond the provision of the necessary technical drawings and will provide a package deal to drawings that you provide. All of them will be concerned to supply a recognisable package deal of materials to the specification set out in their literature and confirmed to you in their quotations. All of them, therefore, will be concerned that you are able to put their kits or packages together and, therefore, most of them will ensure this by being very concerned with helping you obtain or evaluate labour. None of them will go so far as to actually recommend any subcontractor or builder to you but, instead, they will introduce them and then stand by to ensure that you make the correct arrangements with them. Quite obviously, a recommendation, as such, would involve them being a party to the contract that you make with the builders and they will be concerned to avoid that. Nevertheless, if the package deal companies do introduce you to a builder or subcontractor, you can be pretty sure that they've vetted them in some way, in the knowledge that if things go right on site, their job is made all the easier. The package companies often provide advice, again with the same motives, on many other aspects of building a new home, from recommending the right people to design any special foundations that may be needed through to helping with VAT claims but, once again, you will find that the package deal company will not be a party to any ensuing contract.

Of course, none of these reservations apply to the 'design and build' or 'turnkey' packages that are available where the package deal company is actually going to be responsible for the construction of the new house, probably also providing an NHBC warranty at the end. In essence these companies are really building companies who have adapted their business to be able to work and promote themselves within the selfbuild market, sometimes on a nationwide basis, but often, in a limited regional area. They really replace the builders of old who often provided such a service in their local areas but did not have the forums to promote themselves in the professional way that is possible for their successors. Oftimes these design and build arrangements involve the selfbuilder in little or no work and take the project right up to completion, handover and moving in. Sometimes, however the contract can be for the weathertight shell only and, in those cases, the selfbuilder becomes responsible for the fitting out and second fix trades. In these instances the position is no different from any other selfbuilder using a builder and subcontractors and the later chapters of this book dealing with the use of subcontract labour and a contract with a builder are equally applicable.

Payments to package deal companies are something that I have already written about in the chapter on finance but they do bear repetition. The kits sold by package companies are specific to a particular house or bungalow, and the elements like the roof, walling panels etc. have to be made weeks before they are delivered. For this reason companies expect to be paid a substantial deposit when an order is placed, and usually require the balance of the contract sum in advance of the delivery of materials. These sums may be over half of the total cost of the new home, and selfbuilders are naturally concerned that this arrangement is 100% safe. Before any order is signed the selfbuilder will undoubtedly have taken up references on the company or asked their bank to do so on their behalf. It is important, especially in light of the very different services and level of service that the companies provide, that the selfbuilder makes absolutely sure that they understand exactly what they're getting for their money. It's also important to know just when those monies will be required and to allow for this in any cashflow projections that you make. Most of the larger and more reputable companies now operate 'clients accounts' into which the monies that are, quite naturally, required in advance of delivery are

placed. This money then remains in the legal ownership of the client until such time as a trustee of the account gives authority to pay it across to the company. This has advantages to the company because they can raise money against the sums in the client accounts that they operate. If you accept this arrangement, make sure you ask your solicitor or bank to check out the status of this client account, always make out cheques to the client account and not simply to the company, and if the money is going to stay in the client account for any length of time enquire who gets the interest. Finally, there is a legally implied assumption that the package deal service and the goods supplied and /or manufactured will meet the requirements of the Building Regulations as well as the relevant British Standards. However, if the work is to be inspected by the NHBC or by an architect, then it is possible for there to be some variation in their requirements and in these cases, unless it is already there, when accepting the quotation of the package deal company, you should confirm that everything should also comply to their standards. If necessary write it on the acceptance or authorisation above your signature.

Package companies provide excellent services to thousands of selfbuilders, but in the natural way of things there are sometimes problems or disagreements. If you meet difficulties which cannot be resolved at a local level you should take pains to deal with them promptly, but in a way that demonstrates that you are a most reasonable client. Avoid letters that are written in anger. If appropriate, arrange to call at the Head Office by appointment and explain the difficulty in a friendly but very firm way to someone at director level. No firm can afford to ignore a customer who has a five figure contract, and you will be treated accordingly.

Timber frame

One of the most common misconceptions is that all timber framed houses are alike. In fact, nothing could be further from the truth and the reality is that there are many differing methods of construction which for the sake of convenience, usually get lumped together under this heading.

All the methods of building new homes, that are promoted by the major companies, are of equal validity and, in the end, the selection of which method you employ comes down to personal choice. In all probability the impetus for this choice has much more to do with the selfbuilder being comfortable with the people they're dealing with, the level of service they are providing and the cost they are providing it at, than it does with any construction method. Once, however, the choice is made, it is usual for the customer to become a devotee of the construction method. The zeal, with which the finished selfbuilder defends his choice, when I visit them for the case histories, has to be seen to be believed.

The word 'traditional' got bandied about and fought over, for some time, by the various competing interests. Proponents of building in 'brick and block' claimed that theirs was the traditional way of building, in an attempt to brand timber frame as, somehow, being 'new' and therefore untried. The timber frame exponents immediately hit back with the assertion that timber frame was an old and well tested method of building, tracing its roots right back to the middle ages. In fact, and in the end, all of them realised that they were on a hiding to nothing and, whilst the 'brick and block' enthusiasts now prefer to describe themselves as such, the timber frame interests now prefer to promote themselves as 'timber and brick'.

The principal method of building with timber frame is the *open panel* system and when most people describe or think about timber frame, this is what they're talking about. It is the inner skin of a cavity wall that supports the roof and gives the building its structural strength. In a timber framed house this is formed by panels that are usually prefabricated and then raised up into position and fixed together to form a rigid structure. The panels are manufactured from softwood timber framing over which a structural sheet material, such as plywood, is fixed, known as the sheathing. A vapour permeable, but waterproof, breather membrane is then fixed to the outside face of this sheathing. Of course it's a lot more involved than that and if this were a technical manual I would move on to descrip-

tions of noggins, cripple studs, headbinders et al. But it's not, so I won't. The insulation which fills the space between the studs is normally put in on site, once the house is weathertight and the electrical and plumbing carcassing have been done. The wall is then finished off to the interior, and a vapour barrier and the internal boarding trap the insulation.

Now, although most of the literature you'll pick up referring to timber and brick, assumes the use of a cavity wall, there are instances where this is not so. It is possible that the outside leaf can be done away with altogether by the use of a vertical counterbatten, creating a cavity, to which either expanded metal wire mesh is fixed for rendering or an external timber finish, such as shiplap boarding, can be fixed. Tile hanging can also be fixed against a single skin of timber frame. Again, the vertical batten is used to bring the horizontal battens away from the breather membrane, and the tiles are then hung from these battens in the normal way. Many of the houses from the Potton 'Heritage' range use this 'single leaf' construction and many others may use it in combination with timber and brick cavity wall construction to the ground floors. It is also worthwhile noting that, with timber and brick cavity wall construction, the cavity is always left clear and is never filled or interrupted other than by fire stops and cavity barriers which have to be inserted at certain points, as required by the regulations. Custom Homes and Potton are amongst those who use the open panel system.

The Scandinavian timber frame houses, whilst generically similar, utilise a slightly different form of timber framing, known as the *closed panel system*. Scandia-Hus have carried this principle forward with the development of their 'Fabrik 25' construction, where the system and the panels are designed to be 'airtight'. By the very nature of the beast this means that each panel has to be manufactured in carefully controlled factory conditions with each panel being assembled, complete with the insulation and vapour barrier installed, the internal boarding fixed and all windows (usually triple glazed) and door linings fitted. The vapour

Inner Lining of Plasterboard
Vapour Check
Preservative Treated Structural Timber Frame

Thick Insulating Quilt
Sheathing Board
Waterproof Breather Membrane
Stainless Steel Wall Tie

Clear 50mm Wall Cavity

Brick Outer Cladding

barrier is installed in such a way as to create a seal not only at any abutment to an adjoining panel but also at the roof level where it is also tucked into and joined with the roof felting and boarding. Building a home that is insulated to these degrees means that thought has to be given to ventilation and it's normal for a mechanical ventilation and heat recovery system to be employed. The arctic weather apart, there was

another imperative which inspired the creation of these systems. Daylight is at a premium in northern climes and, quite simply, the more that could be done under controlled factory conditions and the less that needed to be done on site the better. This feeds through into the ethos behind the level of fixtures and fittings included by most of the 'Hus' manufacturers and suppliers. Daylight and the need to husband as much sunlight into the house as possible also reflects in many of the designs and layouts. In the early days of the marketing of Scandinavian houses, the designs, with their timber external cladding and 'A' frames found little favour with planners conscious and protective of the 'local vernacular'. What the companies marketing these products managed to do, and to do successfully, was combine all of the design ideals and construction imperatives of these homes with the traditions of British architecture.

Aisle framed buildings are another form of timber frame construction where the major loadings, instead of being borne, solely, by the walling panels, are taken by massive timber

Right - A section of a Potton house showing the aisle frome construction which is completely different from most other timber frame systems.

Far Right - The aisle frames up and the studwork well on the way in this Potton House.

Left - A Timber and Brick Wall Section.

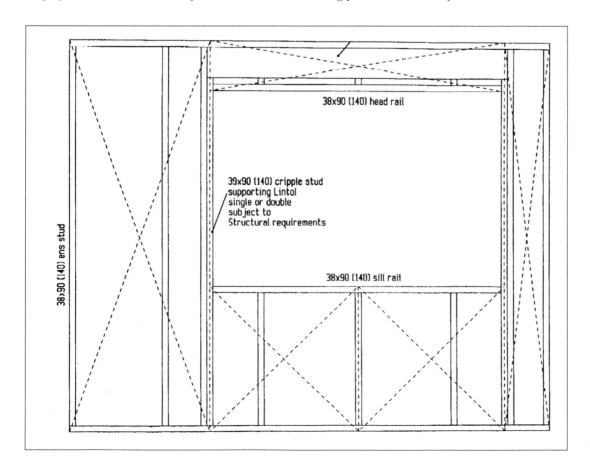

38x90 (140) head rail

39x90 (140) cripple stud supporting Lintol single or double subject to Structural requirements

38x90 (140) sill rail

38x90 (140) ens stud

Left - Elevation of typical external load-bearing external panel.

Right - Medieval technology and style brought up to date by Border Oak.

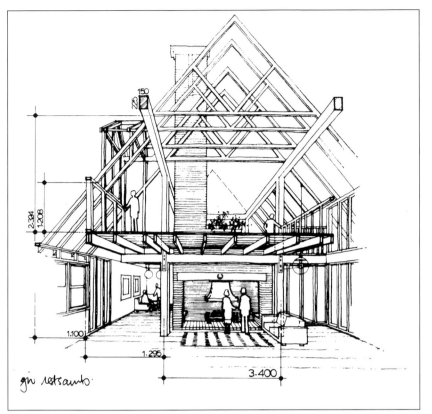

uprights supporting a skeleton frame. Potton are the major exponents of this system of building and many of their well known designs utilise it. Design apart, the essential features of these houses and, in particular, the walling panels follow the same patterns as for the open panel systems described above.

Traditional oak framed houses are, perhaps, so completely unique as to warrant consideration under a heading all of their own. Pioneered by Border Oak, this is fifteenth century building technique brought into the modern age with a massive skeleton of heavy oak timbers forming the frame. The important difference with this system is that this frame is visible internally and

externally and that the building is of single skin construction. The spaces between the oak timbers on the external walls are filled in with urethane infill panels with galvanised perimeter trims and mesh reinforcement. A sophisticated system of trims, water bars, weather seals and drainage channels then ensure that the building meets the proper standards and can deal with the worst that the British climate can provide. To sit in one of these houses is to literally go back in time, and I can vouch for the fact that the feeling inside one of them is no different to that inside my brother's 450 year old farmhouse in Essex. Needless to say each one of these houses has to be manufactured individually and it is normally

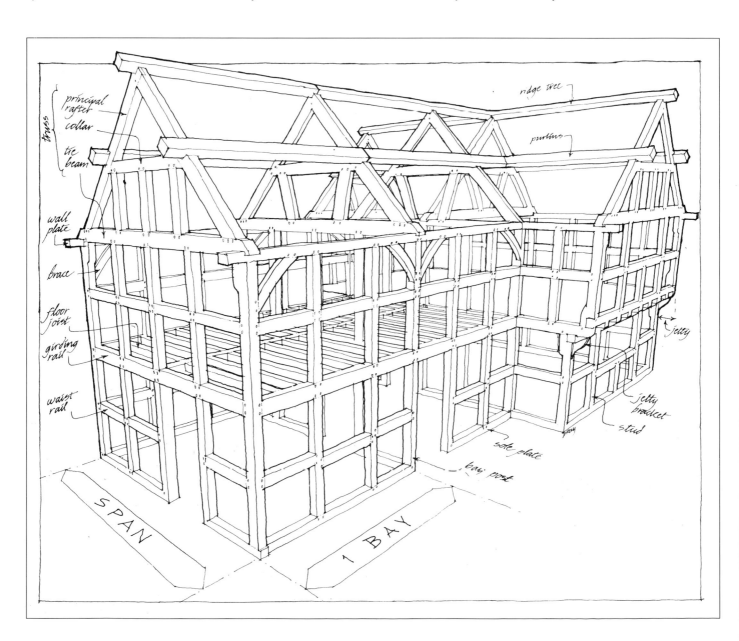

put together on a test run at the works before each part is carefully marked and shipped out to site.

Although many of the timber frame companies will provide you with their services based on your own plans and designs, there is no doubt that for most of them, working within the selfbuild industry, design is the 'hook'. However, whether or not they get involved in the preparation of the plans and the planning process itself, is immaterial to the fact that all of them will, if you accept their quotation, have to be involved with the preparation of the detailed and working drawings. Developers and builders often take the timber frame supply and arrange their own erection but it is more usual for the selfbuilder to use the erection services provided by the company. The specification for the supply and erection will vary from company to company, according to the method of timber frame they employ. Some of the companies can properly be described as 'kit' suppliers in that they supply a large proportion of the component parts for the houses, including second fix materials. Some would probably be best described as 'panel manufacturers', whilst others fall somewhere between these two stools. In many cases, but not always, the supply and fixing of windows and door frames will also be within the package deal companies' remit, as will the supply and fixing of the prefabricated roof trusses. Some companies will go on to felt and batten the roof, fix the insulation material, the vapour check and the internal plasterboard but most times these are quoted as extras. The important thing, as ever, is that everyone, and especially you, knows just what you're getting and just what your contract with the timber frame company comprises. Almost certainly the external cladding will be down to you and in most cases this will take the form of an external leaf of the cavity wall, constructed in brick or stone although, in some cases, as I have previewed above, the external finish will be render or tile hanging.

In any consideration of timber frame, the same hoary old chestnuts of questions keep coming up. Why should this book be different? It's not, except that we can answer those questions without any axe to grind and any answer we give can be read in conjunction with all of the other choices which face you and which are outlined in this chapter.

What's the main difference between a timber and brick house and a brick and block house? Visually very little, internally as well as externally. Structurally, the inner leaf of the cavity wall is built out of prefabricated, engineer designed and insulated panels instead of blocks.

Can a timber frame house be built quicker than a brick and block house? Yes it can, although the speed of the build has as much to do with the selfbuilder's ability to organise and finance things, both on and off site. If there's a long wait for the delivery of the frame after the groundworks, you'll lose any advantage.

Is a timber frame house as strong as a brick and block house? Yes, just as strong and just as structurally integral. Each house has the benefit of computer aided calculations to prove that the frame will not only support the structure and the roof but, that it will withstand windforce and all other exposure factors.

Will a timber frame house last as long as a brick and block one? Of course it will. Some of the oldest houses in the land are timber framed and with modern technology and precision engineered stress graded timber, many of the modern houses will do as well.

Is a timber frame house more susceptible to damp? Not at all. All of the building practices in this country have always been concerned to prevent the ingress of damp. With a timber and brick construction the cavity, which was first invented to prevent the transference of damp, is maintained as a clear cavity, thus fulfilling its original role. Leaking pipes or incorrectly fitted flashings and trays are not peculiar to timber frame and can cause just as much damage to other methods of construction.

What happens about fire and in the event of a major fire how does timber frame compare? Timber frame is as safe as any other form of construction with death or injury no more likely to occur. Even if the frame did catch fire, much of its integral stability would be retained.

What about bad workmanship on site? What

about it? Bad workmanship doesn't confine itself to any one method of building. However, with a large part of the construction and manufacture usually carried out under controlled factory conditions the chances of anything going wrong are limited. In any event, the inspectors from the Building Control departments and the warranty inspectors will watch out to make sure that everything is done properly and, as a selfbuilder, I bet you will as well.

What about hanging things like cupboards on the walls? It isn't really a problem and in any event it's not one that's confined to timber and brick as many brick and block houses are now dry lined. As long as the proprietary fixings are used for normal loads such as kitchen cupboards, shelves, pictures and the like there will be no problem. Otherwise for very heavy bookshelves, you might need to locate the studs and fix through to them or to fix a batten on the wall.

Can you extend a timber frame house? Of course you can. In fact in many instances extension is even easier than with a brick and block house and not half as messy. You do obviously need to check things out with either the original frame manufacturer or with a timber engineer. But there's nothing different about that and one would hope that whatever the method of construction is, professional advice is sought before anybody goes around hacking holes in a structure.

What levels of thermal insulation can one expect? How long is a piece of string? The fact is that the sky's almost the limit and it really is down to you to evaluate your own requirements and to weigh up the competing claims from the various manufacturing companies. The thermal insulating properties of timber and brick are well known and usually exceed the regulation requirements. Timber and brick houses heat up very quickly and their level of insulation means that they then stay warm for longer. In addition with no 'cold spots', they are not prone to condensation.

What about sound transmission? Most sound from outside the house comes through the windows rather than the walls. Internal sound transmission is most often the biggest bugbear

and there's no doubt that this is the one area where timber frame has to fight hard to beat brick and block. Internal sound transmission between rooms can be improved quite dramatically by making sure that there are no air gaps at the top or bottom of any partition. Filling the void in the wall with insulating or sound deadening material can help, as can additional layers of plasterboard. Sound transmission through floors can be alleviated by filling the void with mineral wool or by the use of specialist screeds.

Does one have to use a package deal company or timber frame manufacturer? Not nowadays. Most timber frame houses in the Kingdom are probably built with the aid of one of the companies, even if it's only for the manufacture of the panels rather than for the full service. Stickbuilding is, however, gaining in popularity and I'll go into that in the section that follows, entitled 'Going it alone'.

Will a timber frame house be as valuable as a brick and block house and will it be just as easy to get a mortgage or take out insurance? There's no difference at all.

Are there environmental benefits from building timber frame? Trees are the earth's lungs. They absorb and lock up carbon dioxide and they give out oxygen. Renewable forests are an undoubted benefit not only in the fight against global warming but also for their pure beauty and wildlife habitat. Thermally and energy efficient housing means less use of non renewable fuel sources and the effects of that go far beyond the undoubted benefit to one's pocket. Although these qualities are not the sole province of timber framed houses, they undoubtedly lead the way and their very existence has provided the spur for environmental consciousness in the housing sector.

I don't want this section to turn into a puff for any company in particular and the mention of any company name is a reflection of the help they have given in the preparation of this book as well as its companion volume *The Home Plans Book*. In certain cases, it is also as a result of their having a unique product or service. All of the major timber frame companies working within the selfbuild industry, many of whom are household names, have a wealth of experience which they can draw on to your benefit, and you'll find a list of them at the back of this book. All of them provide a slightly different service in terms of both design and specification. My task is to make you aware of the choices, as they apply, and to lead you into your further discoveries. Your job is to sift through their brochures and decide which ones you feel can best help you express and realise your dreams of a new home. The only guidance I can give is that with the diversity of levels of service, you must make sure that, when comparing between any of them, you are comparing like for like.

Brick and block

Most new houses built in the Kingdom are constructed in brick and block and, because of its familiarity, there doesn't seem the need to defend it or extol its virtues in the same way one has to with timber frame. Equally, the very universality of this familiarity means that many a discussion will hinge on the advisability of its use and the foolhardiness of departing for another system. From what you've just read above, you'll realise that these opinions are very often invalid and that brick and block is just one of the choices that you have to make, rather than being the only option. Nevertheless, it has to be admitted that most people feel themselves instinctively drawn to the idea of building in brick and block and for those that do so, the

Michael and Emma's house taking shape. The blocks are laid fast but the stonework will take longer to catch up.

choice is justified with as much zeal as any proponent of another method can muster.

With a modern brick and block, cavity wall construction, it is the inner leaf of the cavity wall that takes the load and provides the structural stability for the house or bungalow. Whilst this block may well provide, either all or part of the thermal insulation, it is often the cavity, and the insulation that is built into it, that provides the most. It wasn't always thus. When the cavity wall first started to replace the solid wall it went on to gain full acceptance due to its undoubted ability to prevent damp from getting from the outside face of the wall across and in to the inside. This remained as its principal reason for many years and, without dating myself too much, I can still remember the tooth sucking that went on when the ideas of interrupting or even filling the cavity with insulation, were first mooted. That the doubters were often proved right by a whole host of cowboy operators who blew all sorts of unsuitable material into cavities which had never been designed to be anything other than clear, did nothing to stop the onward march of progress and the refinement of materials and techniques into the systems we have today. It is still possible to have a completely clear cavity and to conform to the modern Building Regulations requirements but I wonder if, in the end, it's really worth it when so much more can be achieved with less cost and without the need to have to resort to special materials.

155

I suppose our preoccupation with the costs of heating and running our homes really began, as far as I can remember, with the 6 day war in the Middle East in June 1967. Prior to that, maybe a few souls really cared but, for the majority, thermal insulation could have been confused with something to do with nuclear bombs, which, to me at least, were a far greater source of worry. In the early sixties many brick and block houses were still being built with open cavities, common brick or breeze block internal wall leafs and large areas of window, often single glazed. It's not that we were any hardier in those days or that we enjoyed being cold or sitting in draughts, rather, it's the fact that heating costs were such an insignificant part of our income and expenditure. I can still remember the 'U1' block replacing the old breeze block and I can remember too the introduction of the 'modern' idea of insulating the roof, although, to be fair, that had much more to do with the prevention of mould. The ratchet tightened inexorably from then on with the miner's strikes of the seventies, further troubles in the Middle East in the eighties and our nineties concern over global warming. Brick and block construction couldn't stand still in the face of all this and it had to move with the times and the ever increasing and tighter regulations on thermal efficiency. It had, too, to answer the challenge from timber frame and there is no doubt in my mind that the high levels of thermal insulation, found in modern brick and block houses, owe a lot to it having to keep pace with this competition. Be that as it may, the end result is that brick and block construction can now equal mainstream timber frame construction in its provision of thermal efficiency and many houses built with this method go on to exceed the level of requirements.

In much the same way as with the timber frame heading, there are quite a few ways of going about constructing a brick and block cavity wall. Although there aren't the number of companies specialising or promoting one particular method or another, there are, nevertheless, a bewildering array of different blocks to choose from and a whole host of combinations that can be used to provide you with the wall that will conform to all of the regulations. Whether you're using a package deal company or an architect, they'll be concerned to match your aspirations with the budget and the particular or peculiar requirements of either the design or its exposure. Some blocks can cost two or even three times more than others and some of them, whilst seemingly appropriate may not actually be suitable for your particular situation.

Perhaps one of the most common ways of building is the use of a 100mm 'Type B' insulating block as the inner leaf of the cavity with a 75 mm cavity full filled with insulation and either rendered block, brick or stone as the outside leaf. The two leafs of the walling are held together by special galvanised wall ties and, whilst the external leaf does not provide any load bearing ability to the structure, it does, nevertheless, provide it with stability. That's also probably the cheapest way of constructing the wall and the 'U' values achieved are about the same as for a standard open panelled timber frame wall using 39mm x 89mm studs. However, in high exposure situations, even though modern cavity insulation materials resist damp and allow moist air to pass through them, it is often advisable, and the authorities may insist, that you maintain a clear cavity. In these cases, this is achieved by increasing the cavity very slightly to 80mm and then using a more dense insulation material, held against the outside edge of the inside leaf by special wall ties, maintaining a 50mm cavity.

If you want to up the specification even more then there are a whole range of lightweight blocks to choose from, most of which, measured by the square metre, will cost you more to buy and most of which might prove to be more popular with your bricklayers or whoever's got to carry them up to the top lift of the scaffold. Some of the higher insulation blocks gain much of their property by the use of a lightweight aggregate trapping air. What they gain in thermal efficiency, they can often lose in crushing strength and if there are point loadings or even heavy floor loadings they can prove unsuitable for that situation. Chopping and changing external walling materials around the house isn't always a good idea and can lead to cold bridging.

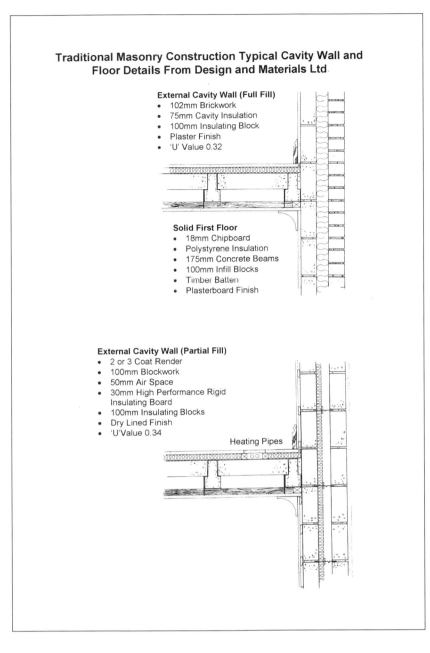

Traditional Masonry Construction Typical Cavity Wall and Floor Details From Design and Materials Ltd.

External Cavity Wall (Full Fill)
- 102mm Brickwork
- 75mm Cavity Insulation
- 100mm Insulating Block
- Plaster Finish
- 'U' Value 0.32

Solid First Floor
- 18mm Chipboard
- Polystyrene Insulation
- 175mm Concrete Beams
- 100mm Infill Blocks
- Timber Batten
- Plasterboard Finish

External Cavity Wall (Partial Fill)
- 2 or 3 Coat Render
- 100mm Blockwork
- 50mm Air Space
- 30mm High Performance Rigid Insulating Board
- 100mm Insulating Blocks
- Dry Lined Finish
- 'U' Value 0.34

Heating Pipes

cool down. In a block built house, when the heating goes off at night, the blockwork will retain the heat for longer. In similar vein in summer, the effects of a really hot day will be delayed as warm air coming into the house, gets cooled by the walls. Well, that's the theory and one that's put forward by those wishing to persuade you to use brick and block. It is true, of course, but if you also dry line the house instead of using a wet plaster, the effect is largely negated.

Without a doubt the biggest innovation that's come about in the field of brick and block construction has been the introduction of solid first floors. Some time ago a large proportion of the claims the NHBC received, related to failed oversites where either the concrete and screed had cracked or the infill had failed and the whole floor had sunk. In large part this was occurring on sites where there was a slope that made it necessary for the fill material to be greater on one side or at one end of the building than it was at the other. The solution was normally to thicken up and reinforce the oversite slab which was then cast so as to be capable of suspension. It was an expensive option with several inherent problems and it was extremely time consuming. Then the floor beam manufacturers started to move in on the house building market, having previously, largely, confined themselves to factories, office blocks and commercial buildings. It very quickly became common practice for the ground floors of houses, whether timber frame or brick and block, to use floor beams, and the NHBC and Building Control departments of many of the local authorities actively encouraged this, especially in situations where there was the slightest risk of differential settlement. There was resistance at first, there still is in some quarters, but gradually people began to realise that, although the costs of the flooring were slightly more than the equivalent in concrete, there were definite savings to be made in time and labour costs. A ground floor could be prepared and ready for the superstructure in under half the time taken for a consolidated, filled and con-creted oversite and, moreover, the costs were a known rather than an indeterminate factor.

Before I go on I'd better just describe a floor

Padstones under, say, a purlin, to take a point loading may still require dense concrete blocks beneath them to spread the load downwards and outwards and, in that situation, you may have to provide additional insulation. Again, talk these things through with your architect and, as always, weigh up the pros and cons for your own situation.

One factor that you might like to consider is that, quite apart from the level of thermal insulation that's possible with a brick and block house there is another, less well known, but, nevertheless, obvious benefit. When a dense material is heated up, it takes a longer time to beam and what is known as a 'beam and block floor'. The beams are shaped like railway lines in a 'T'section. They are laid, with the head of the 'T' downwards, from foundation wall to foundation wall, spaced one block apart. Blocks are then placed in the web between the beams to form a floor that is then brush grouted.

When I first saw these blocks being used on a first floor, I felt quite foolish. Why on earth hadn't I thought of that before? Why hadn't anyone else, come to that? It was so obvious and it had been staring everyone in the face for years!

One of the reasons people went to brick and block was because they didn't fancy the idea of studwork walling between rooms. They then discovered that, with a timber first floor, that's just what they ended up with upstairs. Now, with a beam and block first floor, partition walls to the upper part could, almost always, also be in blockwork. The advantage of sound insulation that was achieved between rooms on the ground floor could now be realised with those on the first floor as well. There were other advantages. Solid first floors meant that transmission of sound between floors would be almost eliminated and there would be greater fire protection, especially where garages were integral with rooms above them.

The finishing of the upper floor takes exactly the same form as it would for any of the ground floors and it can either be boarded on insulation panels as a floating floor or it can be screeded. The provision of services can cause some scratching of heads amongst the uninitiated but in fact they too find their way around in much the same way as they do for the ground floors. In addition there is a built in 'service duct' between the bottom of the infill blocks and the bottom of each floor beam and this is increased by the battens that are put in place to hold the plasterboard ceiling on the underside.

Wet plaster is a choice that is unique to brick and block construction and there are many devotees of this 'hard' form of finishing off the internal walls. Without a doubt there are benefits in the very durability of hard plaster and without a doubt, also, there are drawbacks to the length of time that such a finish takes to dry out and

become capable of being decorated. Timber frame houses are finished off with a dry lining of plasterboard, or similar, which is then either, taped and filled or skim coated. The advantages of this system of wall finish are obvious and they will become even more obvious as the end of any selfbuild project approaches and the time for decorating and finally moving in becomes ever more urgent. There's no reason why brick and block houses can't enjoy the same benefits as their cousins by using the dry lining method. The only difference in the technique is that, instead of being fixed to the studs by nailing, the plasterboard, in a dry lined brick and block house, is usually fixed by either dabs of plaster or by the fixing of battens to the walls. Which is best, dry lining or wet plaster? Neither really, both have their benefits and drawbacks. The pictures, shelves and cupboards that hang on the dry lined walls of my current abode have hung as well on the wet plastered walls of my previous houses and, as long as one knows which sort one has and allows for the correct fixings, one's enjoyment of either method is no different. Design & Materials, a package deal company specialising in brick and block construction tell me that, of their clients, 90% choose a post and beam first floor instead of a timber one and 80% choose dry lining. Whether that has more to do with their promotion of both ideas than it being an indicator of people's preferences, I don't know.

As with the timber frame construction, there are a series of questions which constantly crop up and, as with the timber framed section, I can answer each one without fear or favour.

Do the foundations for a brick and block house have to be stronger? The foundations for brick and block houses are almost always just the same as they are for timber framed houses. Ground conditions are what dictates differing solutions to foundation problems although, in a very few cases, calculations can be used to prove a lighter structure which can then, for instance, find a bearing on an oversite.

Can the same level of thermal insulation be achieved? Yes, but some of the solutions to a requirement far in excess of the regulation's requirements, can involve one having to use special lintels and wall ties, and that can sometimes be expensive or time consuming, as many of the merchants don't carry them in stock.

Does brick and block construction have better sound insulation? Generally yes, especially within the house itself. Low base notes have more power than higher frequency sounds and solid mass absorbs them more easily. I shudder to think what it must be like to live in some houses if the young male drivers with their 'sound systems' also enjoy the same facilities at home.

Will it cost more to build in brick and block? Not at all. The costs experienced by most selfbuilders, whether they build in timber frame or brick and block, are remarkably similar, although those building in brick and block are represented in greater numbers within the group that experience very low costs. It is, however, design, external materials and the size and expectations of a house, which dictate its cost, more than any method of construction.

Will it be easier to find labour? Not easier – no different really. Most labour knows all about building in brick and block but, as I've said, timber frame isn't that different in concept and if one uses a package deal company, they'll undoubtedly help with the introduction of builders and subcontractors who understand their system.

Can it be extended? Yes of course it can but always with advice and in accordance with the regulations. No building can have holes cut into it without proper thought and consideration of all of the consequences.

Will it take longer to build? There's no doubt that building in brick and block usually takes longer and that this method of construction is much more susceptible to bad, and particularly wet, weather. Having said that, for most selfbuilders, the time taken from starting on site to moving in is remarkably similar, whatever the construction method.

Going it alone

A selfbuilder, by the very definition, is someone who has consciously decided to step outside the norm and to do their own thing. The very factors that go towards their character makeup, make it all the more likely that a significant proportion will eschew any 'help' which might seem to coral them into any semblance of conformity. But just how far should this quest for individuality be taken? Well, the answer to that comes down, once again to our old friend, choice, but this time the choice has to be carefully thought out in relation to the selfbuilder's own abilities. Going it alone doesn't mean that one should forgo all advice whether given directly or indirectly. If you're a qualified architect or an extremely competent designer, then, by all means, why not do your own drawings and get your own planning permissions? If not, then to attempt to do so would be to enter a minefield. If you're a bricklayer then it makes sense to do all or most of the labour on your new home, assuming you've got the time. But, if you're in your mid fifties and have worked in an office all your life and never laid a brick, to do so would risk the success of your project and, probably your own life as well.

In terms of design and the preparation of drawings, especially those for the later stages of Planning and Building Regulations, I really believe that this is best left in the hands of a professional. On the other hand, I don't see any reason why the selfbuilder can't be involved in the negotiations for what is, after all, their project and as far as the 'outline' stages of planning are concerned I often believe that the private individual can do a better job. Estate agents often charge £200 or more for 'handling' applications for 'outline planning permission'. In fact all many of them do is take a photocopy of the OS sheet that's in their office, fill out the forms that the local authority hand out, attach their clients cheque for the application fees and send it all off with, or without, a covering letter. That's all they do, except of course, tell their clients the result some six to eight weeks later. If you turn forward to the chapter entitled 'The planning scene', you'll see in there that there's a lot more that can be done to try to make sure that such an application is successful. Some of the lobbying, I refer to, can only really be done by the applicant as a council tax payer and as a potential voter. A planning officer can talk to a professional in a different way than is possible when talking directly to a member of the public. With a professional he can be quite rude or dismissive about a proposal, by hiding behind the detached relationship both of them have to both the application and the applicant. Faced with the applicant in person, or in writing, the answers given have to be couched in more conciliatory terms and any reasons for objections have to explained and expanded. Again, that's not to say that there aren't situations where a professional could be usefully employed but, what I'm trying to illustrate is that it isn't always so.

Employing an architect or designer to do your plans doesn't mean that you lose control of your project. If you turn back to the section on architects you'll see that the measure of a good one, especially in the selfbuild scene, is their ability to be able to translate *your* ideals, *your* requirements and *your* wishes. The same goes for anybody else or any other company. If you decide on an architect and he doesn't produce initial or sketch drawings by the second or third attempt that are to your liking, then pay him off and move on to another choice. Do not just stick with something you're not comfortable with, just because you either don't want to admit you've made a mistake or in the vain hope that things will get better.

If a package deal company is providing you with what you want, then there's no loss of sovereignty. If you're being forced into a straight jacket that you're not comfortable with then the thing to do is pull out and pull out quickly and although this chapter is about making the choices and moving forward, that doesn't mean that, having made a decision, one shouldn't proceed through the next phases without keeping a constant enquiry going as to whether you've chosen the right route. An initial choice to run with a package deal company may well commit you to payment for initial drawings, design studies and/or feasibility studies. When that part of their service is completed they normally won't go any further until you've committed yourselves fully to them and signed up for their full package. You do need to think carefully before going beyond those stages and I'll discuss that in the

next chapter. Remember what I said earlier on, though, about not cherry picking. If you decide that you don't want to play with a package deal company then that doesn't mean that you can run off and build the house they've designed for you – the designs remain their copyright.

All selfbuilders are alone to some extent whether or not they take on a mentor. The selfbuilder who gives the whole job over to an architect who then goes on to employ a builder, still can't get away from the fact that at some stage the choices are down to him. That is, unless he's prepared to move in and only then discover that everything's just as wrong as if he'd gone out and bought a developer's house in the first place. The selfbuilder who uses a package deal or timber frame company will find themselves alone to some extent when it comes down to them sourcing the materials that aren't included in the package.

If you're building in brick and block then the choice has always been there to 'paddle your own canoe' and source the materials from a builder's merchant and that's just what the majority of selfbuilders do. What's changed over the last few years has been the attitude of the builder's merchants and the fact that the ordinary mortal rather than just the initiated can now expect all the help and advice necessary from them. If you're building in timber frame then, again, many of the merchants will arrange your frame purchase in just the same way as they always would have done with, say, an order for trusses. And, if you don't want to use a frame manufacturer then, as I've prefaced in the section on package deal companies, there's always the option of stickbuilding.

The very success of the package deal and manufacturing companies in the timber frame industry, has given rise to a whole new level of professionals, able to provide services and advice on the design and construction of a timber framed building. Architects can now draw on this expertise to design a timber framed building that can be completely constructed on site. In Scotland a large proportion of buildings are now built in this way and the practice is growing in England and Wales. What are the advantages apart from the fulfilment of a desire to go it alone? Well, flexibility really. Flexibility of design in that even once the drawings have been done and work has started on site, design changes such as moving windows or internal walls can be accommodated, subject of course to their being structurally feasible and to the planners agreeing. Flexibility of construction. One house I've seen in Wales used 100mm x 50mm regularised, pressure impregnated and treated timber for the external panels, which were then filled with solid insulation. The vapour barrier then went against the inside edge of this panel in the normal way but then, instead of the plasterboard, another framework of 50mm x 50mm timber was formed. All services were taken through this internal framework which was then filled with fibreglass insulation before the plasterboard was fixed to the inside face. In houses where there's only one panelled leaf, "it can end up like a Swiss Cheese", said the selfbuilder and occupant, and he's right. His house had a feeling of solidity I've rarely experienced. Now, there are systems out there from package deal companies that can emulate and, for all I know, exceed what he gained but, the point is that, that selfbuilder achieved what he wanted from within his own resources, which leads me onto the last of the gains in flexibility for this choice. Money. Building a timber framed house on site from lumber which is delivered from a local merchant or timber yard is never going to be as quick as if the panels were delivered already made up for quick assembly. And that's the point, because it means

that if finance is tight or, if it's not available in fairly front loaded stages, the purchase of materials can more or less follow the progress on site, evening up the cashflow. You don't have to be anything other than a reasonable carpenter to do this but you do need to follow recognised procedures and you'll probably need help of some sort, either in a professional or a labouring capacity.

Which leads me on to the last point of this section – labour. There are a few hardy souls who are selfbuilders in every sense of the word. They're the true 'go it aloners' and I take my hat off to them. For most of us living in the modern world, our selfbuild aspirations have to fit in with a job of work and that means that we have to usefully divide our time between what the boss would consider an extra curricular hobby and what to us is, possibly, the biggest financial undertaking of our lives. If you're going to be crawling into work late and falling asleep at your desk, then the chances are that the job that pays for the mortgage, that pays for the house, will fall away. And when that falls away so will your house. Most selfbuilders choose to either use a builder for all or part of the construction or to use subcontract labour for all or some of the trades and I'll cover that in later chapters. If you do waive the use of any other labour on site to truly go it alone, make sure that you do know what you're taking on, make sure that you do know what you're doing and make sure that you keep an open enough mind to recognise when you need to back off and seek help.

12 The initial drawings

Design study, initial drawings and sketch drawings. All words for the same thing really and all of which should lead you into an assessment of what you're aiming at, what it's likely to cost and whether it's feasible, which is why some of the package deal companies, working within the selfbuild industry, expand upon things and include these drawings in what they call a 'feasibility study'.

The way things happen depends, to some extent on the choices that are made with reference to the previous chapter, insofar as architects and designers often want to do things in a different way and package deal companies also have their differences, depending on whether or not you're using a standard design.

Some architects and designers don't really want to go through a design study stage. This is because they don't want the client to ask themselves, "do I want to use this architect and is he interpreting my requirements correctly?" Such an architect would far rather keep the arrangements moving gently along, until it reaches a compromise between his professional advice and the client's ideas, and he is established firmly as the client's professional agent. Maintaining this role is difficult because the client, wanting a modest house within a fixed budget, feels that he wants a clear idea of what he is going to get before he commits himself. Also, at some point in the design process, costs have to be quantified, and the decision made that the design proposed is practicable within the budget. One could question whether such an architect is really suitable for the selfbuilder but, nevertheless, it's worthwhile trying to establish if they'll agree to carry out a design study for an agreed fee. Some won't want to play on this basis and, perhaps, then, it's better to move on to another choice. Certainly the *ASBA* architects factsheet quite clearly details a sketch design stage and although it's not always done as a formally quoted design study, the procedures they adopt do allow for a continuous evaluation of just where each project is going. Typically, an architect will probably have up to three meetings with the client before pen is even put to paper and they'll only go to the drawing board when they have fully evaluated the client's

needs and requirements under all of the headings that I've described in the section on architects, in the previous chapter. At any stage in this process, therefore, the architect will want to know that they're on the right lines and the selfbuilder will want to know that, yes, the drawings are what they want and, yes, they are probably going to be acceptable to the planners and, that they can be built within their budget. If the answer comes though, at any time, that one or more of these goals is not achievable then the whole thing must stop and be re-evaluated or redrawn until it is right. If necessary, if, after several redraws, it's still wrong then there may be no alternative but to change architects. In that case the relationship should be terminated by payment of a fee based on the work done so far and that fee should, in all normal circumstances, reflect the level of fees charged for design studies by other companies. Of course I'm talking here about worst case and the chances are that when you went out shopping for an architect you picked him or her for their general level of abilities and the flair that they undoubtedly demonstrated to you in their portfolio. The architect will in all probability, already have asked themselves the questions you generate, in their desire to obtain your custom. They'll be as keen as you are to know that everything's on the right lines and the drawings you get back as sketch drawings will probably reflect your original choice and the brief you gave. But, if not, then you must remain in the driving seat of any relationship. This is *your* selfbuild.

If you're using a package deal company for the design process, whether timber frame or brick and block then the way things proceed depends to a large extent on the choices you have made on how to arrive at the design. Many of the companies have brochures with designs within them that can be adapted or changed to varying degrees. Most of them will be concerned that the designs that originally attracted you to their services can be proven to be feasible for your circumstances. Even if a selfbuilder chooses a standard design from a brochure, the company will know that it may well need alteration of some sort to find favour with the planners and they will know also that those alterations, whether or not it affects their own particular price or service to you, may well have an effect on the total costs of the building. In some cases, therefore, it is still necessary to go through a feasibility study stage with a standard design and there may well be a charge for such a service. It is money well spent and you can use the completed study to demonstrate to yourselves, to your lenders and to the planners that you are on the right lines.

If you've gone to a package deal company on the basis of having a bespoke design then, in many respects, your initial relationship with them is no different to what it would be if you'd gone to an architect or designer and later in this section I'll discuss just how you should approach the initial contacts and the preparation of the brief that will lead to the initial drawings. The purpose of any feasibility study is to establish, firstly the design, secondly the costs and thirdly the likely acceptance of the proposals as far as the planners are concerned. The last two depend upon the first and the first has to be undertaken with the last two in mind. Costs can be established in broad brush strokes and most of the representatives of the companies will be able to tell you right off whether or not you're on the right lines, even before the initial drawings are ready. When they are completed they'll also, probably, be able to demonstrate their faith in their own abilities by getting quotations not only for their own services but from builders and others that prove the feasibility of the project in cost terms. In planning terms the architect or the company representative will always be keeping a weather eye open for the project to remain within the requirements of the local authority and they'll probably steer your thoughts, and the design process, to keep within those parameters.

So, back to the first one, the design itself. Almost certainly you've diligently read through the four chapters on design and just as certainly you've got a long list of your requirements, a bulging scrapbook and done some sketches of your own. If not, then the time to get them done is before you meet the architect or company representative so that you can make sure, as far as is possible that the brief they depart with and

therefore, the initial drawings that come back, are what you're after. Start off any meeting with a request for a general appraisal of just what the company can do for you and, whilst you're probably not that interested in being 'sold to', ask just what it is that this company or practice has to offer which makes it worthwhile to choose them above all others. A package deal representative will be trading on the designs and the case histories within his brochure and, to be fair, they're probably the reason you've called him in the first place. An architect or designer will, in just the same way, be trading on his own track record in the form of his portfolio or else the recommendation that has brought him to your door.

The first of their questions to you should probably revolve around what you want to build and what your budget is. If the plot hasn't already been seen by the architect or representative then they'll be concerned to go and inspect it before they get into a detailed discussion. Possibly they will have ideas of their own which they can sketch out with you and it's always a good idea to try and establish just what their thought processes are and just what their level of competence and understanding is. Most of them will have fairly comprehensive check lists and questionnaires to fill out with you, these having been refined over the years to make sure that when the project gets to the drawing board, all the relevant information is to hand. Your list of requirements should accompany any brief that has been prepared and although it conflicts with advice given in previous editions of this book, I believe that there's no harm at all in showing the representative your own sketches. Don't be bashful – he won't scoff, I can assure you and, however amateur the plans are, they will give him a thoroughly good guide to just what you're trying to achieve. He may have seen the plot for the first time that day and then for only a short time. I bet you've spent days looking at and thinking about that plot and you, more than anyone will have worked out just where you want particular rooms to face, what views you want to maximise or even lose and what type of property you feel will fit. Have some paper handy so that when the chap

CUSTOM HOMES

This is the original of the feasibility study plan for Michael and Patricia. They did not draw out any plans of their own and, instead, the architect came up with the design from a list of their requirements. When the planning application was made the upper part was referred to as storage and the dormers were deleted.

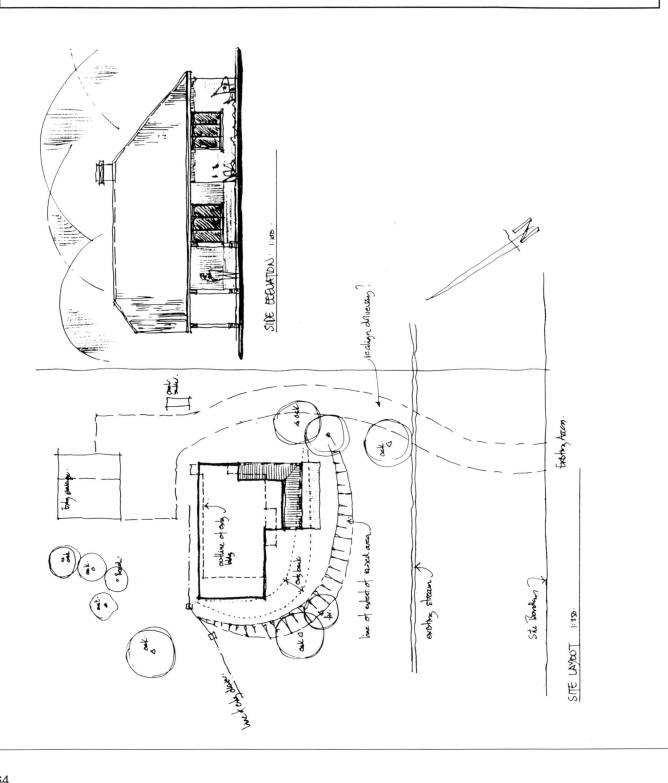

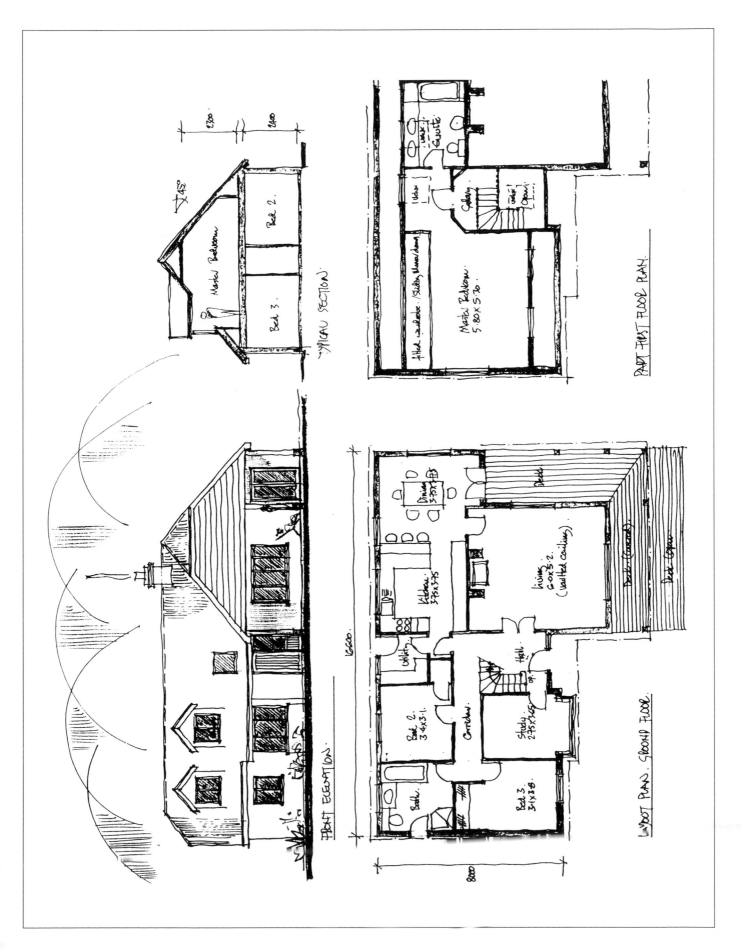

FRONT ELEVATION.

TYPICAL SECTION.

PART FIRST FLOOR PLAN.

LAYOUT PLAN. SECOND FLOOR.

DESIGN & MATERIALS

This initial drawing shows a substantial family house to be built as a replacement dwelling. The footprint of the new house is not significantly different to that of the existing dwelling but it has been set back behind the old one. As long as access is available for building materials and site traffic there is no reason to think that the existing house could not be occupied during the construction.

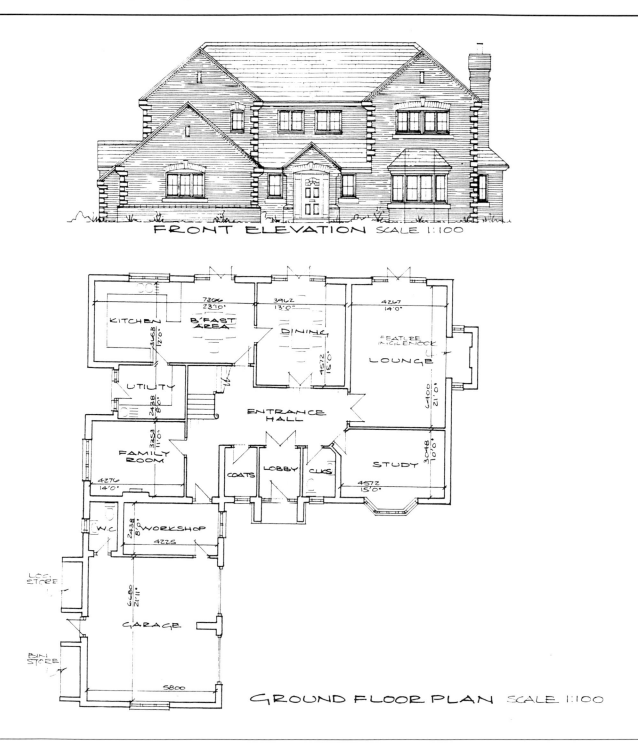

FRONT ELEVATION SCALE 1:100

GROUND FLOOR PLAN SCALE 1:100

REAR ELEVATION SCALE 1:00

UPPER FLOOR PLAN SCALE 1:100

POTTON

This is a deceptively large house that manages to show a compact looking frontage and, with the garage entrance at the rear side elevation, manages to avoid the garage doors being the dominant architectural feature. The lines are simple and borrow from several different heritages, the dominant one being the Victorian influence.

FRONT ELEVATION.

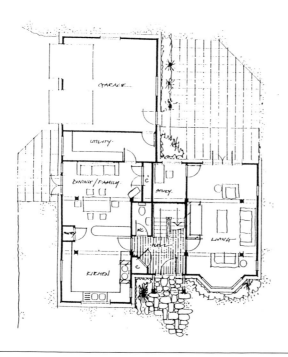

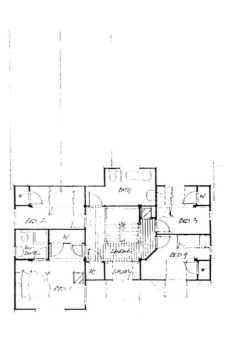

has had a look at your plans, he can draw out his own ideas based on your plans, probably rationalising a jumble of barely connected rooms into something approaching a plan capable of construction. "Why should we do that", you may ask. "Surely it's his job to come up with a design?" "Why should we do his job for him?".

This is not a 60's demarcation dispute, this is a selfbuild project and any means which serve to ensure that you get what you want in design terms are right and proper. Two parties working in isolation of each other's thought processes are unlikely to produce the best results. By comparing your ideas with the professionals input you can sometimes see the realisation and expansion of your plans before your very eyes.

When the initial drawings or sketch drawings are completed with any alterations drawn up or noted, with the costs established as far as is feasible then it's time to stand back and evaluate just how far you've got and what happens next. If you're happy with what's on offer and the price

that it's on offer at then you're ready to commit yourself to the next stages and you should be ready to commit yourself to one company or practice. If not, then stand back even further and ask yourself just what it is that you're not happy with and ask the people you've been dealing with to answer your questions. If the answers don't come back right, if you're still not happy, then cut loose and take another tack with a different company or architect. Don't just let things run on – after the initial drawing stage you could well find that, if you agree to a company doing more work or going for planning, you're legally contracted to them for the whole of their service. If that's not what you intended but you've just let it all happen, it'll all end in tears.

But enough of this gloom. Chances are that the feasibility stage will have demonstrated to you that you've made all the right decisions, all the right moves and that now's the time to think about the next stage of your selfbuild project - the planning permission.

13 The planning scene

To a degree, I've already pre-empted some of the contents of this chapter when dealing with the important business of the evaluation and purchase of a site. However, much of what I've said will bear repetition and expansion, and an understanding of the planning scene is an essential prerequisite for any successful selfbuild project. This applies as much to those who are going to leave the application in the hands of their chosen professional as it does to the selfbuilder who decides to handle the application himself. Even if you engage the services of a professional, you cannot divorce yourself from what follows and it's important that you and your advisors act in concert and work as a team.

Planning is law, but it is law, which is translated by opinion, and opinions can vary. Each local authority will interpret advice from the Department of Environment in its own way. Each planning officer will interpret his own role in the administration of the Planning Acts in his own way and a change of personnel can make a marked difference to the progress of an application. The Planning Acts are concerned with whether or not a dwelling can be built at all in a particular locality, and with its appearance and the way in which it will relate to its surroundings. This control is exercised by the Local Authority, to which an application has to be submitted to erect any new dwelling. Members of the public are entitled to appeal to the Minister for the Environment against any decision of the local authority in a planning matter. In theory all planning applications are considered by a committee of councillors who are advised by the council's professional planning officers, but in practice they often just rubber stamp the recommendations of the planners for run of the mill applications. In some local authorities, applications for Approval of Reserved Matters and uncontentious applications are not even put before the committee and, instead, the planning officers themselves have the power to determine the application using Delegated Powers handed down to them by the authority.

One of the things many professionals hear when talking to their clients, is that such and such a planning officer is very difficult to deal

with or is always negative in their dealings with any application - actually the character descriptions are often a lot earthier. The professional will usually listen politely but he will know the reality, in that, that planning officer, who may well be known to him, is a person who does nothing more nor less than their job. They can never really win. The person who doesn't get planning for exactly what they want will feel aggrieved and the next door neighbour of the man who does get exactly what he wanted, may feel just as aggrieved. All a planning officer can do is try to act within their powers, fairly and in an even handed a manner as their brief allows. Again, at meetings with planning officers, clients who are not getting their way may become extremely upset, as is evidenced by the panic strings that you'll see in most meetings rooms. If the professional doesn't share their anger, some may even turn their resentment against their own advisor, failing to see that first and foremost, their approach won't get them very far and that secondly, and most importantly, their architect is there in a professional capacity. As such, he has to bear in mind that he may well have dealings with the planning officer on behalf of other clients and that, if he allows himself to become as personally involved as his client, he may well disadvantage his other clients and jeopardise his future business. Having said that, the experienced professional will understand that, although for him this is just another job, for his client it is *the* experience that colours his whole existence at that time and that they're bound to be much more personally involved. It helps if each party understands everyone else's roles and starting points and, if this book can assist in that understanding, then fine.

The planners make their recommendations in accordance with set criteria after going through set procedures. The way to obtain a planning consent quickly and easily is to ensure that it meets all the established criteria for an approval. This fact is often forgotten. A planning officer does have the discretion to make recommendations which are at a variance with planning policy, but this is unusual. The golden rule is to avoid applications which may be contentious, and to present anything unusual in a non-contentious way. It is always the land that acquires the planning permission, not the person who applies for it. If land with planning permission is sold, the consent is available to the new owner. You don't even have to own the land in order to make an application on it and many selfbuilders, as we explored in the chapter headed 'Evaluating a site', make applications on sites which they are in the process of buying, long before they actually have legal title. It is necessary to serve notice on the owners of the land and it is advisable to tie things up with them to make sure that, if you're successful, the land doesn't get sold to someone else. This can be in the form of a legal option to purchase in the event of planning being successful or alternatively you can buy the land, subject to receipt of satisfactory planning permission.

There are various types of consent, and it is important to appreciate the differences between them and their relationships to each other.

Outline planning consent gives permission, in principle, for the development of land. It means that some sort of building or development may take place and it is what confers the value on the plot. 'Outline' consent does not, in itself, allow you to commence work but, rather, it allows you to move on to the next stage of the planning process. It is always given subject to conditions, the first of which is that it is valid for a period of five years from the date of its granting *but*, that application shall be made within a period of three years, from the date of its granting, for 'approval of reserved matters'. These reserved matters are usually the siting, design and access arrangements, which are not normally dealt with at the 'outline' stage. There may well be other conditions and, at the next stage in the planning process, these conditions will have to be satisfied.

Approval of reserved matters is the next stage in the normal planning process. It is sometimes referred to as Detailed Permission and it concerns itself with the actual design, siting and access arrangements for the development. In normal circumstances, it does not confer any extra value to the plot, over and above

that already given to it by the 'outline' consent. Within this application any conditions imposed by the 'outline' consent have to be satisfied and it is possible that fresh conditions may also be made. An 'approval of reserved matters' never stands alone – it is always related back to and is a part of the original 'outline' consent. As such, and as an example, if there is a condition on the 'outline' consent, that the development is for a single storey dwelling, and the planning officer agrees that you may, in fact, make application for a two storey dwelling then, you cannot do so as an 'approval of reserved matters' pursuant to the original 'outline' consent, and a fresh application will have to be made.

It is necessary to understand, however, that even though the 'approval of reserved matters' cannot stand alone, it does not follow that it is a mere formality. The granting of an 'approval of reserved matters' does not preclude further applications for quite different schemes relating back to the original 'outline' consent and the refusal of an application for 'approval of reserved matters' does nothing to negate the original 'outline' consent.

Full planning permission is really nothing more than a rolling up together of the outline and detailed stages of an application into one consent. It grants permission in principle and at the same time considers and approves the full details of the proposed development. As such, it lasts for a period of five years from the date of its granting and it confers value to the plot in just the same way as an 'outline' consent would do. Where the issues of whether or not the land should be developed are not in contention and it's more a question of establishing what will be built, then the 'full' application is wholly relevant. On the other hand, any attempt to confuse or obscure the issue of principle by making a 'full' application, rather than an 'outline' application, is likely to backfire.

The words *permission* and *consent* are interchangeable in all that you read here (or anywhere else) about planning matters. Planning permission says that you *may* develop land, it does not say that you *can* develop land and it confers no other rights or obligations. If you get a

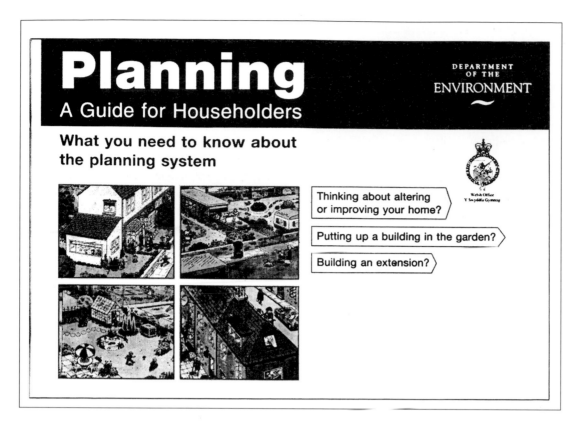

consent, and for physical or legal reasons that consent cannot be operated then there is no liability on the local authority. Consents for 'Approval of reserved matters' and 'Full' consents can still have conditions attached to them which have to be satisfied before any commencement of work. An example of these may be that, before any work commences on site, the approval of the local authority shall be obtained, in writing, for a landscaping and tree planting scheme. Another common example is that, before any work commences on site, the approval of the local authority will have been sought and obtained in writing for the use of any external materials such as bricks or tiles. In these cases the approval of these items is delegated to the officers and in the latter example they may wish to see samples of the intended materials. The condition may go to say that this approval shall be sought, notwith-standing the materials mentioned or stated on the plans, but whether or not it does, these words are implied and you cannot rely on the fact that another material was indicated.

There are other conditions which can be attached to any consent and which have the effect of making that consent inoperable until such

time as they are satisfied. We have already discussed visibility splays in the chapter 'Evaluat-ing a site' and you will recall that a consent can be issued with the requirement that these are proven to be operable before any consent is brought into operation. Beware - it is possible to commence work on a project and even to get to the stage of a practically finished dwelling without addressing the problem but, occupation and full operation of the consent will be illegal until such time as the formalities are sorted out. We have also discussed the issue of encumbered consents, particularly those relating to or limiting the occupation of the dwelling to someone wholly or mainly engaged in agriculture or the widow or widower thereof. Whilst this condition exists in perpetuity, many local authorities will want to strengthen their hand and require the land owners to enter into a legally binding agreement giving extra force to their requirements. They may even insist that the agreement goes further and either ties the dwelling to a farm as a whole or further encumbers an existing farm dwelling, or dwellings, which, up to then, had been free of any planning conditions. In such cases the consent will be issued subject to the preparation and execution of the agreement and until such time as the legal wheels of the local authority have turned their exceedingly slow turns, no work can commence on site.

Well, that's the consents but, perhaps we need to take a step backwards and consider the business of:

Making a planning application

As I've said earlier, the majority of selfbuilders should be purchasing land, which already has planning permission. But there are circumstances where it is appropriate for the selfbuilder to consider making an 'outline' application or even a 'full' application on land that does not have consent. There are also circumstances, which we've already explored, where, with the right safeguards, it is appropriate to make an application on land that you don't yet own. If you do own the land already then, to some extent, you've very little to lose and a lot to gain from the possibility of planning permission being granted. In certain circumstances, such as with farmers, the imperative for seeking a consent may not have anything to do with enhancement of land value, and a lot more to do with the successful running of a business.

Most land in this country is 'zoned'. That means that within the local Development Plan adopted by the Planning Authority, the land is parcelled up and allocated to specific purposes. The titles used in this allocation are probably familiar to most people with, for instance, 'Green Belt' referring to land where the policy is that no development shall be permitted. Land may also be designated as being for Residential, Industrial or Recreational use and other land may be zoned as 'White Land'. This is land that, while not being designated as 'Green Belt', has not been zoned for any other specific purpose. Most agricultural land falls within this category. District plans will clearly show the designation of land for specific purposes and village plans will indicate the 'envelope' or boundaries within which any development is expected to take place. None of this means that just because land falls within an area designated as being for residential use or a plot falls within the village envelope, it will

necessarily get planning consent for development. It's difficult to put into words, because it relies partly on a gut feeling built up over years of practise, just why one plot of land should get planning consent whilst another most certainly will not. I say again, planning is law that, perhaps more than any other branch of the law, is translated by opinion. Prior to any consent or refusal, therefore, all opinions are equally valid, but some might be a trifle more accurate than others. Professionals working within the planning scene have, probably, long since ceased to be surprised by the outcome of many applications and many will have stories of the plot they were certain would get planning, which didn't, and the plot they were convinced would never get planning, which did. If you're employing a professional at this stage then their opinion might be the spur or the disincentive for you to take matters any further. On the other hand, many of you will want to make your own mind's up on this issue and might like to form your opinion on what course of action you take by getting information first hand rather than second hand. There may also be a slight suspicion that there are financial axes to grind if you agree to adopt a particular course of action or commission someone to do something for you based on their own advice alone.

In the chapter on 'Finding land' I talked about obvious plots left by circumstance and there are many of them in many different situations around the country. If you either own or come across such a plot, then perhaps the first thing you should do is make general enquiries at the planning office about their attitude towards that piece of land. Come to that, the same advice will apply to any probable plot. Keep your questions on the broad theme of whether or not the piece of land would be considered as a building plot. Listen carefully to the answers and, without badgering the officer to make statements that he would rather not make, read between the lines of what they say. Now, you may think it preferable for the officer to come out to site, and in some cases it is certainly true that a visit to a site will serve to sway a wavering opinion one way or another. In most cases, however, and particularly at the first enquiry, it's likely that the officer can give an opinion by reference to plans and their own local knowledge. Words like, "every application will be treated on its own merits" mean little or nothing in this context and most planning officers will not usually use them when answering questions on the principle of whether land should be developed or not. "We would resist such an application", or, "Such an application would run counter to the policies of this authority", are much more clear cut and I would invite you to consider, in such circumstances, whether or not you should pursue that particular plot any further. Of course whether you accept such advice depends on many things, not least whether you already own the plot, but again I invite you to consider whether a long history of planning rejections will aid your case at some future date when perhaps the authority's attitude might be slightly different. Certainly getting involved in an argument about the planning policy of the local authority is pointless. The officer will not debate the policy itself and he must, and will, confine himself to dealing with your enquiry on the basis of the implementation of that policy. Sometimes, however, the lay person will pursue the argument and may even convince himself or herself that the planning officer has given way and agreed with their contentions. Normally nothing is further from the truth and the reality is that the planning officer has merely extricated himself from a tricky situation by using words, which seem to satisfy or partially mollify the member of the public he is faced with. In the end planning officers will know that, prior to any actual determination of an application, nothing they say either in writing or verbally is binding on the local authority, a fact that has been tested in the courts and is established in law by precedent.

Of course, the planning officer could look at your proposals and decide that, perhaps, an application would be acceptable or even welcome. In which case your next question should be whether they would like to see any application made in 'outline' or whether they would prefer it to be a 'full' application. If they ask for a 'full' application then, in most cases, it's a pretty sure bet that, at officer level, the land is thought of in terms of being a potential plot. Beware, you're not home and dry just yet and, although rare, it is not unknown for committees to take a differing view on things. There can also be an element within the planning officer's thinking that they feel that it would not be possible to consider the matter in outline, and that they therefore need some detail in order to also reflect on the issue of principle. This same school of thought can apply to some cases involving an 'outline' application, in which case the planning officers do have the power to insist on more detailed plans being considered at these stages. Although it's not a certainty, in many cases where these additional plans and details are requested, it is the precursor to an eventual approval of some sort or another.

If it's to be an outline application then although you're a lot further forward than the chap who got brushed aside, you must not count your chickens before they're hatched. At this point you really need to consider whether you should be using a professional to handle the application or whether you could handle it yourself. It all depends on your own circumstances and abilities but the chances are that if you were a complete no hoper you wouldn't have got to this point anyway. Maybe the reason the planning officer has asked for an 'outline' application is that he's not really sure about whether or not your particular proposal or the development of this particular plot will find favour with the planning committee. Maybe he knows that it will but, by taking it through the 'outline' stages of the planning process, he will then have a chance to influence the eventual outcome by the imposition of conditions. Maybe, you've been advised to make this application because the planning officer felt that you weren't prepared to accept his reservations and he feels that the only way to prove them to you is for you to make an application which he hopes and believes will be turned down. Whatever the reason for arrival at this point, there is a lot that the lay person can do to ensure that the application stands the best chance of success, whether or not a professional is employed to prosecute it.

Most 'outline' applications are considered by committee and it is perfectly legal to lobby the members of that committee to vote on your behalf. In the first weeks of May most councillors will be asking for your support at the ballot box and, in turn, you are perfectly entitled to ask for theirs. They don't have to do so, of course, and if your request for their support is accompanied by a bottle of whisky, then you have stepped beyond the bounds of lobbying and into the realms of bribery.

When the local authority receives an application they will normally acknowledge it and give it a reference number. After this they should determine the application within a period of eight weeks unless they obtain your written consent for an extension of time. It doesn't make sense to refuse this consent as in that case the authority may well simply determine the application by a refusal, citing a lack of time for any proper consideration. Sometimes there will be repeated applications for extension of time. This may be because they and you are still in active negotiation but it may also be a simple failure on the

part of the authority, in which case you do have either the right to refuse the extension of time, bringing matters to a head, or appeal to the Secretary of State against their failure to determine. I shall discuss that in the section on appeals but for now let us stay with the outline application. Assuming that all is going normally, a date will be set down at which your application will be considered by the committee and you and/or the professional working on your behalf should make sure that this date does not pass by without you knowing of the event. Two weeks before the committee is to hear the application, contact the members of the planning committee that your local councillor has identified as being the ones most likely to have influence and ask them for their support. If you feel it necessary, give them a written appraisal of why you think your application has merit and, if you think it would be helpful, offer to meet them on site to discuss the application. Don't leave things any later or they won't have time to do anything and don't do it any earlier or it will not be fresh in their minds when the meeting comes up. *Do not*

Scandinavian influences on a suburban home.

175

take things any further and *do not* badger them in any way – having made your submission leave the rest up to them. When it comes up at committee, you'll have made sure that it will be considered by as broad a cross section of opinion as is available and that it will not just be swept into a decision based on a single report – that is as much as you can, and should, do.

If the planning officer asks for a 'full' application, or if you are buying land with the benefit of an existing consent, then the following stages of the planning process are the ones that determine, not the principle but, the actual details of your proposed new home. In which case I earnestly believe that these stages are best handled by a professional. The issues of principle are ones where the democratic process can be brought into full play and where the lay person, by virtue of his ability to lobby, can seek to influence any outcome. An 'outline' application requires the minimum of drawings and may indeed only require the drawing in of a red line around the perimeter of a plot on a copy of the Ordnance Survey plan sold to you by the local authority. The merits of such an application can be argued by an articulate lay person. The detailed stages of any application need to be properly presented and the plans accompanying them need to be sufficiently detailed and attractive in order to stand the best possible chances. Whilst I advocate consultation with the planning officers by lay people at the 'outline' stage, I do advise caution at the detailed stages. Planners have an interesting job, and, almost without exception they are interested in it. They are anxious to influence development by advice as well as by control, and there is usually a notice at the reception desk saying they are ready to advise on proposed developments. This means what it says. Unfortunately this advice is usually a council of perfection, and it may not suit you to take it. For instance, suppose you are buying an attractive site with outline consent. As a first stage in establishing a design it may seem sensible to call at the planning office to ask for the free advice on offer. You will be well received, will be impressed by the trouble taken to explain how the site "needs a house of sensitive and imaginative

design to do justice to the position". You may be shown drawings, a sketch may be drawn for you, and it is not unknown for the Planning Officer to drive to the site with you. This is splendid, until you realise the ideal house being described suits neither your lifestyle nor your pocket. You will wonder what the reaction is going to be to your application for the quite different house which you want, and which is the one you can afford. The simple answer is that your application will be dealt with on its merits, and that the planning officer has an obligation to approve what he thinks acceptable, and he should not insist on what he thinks is best. However, presumably he will be disappointed and this disappointment must colour his thinking.

From this it will be seen that a preliminary discussion with the planning officer is not to be taken lightly. As a general rule, the best person to deal with the planning office is the professional whom you employ to submit your application. Some will be buying a plot, which already has a detailed consent on it. If the consent is for just what you want then everything's fine and, so long as you've got a current Building Regulations approval, there's nothing to stop you starting work on site. If there are some minor changes that you'd like to the drawings then it is possible that the planners will agree to these being carried out on the basis of a 'minor amendment to the existing consent'. They'll require a letter and drawings listing and showing the amendments, but it's better to talk your ideas through with them beforehand. If they feel that they cannot accept your amendments, or if your proposals are radically different to the existing consent, then you may have to either make a fresh application for 'approval of reserved matters' pursuant to the original 'outline' consent or else make a 'full' application. The failure of either of these methods of application, will not, of themselves, invalidate the original consents but nevertheless these may lapse of their own accord by virtue of their being out of time, so watch out for that eventuality.

When your planning application is made you will have to pay a standard fee to the local authority and this is payable whether it refers to an outline application, a full application, or an application for approval of reserved matters. There is no refund if the application is refused. The level of fees is reviewed at frequent intervals, and always adjusted upwards! The consideration process of any application follows a general pattern in that, once the application is registered, it will be assigned to an officer who will then send out for what are known as Statutory Consultations. These are made to bodies such as the Highways Authority and the Environment Agency as well as to the local parish council. Basically, although the officer may discuss the application within the consultation period, nothing much will be decided until such time as they are complete and it's better, therefore, to wait until the application has been with the local authority for about four weeks before endeavouring to enter into any meaningful discussions with the officer. If the Parish Council approve of your plans then that's

fine. If they reject them then it's by no means the end of the world. Parish Councils have a long history of rejecting what is put before them and there is no other way of saying it other than to say that they have long since 'shot their bolt'. Statutory as their consultation is, the fact is that their conclusions have little or no bearing on the decisions which the officers will reach in their recommendations, other than to reinforce an existing opinion.

The officer assigned to your case will prepare a report on your application, which will form the basis of the recommendation to the committee. If it is to be considered under 'Delegated Powers' then the same report will be submitted to the senior officer or group of officers who will determine the application. In general the applicant is entitled to see and have a copy of the report and also to see any background papers or documents used in the preparation of the

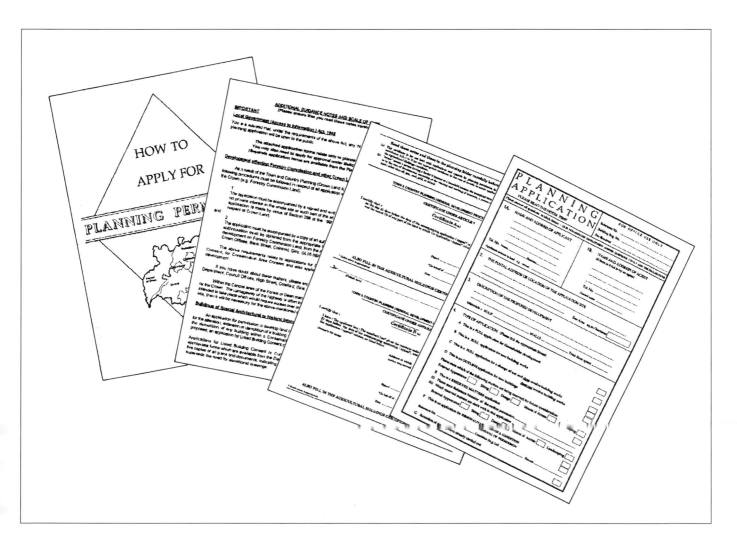

The portion of the letter below lists some typical observations that a planning officer might make on an application.

FOREST OF DEAN DISTRICT COUNCIL

High Street, Coleford, Glos., GL16 8HG.   Tel: (01594) 810000

DX 94102 COLEFORD

Planning & Leisure Services   **Fax:(01594) 812314**
Housing & Environmental Services   **Fax:** (01594) 812230
Other Services   **Fax:** (01594) 812590

Minicom: (01594) 812500

Please ask for: Direct Line:

Our Ref:

Your Ref:

Date:

Dear

Planning Application for the Erection of a Dwelling

I have now had an opportunity to check your planning application and there are a number of points that I want to comment on.

1.   With regard to the siting of the house and its relationship with the surrounding property, it would be better if it was set further forward on the plot and orientated towards the south.   This would enable it to maximise the solar gain and reduce the prospect of any overlooking affecting the privacy of neighbouring residents.

2.   I would suggest that you consider omitting the window to bedroom 2 from the side elevation.   This would reduce the possibility of overlooking of the neighbouring property.

3.   The overall design of the house is acceptable but I am not happy with proportions of the windows or the use of UPVC in this particular situation. The character of the area is fairly traditional and I would like to see the fenestration given a more vertical emphasis and timber used for their construction.

4.   The materials to be used are important and I would suggest that you have a look at the bricks that have been used on the new house directly opposite the post office.   These fit in well with the character of the area in terms of their colour and texture.

5.   The detached garage is sited too close to the western boundary and is likely to affect the trees growing in the hedge.   We want to keep as many of the trees on that side of the site as possible and it should be feasible to move the garage away as part of the revised siting suggested In point 1 above.

\continued.....

Meg Holborow, B.Sc., Dip. T.P., M.R.P.I., Head of Paid Service and Director of Strategy
David A. Matthams, C.P.F.A., Director of Central Services
Tim Perrin, B.Sc., M.C.I.E.H., F.C.I.H., Director of Housing & Environmental Services
Jim Stewart, B.A., M.C.D., M.R.T.P.I., Director of Planning & Leisure Services
Laurence J. Harding, LL.B., Dip.L.G., Solicitor to the Council

Building Control Services

reports. If an objection is received then it is usual for any Delegated Powers to be withdrawn and for the application to then be considered by full committee.

It's a fine line to walk at this stage and your professional is the one to consult. If the application is not contentious but the officers are constantly assailed with requests to consult on the application then you may well stir them into a more detailed consideration of the application than they would have previously considered. On the other hand, if they have reservations on any part of the application and nobody goes near them, then it is possible that they will simply report their reservations to the committee and a rejection may follow for something that could have been altered. The question most professionals will ask when telephoning after the consultation period is the simple one, "Can you tell me the current situation on application reference…?" The answer will then be given in the form of a statement of just where the officer has got with the application and they will usually then go on to explain or set out any reservations or objections they may have. Hopefully, if you've followed all the rules, carefully thought out your proposals and made sure that they are non-contentious, the officers will say that everything is alright. If not then they may go on to list some changes that they would like to see and almost certainly they will then confirm this by a letter, similar in format to the one reproduced above.

It may well be that the reservations, if any, expressed by the planning officer, do not disturb you overmuch. In which case your professional, having consulted you first, will quickly move to incorporate the suggestions within the plan and the application will then receive a favourable recommendation and proceed. On the other hand, you may have doubts about some aspects of the officer's objections, in which case a meeting needs to be convened as quickly as possible. Sometimes the planners will call upon the services and request an input from their own architects or conservation officers and when you attend the meeting, you and your architect may be faced with a whole group of people showing an interest in the outcome of your application and

wishing to exert their influence. Whatever the attendance at the meeting, keep calm and make notes of all of the objections and requirements. If you are able to agree things at that meeting which can later be enacted on the plans then fine. If not, then the best thing to do is to simply take away the list and discuss it privately with your advisors. If you feel that there is no compromise then you have the right to insist that your application proceeds unaltered but it will almost certainly proceed to a refusal. In many cases a compromise solution can be reached that will, at the end of the day, satisfy all parties. What you have to keep in your mind at all times is your objective of to build a new home and that means not only in design terms but also in budget terms. Hopefully by reading the earlier chapters of this book you will have anticipated any peculiar requirements for, say, external materials, and hopefully, their imposition will not come as too much of a surprise to you and your budget will accommodate them.

Sometimes a planning officer can be persuaded that your application has merits that they had not realised. Sometimes a Conservation Officer can be persuaded by a series of photographs that you have taken the trouble to incorporate features that are indigenous to the area. Sometimes a planning officer can see that you have followed a particular style in an area which itself has diverse styles of architecture. It all comes down to preparation and thinking about the application and proposals long before they are committed to paper and long before they finally arrive on a planning officer's desk. And that's the path, and the point, this book should have led you to.

What about lobbying at the detailed stages of planning? You can try it, but it isn't nearly as effective as at the 'outline' stages. Local councillors may well be prepared to argue with a professional planner on the question of principle, but not nearly so ready to engage them in long discussions over architectural details or merits. What you can do by lobbying is to bring about a site meeting where the committee convenes on the site. Technically the applicant is not allowed to talk at most site meetings. In practice, when a group of disparate people have entered *your* land, they'll find it very difficult to ignore you and, in most cases I've attended, several questions have been addressed directly to the applicant or their agent. *Do* be careful to keep any answers or matters you have to raise succinct and to the point. *Don't* go off on a tirade about your application and the ills that have befallen you at the hands of the planning officer. Use your democratic right to put your case and then let the people given the power of decision come to their democratic conclusions. Finally, if you are not satisfied with a decision made about a planning application, you have a right of appeal, but it is often better to make application again, in a way which you think is more likely to be approved. If this seems a possibility, visit the planning officer and ask his advice on this in a straightforward way. If you do not get anywhere, only then should you consider an appeal. I shall elaborate on appeals and the appeals procedure a little later on in this chapter but before we get to that there are a few more headings, which need to be considered.

Highways

A new access driveway entering a class 1, 2 or 3 classified road will need planning consent. This is normally dealt with at the same time as your application for the proposed dwelling and there is a duty on the planning authority to consult with the relevant highways authority although there is no requirement on them to accept their recommendations. With class 4 or 5 roads, no planning application is necessary and, instead, the approval and the consent of the highways authority is all that is needed. Trunk roads are a completely different kettle of fish in that they come under the auspices of the Highways Agency. However the Agency devolves its powers, at the time of writing, to County Councils but, in 1999 these will be devolved to private companies.

Resubmissions

If you do get a refusal on your planning application, you can make a resubmission, with no additional fee payable, within twelve months of the date of the refusal. This only applies to the first refusal and not to any subsequent or serial refusals and it must be the same applicant and relate to the same site. If you choose to withdraw an application, you again get another free go but this time it must be made within twelve months of the date of the original application.

Demolition

If you do decide to demolish an existing building, whatever its state of decay, it does not automatically follow that you will get consent to build a replacement. If it is your intention to knock down an existing sub standard dwelling and replace it with a new house, do not do so prior to receipt of planning unless you have specifically cleared it with the planners. Technically demolition is classed as development and it is therefore a better idea for it to be included in the wording of the description of the application for the new house.

If the building is 'Listed' you will need to apply for listed building consent if you want to demolish all or part of it. If it is in a Conservation Area you will need Conservation Area Consent to demolish a building with a volume, which exceeds 115 cubic metres, or any part of such a building. You will also need consent to demolish a wall, gate, fence or railing over 1 metre high adjoining a highway (including a footpath or bridlepath) and over 2 metres high elsewhere.

Permitted development rights

These have been extensively set out in the chapter headed 'Designing a new home – to suit your lifestyle'. Suffice it to say, within this chapter, that the local authority do have the power to restrict or remove some of your Permitted Development Rights by the issuing of what is known as an Article 4 direction. This is normally issued pursuant to an area being made a Conservation area or where the character of an area of acknowledged importance would be threatened by unauthorised or haphazard development. Flats and maisonettes, whilst not falling within the usual selfbuilder's orbit, do not have Permitted Development Rights in the same way as a house does and it is necessary to apply for planning permission to build an extension, an outbuilding such as a garage, shed or greenhouse.

Agricultural consents

In 'Evaluating a site', I warned against the lay person being inveigled into buying a plot with an encumbered consent. However, many selfbuilders are farmers who either wish to create a new home for themselves on the farm or need additional housing for farm workers. Agricultural consents cut across many of the norms in planning and the chances are that if you see a new house being built in a rural position outside the village envelope it is an agricultural consent that has allowed it there. Most development plans state that "development in the rural area shall be resisted unless it is of proven necessity for the proper maintenance or running of agriculture". Before, therefore, any agricultural dwelling will even be considered by the local authority, it is necessary for the applicant to prove the necessity for the new dwelling and the ongoing viability of the farm unit that will support it. A special form will have to filled in to accompany the application, listing the acreage of the farm, its useage and stocking and the number of people employed. This form will also ask what other dwellings are already on the farm and whether any have been separated from the farm or sold off. Some local authorities will evaluate the agricultural viability in house, some will ask for an Agricultural Appraisal from a recognised authority on farming such as an Agricultural Consultancy or a Planning Consultancy specialising in agricultural matters. In all cases, it's best to provide such a report and if, in commissioning that report, it does not come down completely in your favour, it is perhaps best to delay, and to carry out any recommendations made within it before actually making any planning application. On occasion it may be best to consider making application for the temporary siting of a mobile home on the farm until such time as financial viability can be firmly established. Local authorities will often be more amenable to this course of action and after a few years when your presence is firmly established on the farm, when your development plans are sufficiently advanced and your finances are more secure, application can be

made for a permanent new home. I write this, by the way, knowing of the groans of disappointment that will follow, but as the best advice in many a circumstance.

For those for whom viability is not an issue and where the Agricultural Appraisal is full blooded in its support for the new home, it is open for them to consider skipping the outline stage of the planning and going straight to a 'full' application. If no development is to be allowed in the rural area, unless it is of proven necessity for the proper running and maintenance of farming, and you have proved beyond reasonable doubt that your requirement *is* necessary for the proper running and maintenance of your business, why should you bother about the issue of principle? Surely it is already established? What you need to talk about is *what* goes there, not *whether* anything goes there.

Listed building consent

Although this book is primarily aimed at those building their own new home, I appreciate that many who are considering extending, altering, renovating and converting an existing property will find a lot to read about within these pages. Listed building consent is required for any alterations or extensions, to listed buildings including gates, walls and fences. It is also required for any significant works, internal or external, and for the erection of any structure in excess of 10 cubic metres. Also the Permitted Development Rights are severely curtailed, as is the right to demolish, as set out above.

Conservation areas, National parks, Areas of outstanding natural beauty and the Broads

I've covered most of the effects on properties within these areas in the section on Permitted Development Rights both here and in Chapter 8. I would also refer you to the section on demolition above. You will also need consent before cladding the outside of your house, or any part of it, with render, stone, tiles, artificial stone, plastic or timber and, in many cases, all I can say is, a good job too!

Trees

We've also covered trees in quite a lot of detail in earlier chapters. Many trees, or groups of trees are protected by what are known as *Tree Preservation Orders* which mean that you will need the councils consent to prune, lop or fell them. In addition there are many other controls over trees in Conservation Areas.

Rights of way

A footpath cannot be diverted or closed without an order being made by the council. This order must be advertised and anyone may object. Unless such an order is confirmed you do not have the right to obstruct or divert a footpath and there are powerful organisations whose major interest is in the preservation and maintenance of footpaths. If you have one crossing your plot, do not think for one moment that you can re-route it around the outside of your garden without the express order of the council and do not think that its granting will be in any way automatic.

Mobile homes

Everyone gets the jitters when a large mobile home suddenly arrives on a site. Neighbours think that their leafy suburban street is about to be turned into a Tinkers' encampment and many planners act as if they are about to be besieged by hordes of New Age travellers. If you are putting a mobile home on your site, either to use as a site hut or to live in whilst you selfbuild, it's useful to know where you stand and just what your rights are. Provided the caravan is there to facilitate the building works, you do not need consent for it, even if you decide to live in it. If possible delay the siting of the new home until such time as you have at least made an application for planning permission and preferably just before work actually starts on the site. If you do have to move in prior to any of this, then you'll find it much more difficult to maintain that the mobile home is sited in connection with any building works and you might be required to apply for planning consent. Otherwise you might like to consider that most of the processes which the authorities can take to remove you will take quite a long time and that, in all probability, by

the time any final judgements are made, you'll have long since moved into your new house and disposed of the mobile home.

Wildlife

All of us are concerned in some way to preserve our wildlife and flora but, sometimes our concerns come into conflict with our wish to build a new home. It is illegal to disturb a badger set and it is also illegal to dig up or disturb some extremely rare plants. Some houses may hold roosts of bats or provide a refuge for other protected species. English Nature or the Countryside Council for Wales must be notified of any action including remedial timber treatment, renovation, demolition or extensions and they must be given time to consider and advise on the best course of action.

Appeals

An appeal is always made against the reasons for refusal and although other arguments can be brought into play it is the reasons for refusal which must be concentrated upon. You can appeal against the refusal of a planning application and you can also appeal against any conditions that are imposed within a consent. In addition you also have the right of appeal against the local authorities failure to determine an application.

If there are conditions on an approval by the local authority, that you feel are unfair or unreasonable, and the local authority refuse to vary or remove them, then you can appeal against the imposition of those conditions. *Beware* – the Inspector will consider the whole of the application again and he can change other conditions that you had not previously objected to and he can impose new conditions! He can even reverse the local authorities decision altogether, although if he is thinking of doing so, you will be informed and given an opportunity to withdraw the appeal and stick with the local authority's original approval and conditions.

An appeal against a local authority's failure to determine is all well and good on paper but the reality is that most authorities, faced with such an appeal, will move to determine the application

prior to the appeal being actually conducted. There is nothing to prevent a new application being made at the same time as an appeal is being entered into.

Costs are normally borne by each party, whichever method of appeal is decided upon. It is open for either party, however, to request that the other party pay their costs either in part or in whole, and the Inspector will decide the merits of such an application. He will only award costs against a party if he feels that they have acted in an unreasonable, vexatious or frivolous manner.

The first thing to do when thinking about an appeal is how, or whether, you can avoid one. Seek out an early meeting with the planning officer to discuss whether or not there is another way forward. At this meeting it is most important that you are not aggressive, sarcastic, or waste his time by explaining how unfair you consider the planning laws to be. You should be seen to be a most reasonable person, and take an early opportunity to say that you know he cannot commit the council in any way in his discussions with you. This will make him much more likely to be helpful, either by suggesting a way in which you can frame a further application which he may be able to support, or by giving you a clear idea of exactly what the council thinks about the issue, which is going to be useful when you are considering appeal tactics.

If the planning officer will not discuss the matter in a helpful way, do not assume he is being deliberately unfriendly. It may be that your category of application is a very hot political issue locally, and that he feels obliges to deal with you in a very formal way. If this is the case, you can at least ask him to advise you about the planning history of the area and ask for a copy of the recommendation which he made to the council in respect of your application. Of course, you should have been aware of the planning history before you made your application, but you may find to your surprise that there have been a string of previous refusals on applications made by other people, and that this was a major factor in the council's decision.

Sometimes local politics come into play in such a way that the local authority does not want to be seen to be granting consent for certain types of development even though they know that they cannot sustain that argument at a higher level. It will be denied, of course, but there are cases when it appears that it is almost a deliberate policy to refuse applications knowing full well that their refusal will be overturned at appeal. What happens here, of course, is that when the applicant is finally successful, the local authority can turn around and claim that it was all none of their doing, thus keeping on the right side of their local critics.

It may be that the council considered that the design, siting, materials or some other feature of the proposed dwelling was inappropriate. If this is the case, it is even much more important that you establish an effective relationship with the planning officer to see if you can reach an agreement on features which he will find acceptable.

All of this adds up to the advice that you should try every way of getting approval by making further applications. A planning appeal should be your last resort, both because it effectively closes the book if it is unsuccessful, and also because it will take between five and nine months to get a decision. This time lag is usually critical to those building on their own.

What are your chances of success? Well, although most appeals are disallowed, quite a few are successful and all in all you've probably got a 50/50 chance. It all depends on so many things. The Inspector will consider any appeal on the basis of its planning merits and any personal circumstances are unlikely to influence his decision. An important factor in any consideration is whether or not the proposal fits into the local development plan. This development plan is made up of the approved structure plan and the local plan, if there is one, together with the old style development plan, if it is still in force. You recall that I wrote about 'zoning' earlier and that I also mentioned village 'envelopes'. The Inspector will be concerned that your proposal does not conflict with these adopted plans, or any plan which is being prepared, and he will also be concerned to see that you have followed any published advice given out by your local planning

authority. If you are appealing against a refusal for a scheme which conflicts with these policies or endeavours to create development in the 'green belt', then your chances of success are fairly minimal. If, on another site, within the village envelope or within an area zoned as residential, you can put together a reasonable case, with details of precedents in your area, then your chances are greatly increased. Tour the area and look out for similar buildings in similar situations which have obviously recently been built. Ask about them and find out the details, from the local authority planning register, relating to their approval and how they came by it. If they were granted on appeal then get a copy of the appeal documents and see if there is any argument in them which you can use on your own appeal. In every case I have been involved in, the Inspector has always taken the trouble to visit these 'precedent' sites beforehand and has referred to them both on site and in his eventual decision.

An appeal must be made within six months of the notice of refusal and the first thing you should do is to write to the appropriate office of the planning inspectorate and obtain, firstly the necessary forms and, secondly, and most importantly, a copy of their excellent booklet entitled 'A

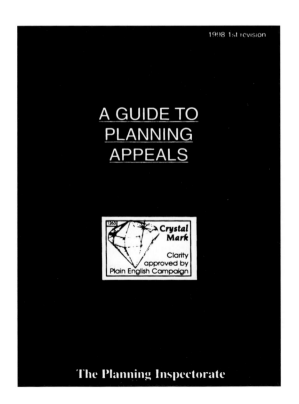

1998 1st revision

A GUIDE TO
PLANNING
APPEALS

Crystal
Mark
Clarity
approved by
Plain English Campaign

The Planning Inspectorate

guide to planning appeals'. From this you will discover that there are two sorts of appeal process, the written procedure and the inquiry procedure, with the latter type being subdivided into the informal hearing and the full blown local inquiry. The booklet explains the differences between them and gives excellent general advice accompanied by flow charts showing how each type of appeal progresses.

At this point you have to decide whether you are going to handle the appeal yourself, or whether you are going to retain someone to deal with it for you. Many people do handle their own appeals, and the procedures are not difficult. The inspectors are not influenced one way or the other by finding they are dealing with the appellant rather than with a professional. However, the professional may be much better than you at marshalling and presenting the facts, and it is the facts on which the appeal will be determined. You should be very sure of yourself before you decide to handle your own planning appeal.

If you do not do so you will have to find someone to deal with it for you, and it is important that he or she has a great deal of relevant experience of handling appeals against refusals to allow individual houses to be built on individual sites in your local area, preferably with a track record of winning! It may be difficult to find the right man: your solicitor or architect should be able to advise you, or if you are on good terms with the planning officer he may be able to point you in the right direction. If you then take your papers to the person concerned they should be able to quote you a fixed fee for which they will handle everything for you. Beware anyone who says they will require a fee just to read your papers and appraise your situation. He or she is probably far too high powered for your job, and is probably more used to conducting planning appeals for supermarkets. You can simply ask a planning consultant "Are you the right person to deal with this for me? If not, can you suggest someone else who I should go and see?".

Any full description of how to conduct a written planning appeal is beyond the scope of this book, but the key points are as follows.

An appeal is against the reasons for refusal,

and starts off with your written submission explaining why these reasons are inappropriate. You do not have to set out the reasons why your application should have been granted. You must deal only with the actual reasons for refusal listed on the refusal certificate, and explain that they are unreasonable. It will require a considerable mental discipline to restrict your submission to this simple formula, but anything else which you write is irrelevant. If a professional is putting this document together for you, you should ask him to let you have a look at it before he sends it off. If you are dealing with the appeal yourself, then somehow you should try to look at papers relating to other appeals. The English used is not important, nor is the quality of the typing or handwriting, but it is essential to restrict yourself to dealing with the reasons for refusal. Avoid any extravagant language. Do not describe the council's decision on your application as a diabolical liberty: the correct phrase is that it "failed to take all the circumstances into account"!

A copy of your opening broadside is sent to the local planning authority, which then has four weeks in which to produce its own written reply. If it does not reply within four weeks, then the appeal carries on without the council having a say.

It is quite amazing the number of times a local authority actually fails to respond and instead relies only upon the terms of its original rejection. Sometimes this is because of the pressure of work. Sometimes it is because personnel have changed, or are on holiday, and sometimes it is because the local authority have nothing more to add to their original reasons for refusal. You will receive a copy of the council's written statement, and you have two weeks in which you can submit your comments on the council's comments. It is unwise to arrange to be on holiday during this period. Following this exchange of statements there is a long pause, and then after some months you will receive a letter from the planning inspector concerned saying that he proposes to visit the site on such and such a date. The site visit is important. The local authority will be represented, and of course you will go along yourself, accompanied by anyone representing you. At the visit the inspector will not allow either party to make any further submissions, nor will he discuss their written submissions with them. His purpose in visiting the site is simply to see the situation on the ground, and you and your agent, and the planning officer, are simply there to answer his questions. With some inspectors this will take the form of fairly perfunctory questions like, "Is this the brick wall you will be removing in order to create the visibility splays?" But, with others, the conversation can widen out to a quite detailed discussion of each aspect of the appeal that he identifies. The important thing to do is to realise that the Inspector is in the driving seat. If you try to browbeat him and launch into a detailed speech about your application and why you feel that he should support you, you will be doing little else other than harming your case. Respond to his questions quietly and get your points across within your replies. Stay close enough to the group as they walk around to be able to hear the answers given by the representative from the local authority so that, at an opportune moment you can counter anything that you feel to be untrue. Avoid any display of enmity between yourself and any other representative and at all costs avoid any direct argument with any other party. If any other representative gets angry remember that by your very calmness contrasted with their anger, you are probably doing your case a lot of good. Above all, let the Inspector make the running in much the same way as you would a judge in court and defer at all times to his conducting of the appeal.

Finally, about a month after the site visit you will receive the Inspector's findings, and these are final. If you have won, they act as your planning consent. If you have lost you must realise that you have come to the end of the road with that application. Only if there is a major change in the local planning situation, or if a substantially different scheme is adopted, is any further planning application likely to be successful.

The whole of this process will probably take between five and nine months. You can do nothing to hurry it up. There is a provision in legislation for the Inspector to give an Advanced Notice of Decision before he issues his official finding, but this is very, very unusual. In over twenty years of dealing with appeals for selfbuilders the writer can only remember one such occasion. A couple wanted a house on their successful smallholding. The council said that the holding could not be economically viable, refused the house but gave temporary consent for a caravan for twelve months, indicating that consent for a house would follow if the venture had not failed. Four years later the smallholding was prospering, but four further applications for the house had all been rejected on the grounds that the holding was not economically viable. There was an appeal. At the site visit the inspector was totally noncommittal. When he had seen everything he turned to the lady who had coped with living in a caravan for four years with small children and said that he had seen all he wanted, and that he would issue his decision in a month's time. He paused, and for the first time he smiled. "It will seem a long month", he said "I suggest you spend the time choosing curtains".

But it isn't always like that.

Scotland

The observant amongst you will have noticed that in many of these headings, details are given for England and Wales, whilst none are given for Scotland. It wouldn't make sense, within this book, to fully explore and comment on the differences between the legal systems of Scotland and England. Suffice it to say that the legal system in Scotland is different in many respects, although many of the principles remain. The planning system is also slightly different but, again, many of the principles and all of the procedures are essentially the same.

14 Building Regulations, drawings and specifications

Planning permission is subjective and deals with whether you build a new home at all and, if so, what it will look like. Building Regulations Consent, on the other hand, is objective and confines itself to the structural aspects of the build by reference to the regulations themselves. An application for approval under the Building Regulations either conforms to those regulations and is approved, or else it fails to conform to them and is rejected, unless, in very peculiar circumstances, such as with a thatched roof, a relaxation can be negotiated.

The Building Regulations cover the structural and safety aspects of any construction and draw together a mass of other health and environmental issues. They are set out in denominated parts that deal with each aspect of building and it would not make sense for this book to examine in great detail or discuss anything other than generalities. The regulations are changed on a regular basis and it is the job of architects, designers and other professionals working within the industry to keep themselves up to date with those changes and to incorporate their requirements within any plans that they prepare or process. It is also their job, by inference, to make themselves as aware as possible of any impending changes to the legislation and these are usually warned of in advance by way of published discussion papers and consultations.

The Building Regulations are usually administered by the Building Control department of the local authority who have a statutory obligation to enforce them and oversee their functions within their boundaries. However, the government has also devolved the authority to inspect and certify compliance under the Building Regulations to other bodies, such as the NHBC, and in addition it is open for architects with the appropriate professional indemnity insurance to register to carry out this work, although my impression is that very few, especially those appropriate to the selfbuild industry, have done so. I have discussed the possible role of the NHBC in all of this in the chapter on 'Finance' so in this chapter I will confine most of my comments to the service and administration of the regulations being carried out by the local authority.

In most local authorities the planning department and the Building Control department are situated in close proximity to each other and are usually lumped together as 'Technical Services'. Make no mistake though, these are separate departments operating and receiving their powers through and from completely separate Acts of Parliament. Although they can, and usually do, co-operate with each other, there is no certainty of this and it is possible to fall between conflicting legislation and interpretations. Planning says you *may* build something – it does not say that you *can* build something. If you get express planning permission for something or it is implied that you have planning consent for, say, Permitted Development, then it does not absolve you from having to seek Building Regulations approval for that development, either expressly or, by implication due to exemption.

In like manner, if one achieves Building Regulations consent for a structure, it does not mean that you can build it without planning permission, again, either expressly or implied. A porch, for example, may well be exempt from the Building Regulations in some circumstances and, in many locations, its construction could well take place under the Permitted Development rights laid down by the planning laws. In a Conservation area those Permitted Development rights could well be curtailed or removed and the fact that the porch could be built under a Building Regulations exemption would do nothing to change that situation.

Building Regulations approval is required if you intend to carry out any of the following works:

* Erect a new building or extend an existing building (unless it is covered by the list of exemptions below and later).

* Make structural alterations to a building, including underpinning.

* In certain cases, a change of use.

* Provide, extend or alter drainage facilities.

* Install a heat producing appliance (with the exception of gas appliances installed by

persons approved under the Gas Safety regulations).

* Installation of cavity insulation.

* Installation of an unvented hot water storage system.

You do not need Building Regulations approval to:

* Install or replace electric wiring.

* Replace a roof covering, so long as the same roof covering is used in the repair.

* Install new sanitaryware, so long as it doesn't involve new drainage or plumbing arrangements.

* Carry out repairs as long as they are of a minor nature and replace like for like.

I appreciate that much of the above will not apply to those building a new home but it may be of interest to those carrying out extensions or refurbishments to existing dwellings. It's as well to contact the Building Control department if you're in any doubt about whether, or not, you need to apply for Building Regulations approval.

In addition to the exclusions listed above there are common types of building work that are exempt from the regulations:

* The erection of a detached single storey building with a floor area of less than 30 square metres, so long as it does not contain any sleeping accommodation, so long as no part of it is less than one metre from any boundary and so long as it is constructed of non combustible material.

* The erection of any detached building not exceeding 15 square metres, so long as there is no sleeping accommodation.

* The extension of a building by a ground floor extension of a) a conservatory, porch, covered yard or covered way, or, b) a carport open on a least two sides, so long as, in any of those cases, the floor area of the extension does not exceed 30 square metres. In the case of a conservatory or a wholly or

partially glazed porch, the glazing has to satisfy the requirements of those parts of the Building Regulations dealing with glazing materials and protection.

At the risk of being repetitive, I must stress that one may well still need planning permission for any of these works and that, if there is any doubt, you should consult the planning department of your local authority.

For the selfbuilder, the timing of any application for Building Regulations approval is an important issue, as most selfbuilders want to make a start on site just as soon as planning permission is granted. In England and Wales a Building Regulations application has to be accompanied by the necessary fees for the approval stages, after which the local authority has five weeks to process and determine the application. In practice, many applications cannot be determined within the statutory period and it has become almost commonplace for applications to be rejected several times, with each fresh, and happily free, application dealing with different points raised. Such a system, which often seems almost incredible to the lay person, would not have evolved were it not for two important points. Firstly the legislation is worded such that it is necessary to have *made* an application for Building Regulations Approval or issued a Building Notice, prior to commencement of works and, secondly the fees for the necessary inspections stages are separated and, with a Full Plans application, payable *after* the issuing of an approval.

This means that, as long as 48 hours notice in writing is given of one's intention to start work on a site, following an application for Building Regulations approval or the issuing of a Building Notice, then there is nothing to stop you doing so. The building does, however, still have to be inspected and approved as it proceeds and the Building Inspectors will, therefore, come along and inspect at the relevant stages. If they approve of the work, you may then carry on to the next stage in the normal way. If they do not approve or cannot sanction what you are doing, then you have to stop until either the approval is granted, or the necessary information is received that will allow them to agree to your continuing work.

Effectively that means that, although you will be advised that by working prior to the formal approval of the plans, you are proceeding at risk. So long as you do not go beyond that which the building inspector has agreed and approved on site, you aren't really in any different a position to the chap who already has Building Regulations approval. The essential rule is that nothing is built that fails to conform to the regulations and, if therefore, the inspector feels that the work is contrary to the regulations then, whether or not you have a formal approval, he will stop you and he has legally enforceable powers to do so. I don't think it's bandied about too much but my guess is, on personal experience, that maybe as many as 60% of new selfbuild dwellings commence work without having a formal Building Regulations approval.

In Scotland the application has to be accompanied by a fee that encompasses both the application and the subsequent inspections and that then puts the making of the application into more or less the same category as the person in England and Wales, who has to decide whether it's a good idea to make the application at the same time as the planning application. Obviously there is merit in the idea of having both approvals on the table as one commences work on site but there are some possible financial penalties involved.

With a planning application it is possible for plans to be radically or even completely altered, yet still remain under the auspices of the original application. No such sanction is given with a Building Regulations application. If the design changes then a completely fresh Building Regulations application will have to be made, attracting an equally fresh fee. As if the fee to the local authority weren't enough, you could also find yourself having to spend considerable monies on the preparation of new detailed plans with any expensive calculations or engineer's details having to be repeated. You can see, therefore, that care needs to be taken and that a Building Regulations application should only be made when it is pretty certain that you know

what you are going to be building.

There are two alternative procedures available to choose from in order to obtain Building Regulations approval – Deposit of Full Plans or The Building Notice.

Dealing with the last one first. If you choose this option then no detailed plans are generally required, as a far greater emphasis is placed on site inspection and supervision, although, further details and/or plans may be requested during the course of the build. The fee is the combined total of the relevant application and commencement fees, so there is no saving to be made by this method as far as local authority fees go. This procedure is really only applicable to works of a completely straightforward nature where the party carrying out the works is totally conversant with the requirements of the regulations as, without plans there is no detailed check on the proposal before the work is carried out, and therefore, no official decision notice is issued. The advantage is that there can be a saving in time and costs due to not having to prepare and submit detailed plans. The disadvantages are that, firstly, there is no approved plan to work to and, whilst the Inspector will try to anticipate problems there can be delays and/or costly remedial works if any of the work fails to comply with the regulations. Secondly, building estimates may be inaccurate without the benefit of detailed plans to work to. In all the years I have been in the industry, I have no experience of any selfbuilder using this procedure. Whilst many selfbuilders proceed with the construction of their new homes without a formal Building Regulations approval having been issued, to do so without the benefit of detailed plans and full constructional details would seem to be singularly inadvisable.

A *Full Plans* application has to be accompanied by plans showing the full constructional details of the proposed work and, whether or not you managed to do the plans yourself for the planning application, these plans need to be prepared by a professional. If that's you, then fine. If not then you really need to examine your motives, swallow your 'go it alone' pride and engage a professional for this bit.

A full plans application should include:

1. The relevant application forms fully completed and with the appropriate fee. (This fee is for the application only and there is another fee payable at the commencement of works that will then cover the necessary inspections.)

2. Detailed drawings at 1:50 scale for floor plans, 1:100 for elevations and 1:500 for site plans. These should include floor plans, typical and particular sections, elevations and site details and boundaries.

3. A full written specification which can either be noted on the plans or provided separately and then cross referenced.

The advantages of the Full Plans application procedure are that you will then be working to set plans along set guidelines and in strict accordance, at all times, with the regulations. Many of the lenders require that a Building Regulations application is made and some, but not all, will require a formal approval before commencement of work. The disadvantage is that time needs to be allowed for the preparation of the plans, prior to application and commencement of work. In the end, both that and the cost of the preparation of the plans are, perhaps, a constant factor and, as I've said, the thought of a selfbuilder trying to build their own home without the benefit of detailed plans gives me the jiggers.

When the plans are received by the Building Control department they are then checked out thoroughly, often by means of a plan vetting checklist similar to the one reproduced here. If the proposals are straightforward and the work shown on the plans complies in all respects with the regulations, then an approval will be issued as soon as possible and certainly within the five weeks deadline. If, for any reason, your proposals do not satisfy the regulations or there are some unclear areas or points, then the Inspector will write to you inviting you to amend the plans accordingly, in order to bring about compliance.

When dealing with planning applications it is wonderful to dream that your finished home will look like this.

Negotiations on a Building Regulations application: what to expect

The letter below is a typical communication from a local authority following a Building Regulation application. It is in no way unusual, and irrespective of the amount of detail shown on the drawings submitted, queries of this nature can be expected from most local authorities.

FOREST OF DEAN DISTRICT COUNCIL

High Street, Coleford, Glos., GL16 8HG.   Tel: (01594) 810000

	Planning & Leisure Services Fax: (01594) 812314
DX 94102 COLEFORD	Housing & Environmental Services Fax: (01594) 812230
	Other Services Fax: (01594) 812590

BUILDING CONTROL SERVICES
J M CHETCUTI - FCIOB FBEng FASI MIBC WOBO

Minicom: (01594) 812500

Mr A. Anybody	Please ask for:	Myself	Direct Line:
12 Acacia Avenue			
Anytown	Our Ref: M/1		
Anywhere			
GT LFE	Your Ref: Y/1		
	Date: 1/1/1		

SCHEDULE OF AMENDMENTS NECESSARY
OR ADDITIONAL INFORMATION REQUIRED

1)   Confirm:-
   a)   Species of trees/shrubs shown on site plan
   b)   Width of foundation taking into account the proposed foundation depth (slenderness ratio)
   c)   Material to be used for anti heave precautions and its thickness. Forward detailed drawing of foundation and anti heave material.

2)   Forward manufacturer's details in respect of precast concrete floor.

3)   Forward lintel schedule inclusive of timber lintels above first floor windows.

4)   Justify adequacy of the 147 x 47mm rafters to the 20 degree pitch roof over bathroom area.

5)   First floor joist layout required – show support of all first floor walls and detail stair trimmers. What beams are required where the two No. ? marks are shown on the structural engineers drawing No.3857/2?

6)   Structural engineer's drawing No.3857/1 appears incorrect in relation to position of chimney stack. Show trimming of floor joists and roof timber around stack.

7)   Stud partition wall between bedroom 2 & 3 to be 40mm off brick stack or 200mm from flue.

8)   Indicate position of smoke detectors on floor plans.

9)   Wall between garage and utility to be fire stopped to underside of roof above.

10) External render to comply with BS 5262

11) Provide cavity trays above air bricks.

12) Specify roof tiles suitable for all roof pitches.

13) Method of weather resistance to dormer cheeks/walls etc. Provision of vapour barriers, breather papers etc. beneath cladding, as appropriate.

14) Show connection of kitchen gully to foul drain. Provision of rodding access.

15) Forward surface water drainage plan.

16) Provision of guard to boiler terminal if within 2M of ground level. Show position of boiler in relation to openings for the dwelling. Confirm type of boiler/fuel etc.

17) Confirm cill height of first floor windows, in particular to bathroom (protection from falling).

18) Forward details of blockwork to cavity walls to achieve 0.45 'U'value.

19) Specify air gap to double glazed units.

20) SAP rating to be provided within 5 days of completion of dwelling.

Meg Holborow, B.Sc., Dip. T.P., M.R.T.P.I., Head of Paid Service and Director of Strategy
David A. Matthams, C.P.F.A., Director of Central Services
Tim Perrin, B.Sc., M.C.I.E.H., F.C.I.H., Director of Housing & Environmental Services
Jim Stewart, B.A., M.C.D., M.R.T.P.I., Director of Planning & Leisure Services
Laurence J. Harding, LL.B., Dip.L.G., Solicitor to the Council

Building Control Services

There may also be additional details and calculations that are required and in some cases it is possible for an approval to be issued conditional upon the subsequent receipt of this information. If you're building in timber frame then the details and calculations for the timber frame itself may not actually be prepared and available until the frame is in the process of being manufactured. In these cases, as with roof trusses and steel purlins, the consent will be issued as a conditional consent and work may well be allowed to continue up to and until these elements are reached. On the other hand, if the inspector has reason to suspect that there are conditions in the ground that will require a site/soil investigation and the design of special foundations, then it is not possible for any work to commence and therefore no conditional consent could, or should, be issued. In this case you will need to turn back to the chapter 'Designing a new home – to suit your site' and refer to the section on foundations and you will need to find out the names of the appropriate professionals who can act on your behalf. Your architect, designer or package deal company can probably assist and, in truth, they will probably already have anticipated this requirement. Alternatively, the Building Inspector, himself, may well be able to give you a few pointers, although he'll be careful not to recommend one party and will, instead, give you a few names to choose from.

The detailed plans will also have to be sent to your warranty company and in most cases if there is any suspicion of bad ground or a special foundation situation, they will require exactly the same information as the Building Inspector wants and may well require at least 3 weeks notice of any intention to start work in those circumstances. If the NHBC is carrying out the role of inspecting and approving under the Building Regulations or if they are merely acting as your warranty company, and you are building in timber frame, they will also require an HB353B certificate to be supplied by the frame manufacturer or designer.

The Building Control department, in much the same way as the planning departments, have a statutory duty to consult with certain agencies and departments. If a proposal for a new building involves drainage and the discharge of effluent either into the subsoil or to a watercourse, then they have to consult with the Environment Agency. If the Environment Agency flag up a problem then the Building Control department will, in effect, act as their agent in enforcing their requirements and in making sure that your application is amended to take their recommendations into account. The Building Control department will also consult other agencies and departments including and especially those dealing with fire, highways and public health.

If, and it does often happen, all of these questions, amendments and additional information cannot be provided within the five week period following the application, then a rejection notice will be issued. If you're already building at this time, then a new application will have to be made as soon as possible but if you haven't started building then you cannot do so until and unless, either a new application is submitted or a Building Notice is issued and the requisite 48 hours notice is given. The principle of serial applications and rejections is, for many local authorities, an established fact and a normal way of proceeding. Others state that they do not regard rejection as a particularly productive exercise and make strenuous efforts to approve Full Plans applications as quickly as possible. They are helped in that endeavour if the relevant information is provided at the application stage and if any anticipated requirements for calculations, soil and site investigations and foundation design details are available before, rather than after or approaching, their five week deadlines. Once again attendance at the school of forward planning will pay off.

If a formal approval has been issued it will usually be done so in attendance with a set of cards, each of which covers a particular stage in the construction of your new home. Even if you don't have these cards or, if you are proceeding with the construction prior to the issuing of a formal approval or under a Building Notice, you are required to notify the inspector at these stages. Obviously for things like loft conversions the stages will be different but in general for new build they are:

* Excavations for foundations

* Foundation concrete

* Oversite

* Damp proof course

* Foul water drains

* Surface water drains

* Occupation prior to completion

* Completion

You will hear stories about not having to wait for the inspector beyond a certain period and of carrying on beyond these stages if the inspector fails to turn up. Ignore them please. The stages are carefully worked out so that no important work is irrevocably covered up before it has been adequately inspected and approved. If the Building Inspector feels that you have covered up something that is wrong or that you have carried out work that is in defiance of the regulations, he has the power to order their exposure and you will bear the cost.

Apart from the obvious example of foundations and below ground work, there is one other aspect of routine inspection that is taken very seriously and that is drains. These need to be inspected *before* they are covered up and they then need to be tested, usually involving pressure hoses and gauges. Now, you may feel that just leaving various sections or connections open will suffice, but you would be wrong and you will find that the inspector will want to see everything and that he will want to satisfy himself, in particular, that they are properly surrounded in pea gravel. In the end he has the legal right of enforcement and he has the right to issue what is known as a 'Stop Notice' that will bring your entire site to a grinding halt until such time as you have either rectified the incorrect work or satisfied him that the work is in order.

All of this serves to illustrate a radical difference between planning consent and Building Regulations approval and one that often confuses lay people. With planning permission,

you have consent to build exactly what is shown on the plans and although the authorities do have some discretionary powers that I've already outlined, essentially, you have consent to build *only* that which is on the approved drawings and referred to in the consent. With Building Regulations, the plans are approved as being in accordance with the regulations but, then, after the consent is issued, the inspector has the power to vary the construction. For example, if your plans show a one metre strip foundation and your Building Regulations approval was granted on that premiss but, when it comes to digging the foundations, the ground is found to be unsuitable, then the inspector can, and will, require you to change tack. He may well require you to have a soil investigation carried out or, a special foundation designed by an engineer and he will require that you stop work until such time as everything is agreed. It is no good pointing to your plans and saying that they were approved with the one metre strip foundations. The inspector's job in assessing your application was to make sure that what was *drawn* conformed to the regulations as far as was foreseeable. The inspector's job, on the other hand, when inspecting your building works, is to make sure that what is *built* conforms to the regulations. If he feels that, due to conditions experienced or evidenced on site, changes need to be made, then he has the powers to require those changes.

It's at this point that selfbuilders can become a trifle upset at this official who's insisting on changes, delaying the job and costing them a great deal more money. In some cases the inspector can almost be seen as being in cahoots with the warranty inspector, with them both conspiring to push your selfbuild project off budget. Nothing is further from the truth. If any of these officials or inspectors feel that it's necessary for changes to be made, then they are doing so in the interests of the stability and integrity of your new home and for no other reason. Their reasons and their objectives, therefore, coincide quite nicely with yours and, if you've taken note of the preceding chapters, then it's quite probable that you've already budgeted for the eventuality or allowed for its possibility

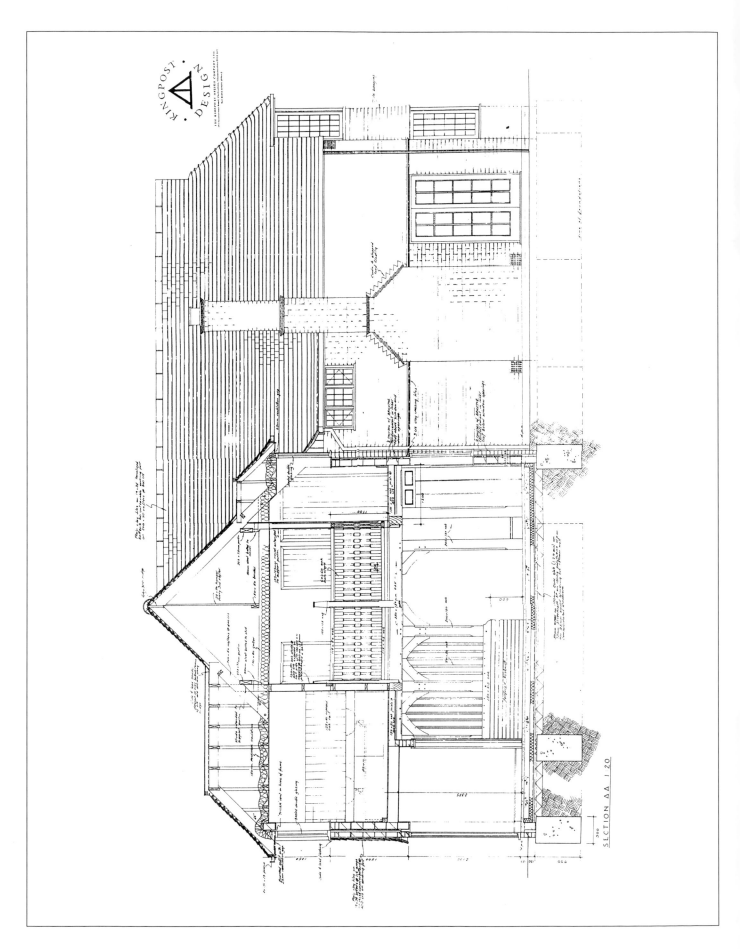

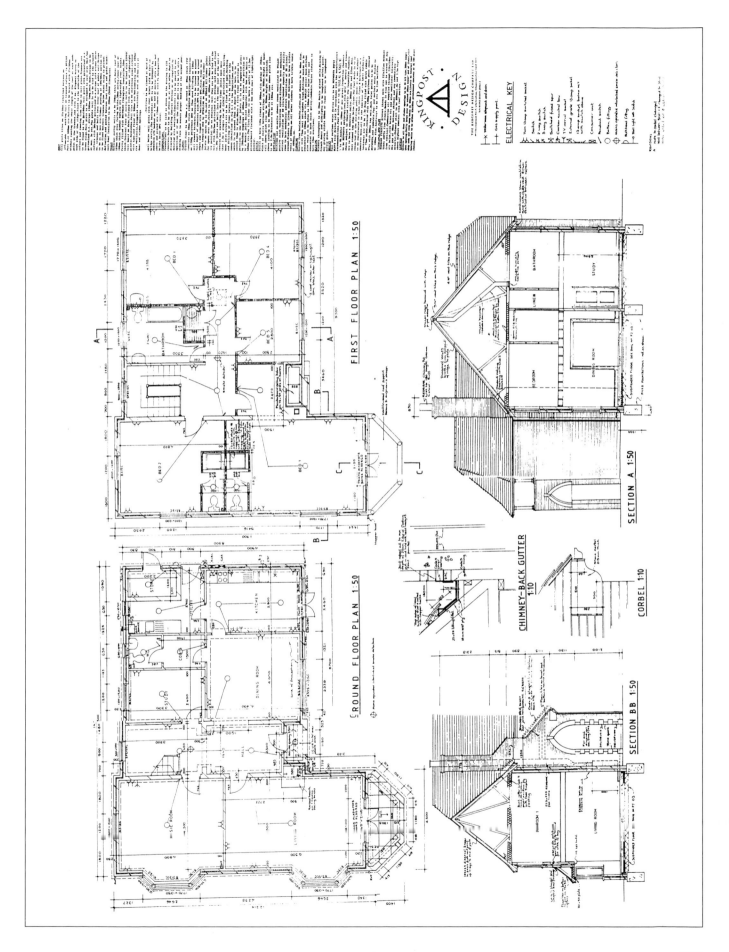

FIRST FLOOR PLAN 1:50

GROUND FLOOR PLAN 1:50

SECTION A 1:50

SECTION B B 1:50

CHIMNEY-BACK GUTTER 1:10

CORBEL 1:10

KINGPOST · DESIGN

ELECTRICAL KEY

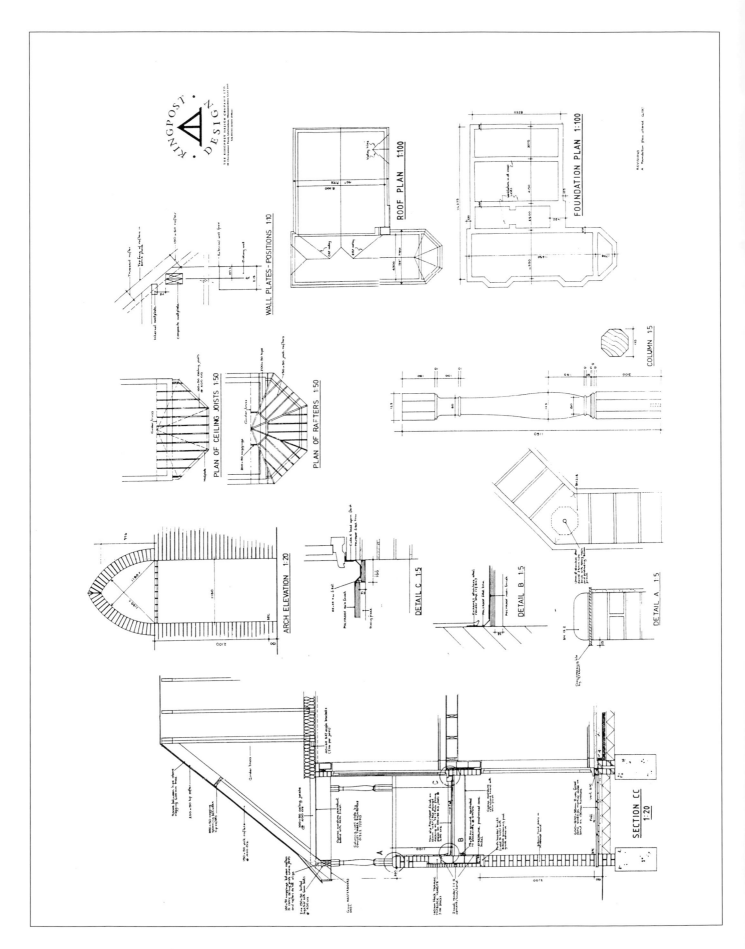

within your contingency fund.

Most medieval cathedrals were built with the aid of fewer drawings than are now considered necessary for the construction of a public lavatory. Nevertheless, many of them suffered failures of some sort and in some cases these were catastrophic. In others the flying buttresses, we now admire so much, were added at a later date, or during the construction when it became apparent that the structure was about to fail. You can't go on like that and today's regulations, and all that has preceded this paragraph, are designed to ensure that, as far as is possible, all that can be known, assessed or calculated to ensure the stability and structural integrity of your new home, is known and appreciated *before* you start work.

The working drawings play a big part in all of this and a properly prepared set of drawings goes an awful long way to making sure that there are as few queries as possible during the construction process. In some cases they are the same as for the Building Regulations application. In others they are elaborate sets of drawings, illustrating aspects of the build as far apart as the foundation design through to the intricate detailing on the corbelling. Either way these are important documents and their treatment on site does not always reflect that importance. Rolled up in a back pocket or stuffed into a bucket of tools at best and left out in the rain at worst, is it any wonder if details become smudged or obliterated and things get built wrongly. Properly pinned up in the site hut or better still laminated, they will remain in pristine condition and fulfil their purpose for the whole of the build.

Construction drawings are also used by subcontractors to design their services. An electrician will require a drawing which he will mark up with the wiring layout, and the plumbing and heating engineer will want drawings for the same purpose. Others will be required when the kitchen is being planned. Central heating drawings are often provided free of charge by the fuel advisory agencies, and the kitchen layouts can be obtained from various bodies, but they all start with a print of the actual construction drawing.

All setting out of construction work should be done in the units used for the design, and the converted dimensions should be used with considerable caution as they are invariably 'rounded off' and, if added together, will give rise to significant errors.

Remember that room sizes on construction drawings are masonry sizes and that the finished dimensions from plaster surface to plaster surface will be about 25mm (1 in) smaller.

Carpet sizes will be about two inches smaller still, allowing for skirting thicknesses.

Revisions to drawings are normally made by altering the master drawing. When this is done the fact that the drawing has been altered should always be noted on it, and the date added. Prints of the unrevised drawing which are then out of date should be carefully collected and destroyed to avoid confusion.

Drawings for complex projects are normally accompanied by a specification (written by an architect), and a bill of quantities (compiled by a quantity surveyor). Between them these highly technical documents describe and define every detail of the building but they are only relevant to a building contract that is being supervised by an architect. However, a simple specification, usually referred to as a short form of specification, can be of use to an individual builder who is not using an architect and who needs to place a contract with a builder.

A short form of specification follows. This sample specification should only be used as a guide for drawing up your own specification for your own particular project. It should not just be copied and you do need to read it very carefully to see whether or not it conforms to what you are trying to achieve. For instance you may not agree that the prime cost sums, referred to in clause No.6, should allow the builder to gain any discounts that are available. Kitchen units and sanitaryware, in particular, often have discounts of 50%, and possibly more, and you might think that this money is better off in your pocket than in somebody else's. In this case you will need to rewrite this clause to the effect that the discounts available should be passed on to you either in all respects, or on named or particular items. If you

Typical short form of specification

A full architect's or quantity surveyor's specification is a long and complex document, couched in technical jargon, and defining materials, methods of construction and standards. Relatively few new homes on clients' own land are built with full specifications, and many are built without the essential definitions of key elements in the builder's contract. This short form of specification covers these definitions, but avoids technicalities by referring to well-known published standards, particularly the NHBC or Zurich Building Manuals. **This specification is an example only, and is intended as a guide to drawing up a specification for a specific contract for a specific house.**

1. This specification relates to a contract established by ... (detail form of contract, if any, or exchange of quotation and acceptance which establishes the contract) and is a schedule to that contract. The contract is between the client ... (name and address) and the builder ... (name and address) and is a simple contract between the client and the builder. Neither the designer, any supplier of materials or any sub-contractor are party to this contract.

2. This specification refers to a house to be built to the drawings attached, which have been initialled and dated by both parties, and all notes on these drawings are part of the specification.

3. The builder shall obtain a NHBC or Zurich Newbuild certificate for the property, and shall provide the client with the documentation relating to this in accordance with standard NHBC or Zurich Newbuild practice before work commences. All materials and work shall be to the requirements of the NHBC or Zurich Builders' Handbook, and shall follow the further recommendations laid down in the NHBC or Zurich site manuals and practice notes.

4. Time will be the essence of the contract and the builder is to start the works on ... (date) or as soon as practicable thereafter, and shall finish the whole of the works in the time stated in the tender.

5. Six sets of working drawings will be furnished to the builder for site use, and any further prints reasonably required shall be supplied on request.

6. The term prime cost when applied to materials or goods to be fixed by the builder shall mean the list price of such goods as published in the supplier's catalogue; any trade discounts obtained by the builder shall be an advantage enjoyed by the builder. Prime cost sums shall include suppliers' charges for delivery. All expenses in connection with the fixing of such goods shall be allowed for by the builder in the contract sum.

7. All work and materials shall be to British Standards and Codes of Practice and shall comply with Building Regulations. Proprietary materials and components shall be used or fixed in accordance with the manufacturers' recommendations.

8. The builder shall be responsible for the issue of all statutory notices and shall comply with the requirements of the Local Authority and statutory bodies. The client warrants to the builder that all necessary planning consents and appropriate building regulation approvals have been obtained, and shall be responsible to the builder for any delay or cancellation of the contract consequent on their not being such consents or approvals.

9. The builder shall be deemed to have visited the site and to have satisfied himself regarding site conditions.

10. The builder shall be responsible for all insurances against all risks on site, including public liability and fire risk, to date of handover. The builder shall make security arrangements for the proper storage of materials on the site as appropriate to the local circumstances. The builder is to avoid damage to public and private property adjacent to the site, and to make good or pay for reinstatement of any damage caused. The builder shall extend to the client the guarantees available to him on proprietary materials and fittings, and shall provide the client with documentation required to take advantage of such guarantees.

11. The builder is to cover up and protect the works from the weather, and to take all action for the protection of the works against frost in accordance with the requirements of NHBC or Zurich Newbuild.

12. Top soil shall be stripped from the site before commencing excavation of the foundations in accordance with the requirements of NHBC or Zurich Newbuild, and shall be ... (spread or left heaped). Any trees removed shall have the whole of their roots excavated, and the back fill shall be with materials appropriate to the works to be executed over the excavation.

13. The builder is to set out and level the works and will be responsible for the accuracy of the same.

14. Foundations shall be as per the drawings with footings under partition walls taken down to solid ground. Depth of the foundations shall be as per drawings, with any additional depths required by the Local Authority paid for at measured work rates.

15. Concrete for the foundations and solid floors shall be truck mixed concrete as specified. Foundation brickwork shall be in bricks or blocks to the requirements of the Local Authority. Fill shall be clean material to the requirements of NHBC or Zurich Newbuild.

16. Ducting shall be provided for service pipes and cables through the foundations, and chases shall be formed in concrete for pipework inside the building in accordance with good building practice.

17. The ground floor, if to be of solid or beam and block construction shall have a sand cement screed, finished to receive ... (tiles as defined or carpeting), or if suspended floor construction shall be as per drawing with floor boarding to be ... (define whether tongue and grooved boarding or interlocking flooring panels or other material).

18. Mat wells shall be provided at the front and back doors to be ... (define type and size).

19. The shell of the building is to be built with the materials specified on the drawings. The external walling material shall be ... (make and type) and shall be laid and finished in a manner detailed on the drawings. The windows shall be ...(make and range) and shall be finished ... (define finish). The external doors shall be ... (make and types) and shall be finished ... (define finish). Internal door frames shall be ... (material and finish). Window boards shall be ... (material and finish). Staircases shall be ... (material and style, particularly style of balustrade and rails).

20. The roof and any vertical tiling shall be ... (define tiles by manufacturer, type and colour) and the tiling work shall be carried out by a tiling contractor approved by the tile manufacturer so as to obtain the most favourable guarantee available from the tile manufacturer. The sub-contract for this shall be between the builder and the sub-contractor.

21. First floor boarding shall be ... (define whether tongue and grooved boarding or interlocking flooring board or other material).

22. Access to the roof shall be provided to NHBC or Zurich Newbuild requirements and a loft ladder shall be fitted within the contract sum.

23. All walls shall be plastered in ... (define lightweight or traditional plaster) to the plaster manufacturer's full specification, and all materials used shall be from the same manufacturer. Caving and other plaster features shall be extras to the contract, to be specifically defined in a quotation and ordered with a written order.

24. Ceilings shall be boarded to suit the ceiling finish specified, which shall be ... (define).

25. The under surface of the stairs shall be ... (define arrangements for below the stairs if a visible feature).

26. Architraves and skirtings shall be ... (define material, size and moulding shape after discussion of samples).

27. Internal doors to be ... (define doors specifically, by manufacturer and model).

28. Any sliding patio doors shall be ... (manufacturer and type).

29. All windows shall be double glazed with sealed double glazing units to be ... (manufacturer and type). All glazed doors shall be single glazed. Obscure glass and shatterproof glass shall be used where required by Building Regulations or where shown on the drawings.

30. Garage doors shall be ... (manufacturer and type).

31. The door furniture to be as the schedule attached. (The schedule should

detail which internal doors are to have latches, which are to have locks, security locks to external doors, letter plates as required, plus any other fittings. Windows are supplied complete with furniture, but if security bolts or special fittings are required these should be specified.)

32. The central heating system shall be installed against a prime cost sum of £... and the proposals for this system shall be as detailed separately. The system shall be designed to meet the heating requirements of the NHBC or Zurich Newbuild, and all work shall be to the appliance manufacturer's requirements. If the heating system requires the installation of an oil tank the position and height of this shall be agreed, and the structure to support and/or conceal the tank shall be ... (define).

33. The chimney and chimney breast shall be built as per drawing, and the fireplace opening provided shall be for a ... (name appliance). This appliance and the fire surround shall be provided against a prime cost sum of £... All work to the fireplace opening and chimney shall be to the appliance manufacturer's requirements.

34. Sanitary ware and bathroom fittings shall be provided against a prime cost sum of £....

35. The cold water tank shall have capacity of ... litres and shall be situated in the roof in a position agreed, to give ease of access, on a stand to NHBC or Zurich Newbuild requirements. It shall be fitted with a lid, and frost protected as required under the Building Regulations. The hot water cylinder shall have a capacity of ... (discuss) in a position to give ease of access while providing for the maximum space for shelving alongside. The hot water cylinder shall be fitted with an immersion heater, to be ... (discuss, including whether this is a dual model to provide both full and top-up heating). The cylinder shall be lagged to NHBC or Zurich Newbuild requirements.

36. The kitchen fittings shall be provided against a prime cost sum of £... and this shall include all sinks shown on drawings. Hot and cold water and drainage connections to a washing machine/dishwasher situated ... (define) shall be provided.

37. Wardrobes, cupboard fronts and other fitted furniture shall be provided against a prime cost sum of £...

38. The electrical installation shall allow for lighting points, power points and switching arrangements to be to NHBC or Zurich Newbuild minimum requirements, and the builder shall quote the additional sum required for each extra ceiling light, extra wall light, and each extra socket outlet. Light switches and socket outlets shall be ... (manufacturer and range). Simple pendants shall be provided at all lighting points, or alternatively the client's fittings will be fixed if provided to programme. The fuse box shall be ... (define fuse board and circuit breaker system). Provision shall be made for television sockets and telephone points in ... (define rooms and position in rooms). Electricity meters shall be in a meter box fitted ... (define position: the Electricity Board may try to define where this should be). Provision shall be made for bells at the front and back door, and a simple bell shall be provided, or alternatively the client's chimes or other fittings to be installed if provided to programme.

39. All interior plaster surfaces shall be finished with ... (define emulsion paint and colour) which shall be applied in accordance with the manufacturer's recommendations for new work to give a consistent colour.

40. Wall tiling shall be quoted as a prime cost sum of £... per sq. yd. for a stated minimum area.

41. All softwood joinery shall be knotted, primed and treated with two undercoats and one gloss finishing coat of interior paint to be ... (define paint and colour).

42. All timber surfaces which are not to be painted shall be protected by using protective stain to the manufacturer's requirements, and shall not be varnished (or other requirements as considered appropriate).

43. Foul drainage shall be as detailed on the site plan, in the materials detailed on the site plan and all work shall be to the requirements of the Local Authority.

44. Rainwater goods shall be ... (manufacturer and range) and shall discharge

open gullies or via sealed drain connectors ... (as defined). Surface water drains shall discharge into soakaways or elsewhere as detailed on drawings.

45. External steps, and the porch or step at the front door, shall be finished with ... (quarry tiles or finish required). A path shall be provided around the whole of the perimeter of the building, to a width of 2 ft., to be ...(specify concrete surface or paving slabs) and shall be laid to the full requirements of NHBC or Zurich Newbuild for external works.

46. Other external works, including any work on the drive, or any fencing shall be considered as extras to the contract, and shall be quoted for in writing and the order for them placed in writing.

47. Any detached garage shown on the drawings is outside the contract, and any work to construct such a garage shall be an extra to the contract, to be quoted in writing and any order placed in writing.

48. Any other work required or fittings to be installed in connection with the contract shall be quoted in writing and any order placed in writing.

49. Any defect, excessive shrinkages or other faults which appear within 3 months of handover due to materials or workmanship not in accordance with the contract, or frost occurring before practical completion, shall be made good by the builder, and payment of the retention detailed in the payment arrangements at paragraph 50 shall only be made on completion of this making good.

50. Payment to be made on a progress rate of:

20% of contract price at dpc
25% of contract price at roof tiled
25% of contract price at plastered out
30% at handover.

The above all subject to a 2% retention as provided in paragraph 49. All payments to be made within 7 days of notice that payment is due.

51. The client may but not unreasonably or vexatiously by notice by registered post or recorded delivery to the builder forthwith terminate the employment of the builder if the builder shall make default in any one or more of the following respects:

(i)   If the builder without reasonable cause fails to proceed diligently and properly with the Works in accordance with this specification, or wholly suspends the carrying out of the Works before completion.

(ii) If the builder becomes bankrupt or makes any composition or arrangement with his creditors or has a winding up passed or a Receiver or Manager of his business is appointed or possession is taken by or on behalf of any creditor of any property the subject of a Charge. Provided always that the right of determination shall be without prejudice to any other rights or remedies that the client may possess.

52. The builder may but not unreasonably or vexatiously by notice by registered post or recorded delivery to the client forthwith terminate the employment of the builder if the client shall make default in any one or more of the following respects that is to say:

(i)   If the client fails to make any interim payment due within 14 days of such payment being due.

(ii) If the client or any person for whom he is responsible interferes or obstructs the carrying out of the Works.

(iii) If the client becomes bankrupt or makes a composition or arrangement with his creditors.

Provided always that the right of determination shall be without prejudice to any other rights or remedies which the builder may possess.

53. In the event of a dispute between the parties arising out of the contract, the parties shall agree jointly to engage an architect independent of either of them to arbitrate between them, and shall be bound by the architect's findings as to the matter in dispute and to his apportionment of his fees as an arbitrator.

are building in timber frame you will also need to adapt the specification to suit the supply and/or the erection of the parts of the work that your frame supplier is carrying out and you might like to attach a copy of their specification to yours to form part and parcel of the same contract. If you are using a brick and block package deal company then you will need to go through and delete the items that the company will be supplying and you might, once again, like to attach a copy of their specification and the list of their supply items to the resultant specification so as to make it part of your contract with the builder.

Now, you make think it strange that having said all of the above and having gone to the trouble of reproducing the specification that follows, I should seek to decry it, but I would like to introduce a word of caution here. The tighter you try to draw a contract the more likely it is that something will be left out or overlooked. Many successful selfbuilders complete their projects with a builder on nothing more than a simple exchange of letters referring to plans and specifications no more detailed or complicated than those prepared for the Building Regulations applications, possibly with the specification from the timber frame or package deal supplier attached. It is important, though, that you do make it clear, in some way, just what the builder's responsibilities are and that you do stipulate that any work has to be carried out in accordance with the Building Regulations, and/or the NHBC/ Zurich Municipal standards.

15 A contract with a builder

Whenever you arrange for someone to do some building work for you, you make a contract with them. In it they undertake to do the job, and you undertake to pay them. You cannot escape it: even if you simply say 'get this done, Ted, and I will see you right', you have established a contract. However, you will want to make sure that the arrangements that you make to build a new home are a good deal more specific than that!

Now there are many textbooks on the law of contract, and they are both heavy going and omit to mention that very few people arranging to build their own homes establish contracts in the way that the textbooks advise, or indeed in the way that their solicitors would advise. There is a great gulf between theory and practice.

A contract is a way of expressing an arrangement which both parties enter into without reservations, believing that they know exactly how everything is going to happen. When they make the contract, whether verbally or in writing, they regard it simply as a convenient way of recording what they have agreed. If all goes well, everything is fine. If there are unforeseen circumstances or problems, they turn to the contract to see where they stand in the matter. If they should fall out over this, it is the contract that determines their legal position. The contract should thus define exactly what the parties have agreed and, if there are problems, how they are to be resolved.

The best way of establishing a formal contract that deals with all of this involves solicitors, quantity surveyors, and documents that are dozens of pages long. If you ask a solicitor what is the best way to arrange a contract or contracts to build a new house, he must recommend these involved procedures. However, such contracts will scare off most small builders and using them automatically puts you in a special league. For this reason only a very few of those building for themselves use them. The choice is yours. This book cannot advise you to ignore the best legal advice, but it does describe how most people arrange these affairs. If it is a matter which worries you, then discuss the whole business with your solicitor.

What follows is about single contracts placed to arrange for the whole of the work involved in building a new home. Contracts with subcontractors will be dealt with in the next chapter. Technically anyone placing a contract for the whole job is an individual builder, not a selfbuilder, as a selfbuilder is someone who reclaims his own VAT. An individual builder has the VAT reclaimed by his building contractor, and his bill from the contractor will not include VAT.

There are two very different ways of arranging for a builder to build a house for you – using an architect to establish and supervise the contract, or arranging and supervising everything yourself. If you use an architect he will invite tenders from builders, advise you which one to accept and will draw up a suitable formal contract which he will supervise on your behalf. This is the Rolls Royce way of doing things. The architect will charge fees of around 10% of the value of the contract, and although he or she will be concerned that you get the best value for money, he does tend to operate at the very top of the market. If you are using an architect then you must make sure that you have made proper arrangements with him.

If you are making a contract with a builder yourself it is important that you do not simply accept any arrangements that he suggests, and that you settle things in a way that you are happy about. Negotiating this in an amicable way may not be easy, but you should insist on what you want while avoiding giving the impression that you are going to be a difficult customer who should be charged extra for being a potential nuisance! If your builder is taking the initiative in this matter he is likely either to present you with one of the standard building industry forms of contract or with a detailed quotation which he will hope you will accept by sending him a written order.

Beware the pre-printed contract: these are excellent for professionals but are unintelligible to the layman and contain all sorts of clauses which you might not want if you knew of them. If such a contract is to be used then ask your solicitor to advise you of any clauses that should be struck out. A contract established by exchange of letters, or by a quotation and an order, is much better provided that you refer in it to an agreed specification and approved drawings. You must make it your job to ensure that the specification and drawings deal with everything that you want to establish, and they should be initialled by both parties so that they are firmly part of the contract.

Some of the matters to be dealt with are listed in the draft specification on the previous pages. Obviously special situations require special clauses in the specification, and the best person to advise you on this is the person, or company, who drew up your plans.

The draft specifications make extensive use of Prime Cost Sums, otherwise known as PC sums. At the stage when you are negotiating the contract you have probably not decided on the particular fixtures and fittings that you require, and so a 'Prime Cost Sum' is allowed for the items concerned. A PC sum of £3,000 for the kitchen units means that the builder must allow this much for the kitchen units. If you spend less then the contract price will be reduced. If you spend more then it will be raised by the difference. Does it, however, refer to the purchase price of the units, or does it also include the cost of fitting? These things need to be specified. If you do not use the wording in the draft then you will need to establish just how much is allowed for the fixing element and you will also need to understand that if you buy kitchen units cheaper because they are flat packed there may well be a corresponding increase in the fixing costs if you also want the builder to be responsible for their assembly. As I've said in the previous chapter, you may well also want the PC sums of certain items to reflect the huge discounts that are available and to reflect them in your favour. Materials usually covered by PC sums are, kitchen units, bedroom furniture, sanitaryware, fireplaces, staircases and wall and floor tiling. Trades that are often covered by a PC sum are the plumber and the electrician where the initial quotation, in the absence of detailed information, may include a PC sum that will reflect the bare minimum needed to provide systems that comply with the regulations and the minimum standards laid down by the NHBC.

In certain instances it may be as well to remove the items covered by the PC sum from the builder's remit. If you do, then you do need to establish whether or not there was any profit element included in the total contract sum, for these items' something that is more likely in the more formal contract situations and not usually attributable to selfbuild projects. You might also like to consider whether by removing items from the builder,s remit, you also remove them from his insurance liability and whether you then need to make sure that they are covered by your own policies.

Another important matter to deal with is the cost of any alterations to the agreed work, or any extra work. This is a potential minefield: a simple request from you that something should be fixed the other way round can involve the builder in a great deal of expensive work, and, unless it is agreed in advance, the cost can be a source of dispute. The cost of all alterations and extras should be discussed and should be confirmed in writing, and the specification should say so.

Assignment of the work is also something to be discussed. If you take on builder A because you have admired his work on another house, you want his same workmen to build your own new home, and you do not want him to assign the contract to builder B, or to use other workmen. If this is important to you it should be set out in the contract or in the specification.

The stages at which payment is made, the arrangements for payment, and retentions to be held for a maintenance period should also be clearly established and never, never should any payment be made other than in accordance with these arrangements. Beware any requests for a payment in advance to enable materials to be purchased at a particularly advantageous price, or any other good story. If your builder needs money in advance then it is 100 to 1 that he is in financial difficulties, and you are not there to bail him out.

This leads to the question of what your position is if the builder fails, or dies, or just does not get on with the work. It does happen. On his part, what does he do if you disappear?

All this has to be part of the contract. Finally, when you have the best contract which you consider to be appropriate to the way in which you want to go about things, for goodness sake stick to it. Be punctilious about making payments on time and generally fulfilling your part of the bargain, as to do otherwise may make things difficult if the worst happens and you have to establish your contract in law. If this is a frightening thought, then console yourself with the fact that nearly all individual builders end up by having their new home built without dispute, and retain good relationships with those who are building for them. Having the right contract is a very good beginning to this.

How to find a better builder

Of course you need someone to make a contract with and, for the most part, as I have already presaged, your architect or package deal company is probably going to be the one, either introducing you to, or helping you find, a suitable builder. Recommendation is the key here, that and reputation. Subcontractors can move on with relative anonymity from a less than successful job but builders cannot leave their failings behind quite so easily. If you are on your own in the search for builders then try asking at hire shops and at the local builder's merchants and remember, they are hardly likely to recommend the guy who brings back machinery late or damaged and they are equally as unlikely to put you onto someone who fails to pay their bills on time. Apart from that most of the sources of

subcontractors and practically all of the recommendations made in the chapter that follows on the use of subcontractors, apply with equal measure to the choice of a builder. In addition, even if you are going to use a builder and have the minimum of involvement with the various trades, I still think it is a good idea to make yourselves conversant with what goes on and, as far as is possible, the general sequence of events that flow through a building project.

Always ask to see a builder's previous work and always ask to be put in touch with a previous client. I can virtually guarantee that they will have a few moans, what building site does not have a few hiccups, but it is the general standard of workmanship that you are interested in, the level of commitment shown and the trustworthiness of the man or company. And if there are shortcomings that are identified by this previous client? Well, if they are serious enough then you will need to move onto the next name on your list but if they are minor and you are tipped on what to expect then, with the advice of your professional friend, you might still employ that builder, only with, perhaps, a few reservations which you might like to draw to the attention of the builder, in writing. Alternatively, if you are told that such and such a builder is marvellous at most things but is hopeless at one particular aspect of the build, you might like to consider removing that part of the work from his remit, in which case, as I have been pushing for you to do for the last two paragraphs, you will now turn to the chapter on building with subcontractors.

16 Selfbuilding with subcontractors

A selfbuilder opting to build using subcontractors effectively becomes the builder, only with one big difference. There is no contract to fall back upon. When you build with subcontract labour it is with you that the 'buck stops' and it is up to you to manage and co-ordinate the various trades, materials, plant and services. Any unforeseen factors that affect the cost or the progress on site are your responsibility. It is you, the selfbuilder, who will have to sort them out, and if there is any additional cost then it is you who will have to bear it. There are great savings to be made by opting to build with subcontractors but the reverse side of this coin is that, in turn, you have to take on the responsibilities that the builder would have undertaken, and for which he would have charged.

Management is the key, of course, and that means attention to detail and forward planning. Subcontractors price for their specific trades only and any grey areas are the responsibility of the selfbuilder. A tidy site where all rubbish is collected to a given point, where all materials are placed and stored correctly with due regard to their accessibility and the accessibility of other materials, is likely to be far more successful than a site that resembles the aftermath of a terrorist bomb. Of course there are degrees. I'm not suggesting for one moment that you should stand behind each tradesman in a white coat, pointing to each broken brick or picking out the odd fallen leaf or pebble from within the mortar. Such overt interference would be resented and would very quickly lead to a breakdown in relations. No, what I'm suggesting is that in the evenings, when the chaps have left site, you tidy up the old cement bags, pick up the bindings and rake the sand heap into a neat cone and cover it. That you discreetly pick up some of the better half bricks from the ground and neatly stack them beside the other loaded out bricks. There's no guarantee that they'll use them and you still may have to wince as yet another whole brick is deliberately cracked in half, but there's a chance. I remember writing a case history for *Homebuilding and Renovating* magazine, about a couple called Peter and Enid who had built a lovely bungalow in the Midlands. Peter took it upon himself to tidy up

the site every day and then halfway through the job he suffered a hernia (nothing to do with the selfbuild) and wasn't able to continue his nightly duties. The subcontractors took it upon themselves to continue his work until such time as he was better!

Perhaps, what that serves to illustrate is that, not only does everyone appreciate a well managed site but that the relationship between Peter and Enid and their subcontractors was particularly good. And that is another important factor to consider. These are self employed men who, very much like the selfbuilder, have quite deliberately stepped outside the system. In doing so they have opted for the insecurities and uncertainties that go with their choice, in preference to the relative comfort of the factory floor. Confident in their respective and individual skills, they have removed themselves from regular employment to enter the world of hire and fire, or start and finish as it is called. In effect, each and every one of them, even the one man band, is, therefore, the representative of their own company and they need to be treated as such rather than as employees or servants. Like any small business they deserve to succeed or fail on the strength of their service and their product and it's necessary for you, the selfbuilder to make sure that, as the one doing the paying, you get what you want. Some subcontractors are completely disorganised in their approach to obtaining and quoting for work and they often prove just as disorganised in their attitude to the work itself. I would suggest that you take all possible steps to avoid these fellows. Others are splendidly efficient in dealing with enquiries, giving out quotations and, as a result, the work itself. I would suggest that these are the chaps you should seek to engage and there are several ways to go about finding them.

By far the best way of identifying which subcontractors you should employ is by recommendation and many of the better ones don't need to advertise or look for work at all, preferring to rely on a constant stream of work that comes their way by word of mouth. Indeed many subcontractors seem almost reluctant to talk to potential new clients unless they approach them by or through some form of recommendation or third party.

As I've said before, selfbuilders love to talk to other selfbuilders and selfbuild sites are a terrific source of recommendation. What you'll get there is, of course, often going to be about price but that's not all you should look for. Good doesn't just need to mean capable of doing a good job at the right price – it also needs to mean reliable and above all helpful. It's no good having, arguably, the best bricklayer in the world if he turns up one Monday morning and is absent by Tuesday with a promise to come back some day. You need to know that the tradesmen you employ will dedicate themselves, in the main, to your job and that they're as interested in continuity as you are. Now, before you run off thinking that means that once on site they should attend all day and every day until the job's done, that doesn't mean that there aren't times when subcontractors will be away from the site. All tradesmen have to go away at certain points in the construction, but the indicator of a reliable man is his ability to juggle the various jobs he's on, in order to maintain continuity on them all. If a bricklayer has to leave your site because he's waiting for the roof construction to be completed, then he's not going to just go home and sit and watch Richard and Judy on television. No, he's going to go and do someone else's footings for a couple of days and then, whilst the groundworkers deal with the oversite on that one, he'll come back to your job in order to do the gable ends. All of this is perfectly reasonable. Where it can go wrong, however, is if your relationship with the trades- man is on the wrong footing, if the man is unreliable in the first place, in which case you haven't done your homework properly on him, or if you've paid him too far ahead of the work.

Before I go on with finding labour, I'll stay for a moment on this subject and explain just what I mean by that last phrase. Say you have a house with two gable ends and when you get to plate height (where the roof starts), the bricklayer has to leave to let the carpenters construct the roof. If you've paid that bricklayer all but a few hundred of his total price for the job then, unless he's an extremely reliable man, there might be trouble

getting him to come back. Gable ends, especially cut verges, are very time consuming in propor- tion to the amount of bricks to be laid. If there's only a few hundred pounds on the job, then a less than reliable man could reason that he, and his gang, could earn ten times the amount on straight work on another job. You see it all comes down to management and to making sure that you're on top of each situation and that, most importantly, you've chosen the right guys in the first place. A golden rule, of course, would be to say never pay any monies up front or in advance of the work but all rules need to be broken at some time and when, and if, they are broken it's down to your skill in managing people and situations. Certainly with labour only trades the tendency should be to keep a tight rein on money going out and to try, as far as possible, to make sure that the payments schedule reflects, at least the work done or, even better, keeps you well ahead, moneywise, with an incentive left in at the end for the man to finish. On the other hand, if a plumber on a supply and fix contract, having done a pretty good job for you on the carcassing, comes to you and requests a down payment towards the purchase of an expensive boiler, then it's a slightly different matter. Such a request should be calmly considered. If you're completely confident in the man, then, by all means, go ahead but, I would suggest that a better way around such a problem would be for you to purchase the item yourself and then deduct either the cost, or the agreed PC sum, from your contract with the subcontractor. That way title in the goods is always yours and if anything goes wrong, you're in a far stronger position.

Never put yourself in the situation of effec- tively lending money to tradesmen, builders or anyone else for that matter, in order for them to work for you. That's the job of the banks and if they feel that they shouldn't be advancing money to someone, despite the attraction of his contract with you, then you can rest assured that they know a lot more about the guy than you do and that they have perfectly good reasons for acting as they do.

But back to the business of finding labour. If your trips to other selfbuild sites draw a blank then try ordinary building sites. Even if a local builder or developer is developing a project, then it's a fair bet that most, if not all, of the labour on site is self employed. It's an equally fair bet that a good many of them don't actually know where they're going from there, relying as they do on the fact that something usually comes up. That something could well be you. Now, I'm not suggesting that you go clambering up the scaffolding in a howling gale to talk to a busy tradesman. No, wait 'till they come down for their break and then just start off with the statement and the question "I'm building my own home. Would you be interested in pricing for it?"

Maybe he's not interested. Maybe he is but he's tied up for the next six months, in which case, he's probably no good for you but that doesn't mean that you necessarily have to leave it there. Try asking him for the names of anyone else he thinks you could approach. He may not give you names of men within his trade but he may well give you names of other tradesmen and, in particular, he may give you the names of subcontractors who operate in the trades either side of his own. You see, although subcontractors are all individuals concerned with their own trade, they do tend to work in groupings, little extended families, if you like. A good tradesman doesn't like to follow a bad or an unreliable one. It holds him up and makes a difficult job harder. A bricklayer who is interested in continuity isn't going to recommend a carpenter who has proved unreliable in the past by not turning up to do the joists on time, and, in turn, a carpenter isn't going to put you onto a bricklayer whose work is so out of level that it takes him twice as long to level up those same joists. Get to one good tradesman and from that, you'll be put on to others, in other trades, who are just as good.

Other sources of names for both subcontractors and builders are, of course, Yellow Pages or the classified sections of your local paper and a relatively new source of names are the folders that the Building Regulations forms come in. A chap who's prepared to spend money on advertising in such a medium is a chap who's obviously got very little to hide and in any case you could ask the Building Inspector himself which ones he would recommend. He probably won't stick to one name but instead may mention two or three which of course is all to the good. Martin, one of the selfbuild stories at the end of the book, also asked around at his local builders merchants and hire shops for names and was particularly successful in getting hold of good tradesmen.

The impression given by the strict division between the preceding chapter and this one is that one can either build with a builder or that one can do so with subcontract labour. The reality, of course, is quite different and the facts are that there are a number of permutations between the two methods. Indeed, one of the most popular ways of getting a house built is to use a single builder to take the project up to the weathertight shell and to then use subcontractors for the remaining stages of the build.

In the last chapter we discussed placing contracts with builders who are responsible for every aspect of the work on a new home, with clearly defined obligations all round and provision made to cover all eventualities. Detailed and legally enforceable contracts like this are rarely made with labour only sub-contractors, who often work simply on the basis of a verbal agreement. The best you can hope for is a quotation on a piece of headed paper. A quotation on a labour and materials basis may be quite detailed, but it will not deal with unforeseen contingencies in the way that a builder's contract does.

As a result you have to rely on finding the right man, coming to an amicable agreement with him, making sure that he does the right job, paying him only for work done, and terminating the arrangement promptly and without rancour if things are not working out. The key word in this is amicable. Arguments between selfbuilders and sub-contractors are rarely won by either party, as either the sub-contractor will walk off the site, or else the work will proceed in an atmosphere that does not make for a good job. It is virtually impossible to enforce an arrangement made with a sub contract workman in any legal way, and you have to handle problems on a give and take basis. Builders have experience of this: most selfbuilders have not. You may feel that, in order to prevent any disagreement over what exactly is included in the subcontractor's quotation to you, you should attempt to define and list the precise nature of his duties and obligations under the contract. Do be careful about this. If, for example, you receive a quotation from a carpenter that merely states 'All labour for first fix, roof and second fix carpentry for new house at 19 Acacia Avenue, Anytown' then it would be next to nigh impossible for the carpenter to subsequently turn around and claim that the fixing of the facia board and soffit was not in his remit. On the other hand if you've attempted to list all of the carpenter's duties and, for some reason, you've forgotten to list these items, then an unreasonable carpenter, or one where the relationship with you has become strained, could well argue that he is due some extra monies.

Fortunately there are ways in which you can take action to avoid misunderstandings and problems. Firstly, reinforce the arrangements made by giving the subbie a letter or a note which is either your acceptance of the written quotation if you received one, or, more usually, confirms a verbal arrangement which you have made. Secondly make sure that any acceptance is tied back to the plans and specification of the proposed building and that you have a note of the subcontractor receiving them, together with a note of the plan numbers and any dated amendments.

The business of payment is important. Labour only sub-contractors expect to be paid promptly, and in cash. If you do not do this you are asking for problems, and running the risk of your sub-contractors going off to other work. Although you should keep a record for your own accounts of who you paid and how much you have paid them, you have no responsibility to notify the tax authorities of the payment, although a builder is obliged to do so under what are called the '714 arrangements'. This is a complicated business and its very existence gives the selfbuilder an edge, in that the subcontractor who works for you, as opposed to the local developer, will, if he is paid the same rates, be approximately 20% better off. This is something

that is only ever obliquely referred to in the industry but it is something that it is as well for you to be aware of.

Although the sub-contractors working for you will not be employees in the strict sense, you should ensure that you have employer's liability insurances. The tiler who falls off your roof will decide that he had a 'Deemed Contract of Employment' with you before he hits the ground, or if he does not remember this, his solicitor will! Dealing with a resulting claim will be expensive whatever the outcome, and it is best left to an insurance company. Appropriate cover is part of standard selfbuilders' insurance policies, and is discussed in a later chapter.

Labour only sub-contractors will expect you to provide all the plant required for the job, and to have it there on time. If there is a difficulty with this, such as a mixer breaking down, they will expect you to solve the problem at once, otherwise they will want to be paid for their wasted time or will go off to another job. The same applies to delays in delivering materials, or in arrangements to replace materials stolen from a site.

Selfbuilders should always employ sub-contractors on fixed prices. Builders often do not, and there are complicated systems of measured work, where for example, a bricklayer is engaged at £xxx per thousand bricks laid. This may sound simple, but building industry practice is that some bricks at cills and reveals count as one and a half bricks, or even two bricks. Measured work rates for plastering are even more complicated. Get lots of copies of your drawings so that you can given them to prospective sub-contractors, and make it quite clear that you will be employing them to do the job that you want doing as shown on the drawings at a fixed price, and not in accordance with the mysterious rites of the building industry.

Avoid, at all costs, the subcontractor who wants to carry out the whole of his trade on the basis of 'daywork' or 'timework'. I once made this self same statement in an article for *Homebuilding & Renovating* magazine and then had to defend myself against an irate subcontractor who reckoned that I was giving bad advice.

He maintained that it wasn't always possible to know exactly what was required with a job and that timework was a perfectly fair and reasonable way to proceed. I didn't retract my opinion then and I'm not going to now.

Many of the trades work out their prices for a job on the basis of measured rates for work and, if they're sensible, they'll qualify their quotation to you by reference to those assumptions. For example a builder or groundworker quoting for work below ground may well quantify the depth and width of the dig, the amount of soil to be disposed of and the amount of concrete and blockwork to be used in the foundations. If he's, therefore, allowed for 10 cubic metres of concrete in the bottom of foundation trenches which are a maximum of 1.2 metres deep and he hits a soft spot where the Building inspector wants him to increase the depth and fill up the trench with more concrete, then you could find yourself with a bill for the extra time taken to dig, the extra spoil to dispose of and the extra concrete used, over and above the specified amount. If it all ratchets up to a trenchfill foundation then the amount of concrete could rise to two, three or many times the original. That means a very big bill for extra concrete but, there may well be a corresponding saving in below ground blockwork and, when this is quantified and compared, you will almost certainly be able to set one off against the other. You'll still come off worse, I'm afraid, but the bitter pill will be sweetened a little and, if you've read the earlier chapters carefully, you'll probably already have anticipated the problem and it won't come as too much of a shock, in any event.

Some of the trades, carpenters for one, do indeed work out their prices on the basis of the number of man hours that they will have to put into the job. For example, if a carpenter thinks that the job of constructing your roof will take two men ten days to complete, then he'll arrive at his price for the job on the basis of 20 man days. Now, that won't necessarily be his price to you as he may well have ancillary things to add to that and he may well, depending on the nature and size of his business, have profit to add, before arriving at the quotation he wants to give you.

But the principle remains – he has arrived at his price to you by reference to the time he estimates that the job will take him. When such a man gives you a fixed price quotation for the job, he is demonstrating his confidence in his own abilities both in arriving at the price in the first place and being able to achieve the targets he has set himself in the second place. These are the kind of chaps you should be playing with and as far as those guys who want to do the whole job on daywork are concerned, I have only one piece of advice – sup with a very long spoon.

That's not to say that there aren't times when daywork isn't right and proper. In certain instances and in certain situations, it is totally appropriate. A bricklayer who is on a price may well put, at the bottom of his quotation, a rate for daywork. This may well be to cover for having to stop work and put men onto unloading materials or it may be there for things like the fancy fireplace, the precise design of which, you haven't yet decided on. All of this is perfectly acceptable and perfectly normal and the quoted daywork rate in these situations is the mark of a man who is thinking forward.

An long time ago, I was building my first house and there was a bricklayer working on the site on the basis of a price per thousand bricks, something that I've already said isn't that appropriate for the selfbuilder. In any case, there weren't books like this around and I was relatively inexperienced anyway. The bricklayer came to me half way through the job and asked that, as it was quite a way for him to travel, could he go on daywork? In my innocence, I agreed to his request. In the last week of him working on measured rates, he had laid an average of 1500 bricks per day. From the time he went onto daywork, that dropped to 400 bricks per day. It wasn't a lesson I shall easily forget!

You'll remember the 'know it all' we encountered in the pub in the chapter on evaluating a site? Well that same chap will also tell you that you've got to get at least three quotations from each trade and that anything less is laying yourself open to ruin. Balderdash is the word that springs to mind. Most subcontractors in a local area are in almost constant touch with each other either at work or in the pub. If you flooded the local labour market with requests for prices then there's a chance that none of them would bother to do the large amount of work necessary to provide you with a quotation, thinking that the odds of them getting the job are too slim. Certainly get more than one quotation, if you've got several names, but, equally as certainly, if a particular tradesman is recommended by, say another selfbuilder, and his price comes within what you've budgeted for, why waste anybody else's time? More importantly, why risk missing the first guy's window of availability on a futile gesture?

Even if the recommended guy's price is a little higher than other quotations that may not be a good enough reason to discount taking him on. Prices that you are quoted have to be related to your budget and to the big picture. A man who impresses you as someone in whom you can really have confidence may quote more than someone else, but he may be the best man for the job. A golden rule is to get a clear idea of the general level of prices for a job like yours before you start discussing the matter with any potential sub-contractor. This, again, is part of learning all that you can about selfbuild before you actually get involved on the site.

Negotiation is a large part of management but, do be very careful about trying to knock a price down. Certainly there is nothing to say that you can't tell a man that you fancy using, that his price was a little high in comparison to others. He may well be able to look at things again and he may well find that he has either made a mistake or some wrong assumptions. On the other hand, do be aware that if he does come down in price reluctantly, he may well try to claw back the amount he perceives that he's 'lost'. He may do this by finding extras or he may do this by skimping on the job itself – either way, you may find that it would have been better to stick with his original price or to have engaged the other fellow.

The last real issue to explore before I go on to consider each of the main trades in sequence, is that of competency. Are they any good at what they do? Well, if you've arrived at the fellow by recommendation then you already have the answer to that one but, if you found him by some other method, what do you do? The answer is you do exactly the same, only in reverse – you ask around. Ask the tradesman himself for the names of the people who he last worked for and then go and visit their site and ask them what they thought of him. Chances are that he won't give you the name of the last site he was ignominiously expelled from and chances are, therefore, that, if he's willing to give you the names in the first place he's probably alright. Nevertheless do check it out. And when you're there, don't just listen to what you're being told but use your own eyes to see for yourself. If it's a bricklayer you're investigating, you may feel that, as lay person, you have no powers of judgement when it comes to such an important skill. Nonsense, anybody can see if the bricks are all smudged with mortar, and if the general standard of work is untidy. Anybody can stand back and see if the perps (the vertical joints) are neatly in line and anybody can see if the beds (the horizontal joints) are straight. If it's a carpenter then look for the joints on the skirtings and architraves. Are they finished well or are they gappy? Do the doors, and in particular pairs of doors, hang nicely with even spacing all around? The eyes in your head and the tongue in your mouth can find out a lot. Remember, a good tradesman is proud of what he does and what you've got to realise, is that you're entitled to investigate all you can about someone who, after all, is going to be involved with you in probably the most important project of your life.

What follows is a brief description of the nature of each of the normal subcontract trades, together with a note of how they arrive at their prices. I have also included some warnings and specific things to look out for but I don't want you to run away with the idea that all is doom and gloom. I make these suggestions as points that can aid you in the management of your selfbuild site. I do not make them in order to put you off or to frighten you in any way about using subcontractors. Indeed your very knowledge of these things will enhance your standing with any tradesmen who work on your site and serve to assist them in doing a good job for you.

The subcontractors with whom selfbuilders are most likely to be involved are:

Groundworkers

Of the eight stages of inspection required by the Building Inspector, six concern the groundworker. Of the nine inspections stages listed by the NHBC, five involve the groundworker. Of all of the trades, this one, most of whose work is eventually covered up and hidden from view forever, is, without doubt, the most important. It is also the one where unforeseen problems and cost overruns can occur and much of what has been written earlier on in this book concerns itself with the anticipation, as far as is humanly possible, of any special requirements. The chaps who undertake this trade have to be prepared to react very quickly to changing conditions and they have to be able to adapt calmly to problems as they occur.

In most cases the need for any special foundations will be flagged up at a very early stage and a subsequent soil investigation and survey will lead to a foundation design or system being adopted. In other cases, all the investigations in the world can fail to reveal a problem and it is sometimes necessary to change tack fairly rapidly and adopt a different foundation. I remember the case of a house in Harrow where there was a soil investigation that revealed that the subsoil, found in each of the three bore holes that straddled the oversite, was gravel. The recommendation was standard strip foundations 1.2 metres in depth with 600mm x 225mm of concrete. When it came to digging the foundations for the house itself, the builders encountered a pocket of very wet clay and the foundations had to be dug to over three metres deep, shored up and pumped out prior to pouring them full of concrete.

Nobody had done anything wrong. The selfbuilder had, very properly, commissioned a soil survey. The investigating Surveyor had reported quite rightly on what he had found and the builder's quotation was based upon his recommendations. What this proved was that everybody had taken the right precautions but

that, in the end, the only survey that really counts is the one that takes place when you finally dig.

Groundworkers can undertake to carry out this trade on the basis of the provision of all labour, materials and plant but it is more common for selfbuilders to use groundworkers working on a labour only basis. In most cases this labour only basis includes for the supply of a digger but it will often exclude additional plant such as a dumper and will almost certainly exclude any lorries to dispose of spoil. The guys working on the site will know where, when and whether to get any additional plant but it is important that the selfbuilder understands exactly what is being provided within the quotation.

It is also important to know just what basis the quotation has been reached. The price will be worked out by the groundworker, using a combination of measured rates and estimated time/daywork rates. You need to establish just what depths and quantities are assumed to enable you to identify when and if extras are applicable and you need to be able to establish the rates at which any extra work will be carried out. Of course it's not always possible to anticipate every eventuality with this trade as, in some cases, changes may go beyond matters like extra dig or extra concrete and into the realms of a completely different type of foundation. In those cases you may need to stop and establish a price for the new work, almost as if you're starting again. If the changes are fundamental, then you're probably not going to lose any more time by drawing breath and establishing a new contract with the groundworkers, as the probability is that, first of all you'll have to wait whilst new details are approved by the Building and warranty inspectors and secondly, you may need to order extra materials such as reinforcement or clayboard.

Of course, it goes without saying that if you do start off with one type of foundation and, due to unforeseen circumstances, you have to stop and change direction, then you will, I'm afraid, still have to pay for all of the abortive work that was carried out before the job had to stop.

The groundworker's job usually stops at

All square and level.

A beam and block first floor is a feature of many brick and block homes.

oversite level with the groundworker being responsible, once the blockwork foundations have been laid, for the consolidation and casting of the oversite itself. If a beam and block ground floor is being employed it is sometimes the groundworker who maintains responsibility for the laying and infilling of the beams but in some cases this job can be taken on by the bricklayers. If the first or upper floors are beam and block then the selfbuilder needs to establish just who is going to undertake this. Whoever that is, it's normal for this to be quoted as a separate price. A beam and block floor was described in the chapter, 'Making the choices'. Increasingly they are being recognised as the standard way of achieving the ground floor with the normal concrete oversite slipping into second place and a timber suspended ground floor trailing well behind in third.

With a beam and block ground floor the void beneath it can be left as 'mud' so long as, first of all it doesn't come within 75mm of the bottom of the beams and secondly, any differential between the ground levels inside and outside the oversite is not greater than 600mm. On the other hand, a concrete oversite will require very careful filling and consolidation to avoid differential settlement and if there is any suspicion that the fill or the difference in depth of fill will exceed 600mm the inspectors are likely to require you to use floor beams in any event.

Whichever ground floor you use, the groundworker's job will include all of the drainage for both foul and surface water and their connections and it is usual for them to bring the tails up and into the oversite in the required positions. If plastic underground piping is being used, and I would suggest that this form is more relevant for the selfbuilder, then the rule is that the brown plastic pipes below ground and poking up through the oversite are the responsibility of the groundworker and the grey ones that connect to them above that level are that of the plumber.

For details regarding the various foundation methods and for information on the different sewage systems you might encounter, you'll need to turn back to the chapter on 'Designing a new home - to suit your site'.

One of the most expensive and time consuming operations can be the removal and disposal of spoil from site. Tipping charges can be exorbitant but, on top of this, the digging process often has to stop and wait whilst lorries complete the journey to and from a tip that may be several miles away. Without loading out your site with unwanted and unusable material, it may be as well to consider what you can accommodate and, if there is going to be landscaping in the future, how much, if any, of the topsoil or subsoil may be useful for this. When they had to reduce the levels to satisfy the planners, Michael and Emma, in one of the selfbuild stories at the end of the book, managed to spread most of the soil they dug out from their oversite, onto their raised lawn such as to enable them to consider constructing a Ha Ha to the open land at the side. In similar vein, Michael and Patricia, in another of the stories, spread all of their spoil in the woodlands at the back of their plot and used the hard-core from the old bungalow to form the driveway. Perhaps, more than any of the others, that story also serves to illustrate just how things can change in the ground. But in doing so it also serves to illustrate that, in the end, most, if not all, sites still turn out alright, so long as everyone remains calm and carefully approaches each situation as it unfolds.

Bricklayers, blocklayers and stonemasons

Although they usually get lumped together as being in the same trade there are significant differences, in that a bricklayer will obviously be able to lay blocks but might not necessarily be any good at laying stone. Then again, the laying of natural stone is significantly different to the laying of reformed stone and, to complicate matters further, the laying of random coursed undressed stone is a completely different ball game to the laying of cut and dressed stone.

All of this stresses the importance of seeing a prospective tradesman's work before you take him on and of checking by your own observation and by reference to others he has worked for, that he's the right guy for the job. This book is not meant to be a technical manual so I won't go too deeply into any of the finer points of bricklaying. What I would like, however, to stress, are a couple of pointers that you should look out for. It's quite obvious that the laying costs of the various stones will vary according to the type of stone and when asking for a price for stonework, a reputable tradesman will need to know exactly what material you intend to use. The very questions he asks will give you a pretty good clue about just how competent he is. With bricks, it's all too easy to assume that one brick is the same as another but, again, you'd be wrong. Sand faced Flettons soak up mortar very quickly and can be laid just as fast whereas some of the harder stock or engineering bricks have a very low porosity. When these are laid they do not take up the moisture in the mortar bed and, if too many are laid, they tend to 'float on the bed'. In addition the Flettons are uniform in their size and square, whereas hand made bricks, by their very nature, have an irregular shape. Pointing such bricks can take considerably longer and requires much more thought and skill. Once again the mark of a good bricklayer can be his very questions.

The price is usually reached by reference to measured rates for each aspect of the work and then this is normally totalled up and given as a lump sum price. Occasionally a bricklayer may prefer to work on the job on the basis of measured rates of, say, so many pounds per thousand bricks laid or so many pounds per square metre of blockwork laid, but this is not that usual on a selfbuild site. Oftimes a lump sum quotation will also have a note of measured rates for additional work and I would suggest that if it doesn't, then it's a good idea to seek out that information and agree it before the chap starts. Alternatively there may be a daywork rate noted and, as I've explained before, that's fine for certain aspects of the work but normally, totally unacceptable as the basis for the whole job.

No skilled tradesman, and particularly the very important trade of bricklayer, likes to be stood over when he's working, but there are some very important things you should look out for, hopefully on the other guy's site, before the bricklayer starts on yours, but, if not, then as

soon as he's working for you. The neatness of the visible brickwork itself is something we've already discussed but what I'm referring to here are those aspects of the trade that soon get covered up. Damp proof courses are of vital importance, so much so that they, in effect, form an inspection stage, all of their own. If floor beams are being used then these are often placed directly on top of the damp proof course itself. The beams are heavy and they often have to be moved from side to side to accommodate the infill blocks. Just make sure that when this is done the damp proof course itself isn't torn or rucked up. There are other damp proof courses throughout the building that are of equal importance and it's as well to look out for them and to make sure that they're installed properly and that they're in wherever the plans call for them. These are the cavity trays and tray dpc's that trap water or moisture that may find its way into the cavity, and channel it out though weeper holes. They usually occur at an abutment of a lower roof with a cavity wall and are installed in concert with the various flashings that also occur at these points. Failure to build these in at the right height and position can result in water getting in to either the roof void or the house itself. Once installed, a careful watch needs to be taken to make sure that they are kept clear of any obstruction and, in particular, falling mortar.

Most bricklayers are labour only and the most usual combination to work on selfbuild sites is two bricklayers served by one labourer. This is known as a two and one gang and on price work they will often lay between 2000 and 3000 bricks a day on straight runs, although that figure will drop considerably with corners, openings and fancy detailed brickwork. The only tools they usually provide are their own hand tools but, just occasionally, they may also bring their own mixer. Normally, however the provision of this is down to you as is the provision of mortar boards (spot boards) and of course the sand, cement and any necessary additives. Whilst on the subject of sand, it is the one thing good bricklayers are fussy about and they may well request that it's obtained from a particular pit. This isn't because they get some sort of kick back and it's normally because they feel that that particular sand makes a better mix. If you can satisfy their whim on this one without too many hassles then it's often a good idea, and it does help to start off on the right foot. And talking of starting off on the right foot, do make sure that when they all arrive on site, not only are all the materials there and ready for them but that there is a convenient water supply and hose leading to a butt placed near to the place where they'll be mixing. The first arrival of the bricklayers is always the most important and if they arrive and everything's there, ready for them, then they'll stay and get stuck in straight away.

I'll talk about scaffolding when I get to the bit about plant and machinery but it does need mentioning with regard to this trade. In the past many a bricklaying gang undertook their own scaffold with the labourer raising the lift in slack moments when he'd made sure that the bricklayers themselves had all they needed. I don't think that that's such a good idea any more, with all the new Health and Safety legislation, and my advice is to use specialised scaffolding contractors who provide the scaffolding on a supply and erect basis. They normally guarantee to be on site within 24 hours of being notified and they normally, also, work in with the bricklayers. The scaffold they provide will conform to all of the rules and you'll know that it's safe for, not only the bricklayers but for all of the following trades and for you, the selfbuilder. Oh, and one last word about scaffolding in connection with this trade. On sloping sites it may be necessary to provide a scaffold right from ground level, known as a foot scaffold. Talk to the bricklayers about this and, if it is needed, then you may need to line up the scaffolding a couple of weeks before you would otherwise have done.

More than any other trade, perhaps, the bricklayers have to fit in with and work around the other trades. They are perfectly used to this but you will need to make sure that any interweaving trades are geared up for the correct times. In all probability the task will be made easier for you by virtue of the loose association that I have already referred to and, in equal probability, all the arrangements may well be made each night in the pub. But, don't take that for granted and keep on asking and checking for when following or intervening trades are needed and make sure that they are notified. Continuity is a mark of a well managed site. If the bricklayers reach first floor joists and you're having timber joists then the carpenter needs to be on hand to cut, lay and level them up in good time for the bricklayers to carry on with the minimum of disturbance. If you're using a beam and block first floor and the bricklayers have quoted you for this particular job then you may need to make sure that either a digger is on site to assist with the lifting of the beams or, in some cases, you may need to organise a crane. As with all things about selfbuilding, attendance at the school of forward planning is the key.

Carpenters or joiners

Same thing, different name really, although in the south the word joiner is usually associated with the making of furniture. Once again this is normally a labour only trade but the men will almost certainly provide all and any tools and machinery they need. More than any other trade, this one may need power at a time when it may not be readily available and, if you can't get a line from a friendly neighbour, you may need to hire a generator, although many of the carpenters I know, have their own. Whilst on the subject of power, it is sometimes possible for a temporary supply to be brought into the meter box as it's built in. Alternatively, a temporary supply can be brought into a locked up box, built to specifications laid down by the local board which are fairly draconian and equally expensive. Incidentally whilst many of the power tools available from hire shops are 110 volts, which requires a transformer, most of the tools I have seen carpenters using, that are their own, work on normal voltage.

The trade of carpenter is divided into three sections, 1st fix, roof and 2nd fix and, many prices are given on this basis. The price is normally arrived at, not so much by measured rates, as by the carpenters themselves working out just how long each section of the job is likely to take. If your roof is to be a simple trussed roof that will take two men four days to fix then the carpenters price for this part of the work will be worked out on that basis. On the other hand, if your roof is a cut and pitch roof that is created on site and the same two men estimate that it'll take them ten days, then the price will rise accordingly.

Although there is a rigid division between the sections within this trade and everybody on building sites knows just what jobs fit in which category, the stages do not follow on from each other in strict progression and overlap to a considerable degree. First fix is normally deemed to include the cutting and fixing of the first floor joists, the fixing of door linings and window boards and the fixing of garage door frames. It also includes, although it has to be done at a later date, the laying of the first floor decking, the making up and erection of any stud partitioning, the assembly and erection of the basic staircase as well as the making up and fitting of any loft traps or tank stands. But, before that second lot of work is carried out, the work to construct the roof has to be completed and then the carpenter has to wait for the roof to be covered in by the tiler.

Second fix involves the hanging of internal and external doors and patio doors, the fixing of skirting and architrave and the finishing off of things like the staircase balustrade. It does not normally include fitting of kitchen units unless this is specifically requested. It also does not normally include things like fitted bedroom furniture unless, again, this is specifically requested, although it does normally include things like built in wardrobes. Now, before you go making a list of all of those things, let me say that what I've just written is in no way meant to be a comprehensive list of the carpenters trade. What you do need to do is establish just what is included in any quotation, although I would repeat the warning not to try and be totally specific and to, wherever possible, leave things under their headings of 1st fix, 2nd fix and roof.

Of course the design of the house will have a profound effect on the carpenter's specification, as will the fact of whether or not you're building in timber frame. If there is any internal or external boarding or cladding or if there are mock Tudor beams to be fitted after external render, then you'll have to make sure that these are included. If you're building in timber frame, then, assuming you're not stickbuilding, the majority of the first fix and roof may well come under the auspices of the frame erectors and the carpenters trade will shrink to slightly more than second fix.

The measure of a good carpenter is in the finish and if you've read the previous sections then, when you went out looking for the man to do this work, that was one of the things you especially looked out for. On the other hand there are some other things, very like with the bricklayer, that you do also need to watch out for, that may have already have been covered up on the job you went to look at. If you're having a timber first floor with joists then, almost certainly, there are places where midspan strutting is indicated on the plans and you need to make sure that this is carried out. Basically it's needed to prevent the joists from twisting or acting independently from each other and it's provided by either proprietary struts, angled herringbone strutting using 50mm x 25mm battening or by solid span strutting using offcuts of the joists themselves. You also need to make sure that any necessary noggins are put in between the upright studs of any stud partitioning, both to provide structural integrity and also to provide fixings for radiators, switch and electrical boxes and the like. And whilst on the subject of noggins, it's normally the carpenter's job to fix any necessary noggins to carry and support the plasterboard.

If any of the floors are to be floating floors then their laying has to be done after the plumber has carcassed but, normally before the plasterer starts. The plans will give the specification but from your point of view, you need to make sure that any necessary membrane is both down and integral, that the insulation is properly laid and that the decking is glued and fixed on all edges. One other thing that you do need to check for is that the boarding or decking stops 12mm from each wall to allow for expansion. Failure to do this can result in humping up of the floor.

Roof tilers and slaters

This is normally, but not always, a labour only trade and the only things that the men will provide are their specialist tools of the trade. Tilers will felt, batten and tile a roof and they are also responsible for any vertical tile or slate hanging with their prices arrived at by a combination of rates, according to the material to be used. It'll be up to you to make sure that everything's on site for them, including not only the roofing materials themselves, but also a decent scaffold to work off as well as facilities for them to be able to mix up any necessary mortar. If you do use a supply and fix contractor then they'll obviously undertake to supply as much and as many materials that are needed for the job. On the other hand many of the specialist tiling suppliers and merchants will take your plans and provide you with a quotation for just what's needed so it's not that difficult to think in terms of using a labour only subcontractor who they may, in any event, recommend to you.

The choice of roof covering can have a big impact on cost, not only from the perspective of the price of the materials themselves but, in the knock on costs to both labour and other aspects of the structure. Let's take a simple change from concrete interlocking roof tiles to plain concrete tiles. At first sight, to the lay person, the fact that the plain tiles are just over a third of the cost per thousand when compared to the interlocking tile may seem attractive. But, you'll need six times more tiles, so the reality is that the material cost is going to very nearly double. If you add to that the fact that there will be at least three times the amount of battening and, with all the extra loading out and fitting necessary, the labour costs will also double, you can see that this simple change has quite a profound effect. If you then ratchet things up some more by the use of plain clay tiles then, although the labour content may well stay about the same, the material costs could well double up yet again. And that's not where that one stops, because clay tiles absorb water far more than concrete ones, and that means that the roof structure may have to be beefed up quite considerably to take the extra weight.

And, talking of beefing up roofs, reformed slates may cost under half that of some natural slates with reformed stone type slates priced somewhere between the two. However, the knock on costs of the huge weight increases experienced with stone slates will mean that the overall costs of the roof will be considerably more, making this, by far, the most expensive roof covering. Michael and Emma, in the selfbuild stories, chose this roofing medium, both because they liked it and it fitted in, and because it was one way to convince the planners of the merits of their new home.

So what do you need to watch out for when getting a price from a tiler and, once work has commenced, what do you need to keep an eye on? Well firstly, it's important that you make yourselves aware of the manufacturer's recommendations regarding fixing and laying and that you equate any prices received back to those requirements. The fixing and nailing requirements for a particular tile or slate may well be completely different in different situations on the same house. In addition, in areas of high exposure, there will, almost certainly be a requirement for extra nailing and the overlap that each tile or slate has over the one below it, may need to be increased. Tiles or slates are gauged across and up a roof plane. The distance that the battens are set apart dictates the gauge of the tiles up the roof, and their lap, and you do need to make sure that these spacings do not exceed the manufacturer's recommendations for your particular situation. Interlocking tiles have to be properly gauged across the roof, so as to fit and run to the verge tiles, without the need for the cutting of tiles within the roof plane. Plain tiles have to start at the verge with a tile and a half laid in each alternating course and, as the tiling is commenced from each outside edge, you need to watch out for the gauge of the tiles across the roof plane so as to make sure that you don't end up with silly sized cuts in the middle.

Leadwork needs to be sorted out, as there are many areas of the roof or its abutment to other parts of the structure where lead has to be employed. Sometimes leadwork comes within the plumber's remit, as with flashings, but, even here, although the plumber may well make up the flashings, they may have to be fixed, either by, or in conjunction with, the tiler. Sometimes, for example with soakers, where a dormer cheek abuts a roof plane, the roof tiler will take on sole responsibility. It doesn't really matter which trade carries out this work. What does matter is that somebody does it and that you establish just who that's going to be, right from the outset.

Nailing is the biggest single thing that you need to look out for. Slates of all sorts, on any roof, need nailing for every slate on every course, as they don't have the fixing lip that tiles have. Most of the reformed slates have pre-drilled holes but watch out for some of the natural slates where, either there are no holes or else new ones may need drilling. Vertical tile hanging also needs every single tile to be securely nailed and in addition the battens need very secure fixings to the wall behind. On a roof plane, tiles will have a recommended nailing schedule which will ask for nailing at course intervals and will certainly specify that all verge tiles and under course tiles are nailed. To check that the tiles have been nailed correctly, stand on the scaffold and, with a length of batten, gently push up each course in a vertical line. If they have not been nailed in the correct sequence then insist on them being so. On a calm clear and sunny day you may think that nothing is going to move these tiles but I can assure you that high winds can strip a badly nailed roof very quickly indeed. This is especially true of the leeward side of a roof plane where it is the vacuum created by the wind that, literally, sucks the tiles off the roof.

Plumbers

In the not so recent past, the advice, almost always, was that the trades of plumbing and central heating were to be considered as supply and fix. To some extent that remains true today although, with the advent of so much choice and with so much more being available directly to the selfbuilder, more and more items are being taken out of the supply element of a plumbers price. Certainly it has long been common not to include sanitary-ware in any price, as most selfbuilders have always preferred to buy their own, even if

the fitting of it was left as part of the plumber's job. On the other hand, most selfbuilders, were content to rely on the plumbers themselves devising a central heating system and to accept his choice of boiler and radiators. Now, with a bewildering array of different boilers, with the multiple choices between, not only differing sorts of radiators but, underfloor central heating systems as well, the plumbers are finding that their clients are not prepared to accept just what they're given. Increasingly, this means that the selfbuilder will want to specify his own materials and equipment and in many cases they may also want to take on responsibility for their purchase. As I've repeated time and time again, this book is not meant to be a technical journal and I don't intend, therefore, to go into the various and conflicting claims for the different systems and components, other than as referred to in the chapter, 'Designing a new home- to be energy efficient'. There are, however some important points to consider in all of this.

In visiting selfbuild sites for this book, and for various magazine articles, the thing that has struck me is how often the selfbuilder finds himself way ahead of his plumber in respect of his knowledge about new innovations. Sometimes this has led to problems. Sometimes the selfbuilder makes a choice on the basis of very good advice and adopts a system that he expects a plumber to be completely *au fait* with, only to find that, not only is the plumber quite flummoxed about what he's supposed to be doing but that the selfbuilder, is going to have to spend a lot of time being a conduit of information between them and the manufacturers. It makes it all the more important that, when thinking of engaging a plumber, you should talk to him about what you're hoping to achieve and carry him along with you in respect of the equipment you are proposing to use. If you sense any reluctance or inability to understand what you're trying to achieve, then pull away and try another subcontractor.

It'll all get better, of course. The plumbers will catch up – at least until it all changes again. Take the case of the sealed system versus the vented system that had pertained in this country ever since Victorian times. From being new, cutting edge and very daunting technology to becoming

Some trusses go up by hand, whilst others need a crane.

Stone slates coming together neatly in the valleys.

the norm took barely two years. The same goes for plastic plumbing and underfloor central heating of course, all of which are fast becoming the accepted ways of working, as is the, almost consequent, reversal in the role and operation of the 'familiar' hot water tank. Instead of a coil of copper tubing heating the water in the tank which is then available for drawing off as hot water, many of the modern storage tanks reverse this process. The boiler heats the envelope of water in the tank and the cold water passing up through coils, is heated by the surrounding water, to be drawn off, at the higher level, as mains pressure hot water.

In the meantime, it's important that you take your plumber along with you and that you make sure that you engage the professional who is going to be able to provide you with the system you have chosen for your new home. If you're going to use underfloor central heating or a particular boiler then, in all probability, the company supplying you with the system will also be able to put you onto, or recommend a plumber to do the work. I would contend that it is always better to stick with the guys who know what they're dealing with. You may feel tempted to take a large part in the education of your local plumber and take the credit for leading him into a new technological age but take care that you don't do so at your own expense and at the expense of the good working of your new home.

If, of course, the plumber has been recommended to you by another selfbuilder or by the company or manufacturers of the systems you wish to employ, then the business of getting a quotation will be relatively straight forward, in that you will ask for a price based on exactly what you're after. On the other hand you may want to get prices from more than one source or you may, at the outset of your project, be unsure of just which way you will be going and what boiler or central heating system you are going to employ. In this case it might be a better alternative to simply approach various registered plumbers, asking them to quote you for a standard system of domestic plumbing and central heating to NHBC and local Water Board requirements. Then when you have all of the

prices in you can then choose the plumber that you feel most comfortable with and discuss with him the various options you are considering, prior to asking him to re-quote on the basis of what you actually want.

As with many trades, the plumber's is divided into 1st fix and 2nd fix, with the 1st fix being taken up by the general carcassing and the fixing of vent and soil pipes. It's important therefore, that the plumber is identified by at least the time the roof tiler starts, so that he can work in with him on the vent pipes as well as the leadwork to the roof that I've have already talked about. The plumber will also have to work in quite closely with the carpenter over the plumbing in of any kitchen units and with the electrician regarding power for the boilers and the earthing of any pipework. If you're using a vented system, then the carpenter will have to construct any tank stands in the roof and the plumbers will have to be on hand to put the tanks into the roof before it's closed in, otherwise they might not fit through the truss spacings.

Electrician

This is another trade that is divided into 1st and 2nd fix and it is almost always a supply and fix trade, where the price is arrived at by reference to the time that the chap reckons the job is going to take plus the costs of the materials involved. An electrician will normally quote a fixed price for an installation shown on a drawing, or as detailed in a quotation, plus a fixed extra charge for each additional light or power outlet required. He will supply the switches and sockets (of a make and type which should be specified) but his quotation will often provide for simple batten or pendant light fittings only. As you will wish him to get the installation tested by the Electricity Board as soon as practicable, so that the mains connection can be made, he has to provide these fittings for the Board's test. Very often, however, you will be buying your own ornamental fittings, and if you can give them to him at the right time he will normally fix them free of charge in place of the pendants and battens. Do not ask for rebate for the savings on pendants and battens - this is balanced by the cost of involvement with your own fittings, which you will have chosen for reasons which have nothing to do with ease of fixing! The electrician will also fix TV points (but not TV aerials), telephone ducting and deal with your heating thermostat and boiler wiring. He will supply and fix any immersion heater required.

Any plans that form the basis of the arrangements that you make with the subcontractor should show the position of all power points and light switches together with details of any other specialised equipment or circuits that you are employing, using clear and readily identifiable symbols. To save any argument you should make it clear that you have retained a copy of this plan and you should refer to it in any correspondence regarding your contract with the electrician. In spite of that, I would suggest that, just before the electrician starts work on site, you walk around your house, plan in hand and chalk at the ready. Imagine the rooms with the furniture in place and then check what you envisage with what you've noted on the plans. Think carefully about which way doors will open and upon which side they'll be hinged. You might well find that you want to move a few things around and, if you're going to change things, it's a lot cheaper beforehand than after the wires are all in.

Plasterer

If the groundworker was the most important trade structurally, then the plasterer is, perhaps, the most important of the finishing trades as far as the look and the feeling of quality in your new home is concerned. In a way the analogy goes further, as the plastering stage is the foundation for the flair and the taste that will characterise your home. If the plastering's bad then no amount of paint and wallpaper will ever hide it up.

It's generally a supply and fix trade, although sometimes things like plasterboard are supplied as part of, say, a package deal. In the main that's because plaster has a limited shelf life and a decent plasterer won't want to have to try and work with material that's gone off, anymore than you'll want a bad job that can, and will, be blamed on your supply. It's normal for a lump

sum price to be given for the trade and that is reached by reference to measured rates for each particular element of the work.

The two main methods of internal plastering, wet plaster and dry lining, used to generally fall either side of the timber frame/brick and block divide but in recent years it has become ever more common for brick and block houses to use dry lining. In any event, many brick and block houses had stud partitioning to the upper part and they had to be dry lined so it wasn't a great big step to consider it for the remaining blockwork walls. Dry lining offers far shorter drying out times, enabling painters and decorators to work very soon after the plasterer has finished. However wet plaster provides the harder and more durable surface that many people prefer and, for some, it is one of the principle reasons for choosing to build in brick and block as, obviously, it cannot be employed with a timber frame construction. As a self-builder the choice is, of course, yours and I'm not going to stand on either side of this line, except to say that, in the end, both methods have their respective merits and, as with all the trades, there are things to watch out for.

The best way of considering them is to break the trade down into the various elements.

Walls - If they're dry lined then the plasterboard will either be fixed to the studs, on timber framed and studwork walls or, on blockwork, it will be fixed by the use of either plaster dabs or battens. If it's dabs, then care should be taken to see that there is a continuous line of dab around the edge of the board, so as to prevent cold air transmission from the wall cavity resulting in a draught and heat loss though the cavity between the plasterboard and the wall. If the walls are to be skim coated then the plasterboard is fixed grey side out, whilst, if they are to be taped and jointed, it needs to go on cream side out. Either way, the final finish depends to a large degree on the taping and filling of the joints and the skill of the tradesman is crucial if you're going to avoid visible joints or uneven walls.

Wet plaster is sometimes referred to as render and set, where the walls are given two coats of sand and cement render with a top coat of finishing plaster. Sometimes the render coats are replaced by a specialised plaster that is then finished with a topcoat. The first coat of render may not always be necessary as its main purpose is to 'dub out' the walls and take up any unevenness in the blockwork. The second coat is the 'scratchcoat' and provides a key for the plaster finish, being scratched in a swirling pattern to facilitate this. In any method of plastering, care needs to be taken that the finish coat is sufficiently thick, 3mm is the norm, and that the two applications that go to make it up are finished to a smooth surface. Where plaster fails to adhere, or where there is excessive cracking, the cause may be due to a number of things. One of the excuses most often heard is that the weather has been too hot or that the central heating has been turned on too soon, forcing the plaster and/or the render to dry out too quickly. Whilst either of these may well be the cause, it can just as easily be caused by inadequate preparation of the background material or through the plaster coat being too thin.

Cracking of plaster with any method may be due to movement or shrinkage of the background materials and the remedy is often to wait until all movement has finished and then to cut out and fill the cracks. A point to watch for is where differing materials, such as blockwork and studwork, abut and, in these cases, the joint should be strengthened with at the very least scrim tape or else expanded metal lathing. Fine hair line cracks like crazy paving, with the plaster coming away from the wall in sections, in large or in localised areas, may be the result of the plaster being applied when the render coat is too 'green'. If the render coat is still very wet when the finish coat is applied, then it may well shrink to a considerably greater degree than the plaster, forcing the topcoat to craze and lose adhesion.

Ceilings - The average house has the ceilings either 'Artexed' or set (plastered) and, whilst 'artexing', using the trade material 'Artex' is often carried out by a completely separate trade to the plasterer, it's as well for us to consider them together, for the purposes of this part of the book. If the ceilings are to be 'artexed' then the plaster-

board is tacked cream side down and the joints are then taped and filled prior to the application of the finish, which can be provided in all of the well known patterns. Any coving or decorative roses need to be put up *before* the work commences and the 'artexers', who normally work from the floor with long handled applicators, will often do this job as well.

With a set ceiling, the board is tacked grey side down and then two coats of plaster are applied after all the joints have been scrim taped and filled. A board scaffold will be required to enable the plasterers to reach the ceiling by hand and, with this type of finish, decorative mouldings, roses or coving are fixed *after* the ceiling is done. Which is best? Well again it's down to choice. 'Artex' is slightly flexible making it eminently suitable for new buildings where shrinkage will undoubtedly occur. It cannot be allowed to get wet as it will literally wash off and will almost certainly stain and, whilst most people don't bother to paint it, you really should consider doing so, at the very least, in all wet rooms. Set ceilings provide a 'classy' finish that is, nevertheless prone to cracking, at least in the early years of a new building. However it is easily patched up and filled and redecoration is comparatively easy.

Floors - If a floor is to be screeded then this job falls to the plasterer. The most common reason for choosing a screeded floor in lieu of a floating floor is where ceramic, stone or quarry tiles are going to be used. The choice, however, does need to be made at an early stage of the construction because screed laid on the necessary floor insulation has to be at least 65mm thick and that means that in those rooms where it is to be employed, the floor beams or oversite will have to be set down in relation to other rooms which may have a floating floor. This doesn't create any real problem but you do need to think about the floor coverings for each room if you are to maintain the same levels on all floors. Carpets and underlay are probably not too different in overall thickness to most ceramic tiles and decorative wood floorings but stone slabs are considerably thicker and you will need to take this into account when setting the sub

The electrician getting on with his first fix.

Tacking the ceiling of a Potton home.

Underfloor central heating coils laid before the screed.

Screeding the floor, not a job for those with bad knees.

floor levels in each room. On the top floor if you're screeding a pot and beam floor then it's not that easy to set the beams up or down without affecting the ceiling heights on the ground floor so it's probably just as well to stick to flooring mediums of equal thickness.

Many of the underfloor central heating systems rely and work on the principle of the heating coils being buried in a screed and the various manufacturers and suppliers will have differing requirements for both its thickness and the positioning of the insulation. In some cases the equipment may include elements of backing and insulation to be set in the screed and your plasterer may well have to work in with the heating engineer or plumber on this one. Domestic hot water pipes may also have to run through the screed and in some areas there is a requirement that these are ducted.

Check that any floor to be screeded is clean and free from dust or mortar before any membrane or insulation is laid. In some situations the membrane goes below the insulation and in others it is laid on top of it before the screed is laid. In all cases you'll need to ensure that it is laid and that, having been so, it isn't punctured or rucked up during the work. For a lasting and stable screed the mix needs to be a dryish one, of one part of cement to three to four and half parts of sharp sand, and the temptation to walk on the new screed should be resisted for two days.

Finally a word about garages where a pot and beam floor has been used. These have to be screeded to provide the necessary structural integrity and strength and this is done by means of a screed having a minimum thickness of 50mm with reinforcement mesh set within it.

External render - The rendering of the exterior is normally carried out when the scaffolding is still up, with the topcoat render finish applied as it comes down. Blockwork walling needs one undercoat in moderate conditions, with two in high exposure situations, finished off with a topcoat to which a waterproof additive can sometimes be added. Timber framed sections will need to be wire lathed before rendering and it's necessary to provide a ventilated cavity between the render and the sheathing. With unbacked lathing this needs to be 50mm and with backed lathing it has to be 25mm.

All external corners, drip beading over windows and bell drips where render stops, need to be formed using purpose made metal lathes and beading. It's not necessary to decorate external render but most people prefer to do so and there are any number of proprietary finishes on the market, all with conflicting and competing claims. Perhaps the cheapest and most commonly used is external emulsion and, with many colours, but not with white, the colour pigment can be added to the render mix itself to provide a through colour. Consistency is the watchword with all external render, in terms of thickness, mix and colour.

Decorator

Many selfbuilders opt to carry out their own decoration and most, if not all, make a pretty good job of it. For those who don't want to get involved, the trade can either be supply and fix or labour only with the prices worked out either on the basis of measured rates or by reference to the time the guy reckons the job is going to take. On sites you'll hear the phrase, "If you can't make it, paint it", and certainly in the hierarchy within the building industry, the painter and decorator is at the bottom. That's not a position they deserve because, firstly, the work they do is often the making or breaking of a well finished house and, secondly, quite a lot of their work involves 'snagging' or tidying up work done by the preceding trades. Preparation is two thirds of the painter's job and that preparation includes rubbing down and filling any holes or cracks and generally making good any surface long before any paint is applied.

I'm not going to go into the differing paints and finishes in this forum. Suffice it to say that there are many different products on the market and that you should make your choices by clearly reading the specifications and manufacturers claims, backed up by recommendation from both professionals and from others who have experienced the product.

The tools of the trade are almost always provided by the decorators themselves, including brushes, cleaning fluids, sandpaper, fillers and hard tools but you do need to establish this fact with the subcontractors you engage. The one thing you can make sure of is that the trade is carried out in as clean an environment as possible, given that this is a building site. You remember me writing beforehand about grey areas? Well, this is where they all really come together. The decorator is often in the house at the same time as many of the other second fix trades and many's the time I've seen them working away, painting things like skirtings and architraves whilst, in the same room, piles of shavings and dust are being accumulated by a carpenter hanging a door or a plumber fixing radiators to the wall. At other times I've seen a decorator trying to work around piles of rubbish that have been roughly swept to the centre of the room. I would suggest to you that the best thing to do in this situation is to ask the decorator to go and do something else until the other trades have finished and that you don't get him back to that room until you've arranged for all of the dust and rubbish to be cleared out. It's not the job of the carpenter making the pile of shavings to clear them up and sweep them out any more than it is of the decorator.

Whose job is it? Yes, you've guessed it, it's the management - and that's you.

Glazier

Oftimes this is a specific supply and fix trade but at other times the work can be carried out by either one of the other subcontractors like the carpenter or by the selfbuilders themselves. Most Upvc and aluminium joinery and, these days, quite a lot of the better quality timber joinery, comes pre-glazed, so what we're talking about here is the glazing of timber softwood or hardwood windows and doors.

Any price that you get for this trade will, almost certainly, have been arrived at by reference to the time that will be taken and the amount and scope of the materials that you want the tradesman to supply. Once again I'm not going to use this book to discuss the technicalities of glazing. Suffice it to say that just sticking bits of glass in the holes isn't what it's all about

and that there are specific and carefully formulated procedures and recommendations that need to be followed. Modern double glazing units have to be carefully and scientifically manufactured and their fitting has to follow a precise pattern and sequence that whoever is undertaking this trade should be fully aware of.

If at all possible, the glazing should be done off the scaffold. However, this isn't always feasible as you may find that sometimes the scaffold obstructs the windows. If you do glaze whilst trades are working above then try to make sure that some sort of protection is afforded to the units as well as to the frames and, whilst on that subject, when the units are delivered, make sure that they are properly and safely stored in accordance with the manufacturer's or supplier's recommendations. Poor treatment of the units at any stage may result in their breaking down, or in stress fractures.

Ceramic floor and wall tilers

I'm hesitant to include this as a trade in this book as most selfbuilders opt to do their own. Nevertheless it is a recognised trade and whilst there are labour only guys out there, the most usual combination is that the suppliers will either put you onto them or include the fixing in their price.

Professionals at this trade are extremely fast in comparison to lay people and the job they do is often very much superior. If the suppliers of the tiles can get you a reasonable fixing rate then I would suggest that you earnestly consider it and when you weigh up the time it will take you, you may feel that it's worthwhile. A clean dust and grease free surface is the key to successful tiling, whether on floor or wall, and the quality of the grouting, and its suitability to its situation, is very important.

Health & Safety

There are various statutory requirements for those who run building sites most of which are studiously ignored by selfbuilders and subcontractors alike. Provision of latrine facilities, a hut for meals, protective clothing, a first aid box and accident register are required by the Factories

Inspector who is extremely unlikely to visit your site. However the provisions and requirements still stand and, particularly if you are employing more than five people on your site at any one time, you could find yourself running foul of what is essentially criminal rather than civil law. The Management of Health and Safety at Work Regulations 1992 apply to everyone at work, regardless of what work it is and they require that adequate risk assessments take place regarding every aspect of work. Employers and the self employed must identify any hazards involved with their work, the likelihood of any harm arising and the precautions that they feel are necessary. In particular the self employed must ensure, so far as is reasonably practicable, their own health and safety and that of other workers or members of the public. There are various methods and suggestions contained in the regulations which can be obtained from the Health and Safety Executive (HSE) but they all really boil down to a common sense attitude to safety at work.

One thing that is glaringly absent on most selfbuild sites is the wearing of hard hats. Keep a few handy in your site hut and insist to all of the labour on site that they should wear them. Chances are that, whenever your back is turned or you're away from site, they still won't, but at the very least, when a tile falls off the top lift of the scaffold, if the guy whose head it enters isn't wearing one, it'll be down to him. More importantly, perhaps, if backed up in writing or by a notice, prominently displayed in the site hut, your insurance won't be invalidated.

Building Control and warranty inspections

I've already mentioned this in previous chapters but it does bear repetition here just to remind you that the Building Inspectors and the inspectors from whichever warranty company you've chosen to use will need adequate notice of your reaching various stages in the build. If there are cards then someone needs to be responsible for them being sent in and you need to make sure that no work is progressed further than any satisfactory inspection. Remember, these inspec-

tors, and especially the Building Inspectors, can be very good friends or very bad enemies but if you stick to the rules, and make sure that your site runs to them, they're much more likely to be the former.

Creation of a new access, alterations to the highway and connections to sewers

When a planning consent is issued, the applicant is advised to contact the Divisional Surveyor of the local County Council before any work is undertaken or planned in connection with the highway and there are information packs that will be sent out listing and detailing the procedures to be followed.

First of all, only approved and accredited contractors can carry out any works to the highway and, strictly speaking, that applies to any part of the highway whether metalled or otherwise. There are instances, however, where other contractors can sometimes be authorised to carry out works to the unsurfaced sections of the highway such as the grass verges, so long as they have the appropriate insurances, but I would stress that this is at the discretion of the highways authority. An approved and accredited contractor can be an individual who has passed the relevant tests and satisfied the stringent financial criteria, but it is more likely to be a firm and the local authority will be able to supply you with a list of the names of suitable companies. A Section 50 licence, under the New Roads and Street Works Act 1991, is required to open up or carry out any work to the highway and this is issued by the highways authority, which is usually the County Council to whom the authority has been devolved. A new sewage connection, within the highway, will require not only this licence, but also consent, given under Section 106 of the Water Industry Act 1991, to make a connection to the public sewer. There is a legal right to this connection which is issued by or on behalf of the water authority, although in many cases the local authority act as their agents and application to make the new connection has to be made through them. Some authorities insist on doing this work themselves.

In areas where it has been identified that the

sewer is overloaded, the local authority may adopt a policy restricting further development or connection to the sewers. On the face of it this would seem to fly in the face of the legal right to connect that I have mentioned above but the local authorities get around that one by operating and enforcing the policy through the planning procedures.

Any works to sewers, driveways or roadways, within the curtilage of your site, can be carried out by you and your normal contractors, even if it is intended that they will be adopted when completed. Of course, the works will have to be carried out to the specification and approval of the authorities and, in certain cases, as discussed in the chapter, 'Finding a site', it will be necessary for a bond to be taken out. Once the works stray beyond your site and onto the metalled highway, including the creation of any bellmouth, then the work has to be put in the hands of an approved or accredited contractor. Many groundworkers will quote a selfbuilder for all works to the driveway and sewers within the site but make it clear that their responsibility stops at the boundary with the highway. This is all perfectly normal but it is important that the selfbuilder identifies the fact that there will be an additional contract, and not inconsiderable cost, for the works within the highway.

Selfbuild site foremen

The idea of employing someone to specifically look after and manage a site on a day to day basis is a very attractive one but it's more often thought of than carried out. Nevertheless, from time to time one does come across a selfbuilder who has engaged a site manager or working foreman for the day to day supervision. Invariably this is a retired professional, and I am usually told that they have welcomed the job to liven up their dull retirement. This has always seemed a very sensible thing to do, and if you find the right man who has spent a lifetime working for a builder or developer he should surely be able to save you enough to cover the cost of employing him, particularly if he is paid on an informal basis.

Do be careful to pick the right person for this and beware the 'white coat' syndrome. If it's someone who's retired from the building industry then all should be well but if it's someone who used to be a factory foreman, where everyone clocked on and off, then you could find yourself with an empty site.

Some of the package deal companies have schemes whereby they introduce you to builders who will either undertake the construction as builders or will 'project manage' your new home. In effect they look out for and engage the various tradesmen and purchase the materials for them with you paying the bills plus an agreed fee for this service.

Buying materials

If you are building on your own and are not using the services of a package company you will spend at least £30,000 on materials. Buying them 10% more advantageously than the other chap will give you a saving of £3,000, while buying them 10% less well will cost you an extra £3,000. It is worthwhile giving very careful consideration to your buying arrangements.

A major factor in this is the delivery arrangements. A best buy in materials that can only be delivered on a 40 foot trailer at an unspecified time during the week may be less attractive than the same consignment at a slightly higher price on a small lorry that can get to the back of your site with guaranteed delivery on a Saturday morning. It's also worth a lot to have deliveries made on vehicles with cranes, for unlike a builder or developer, you're unlikely to always have a digger or dumper on site at the right time to unload for you. If the lorry does not have a crane, then you will have to make sure that there are enough people about to unload it by hand. Often you will discover that the delivery arrangements are a key factor in choosing a supplier.

It is well worth while to start thinking where you should buy materials just as soon as you are certain that you are going to build, and you should start to collect leaflets and prices as early as possible. It may seem that there are obvious advantages in putting all your business through one builders' merchant or perhaps through one of the DIY superstores, but in practice most selfbuilders use a number of suppliers. Decisions about this depend on how much time you have to shop around and whether you live in an area where there are plenty of sources of supply. The best way to go about finding the best prices is to get to know the standard list price for the material or component concerned and then to find the salesman and ask him face to face what is his 'best price'. If this is not possible, ask him on the phone. You are unlikely to be offered very competitive terms by letter if you are only buying in one house quantities. There are some materials that you will only order after having given very careful consideration to samples, particularly items like handmade bricks. In this case make it quite clear that you are ordering 'as per sample' and be sure that you keep the sample safely somewhere. When you take delivery of anything which cannot be checked as it is unloaded, always give a qualified receipt on the delivery note, writing 'not checked' above your signature. This will enormously strengthen your hand in any subsequent debate about whether you got what you ordered, but remember that if there are any such problems you must deal with them immediately.

One of the advantages of buying direct from manufacturers is that you can use the services of their sales representatives, and this can be very useful indeed. Of course, it is rarely cost effective for them to spend much time with a small customer like you, but they will often do so, especially if you go out of your way to welcome them with a cup of tea or a walk down to the pub for lunch. A tile manufacturers rep will not only advise on the ranges of tiles likely to be acceptable to the local planning officer, but he will also talk about features such as modern verge systems, patent flashings around chimneys or the local tiling contractors who are most likely to suit you. Reps are also able to advise where their materials have been used locally so that you can go to see them in situ, which is a good deal better than looking at samples.

The sources of supply used by selfbuilders are generally as follows:

Bricks - These are usually ordered though either a Builders Merchant, who will have allocations, or from specialist brick merchants or manufacturers, many of whom, advertise regularly in the selfbuild magazines. For whole houses the bricks are usually quoted at a price per thousand and you should ensure that the price you are given includes for delivery to your site with a crane offload vehicle. If samples are required for yourself or, more probably, the planners then most companies, in anticipation of an order, will arrange for these to be delivered. Builders Merchants often have extensive brick libraries and their staff can be awfully helpful and knowledgeable about alternatives and prices.

If you are using second hand bricks then you should make sure that what gets delivered is the same as the sample. You should also as far as is possible make sure that you've got plenty of bricks and whilst the wastage factor in ordering new bricks might be 5%, with second hand this might well have to double. Remember too that many older bricks are in Imperial sizes and that in some localities bricks were a very peculiar size indeed.

Stone - If it's reformed stone then it's ordered from similar sources to the bricks and in many respects it has all the same properties. Be careful, however, with the different ratios of the differing sized blocks that go to make up the walling and make sure that you are, in fact, getting these in the correct ratio to enable you to end up with the coursing you have chosen. It's perhaps best to put the onus for this on the suppliers by telling them quite categorically that you are relying on their expertise in this matter.

Natural stone will normally be sold, direct, by the quarry and it is either done so as random 'as dug' or as cut and dressed. If it's the former then it's frightfully difficult to establish, as it's sold by the tonne, that you've got the right amount and you'll probably have to rely on the rough guide from the quarry, as to just how many metres of walling you'll get per tonne. It'll all depend on the heaviness of the stone of course, as it will with cut and dressed stone, although, with this, the quarry will probably be able to be much more specific about how many square metres of walling you'll get, usually between 4 and 6 per tonne.

Flint - Usually brought through specialists by the drum, either napped (split) or unnapped. One drum will usually provide about 4 square metres of walling. As this is only really used in specific localised areas, the dealers are usually well known to those in the trade or to local merchants.

Blocks - The main manufacturers of walling blocks only supply through recognised merchants although smaller local companies may deal with you direct. Prices are quoted by the square metre and, as with bricks, you will need to establish the price for delivery to your site on crane offloading vehicles. Packs are usually shrink wrapped in polythene and, on the lorry they are often also on pallets. If you need to retain these pallets there is often a special charge and you will always have to clear it with the depot before delivery. The pallets remain the property of the block company and they will arrange to pick them up one day, maybe with an additional charge.

Joinery - These can be obtained direct from manufacturers but, with the larger companies, they are more usually obtained from merchants and stockists. You'll undoubtedly want to make sure that you're getting what you want with these items and you'll no doubt, make sure that you know all about their properties, benefits and glazing arrangements. The literature from the manufacturers will tell you all about this but you will need to make sure that when they are delivered every item is checked thoroughly for any damage in transit. Establish, as well, which items or ranges are stock items and which are made to order. A replacement or addition in the latter category can involve an awfully long wait.

Roof trusses - These can be ordered direct from the manufacturers or though your Builders Merchant. Don't be tempted to try and define what you're ordering and instead confine yourself to asking for a pre-fabricated roof to suit your particular drawings. That way, if there are any problems then the manufacturers will have to solve them. Sometimes the roof manufacturers will also supply the ancillary roofing materials such as facia, barge, soffit etc and you do need to establish this fact, even if the quantities and sizes are left up to the suppliers themselves.

You will also need to establish just what delivery arrangements there are and when the trusses arrive you may well need some extra labour on site to manhandle them off.

Timber - Timber is priced by the cubic metre at the yard but happily this is normally translated into various prices per metre according to the sections. Most Builders Merchants have their own timber yards or else there are specialist timber importers who will sell direct to the selfbuilder. If timber is required to be treated then this is normally carried out in the yard, for an extra cost, and it may delay the delivery, as that department of most yards is always at full stretch. Be careful about delivery as you may get an extremely big lorry arriving with an awful lot of wood on it and no crane offload, so you may well have to organise extra labour to be on site.

Roof tiles/slates - Tile company reps will often deal directly with the selfbuilder, even if any eventual order is placed through a local Builders Merchant. The merchants themselves will also probably have a library of roof tiles and slates, maybe attached to and part of their brick library, and their staff may be able to suggest suitable alternatives from various companies. Any order should be made on the basis of the supply of the roofing materials that the suppliers have quoted from your plans and the quantities should be left to them. It's unlikely that the quotation will fail to detail the amounts that they're supplying, so, if you're short they may still refer you back to the quotation. But, if you can definitely establish that the fault lies with them, then in the unlikely event, at least they'll move heaven and earth to get the balance to you so as not to delay the job. You need to establish whether they will be supplying any ancillary materials and/or fixings and, in like manner to the tiles themselves, it's perhaps better to let the suppliers recommend the quantities.

Glazing

Many joinery manufacturers will now supply double glazing units to suit their windows, but most selfbuilders buy them separately as they find this more advantageous. If you are ordering glass make sure that the measurements that you give to the supplier are clearly marked as either 'rebate size' or 'tight glass size'. Better still, ask his rep to come and measure up for you, and then if something doesn't fit it is his fault.

Plumbing and heating materials

If you're using a supply and fix plumber and heating engineer then there will be very little that you need to buy for this trade. If you're using a labour only subcontractor in part or in full then materials will be available from either specialist Plumbers Merchants or from normal Builders Merchants. For those who are dealing direct with specialist manufacturers or suppliers of equipment, the like of underfloor central heating or special boilers, the price may well be of secondary consideration to the nature of that which is being offered. Nevertheless do try and check that you're not being taken for a ride by reference to different prices of similar equipment from other manufacturers or suppliers. With 'conventional' systems, some merchants will take your plans and give a lump sum price for any materials.

Kitchen and utility room units and furniture

Where does one start? The offers are endless as are the ranges of differing units and equipment. 40% discounts are often only the start of what's available and in the course of my travels I've met many selfbuilders who bought kitchens at one third of the original price, just because they were in the right place at the right time. Keep a look out in your local paper and an extra look out for kitchen showrooms changing over their displays. Bear in mind that flair and imagination can often count more than just bunging money at something and bear in mind, also that the most expensive units, have many of the physical characteristics of some of the cheaper ones. Try to remember, as well, that in 5 –10 years time your kitchen may look dated and, if its cost was a reasonable rather than an excessive proportion of your budget, you could give your home a face-lift by getting a new kitchen.

Sanitaryware

Much of the same applies to this. The Builders

Merchants often have displays and there are specialist shops and merchants throughout the land, some of which are frightfully expensive and awfully up market. My strictures regarding flair and imagination being more important than money also apply in equal measure. Out of town warehouse companies often have breathtaking bargains and, if you live on the south coast, a trip to France or Belgium might be worth its while. Gordon and Jenny in the selfbuild stories did just that for these items and for many others.

Insulation materials

Insulation quilt for roofs and insulation slabs for cavity walling are often best bought from specialist insulation suppliers, who you will find listed in the Yellow Pages. However Builders merchants and some of the out of town DIY stores often have special offers at huge discounts.

Electrical goods

If you don't use a supply and fix electrician then you'll probably be able to buy much of what you need at your local Builders Merchant. Alternatively there are specialist electrical outlets, some of which may not want to open an account with you and all of whom are not very sympathetic to the general public, preferring as they do, to sell within the trade. As far as light fittings and electrical goods and equipment are concerned you could probably do no better than the out of town stores.

Plasterboard and plastering materials

Wet plastering materials and ancillary materials are best supplied by your plasterer but plasterboard is one thing that it might pay you to supply and this is available from your local Builders Merchants. It may not come directly from them and it may be delivered directly to your site by the manufacturers, in which case, if you don't have a fork lift on site, you'll have to gear up some pretty strong labour to unload it and carry it into the dry.

Plant and scaffold hire.

Every selfbuilder hires plant or equipment at some stage in building a new home, and arranging your hiring in the most effective way is an important part of your project planning.

You need to plan your tool hire arrangements at the same time that you are deciding on suppliers and, indeed, your local Builders Merchants will, in all probability, have a tool hire department. In addition, in most larger towns, you will have a choice of tool hire and plant hire companies that normally have, either a typed list, or a glossy brochure of just what's available. Give them a ring or pop in and see them and ask about their services. If a firm seems keen to have your business they are likely to look after your requirements. If they are casual about explaining their service to you, then they are probably only interested in their established trade customers

Much will depend on where a hire depot is situated, and a small local operation may suit you better than a plant hire super-store. Remember that the firm that you choose is going to be very important to you, and take time to go to see what is on offer, and judge the reliability of both the equipment and the delivery promises that will be made. Most of the leading hire companies belong to a trade association called Hire Association Europe. They subscribe to a national code of practice and have a common form of contract. In recent years this has done much to raise standards generally and particularly to promote safety. HAE also provides an arbitration service when required.

When you have decided on a hire company, consider how you are going to pay them. You may get a better discount as an account customer, or cash terms may be cheaper. The smaller the hire company, the more you can negotiate on this. Remember that they will all want deposits, and two separate forms of identification. A driving licence and a credit card are usually all that is required, although some depots that hire out expensive machines like excavators will ask you to pose for a polaroid photo which stays with them until the machine is returned. All good fun. You may be able to use your credit card for the deposit, and usually the card voucher stays in the till and is destroyed when you return the equipment. This is really a form of 'no deposit' hire, and very useful.

It is important to remember that the plant which you hire is probably the most dangerous

equipment that you will have on your site, and that a juicy accident would really set back your building programme. All HAE hirers are committed to providing proper instruction on the use of power tools, emphasising safety, and have appropriate protective clothing for sale. This instruction is very important and the standard of it varies. Some hire shops have specially trained staff responsible for this and take it very seriously indeed whilst others are perhaps a little more lax. If you feel that you need to be given additional instruction, then ask for it and, if you feel that you're not getting what you need from that company then go and see someone else.

This leads us to consideration of insurance for plant. Many of the hire shops or depots offer an indemnity to cover damage done to hired machinery or plant by an inexperienced operator, for an additional cost on the hire charge. This policy does not normally cover for theft from site and if it gets stolen then you may be liable for the full cost of any replacement, unless, of course, you're covered by another policy such as your selfbuild insurance. If you're only going to have machinery or tools on site for, say, a day at a time, then this is perhaps, still the best way of covering things. On the other hand, the selfbuild insurance policies that every selfbuilder should have, can give cover for plant and machinery on site, whether hired, owned or borrowed, either for an extra premium, or in some cases as part and parcel of the original policy subject to various excesses. It really depends on your individual circumstances and I would suggest that the best course of action on this one, is to talk to your broker.

There are two items of hired in plant that need special consideration. The first is your mixer. Small mixers with less than 4 cu. ft. capacity are unpopular with bricklayers and should be avoided. Larger diesel mixers are ruggedly built, and are often offered for sale very cheaply through small ads in local papers or on notice boards in builders merchants. If you are a fair judge of used machinery it will be cheaper to buy than to hire, particularly as you should be able to sell on your mixer when you finish. Some mixers at Milton Keynes plots have been owned by dozens of selfbuilders, and, incidentally, so have many site caravans.

Scaffolding needs thinking about carefully. It is possible to hire scaffold for erection on site and indeed there may be instances where, at the end of the job, it's necessary to hire in something like a tower scaffold for a particular task. I do not believe, however, that it's a good idea for the selfbuilder to attempt to provide a full scaffold for on site erection by either himself or by one of the other tradesmen. Bricklayers will often volunteer to erect the scaffold as they go and, in the past, I have to admit that that is what I have often done. But in today's climate of awareness about health and safety in general and the new legislation, in particular, I really believe that this is not good advice. Bricklayers may well erect a scaffold that gets them through their trade but, they might not really care about how the tiler is going to get on or how the plumber will get to do his flashings around the chimney, knowing that by the time those chaps are up on it, they'll be long gone. And if the scaffolding's dangerous or illegal and one of the following trades or a member of your family falls off or through it, I'll give you one guess who's going to be liable – yes it's you. Reputable hire and erect scaffolding firms, who will come along to site and erect a proper and legal scaffold, are the answer. Most of them are fairly reliable and will usually come with just 24 hours notice to raise, lower or extend the scaffold, working in with the other tradesmen as they go. To cover yourself even further, make sure that when you engage a company you state, in writing, that their scaffold should conform to all of the Health and Safety legislation and to best practise. Hire is normally quoted as being for minimum period, often ten weeks, with a weekly rate thereafter and it is normally quoted by reference to the plans. Foot scaffolds, for uneven ground or, board scaffolds, for internal plastering of ceilings etc., are not usually included and, if you need these then you'll have to ask for an additional price.

One thing that you should especially watch out for is the treatment of the scaffolding by other tradesmen. Firstly, don't ever let them alter the scaffold by themselves, for that could invalidate any liabilities of the main hire and erection company and any warranties they will have given you. Next, keep an eye out for tradesmen cutting up scaffold boards or using the angle grinder you've hired in for another job, to cut off the end of a putlock. It's you that will be charged for these at the end of the job, as indeed you will for the pile of fittings and clips that get buried, simply because nobody bothered to move them.

Finally, electric tools. These should always be connected through an RCD contact breaker. The hire companies have suitable plug-in units available, but they do not provide them unless you ask for them because most hirers are planning to do jobs at houses that have contact breakers in the fuse box. If your temporary site supply is not RCD protected, hire a plug-in unit.

Caravans and mobile homes

Caravans are often used as site huts, and in this role they are not subject to planning controls. If you are worried about how safe they will be it may be a good idea to remove the wheels and take them home so that the van cannot be towed away.

If you are going to live in it you will be following in the footsteps of thousands of other selfbuilders, and although the authorities may challenge you, you are most unlikely to need planning consent. This is mentioned and discussed in the chapter, 'The planning scene'. However, the sight of your caravan may make your neighbours uneasy, so it is a good idea to reassure them that it will not be a permanent feature of the landscape. Another factor is that there may be a covenant in the title to the plot which prohibits caravans on the land. If it is an old covenant you can probably ignore it, knowing that it would take longer to get anything done about it than you will take to build the home. However, if the person selling the land to you has imposed a covenant of this sort you should get him to agree in writing to your having a caravan while you are building, before you exchange contracts.

Most residential caravans on selfbuild sites are connected up to the services at an early stage, which may give rise to a demand for council tax.

You will have to play this by ear. If children are involved it is essential to fence the caravan off from the building work so that they are not technically living on a building site, which would break Health and Safety legislation. A fence will also provide privacy which will be ever more welcome as the job progresses.

Programming

If you flick forward to the selfbuild story about Michael and Patricia you'll see a wonderful programme that Patricia did before any work started on site. The value of a programme such as this, or indeed one that isn't quite as sophisticated and is simply a list on a piece of paper, is in anticipating when a particular task is to be done or when machinery or materials will be required. Every job programme is different, of course, but on the following pages there are set out, two simple work sequences for bungalows, one built in brick and block and the other, in timber and brick.

Moving in

Selfbuilders are often concerned about just when they are considered to have occupied their new home if they decide to move in with the building work still going on around them. There are no hard and fast rules for this, and for most purposes you can decide what it suits you as the date when you became a householder. Indeed,

there will probably be different dates for different purposes, such as:

* Council Tax. You are unlikely to have any problems if you state firmly when you moved in as a householder (as opposed to being a selfbuild family camping in the house to provide security), particularly if everything has moved along steadily. However be very positive. Some councils still issue completion certificates for Building Regulation purposes, which you can quote, or not, as appropriate. If you have been living in a caravan on the site and have paid appropriate council tax, make sure that you do not find yourself being billed twice when you move into the house.

* Insurances. Insurance companies which are used to selfbuilders accept that selfbuild policies and home owner's policies usually overlap. Your belongings while you are 'camping' in the house are not covered on a selfbuilder's policy, but can be separately covered as the first stage of a home owner's policy. If your selfbuilder's policy runs out before you finish all the non-structural work, you will be considered to be a home owner who is doing normal DIY work on his property. DMS Services or other specialist brokers can advise on this.

Project planning stage one — establishing a budget and a design

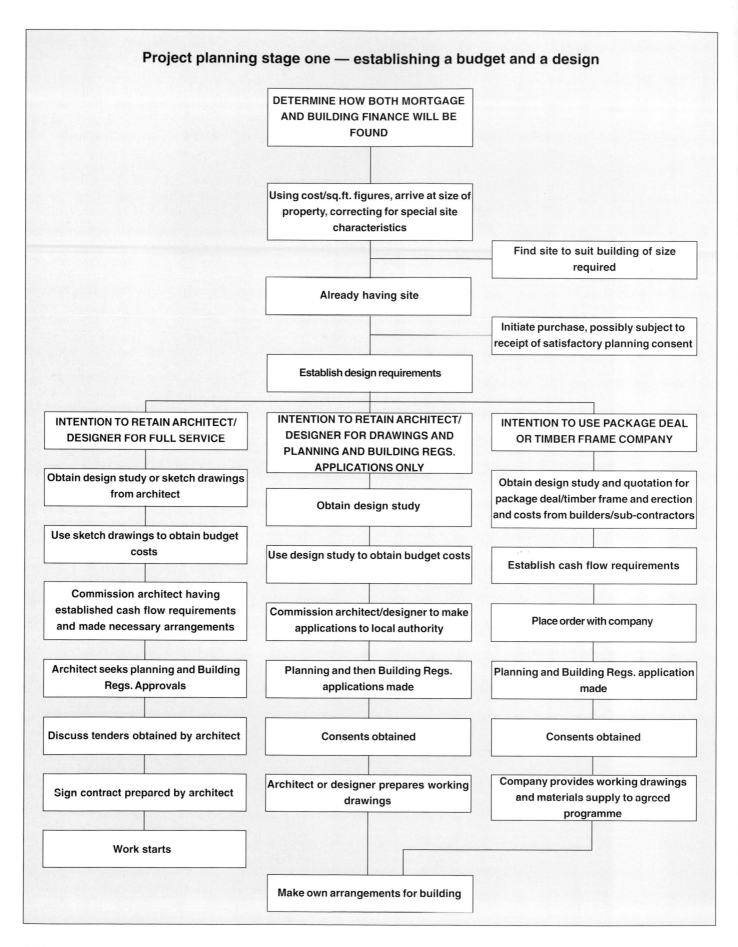

DETERMINE HOW BOTH MORTGAGE AND BUILDING FINANCE WILL BE FOUND

Using cost/sq.ft. figures, arrive at size of property, correcting for special site characteristics

Find site to suit building of size required

Already having site

Initiate purchase, possibly subject to receipt of satisfactory planning consent

Establish design requirements

INTENTION TO RETAIN ARCHITECT/ DESIGNER FOR FULL SERVICE	**INTENTION TO RETAIN ARCHITECT/ DESIGNER FOR DRAWINGS AND PLANNING AND BUILDING REGS. APPLICATIONS ONLY**	**INTENTION TO USE PACKAGE DEAL OR TIMBER FRAME COMPANY**
Obtain design study or sketch drawings from architect	Obtain design study	Obtain design study and quotation for package deal/timber frame and erection and costs from builders/sub-contractors
Use sketch drawings to obtain budget costs	Use design study to obtain budget costs	Establish cash flow requirements
Commission architect having established cash flow requirements and made necessary arrangements	Commission architect/designer to make applications to local authority	Place order with company
Architect seeks planning and Building Regs. Approvals	Planning and then Building Regs. applications made	Planning and Building Regs. application made
Discuss tenders obtained by architect	Consents obtained	Consents obtained
Sign contract prepared by architect	Architect or designer prepares working drawings	Company provides working drawings and materials supply to agreed programme
Work starts		

Make own arrangements for building

Project planning stage two — to use builders or sub-contractors

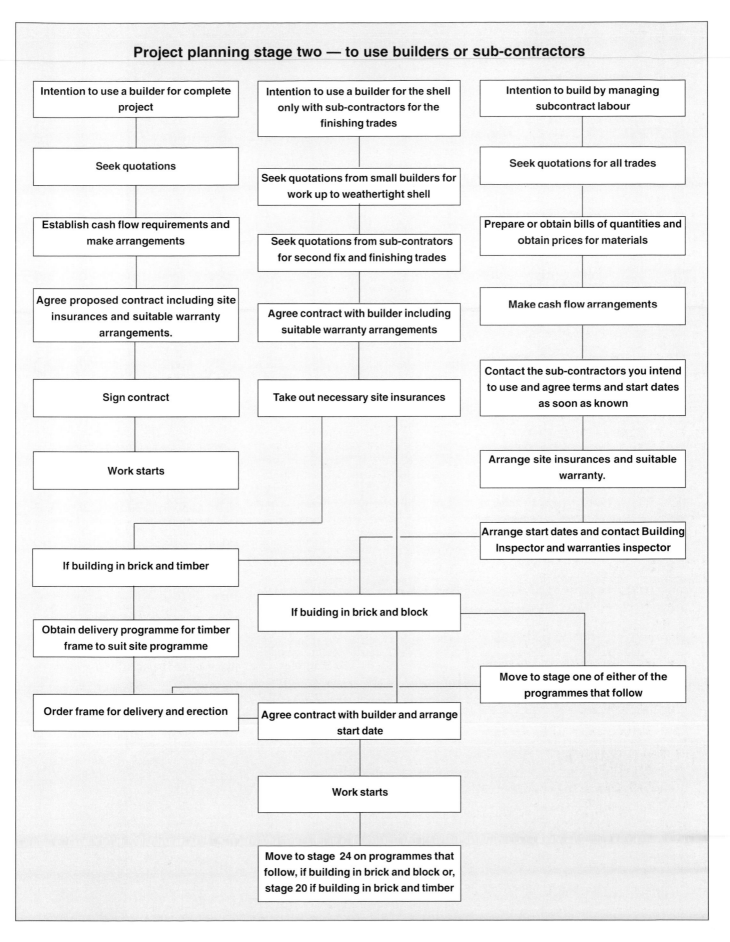

Intention to use a builder for complete project	Intention to use a builder for the shell only with sub-contractors for the finishing trades	Intention to build by managing subcontract labour
Seek quotations	Seek quotations from small builders for work up to weathertight shell	Seek quotations for all trades
Establish cash flow requirements and make arrangements	Seek quotations from sub-contrators for second fix and finishing trades	Prepare or obtain bills of quantities and obtain prices for materials
Agree proposed contract including site insurances and suitable warranty arrangements.	Agree contract with builder including suitable warranty arrangements	Make cash flow arrangements
Sign contract	Take out necessary site insurances	Contact the sub-contractors you intend to use and agree terms and start dates as soon as known
Work starts		Arrange site insurances and suitable warranty.

Arrange start dates and contact Building Inspector and warranties inspector

If building in brick and timber

If buiding in brick and block

Obtain delivery programme for timber frame to suit site programme

Move to stage one of either of the programmes that follow

Order frame for delivery and erection

Agree contract with builder and arrange start date

Work starts

Move to stage 24 on programmes that follow, if building in brick and block or, stage 20 if building in brick and timber

Project planning for a simple brick and block bungalow with a beam and block ground floor, and with the plumbers, electricians and plasterers as supply and fix trades. Plasterboard and santitaryware from self builders supply

	Action	Requirements
1.	Apply for all services	
2.	Apply for building water supply	Water butt and hose
3.	Arrange insurances and warranties	
4.	Provide access, hard standing, site storage	Hardcore, site hut
5.	Strip top soil and stack for future use	Digger hire
6.	Excavate foundations, service trenches and drive and spread hardcore	Digger and hardcore
7.	Building inspector and warranty inspector to inspect excavations	
8.	Pour foundation concrete	Concrete, any ancillary or reinforcing materials required
9.	Building Inspector and warranty inspector to inspect foundation concrete	
10.	Build foundation blockwork	Concrete blocks, wall ties, sand and cement, drainage exit lintels, cranked ventilators
11.	Lay damp proof course	dpc
12.	Building inspector to inspect dpc	
13.	Position floor beams and infill with blocks	Floor beams, infill blocks
14.	Brush grout beam and block floor	Dry sand and cement
15.	Building Inspector and warranty inspector to inspect oversite	
16.	Build superstructure to wallplate	Bricks, blocks, wall ties, wall insulation, door and window frames, lintels, flue liners, meter boxes
17.	Warranty inspector to inspect up to plate	
18.	Carpenter to scarf wallplate, bricklayer to bed it	Wallplate
19.	Rear end trusses as template for gable ends	Roof trusses
20.	Bricklayers to build and cut up gable ends	Bricks, blocks, wall ties, sand and cement
21.	Bricklayers to build chimney through roof	Flue liners, bricks, lead tray, sand and cement
22.	Carpenters to fix remaining trusses and finish roof, including fascias, soffits	Balance of roofing materials
23.	Tilers to felt, batten and tile roof with plumber in attendance for any flashings and to position vent pipes and lead skirts	Roof tiles, felt and batten and any ancillary fittings or fixings
24.	Warranty inspector to inspect roof	
25.	Decorator to decorate fascia and soffits	Decoration materials
26.	Plumber to fix guttering prior to scaffolding coming down	Rainwater goods
27.	Carpenters first fix – door linings, window boards, tank stands, loft trap, external doors and patio doors	Carpenter first fix materials
28.	Lay drains, services and bring into house	Drainage materials including Pipes, inspection covers, pea shingle
29.	Building Inspector and warranty inspector to inspect drains on test	
30.	Backfill drains and service trenches	Pea shingle
31.	Glaze all windows	Glazing materials
32.	Plumbing and central heating first fix	Appropriate materials from sub-contractor's supply
33.	Electricians first fix	Appropriate materials from sub-contractor's supply
34.	Bricklayers to build fireplace	Fireplace bricks, stone or surround
35.	Lay floating floor	Flooring grade insulation and t&g chipboard, glue
36.	Plaster out	Plasterers materials, plasterboard
37.	Warranty inspector to inspect 1st fix complete	
38.	Plumbers second fix and water on	Sub-contractors materials supply, sanititaryware, sink unit
39.	Carpenters second fix, including fitting of kitchen units	Kitchen units, internal doors and furniture, skirtings and architraves
40.	Test out and services on.	Telephone installation
41.	Decorations	All decoration materials
42.	Ceramic wall tiling	Tiles, adhesive and grout
43.	Building and warranty inspectors final inspection	
44.	Clean through and arrange for Householders insurance to take over from site insurance	

Project planning for a rectangular bungalow built in brick and timber, with a beam and block ground floor, cut verges and with the plumbers, electricians and plasterers as supply and fix trades. Plasterboard and sanitaryware from self builders supply

	Action	*Requirements*
1.	Apply for all services	
2.	Apply for building water supply	Water butt and hose
3.	Arrange insurances and warranties	
4.	Provide access, hard standing, site storage	Hardcore, site hut
5.	Strip topsoil and stack for future use	Digger hire
6.	Excavate foundations, service trenches and drive and spread hardcore	Digger, hardcore
7.	Building Inspector and warranty inspector to inspect excavations	
8.	Pour foundation concrete	Concrete and any ancillary or reinforcing materials required
9.	Building Inspector and warranty inspector to inspect foundation concrete	
10.	Build foundation blockwork	Concrete blocks, wall ties, sand and cement, drainage exit lintels, cranked ventilators
11.	Lay damp proof course	dpc
12.	Building Inspector to inspect dpc	
13.	Position floor beams and infill with blocks	Floor beams, infill blocks
14.	Brush grout beam and block floor	Dry sand and cement
15.	Building Inspector and warranty inspector to inspect oversite	
16.	Delivery and erection of timber frame kit	Timber frame kit
17.	Warranty inspector to inspect timber frame erected	
18.	Bricklayers to build chimney through roof	Flue liners, bricks, lead tray, sand and cement
19.	Tilers to felt, batten and tile roof with plumber in attendance for any flashings and to position vent pipes and lead skirts	Roof tiles, felt and batten and any ancillary fittings or fixings
20.	Decorator to decorate fascia and soffits	Decoration materials
21.	Plumber to fix guttering prior to scaffolding coming down	Rainwater goods
22.	Bricklayers to lay bricks to elevations	Bricks, sand and cement
23.	Warranty inspector to inspect brick elevations complete	
24.	Carpenters first fix – door linings, window boards, tank stands, loft trap, external doors and patio doors	Carpenter first fix materials
25.	Lay drains, services and bring into house	Drainage materials including Pipes, inspection covers, pea shingle
26.	Building Inspector and warranty inspector to inspect drains on test	
27.	Backfill drains and service trenches	Pea shingle
28.	Glaze all windows	Glazing materials
29.	Plumbing and central heating first fix	Appropriate materials from sub-contractor's supply
30.	Electricians first fix	Appropriate materials from sub-contractor's supply
31.	Install insulation and fix vapour barrier	Insulation and vapour barrier
32.	Tack plaster board to walls and ceilings, and finish	Plasterboard plus plasterers materials
33.	Bricklayers to build fireplace	Fireplace bricks, stone or surround
34.	Lay floating floor	Flooring grade insulation and t&g chipboard, glue
35.	Warranty inspector to inspect 1st fix complete	
36.	Plumbers second fix and water on	Sub-contractors materials supply, sanitaryware, sink unit
37.	Carpenters second fix, including fitting of kitchen units	Kitchen units, internal doors and furniture, skirtings and architraves
38.	Test out and services on.	Telephone installation
39.	Decorations	All decoration materials
40.	Ceramic wall tiling	Tiles, adhesive and grout
41.	Building and warranty inspectors final inspection	
42.	Clean through and arrange for Householders insurance to take over from site insurance	

17 Trouble shooting and problem avoidance

The whole purpose of this book has been the avoidance, as far as is possible, of problems, by either their anticipation or by their replacement with solutions. Nevertheless problems will still crop up from time to time and, although most of them are not very serious, at least not half as serious as the man in the pub would have you believe, there are times when it's a little difficult to see the way forward. Way forward there is, however, and if you're to find that way forward then it's important to remember that when dealing with a crisis, your objective is to build the right house, within your budget and to the planned timetable. It may mean that you will spend some of the contingency money in your budget if it keeps the job on schedule, or that you will decide to concede a point in an argument with the council. This is not always easy to accept, but keeping everything moving forward is more important than winning a dispute over who pays for a dropped kerb or a broken double glazing unit.

Seizing the initiative is the important thing and part of that initiative is attendance at my oft mentioned, school of forward planning. So let's look at some of the possible problems under various headings, many of which have been presaged within the main text of the various chapters but all of which bear repetition.

Getting off on the right foot

When you start a selfbuild project its whole shape is determined by the very first decisions that you make. Are you choosing the right site? Is your solicitor really interested in working for a selfbuilder who wants to ask him a lot of unusual questions? Do you have the right designer working for you? Or the right package company? These early decisions should be made after careful consideration of all your options, and you should not drift into them.

In particular, employing the people and firms who will be central to the whole operation is something that should be given a great deal of thought, and you should evaluate all your options. If you're not happy with how things are going at the evaluation and planning stages then stop and, if necessary, change course. Don't be

hassled into making the wrong decision and if you do find out that you're going down the wrong road then, before you're legally and irrevocably committed, pull away, look back in this book to the chapter headed 'Making the choices', and think again.

Site problems

Unforeseen site problems that are discovered after you have bought your site can prove a disaster. Examples are discovering that there is a ransom strip which prevents you having access to the site, or that the main drain is not where you believed it to be, or that the highway authority requires a sight line at your entrance and this involves the co-operation of an unfriendly neighbour. These are all the sort of things which you should check out before you sign a contract to buy the land. Remember your solicitor will concern himself with whether your title to the land is good and solid. It is **your** job to make sure that you are going to be able to build on it in the way that you want.

Sometimes, despite all the precautions, despite soil investigations and surveys, the excavation of foundation trenches turns up ground conditions which have not been anticipated and which require a change of foundation design. Above ground, most building is a simple matter of a huge jigsaw going together and extras are normally either completely foreseeable or elective. Below ground, the only survey that is 100% accurate is the one that you effect when you construct your house and any contingency sum within your budget is there, first and foremost, to cover extra costs below ground. If it's not required, then and only then, can it be rolled forward to meet other choices.

If your excavations turn up unexpected ground conditions then the thing to do is to remain calm and to get hold of the very best professional advice as soon as possible. Start with the Building Inspector and/or your architect and get them to put you onto a suitable engineer who'll come out to site whilst the excavations are still open. Give him time to do his tests and to come up with a solution and then when that's prepared make sure that you get approval from the Building Control department of the local authority and from your warranty company for what he is proposing, before you recommence work. If necessary pay your contractors or subcontractors for the abortive work and agree a new price for the revised specification, almost as a completely new contract. They'll be as keen as you to get restarted and their price will often reflect the fact that they're on site already and all geared up to go. But don't let them jump the gun and make sure that, when things do start again, everything's approved and that all and any of the revised materials required have been properly sourced, otherwise your site will just come to another halt.

Selling the existing home

In previous editions of this book there would have been dire warnings over the financial consequences of the existing house failing to sell in order to satisfy a mortgage commitment. The facts are, however, as I write this book, that unless you can adequately demonstrate your ability to service the mortgages on both houses, the chances are that you won't have started building without selling the original house first. For those who do manage to build without having to sell the existing house, that doesn't mean that to reach the end of a selfbuild project, only to find yourself saddled with two homes doesn't have its own problems. If you're going to occupy them both until such time as one of them sells then you're going to have to think in terms of two Council Tax commitments and the lighting, heating, insurance and running costs of two homes. If you're going to leave one empty then you're going to have to think in terms of insurance for the unoccupied dwelling and if the one that's left empty is the one you're trying to sell, remember that empty houses never have the sales appeal of a lived in home. You need to add up the figures and make the decision, long before it's 'stale on the market', about what price is your cut off or break even price. If necessary and if the season's all wrong you might like to consider cutting your losses by means of a shorthold letting for six months but don't forget that you'll have to pay tax on the income from the tenancy

and, if you want to be absolutely sure, you'll probably also have to pay management fees to a letting agency.

Coping with death

If you walk under a bus while you are building the new house, your estate will still have the building finance available to get the job finished. However, in order to arrange for this they will probably want up to a £20,000 of additional money to be able to employ the best builder in town to finish it quickly, perhaps so that it can be sold. If something happens to you, will this money be available in your estate? If there is any doubt about this at all you should take out an appropriate short term life insurance policy. It will not cost very much, and is a prudent thing to arrange.

In the chapter 'Designing a home to suit your lifestyle', I invited you to consider the effects of death on a selfbuild where family were directly involved in the financing and sharing of a new home. As much attention needs to be paid to the unravelling of these arrangements in the event of death on either side, as it does with their creation.

Domestic problems

One of the commonest reasons why work comes to a stop on a selfbuild site is that the couple building have split up. This has a disastrous effect on both the finances of the project and on the enthusiasm to get the job done. These are always sad stories, and sometimes I get the impression that the selfbuild operation was a last ditch attempt to save a marriage that was in deep trouble anyway. If your relationship is going through a sticky patch then avoid selfbuild until things are better. Many's the time a selfbuild project has been seen, usually by one party, as the means by which, striving with common purpose, a couple can bring a shaky marriage back into line. In fact the reality is far different and the stresses and strains that inevitably occur in any building project are the means by which the marriage eventually founders.

On the other hand, many successful selfbuilders will tell you that building their new home gave them an opportunity to tackle something together which made them realise just what an effective team they were, and that they really enjoyed working together. The selfbuild stories at the back of this book, almost all, demonstrate how successful relationships were strengthened and new ones made secure during and within a selfbuild project.

Accidents

The building industry has a bad accident record and selfbuilders are even more at risk than professionals. There is a real risk that you will suffer an accident while you are building. Guard against this by learning of all the hazards, and taking common sense precautions. In particular beware cement burns and I write this as someone who still bears the scars of my inexperience, decades ago.

Problems with the authorities

Dealing with authority can sometimes be likened to charging, head first, at a brick wall without ones hard hat on. Nevertheless it is a skill, which it bodes each and every selfbuilder to acquire, and there are times when one needs to be able to stand back, cool off and think carefully about your objectives. Most authority is there to perform a function and that function is not usually clouded by too much sentiment. Most employees of authorities and statutory undertakers do not have very much freedom of expression in the carrying out of their duties and have to follow strict guidelines and procedures, laid down and adhered to with just as much zeal as tablets of stone from on high. What you need to do is to find ways of expressing your objectives in ways that conform to these regulations and procedures and to do that you may, sometimes, have to put yourself in the shoes of the other man and try to look at things from his perspective.

Planning departments

For some selfbuilders, problems with planning departments will commence at the 'Outline' stages of planning permission and for quite a few of them, those problems will remain insurmountable. In the chapter dedicated to planning I've discussed ways of maximising the chances of an 'Outline' application being successful, but I have also said that on some applications the end of the road can be marked and that it's then, perhaps, better to move on to another plot.

For those dealing with the planning authorities at the detailed stages there are a whole raft of other problems, most of which I've already covered but all of which may need you to stand back at some time to consider that your main objective is to get your new home built within your budget. Planning officers do have some leeway but not enough to allow you to form the vanguard of precedent that will remove or destroy their authority's whole planning ethos. In any negotiation for detailed consent a balance has to be reached between your desires for individuality with the planning officers duty to maintain conformity with the local structure plan, and the planning authority's design guidelines. Keeping the emphasis on the achievement of every one of your desires, however at odds with the local vernacular, can only lead to conflict and a loss of momentum on your whole selfbuild project. The motto has to be to steer clear of contention wherever possible. If you've got the time and the money to turn your new home into a crusade, then by all means take things to the limit but, for the average selfbuilder, time and money are in short supply and reasonable compromise is the order of the day.

Planning consents are fairly concise documents written in plain English on very bad quality paper. The words on them are specific and precise, and they are meant to be read, understood, and complied with. This seems straightforward, but it is surprising how many selfbuilders choose to ignore the conditions of their planning consent. They do not follow the building line shown on the approved drawing, or they decide to move a tree which has a protection order on it, or they simply do not bother to get the formal approval for the bricks and tiles that they choose to use.

Those who do this may decide very lightly that there is no need to bother with what they consider to be unnecessary formalities. Then they find that they are involved in a dispute with the authority that will take a long time to resolve, and may delay all of the work on site until it is settled.

Building Control Departments

The principle problems the uninitiated have with Building Control are the serial applications and rejections that are the hallmark of how many authorities work. Many selfbuilders see these rejections as some sort of failing and, wrongly, tend to blame their architect or package deal company. Don't let any of this worry you and, as long as the relevant procedures are adopted and adhered to, it should not cause you any delay or upset in your programme.

Bad tradesmen will often portray the Building Inspector as some sort of an ogre but, as a selfbuilder, you should always keep in mind that the inspector has precisely the same objectives as you in that both of you are trying to ensure that your new home is built properly and in conformance with the regulations. It's true that some of the older and wiser Building Inspectors can appear more lenient whilst some of the younger more eager ones can appear to be 'going by the book'. The reality is that appearances are almost always wrong in that the objectives are the same. If the older inspector suspects bad ground, he may well throw up the query at the early stages of an application and when he comes on site he may well be able to suggest a course of action or remedy. The younger one, without the background knowledge will, nevertheless, pretty soon come to precisely the same conclusions, just as soon as he sees the excavations and the end result is almost certain to be the same.

Remember that the Building Inspector is on your side. If he thinks that despite what your plans say, another course of action is advisable then he is coming to that conclusion for very good reasons and only a fool would try and flout them. Even if a suspicion of bad ground is not confirmed by subsequent exploration and investigation, the very fact that you have had it disproved is not a victory or a triumph over someone who is trying to do you down. Instead it is, and should be treated as, a worthwhile evaluation which has led you to the point of comfort in the knowledge that what you are doing is right and that the relevant people are looking out for your interests.

Highways and Environmental agencies

To a large degree the requirements of both these agencies will be dealt with by the planning and Building Control departments but there are times when one can fall between two stools. Sometimes a planning consent can ask for 'visibility splays to the requirements of the Highways Agency and the satisfaction of the planning authority'. I have known such a case where the Highways Agency had no objection to an access being formed with certain visibility splays, only for the planning authority to turn around and insist on a stricter specification. True, their objections were over-turned on appeal but the delays and frustrations experienced by that particular selfbuilder were, at times, almost overwhelming.

Remember that before any work can be carried out involving the highway, including creating a new access or connecting to a public sewer in the highway, a licence will be required from the highways authorities, consent will be needed to make a connection to the sewer and periods of notice will be required before the works may take place. Remember also that only accredited or approved contractors can carry out works that involve digging up or disturbing the metalled sections of the highway, including the footpath.

Where any of the agencies are involved, try to ensure that, as far as is possible their require-ments are anticipated and conformed to and try to ensure that, when making your applications, you make the planning and/or Building Control departments aware that you have taken these factors into consideration. If you do find your-selves stuck in the middle of, what will be to them, an interesting conflict of interests, then try to arrange a meeting between the sides and go to that meeting, with your professionals, in the capacity of arbitrators seeking a solution, rather than as an injured party.

Electricity, gas, water and telephone companies

For me these have always been the hardest brick

walls at which I've charged headlong. All of the inflexibilities of both personnel and procedure seem to coagulate within and under their vast monolithic umbrellas. Procedure is the thing, that and timescales which, despite the dictates of your site, have to be adhered to. Make sure that you obtain the necessary quotations for supply in good time and make doubly sure that you send off any payment or order for that supply within the timescale laid down in the documentation. If the water board want six weeks notice of your requirement for a building supply then you can shout as loud as you can that you need it the following day but the chances are that you'll have to wait for the requisite period. The moral must be to read the requirements very carefully and to follow them and the procedures to the letter.

On the other hand, if you get into trouble and accidentally cut a main, you'll be amazed at how quick the response will be and how positive the action taken is, right down to the bill for damages that will follow. If you have a suspicion that a main crosses your land then ask the relevant Board to provide you with a plan and to pinpoint the exact position. That way, if they're wrong, as Keith Axelby, pictured in the chapter on insurances, found out, at least you've got a counter claim against them.

One problem that many selfbuilders come across is meter boxes. The electricity and gas boards provide these, and some of the ducting pipes, within their quotation for supply but they don't often deliver them. Instead they have to be picked up at a depot by reference to an order which, yes you've guessed it, has to be processed within certain timescales. Make sure that you've got all of this organised before your bricklayer gets to the point of needing them to build in. Although they can be cut in and fixed at a later date it's never as good a job.

Difficulties with professionals

Never lose sight of the fact that the man with the string of letters behind his name is, nevertheless, just one of the people *you* are going to employ to assist in the building of *your* new home. He may well be a very important person in his own right but, as far as the building of your new home is concerned, he is just one of many who will have an input and it is you that is in the driving seat and must remain so. Do not let yourselves be intimidated into agreeing to or going along with something that you are not happy with. As I've said before, if you're not happy, then stop and think carefully before going on and, if necessary, and if you are not legally committed, then pull away and seek another avenue.

Of course if you're tied into a legal contract with the professional then you must have been happy with what they were going to be doing for you at some stage, otherwise you wouldn't have committed to them. But what do you do if it all starts to go wrong part way through the project? A bricklayer who is dismissed will, especially if he's paid up to date, just shrug his shoulders and leave site, albeit with a few choice words left ringing in your ears. A professional who has failed to live up to your expectations or even to his own promises, may not be so easy to get rid of. If it's a package deal company that is failing to perform, something that is happily very rare, then there may well be an element of manufacture and supply to which you are undoubtedly committed and, unless you are very sure of your ground, you may well end up with a very large bill for damages, breach of contract and/or loss of profit. All of this makes it ever more necessary that you should satisfy yourself, well before the commitment stage, that you are taking the right course of action and that you're dealing with the right people. If it's another professional, acting for you in a variety of capacities, then any attempt at dismissal may well result in a very large bill for abortive work and a writ if you do not pay very promptly.

It's all very unlikely, but if you do get into this situation then the thing to do is to make sure that you do things very properly. First of all try arranging a meeting with the company or professional with whom you are in dispute and, at that meeting, try to resolve your differences to your mutual benefit. Do not cut your nose off to spite your face. Do not imagine that your differences are irreconcilable or, at least, do not approach such a meeting in this frame of mind. Set down your grievances in writing, clearly and without resort to intemperate language. Commit to paper your earnest desire to find a suitable way forward and, if one can be found, take it. And if, despite all of your endeavours you feel that you have no option but to sever your relations? Well, if you do have to terminate a contract, with a professional, only do so after careful consideration and in consultation with and on the advice of a solicitor who has been given the opportunity to carefully examine all of the facts and, in particular, the contract or terms of engagement.

Forgetting about insurance and warranties

How could you possibly do this after all of the exhortations and hints I've dropped throughout the text? Yet the facts are that people still do forget, or even, at times, feel that they can get away without insurance. Maybe some do but it only takes one gale or one errant child to make a mockery of a whole selfbuild project, sufficient to blight a lifetime.

Never start work on site without adequate selfbuild insurance and always listen to the advice from solicitors and others about single premium indemnity policies where they are deemed necessary.

Again with warranties, these need to be put in place long before work actually commences on site and certainly long before trenches are opened. If there are trees present or if there is bad ground suspected then the lead up period of notice of commencement of works may well be extended and you will need to take this into account in your programme. I've known of selfbuilders building without a warranty, something that's next to nigh impossible if a building society or bank is involved in the project, and I've known of times when all of the bravado disappears in the realisation that a mistake's been made. It's not impossible to sell a house without a warranty, but it's certainly difficult and it involves expensive and extensive structural surveys and complicated insurance policies.

Oh, and one last thing whilst on the subject of insurances. Don't be bashful about asking any of the people you engage for details of their insurance and indemnity policies. Ask your builder for a copy of his insurance policies even if you're playing safe by arranging one of your own. If he's going to be digging up the Queens highway then you need to know that he's adequately covered and if he's not then you either need to insist that he increases his cover or else that you engage another party to carry out that work. Ask any of the professionals for details of their indemnity policies and make sure that the amount of cover provided is sufficient for your project.

Problems with suppliers

First of all, any organisation selling goods or services on any sort of scale sometimes lets down its customers. In the building industry this is a common problem because of the stop/go nature of the market, the fact that deliveries are made to a multitude of different sites, and because often suppliers do not hold buffer stocks. As a result of this, most selfbuilders are likely to meet one or two minor irritating problems with suppliers, and a few have to cope with major problems.

Let us suppose that you have ordered a new type of central heating boiler. You have the technical literature, which shows that the boiler that you want needs a certain sort of flue and a plinth of a certain size. You place the order for the boiler for delivery in three months time, and build your house with the appropriate flue and plinth. You receive a confirmation of your order, which shows that delivery is required at a specific time, and which also has fifty different terms and conditions of sale printed on the back.

Three months later the boiler does not arrive. You ring the supplier's office, and are fobbed off with a junior employee who keeps assuring you that he or she will look into the matter. Fortunately you have kept the card given you by the salesman who called on you to take your order and you manage to get hold of him. He tells you in a very confidential manner that there are problems with the supply of this boiler, but due to his own superhuman efforts he is sure that you will get one very soon. He tells you that he is heart broken that you did not get delivery on time, and that he will do all that he can, etc., etc.

A week later you get a letter from the company saying that the particular type of boiler that you ordered cannot be supplied, but they will supply you with a different and superior model, at no extra cost. They include the specification for the new model, and you note that this will require a different plinth, and, even worse, a larger flue. You ring your friend the salesman, who tells you that he is so upset at the way you have been treated that he would resign from the firm in disgust were it not that he feels he must stay on in order to get your problem sorted out. You don't believe a word of it.

Where do you go from here? Well, first of all, it is useful to sit back and consider why you think all this has happened. There are two alternatives. It is possible that the suppliers are rogues, or so desperately inefficient that trading with the public at their level of competence amounts to a confidence trick. If this is the case, then you must cut your losses and find another supplier.

Have you a claim against the villains who let you down? Possibly, but the real fault is yours. People who buy building materials are considered to be in business, and generally capable of making proper business decisions, like deciding which are reputable firms and which are not. If you have got it wrong there is not a very great deal that you are going to be able to do about it unless you decide to make it a personal crusade. Crusading takes time, and it is unlikely that you will be able to spare the time.

A much more likely situation is that you are a tiny part of huge problems being experienced by a reputable supplier. They may have been let down by the boiler manufacturer. A significant design fault in the boiler may only have become apparent very recently, and until it is sorted out they dare not send any out, and equally they cannot tell you about the design fault because otherwise their product insurance on the defective ones that have already been supplied will be invalidated. Possibly there is nothing wrong with the boiler, but everything wrong with the supplier's financial situation.. However, unlike the rogues or the incompetents, a reputable supplier with difficulties may offer you the best chance of getting things sorted out.

Now let us think about what you want. First

of all, you want a boiler that meets your requirements, possibly with some compensation because of the trouble that you have been put to. You may also feel so aggrieved by all of this that you want to 'warn others' about the supplier, which is simply a way of saying that you want to get your own back. But what good will this do you?

So what do you do? First of all, evaluate your situation very carefully, and do not be in any way unreasonable. Do not threaten the supplier with legal action until you have settled on your plan of campaign in the matter. At this stage the most important thing is to try to find alternative boilers from other suppliers. If you can, then you simply write cancelling your original order because of the supplier's 'non performance of the contract'.

If you threaten the supplier with legal action, you will probably forfeit any chance of him giving special consideration to your problems and trying to do something special to help you. With a large firm it will simply mean that the whole matter will be taken out of the hands of the sales department and dealt with by the company secretary. This does not mean that you should not take legal advice, but you should not shout about it until you are sure that you are going to shout to some effect.

Sending the paperwork to a solicitor will enable him to advise you whether you have a simple contract for the purchase of goods, or whether you have a contract which involves an element of service, and whether 'time is of the essence' in performing the service. He will also tell you what you can hope to achieve by standing on your legal rights, the cost of doing this, and the probable timetable involved. Almost certainly you will decide that the legal route does not make sense unless you are looking at a very serious and very costly problem.

Next, do beware of casually threatening that you will ring a newspaper or a TV show. If you do tell the supplier that you are going to do this, you will probably be told that it is up to you, and you will forfeit any sympathy or special help. If you want to complain to the media, do so by all means, but do not tell the other side!

This does not mean that you cannot use a

threat of legal action if you decide that this is really what you want to do. If so, then it is usually far better for you to continue to be the reasonable customer, writing courteous letters explaining your position, while your solicitor writes separately on your behalf explaining that Mr. XXX is suffering such losses that he has had no alternative but to retain Messrs. Nasty & Sue to press for specific performance of the contract and compensation in respect of losses suffered to date.

If you are going to do this, then make sure that you decide *in advance* exactly how far you will go, and at what expense. Remember that only the lawyers profit from the law, and most judges in civil courts spend their time listening to cases where neither party can be a real winner.

It is much better to concentrate on finding out what has really happened, and to try to persuade those who can help you to make a special effort on your behalf and perhaps to give your order some priority. Two ways of doing this are:

1. to be seen as a nice guy who is being very reasonable in very difficult circumstances, and

2. to try to deal with people as near to the top as you can get on a face to face basis.

See if you can reach the sales director or even the managing director by phone and say that your problems are such that you must arrange to call on him to find out exactly what the position is in order that you can make your own plans accordingly. Do not be abusive, and if appropriate you can say that you appreciate the concern that the company has shown to date, but that you must now come to a firm arrangement with him on a face to face basis if you are to minimise the losses that you are suffering.

Now you may think that this is being rather wet, and the chap really needs to be told his fortune. Stop and think: if you were sitting in his chair would you want to help a customer who was abusive?

What you want is the boiler that was originally specified, or an acceptable alternative, and possibly some compensation. If you are taking

the legal route to claiming this, then leave being nasty to your solicitor. At any rate, what is the point in being nasty and antagonising the other side? Anyone who has worked in a sales office will tell you that this may be a recipe for being put at the end of the queue for the new boilers when they arrive. You think that talking tough will frighten the suppliers? Unless you have a record for GBH you will only make them laugh. On the other hand, if you are seen to be disappointed but philosophical they may try to help.

Another good reason for a personal visit to the supplier is that you may discover what the real problem is, and this may persuade you that under no circumstances do you want the particular type of boiler that you ordered. The more that you can learn about the background to the whole business the better, and the more likely you are to obtain a satisfactory outcome.

If the problem involves a package company it is particularly important to strike the right balance between being a very reasonable fellow and being determined to make sure you get the service you are paying for. Unlike builder's merchants, package companies depend on individual selfbuilders, and advertise that they make things easy for you. If you are not happy, do not hesitate to insist on speaking to the managing director.

Finally, in any dispute of this sort you should always look at the cost of your 'worst case losses' and decide whether or not it would be better simply to walk away from the whole situation. If you are selfbuilding, the target is the right house, on budget, and on time.

Cheap materials and bargains

I've already warned about the guys who come around selling cheap tarmac that, if you allow them to lay it, will very shortly lose all integrity. Cheap doesn't always mean good and where cheap is also bordering on the illegal then it can be a very expensive option. I remember, many years ago, a selfbuilder who told me that he'd got a contact who'd offered him concrete at £25 per load. As he was going to have some pretty deep trenchfilled foundations, this seemed attractive until he told me that, technically speaking, this would then make his house part of the new M11! I warned him against this and then didn't hear from him again for some time. That is, until he phoned me up one evening to thank me for the warning that he'd apparently heeded. It turned out that when the second load of legitimate concrete had come into the site, the lorry had dipped its wheels into the trench and toppled over into the oversite. Now, if that had been a stolen load, how on earth would anyone have explained all that? In the event it took a crane to get it out again and the selfbuilder was more than adequately compensated for his trouble.

Avoiding dodgy materials is one thing but that doesn't mean that there aren't bargains to be had and a quick reference to Gordon and Jenny's selfbuild story will tell of the huge savings they made by literally looking abroad for their purchases. What you need to learn is not to confuse a bargain with something that is cheap and nasty and is likely to be totally counter productive.

Choices of materials, fittings and fixtures

Try to keep things in perspective. I can remember meeting selfbuilders at the very beginnings of their thinking about selfbuild who literally didn't know one end of a brick from the other and to whom I had to carefully explain the differences between a profiled interlocking tile and a plain tile. Six months later, when they'd been into a brick library and chosen a particular brick, there were ructions and gnashing of teeth when the planners indicated that the brick wasn't acceptable. Six months after that when the house was finished nobody cared and everything looked right. I remember another selfbuilder who rang me up one morning to tell me that his wife hadn't stopped crying all weekend because the taps on the bath weren't as she'd envisaged they'd be, even though he acknowledged that they were the ones they'd chosen. It wasn't a re-run of the Biafra civil war, no children had died – it's just that the perspective had been lost. I do like to think that the poor lady is now able to relax in her bath without bursting out in floods of tears and that, either she's accepted the taps or that

they exercised their right of choice and changed them when they could.

Problems with builders

In all of the chapters devoted to seeking out and engaging builders and subcontractors, I have stressed the importance of your eventual choice being made after thorough investigation and considerable personal enquiry and inspection. Nevertheless, it is a fact that any builder is no better than his last job and things can change which make a previously good builder perform in an unreliable or uncharacteristic manner. Family breakdowns, ill health and money problems can all affect a builders performance and it's important that you not only get to the bottom of what's wrong but that, having done so, you take action to ensure that your site doesn't suffer. You're not a marriage guidance councillor, you're not a doctor and you're certainly not a banker, at least in respect of your new home. What you are is a selfbuilder and you must not lose sight of the fact.

The tell tale signs are not always bad workmanship, at least not in the immediately visible form. Normally you'll notice long periods when nothing seems to happen or when there are long waits for follow on trades to arrive on site. You may be told that the plumber is busy elsewhere and that he'll be along in a few days, you may be told that the tilers are all geared up but that there's a delay on the delivery. All of this might be perfectly true but, in equal measure, these excuses may be symptomatic of something going wrong. Maybe the state of the man's mind means that he's lost the will or the ability to organise the follow on trades whilst he's trying to save a marriage. Maybe the plumber won't come or the merchants won't deliver the tiles, because they haven't been paid for the work and the materials they provided on the builders previous job. Maybe a clue to that being true could be your builder's request for forward payment of some money, something that you should resist at all costs. If you can, talk to the plumber directly, and ask him what the problem is or go along to the merchants and ask them to confirm when the tiles are going to arrive. Strictly, they're not at liberty to discuss the builder's status, but by finding out exactly what the situation is regarding the tiles for your new home, you may well be able to draw some pretty firm conclusions. Perhaps, also, the merchants themselves might start pumping you for information about what exactly is going on and they might even have been told that your failure to pay on time is the reason they haven't been paid!

Stick to the contract. Only pay as and when a stage is reached and then only when you and your architect and /or the Building and Warranties inspectors have approved the work. Watch out for corner cutting. A builder in trouble may well try to skimp on important things and in extreme cases, I have witnessed, will even do things that are deliberately meant to deceive. I shall never forget the garage floor that was neatly screeded with a sand and cement mix. The only trouble was, there was no concrete below and the first time a car went on it fell through! Don't panic, something like that is very rare although not so non-existent as to be unable to liven up the text of this book.

That's the value of the contract, whether it's the long and complicated one I set out earlier of whether it's a simple exchange of letters. Either way, the most important things it needs to contain are the price, the stages at which payment will be made and the express or implied requirement that all work must be carried out to the proper standards and to the satisfaction of the Building and warranty inspectors and/or your architect. If you reach a point where the contract has to be terminated you should be advised by your solicitor about what to do at every stage. In this case your concern will be to move from the bad contractor to a new one as soon as possible, with as little disruption and delay as possible. All situations like this are different, but you will probably want to engage a quantity surveyor to give you a report on the work done and the value of materials lying on site, and if there is any question of bad workmanship an independent architect's report may be required. If the NHBC or Zurich are involved remember that they must be consulted.

If your builder fails

Perhaps the most worrying thing that can happen to a selfbuilder is that someone building the whole house for you goes bust, or they simply disappear, or tell you that they are facing bankruptcy and cannot continue with the work on your new home. What do you do?

Well, that will depend on the nature of your arrangements with the builder, your formal contract with him and whether or not that involves either an NHBC Buildmark or a Zurich 'Newbuild' warranty, (not Custombuild).

Your final situation will depend on this, but in either event you must take the following immediate action, at once, without any delay, and ignoring any remonstrations by others.

1. Secure the site by changing all locks. It is not unusual for a builder's employees and subcontractors to try to recoup their losses by helping themselves to 'his' valuables on the site, which will be *your* building materials or fixtures. They will convince themselves that they are entitled to do this. So may builder's merchants and other suppliers to whom the builder owes money, and they may arrive with a lorry waving delivery notes saying that ownership of materials supplied does not pass to purchasers until they are paid for. These vultures are trespassing on your site, and although the law is on their side in many respects, they cannot enter your site without your permission. Simply say '*this is my site, the builder supplied these materials to me, and your problem is one for the liquidator. Go away.*' Wire off the entrance to the site and put up a notice saying something like:

'*Materials on this site are the property of Joe Selfbuilder, and of no other person. Any attempt at repossession against the debts of others will be treated as theft.*'

It may even be worthwhile moving materials elsewhere or engaging a watchman for a week.

2. Next, advise the local police of the situation.

They will not help you in an argument with a repossessor, but they will be concerned to prevent a breach of the peace or a criminal trespass. Their interest may also deter the opportunist thief who notices that work has stopped.

3. Finally, consider the insurance situation. If theft, fire, vandalism, etc., were covered by the builder's insurances, and you can get details of these insurances from him, check out with the company concerned that cover still exists on the site and for how long it will be in force. The answer will usually be 'no'. If so you must arrange your own insurance by phone in the next ten minutes. Do not tell the brokers your tale of woe, simply say that you are starting a self-managed selfbuild project with an uncompleted house and want immediate cover. If they do not take down the details, give you a quote and then immediately confirm that you are on cover subject to you sending them a cheque within 72 hours, find another broker!

Having done all that you can to safeguard your property on your site, you must move on to safeguard your legal position. Take whatever contract documents you have to your solicitor and ask him to send an appropriate notice to the builder advising him that by going bust he has voided the contract, and spelling out where he stands. Your solicitor should get off this letter by recorded delivery the same day.

If there is an NHBC 'Buildmark' warranty in place or if the property was registered under the Zurich 'Newbuild' scheme then you do need to get in touch with their local inspectors as quickly as possible and you will be delighted to hear that there is a considerable amount of help that they can give you.

First of all the NHBC 'Buildmark' scheme. If you are buying speculatively, something that is outside the scope of this book but which may, in some cases form the basis of your contract with a builder such as when the builder was also the vendor of the land, then, if the builder has not started work, the NHBC will refund any amount

you have paid as a deposit, up to £10,000 or, if greater, 10% of the value of the home. If, on the other hand, the builder has already started work under a contractual arrangement and he then fails to complete the job through his insolvency or fraud, then the NHBC will provide some very important help.

They will either:

1. Pay you the amount above the *value of the home* which is needed to complete the home, substantially in accordance with the NHBC's requirements, together with, where appropriate, the cost of putting right any *defect* or *damage*; or

2. They will reimburse you any amount you have paid to the *builder* for the *home* under a legal obligation but cannot recover from him, or

3. Instead of either of the above, they may also, at their option, arrange for the work to be carried out.

Sounds good doesn't it and it is although there are special conditions the first of which is that the NHBC will only be liable for what was in the original contract and that they will not be liable for any extras that were subsequently arranged. In addition, if you have retained any part of the contract price, the NHBC will be entitled to deduct that from the sums it would pay out or, if it is the NHBC that arranges to complete the work, they will require you to pay them the amount of monies that you still owed under the original contract.

The maximum liability of the NHBC for all of this is £10,000 or, if greater, 10% of the *value of the home*. Let's put all of this in plain English by reference to a theoretical example. Let's say you have a contract with a builder to build your new home for a price of £100,000 and when you've paid out the sum of £60,000 the chap goes bust and does a runner. You've got £40,000 left in the kitty. You need to find another builder to take over the job but the best price you can get is for £60,000 as all of the builders know that, first of all the first builder has taken a large part of the profit element with him, secondly you're in a bind and thirdly they need to make allowances for any hidden problems that the first builder may have left. On the face of it you're £20,000 out of pocket but the NHBC will reimburse you this money, so long as it doesn't exceed 10% of the *value of the new home*. So, if the house is going to be worth £200,000 you're alright but, if the house was only ever going to be worth £175,000 then the most you'll get from the NHBC is £17,500. And that's another reason and another lesson which relates back to the earlier chapters where I talked about the carrying capacity of the land and warned you to be careful about not overdeveloping a plot in terms of its value.

With Zurich 'Newbuild', then if it's a speculative sale and purchase, they will reimburse up to 10% loss of deposit in the event of the builder's bankruptcy or fraud. On the other hand they take a very different view to the NHBC when it comes to the business of a contract with a builder for a selfbuild project, in that they believe that, if the builder, in our example above, goes bust and the subsequent builders want more to finish than is left on the job, this indicates that, either the first builders price was low in the first place or that you've paid to far ahead of the work done. They, therefore, maintain that they're not in business to finance a bargain and that they're, equally, not in business to bail out foolhardy behaviour. On the face of it this seems fairly harsh but the truth and total fairness are probably halfway between these two attitudes. In any event, Zurich do say that they have a register of builders and that they are perfectly prepared to consider giving a quotation to cover for an builders possible bankruptcy and that they will base the premium on their knowledge of the builder and any financial checks they may make on him.

All of this goes to repeat the oft given advice never to pay monies up front and never to give advances on payments before the relevant stages have been reached and approved. It is also worthwhile mentioning that, despite the assistance mentioned above, it does not absolve you from a duty of care and any one of these policies will refuse to pay out if it can be proved that you have acted recklessly, improperly or without due regard to proper procedure.

Sometimes, whilst all of this is going on there will be siren voices from the builder, urging you to come to some new sort of financial arrangement with him or another company he owns, to finish the house. Unless there are very special circumstances, I suggest you avoid these proposals which, in any event, especially if they involve payment of any money technically owed by you to the bankrupt company or builder, may put you on the wrong side of the fence as far as the Official Receiver is concerned. Sometimes it's technically possible to make money out of this whole situation where, for example, the builder goes bust just before a stage payment is due. In this case, whatever you do, do not pay any of the monies to the builder. He has failed and any money that you do owe him is properly due to the liquidator who will use it to pay off, firstly preferential creditors such as the Inland Revenue and the VAT authorities and, secondly the major creditors. When you hear from the liquidator claiming money from you, ask your solicitor or accountant to enter a counter claim to include all your losses, including the additional cost of a contract with another builder, and even compensation for your distress and wasted time, etc., etc. The counter claim will be larger than the liquidator's claim. You will not get any money, but it will be set against the liquidator's claim.

The other voices you will hear, of course, are those of the subcontractors and it's open for you to consider, depending upon what stage the building has reached, whether you can come to some suitable arrangement with the subcontractors for them to work directly for you up to the completion of the house. Beware the fact that they may well not have been paid for the first fix parts of their work. That must not bother you. You may well have rightly paid the builder for those stages and the fact that he has not passed the money on is not your fault. Even if this is not technically true, the subcontractors have no contract with you – their contract is with the builder. Make it quite clear that, up until the time of the builder going bust, you have paid him for the work and that any shortfall that the subcontractors have is between them and the builder and /or the receivers. All you're prepared to do is consider employing them, at a fixed price, for the remainder of the work to be done.

I said that it was 'technically' possible to make money out of this situation and the reason I wrote that qualification is that, if you're going to make a claim under the NHBC scheme, if you've withheld all or part of a stage payment, that has been reached in whole or in part, then the monies withheld will be counted in the NHBC's calculations of your claim. That's why it might, in some circumstances, be better, especially if the builder goes down after completion of the weathertight shell, to consider whether a claim would be your best option, or even necessary, and whether you should make other arrangements. Of course, if the reason why you used a builder rather than subcontractors in the first place was that you had neither the time nor the inclination to build all or part of your new home on a self managed basis, then these last suggestions are going to be of absolutely no interest to you.

Problems with subcontractors

Prevention is always better than cure and if you've followed all the earlier advice about choosing a subcontractor and about talking to previous clients of his, then it's unlikely that you've engaged a bad one. On the other hand the same maxim that 'a man's only as good as his last job' applies and there are times when a chaps personal or financial affairs can affect his work. This is where the skill of management comes into play. By self managing your project you stand to make considerable savings compared to the fellow who went and employed a builder. Part of that saving is made up by the management responsibility that you have taken on and, sometimes, that management responsibility means that you may have to dispense with the services of a tradesman altogether or refuse to pay until and unless work is put right. All of this may seem daunting but it is part and parcel of what you have taken on and if you feel that you are going to be incapable of dealing with these situations, then I suggest you question your chosen method of building.

Horrendous as it may seem at the time, there is little likelihood that bad workmanship by one subcontractor will scupper your whole project, although it might set it back a bit whilst you either have the work put right or seek other subbies. Keep a watch out for workmanship and make sure that it's up to the standard you picked the man for. If you're in any doubt about what he's doing then consult with your architect or the Building Inspector and get them to let you know whether everything's alright. If, despite your very best endeavours you and your advisors feel that the chap isn't any good after all then move quickly to terminate your arrangement with him and if you've decided that this is the thing to do, never change your mind. Do not bother about the other chap's feelings: any bad subbie has been finished lots of times before. Pay him in full for the work that he has done, and do not deduct the cost of putting right any defective work: your choice of subbie or lack of supervision was at fault, and you will have to pay for your mistake. It is what the contingencies item in the budget is for.

Depending on others

Never, never let a selfbuild project depend on others. If Grandma is going to let you have the last £10,000 of your finances, she should hand it over before work starts. If your Uncle offers the stone slates on his derelict barn for you to use on your new home, then make sure they are removed from the roof and stacked before work starts. If a neighbour has agreed to let you have an easement to connect your drain into his septic tank, then get it signed at the same time that you sign the contract to buy the land.

Make sure that all key elements in your proposals are always properly tied up before you enter into financial commitments and remember that Grandma, your uncle and your neighbour could all conceivably be in the same car crash and that their executors might not be very sympathetic to your case.- or they could just change their minds.

Trouble over mobile homes

Local Authorities do not like caravans, and they

can be a source of trouble. In your negotiations with the planners you may have explained that you intend to live on the site in a caravan while you are building, and obtained the necessary formal consents, which will be for a limited period. However many selfbuilders don't bother with this, either because it's commonplace for selfbuilders to live on site in the area, or sometimes because they do not want to mention a caravan whilst negotiating the planning application, for fear it might adversely affect the outcome. If you are in the latter class, and you have not yet obtained all the consents that you need, avoid putting the caravan on the site until you have, especially if you think your new neighbours may be sensitive about it. When you have actually started work on site, your legal position is that you do have the right to put it there and, indeed to live in it, so long as it is there in strict connec-

All finished. But are they, perhaps planning their next self build?

tion with your building works. If you have problems with the council remember the council knows it will take longer to get an order requiring you to move it than you are going to take to build the house, and will not usually press the matter. If they do, remove the wheels of the caravan and claim that it is the site hut. Silly arguments can go on until you replace the wheels and sell it to some other selfbuilder who will tow it away.

Problems with neighbours

Almost all neighbours of a plot will have objected to its being granted planning permission in the first place and, even if they're the vendors, they'll be happy to take your money but less than happy at the prospect of you actually building on the land. I bought a plot on the south coast once and wondered just why the neighbours were so uptight with me until one of them told me that

the lady who had lived in the bungalow on one side of my plot had committed suicide for fear of what was going to happen. What makes this worse is that the lady also happened to be the vendor of the land and one of the reasons she had got so distressed was the stick she had received from some neighbours over the fact that she had sold the land for development in the first place! For a while I considered whether to build on the plot, let alone live there. In later years the open piece of land on the other side of my plot got planning permission and the chap I'd sold the house I built to, got so incensed at this that he has never spoken to the subsequent occupiers, even though the chap who now lives there is twice removed from the original builder!

Sometimes a neighbour will seize upon your arrival on the scene to re-assert a claim or re-arrange the boundaries to his advantage, particularly if they're formed by a hedge. He'll swear that the centre line of the hedge doesn't constitute the boundary and that the hedge was originally planted by the chap he bought his house from, that it was planted well inside his land and that, therefore, the boundary is well on your side of the hedge.

What do you do about all of this? Well, first off these people are going to be your neighbours so if you can possibly sort the thing out amicably then that's best all round. And if you can't? Well, get some stakes and some wire and, in consultation with your solicitor, clearly mark out your boundaries and send a letter by recorded delivery to your neighbours telling them that you have established your boundaries and fenced your property accordingly. The onus is then on your neighbour to get in touch with his solicitor to try and establish his claim on *your* land, not vice versa. You have the initiative and, possession being nine tenths of the law, it's your neighbour who has the uphill struggle.

Deliveries are the one thing that upsets neighbours and, I'm afraid, quite rightly so. Firstly if the plot is on a narrow lane and the block lorry arrives in the morning, then he'll put his feet down and proceed with unloading, seemingly oblivious to the queue of angry car drivers who realise that they're going to miss their train. If you're not there or the space to put the blocks is not obvious or clearly marked out, or if there's not room on the site, he'll have no compunction about stacking them on the road or the footpath and you'll have to spend the rest of the day, when you do arrive on site, moving them. I can even recall one site where the lorry driver arrived at a site and decided that the best place to put the blocks was on the side of the plot in front of the garage doors and that the best way of getting them there was to park on next doors drive! The problem was that next doors drive hadn't actually been designed or constructed to take the weight of a fully laden block lorry. Try, as far as is possible to ascertain just when deliveries are going to be made and make sure that, if you can't be on site, somebody else certainly is. If you know that work or deliveries are going to block off the road at a certain time then take the trouble to inform your neighbours and to warn them that they may need to park their cars up the street. They'll never be too happy about it but at least you've done your best. And if the complaints are about noise or smoke, then do something about it. Maybe a diesel mixer could be swapped for an electric one. Maybe the radios could be turned down a little or at the very least tuned in and maybe, fires can either be stopped altogether or limited to reasonable hours with the old tires sent to the tip instead of turning the whole sky black.

Remember, above all, that this is not just any old building site, it's the site of your new home and, as such, the neighbours are going to be an important factor in your enjoyment of it. A short letter to each one apologising in advance for any inconvenience, a visit to those most affected and, perhaps, a few bunches of flowers won't go amiss at all.

Disputes

Once you have started to build a new house it is important to get it finished on time otherwise the interest charges on the building finance will get out of hand. If you do become involved in a dispute with others, settle it quickly so that the whole project is not held up. This may involve making a pragmatic decision to let others get away with things that you think are wrong. If you agree to a neighbours version of where a boundary post should be put, or pay a few pounds more than agreed for materials or services, it may be the right decision if it saves time and keeps up the momentum of the whole job. Don't be a soft touch but, in equal measure, don't cut your nose off to spite your face.

Those who buy a new house from a builder or developer do not then have to pay VAT on top of their purchase price. The VAT authorities, in recognition of this fact, have made special arrangements for selfbuilders, and for those converting an existing structure into a dwelling, to reclaim any VAT that they may pay on their purchases. All of this is arranged through regulations that are set out in VAT Notice 719 which has the simple title, *VAT refunds for 'do-it-yourself' builders and converters.*

The regulations themselves are equally simple and straight forward, and all the details are obtainable from local VAT offices, where you can get a claim pack containing leaflets and the claim forms that you will require.

The VAT regulations are administered by the Customs & Excise. Their simple procedures and straightforward way of doing things stem from hundreds of years of experience in clearing ships between tides and compare very favourably with the ponderous ways of the Inland Revenue, planning offices, services authorities and others who the selfbuilder will get to know. However, their rules require that you are equally business-like, and you should learn what is involved at an early stage.

Everything is set out quite clearly in the leaflet and it wouldn't make sense to reproduce everything said in it here, although there are some comments to make. If you are unsure about anything at all then you can and should contact your local VAT office for advice. Incidentally, they won't be listed under VAT, if you're looking them up in the telephone directory and, instead, you'll find them under Customs and Excise. If you stick to the procedures, submit your claim on time with all your invoices properly listed, and answer any questions promptly you should receive your refund in well under a month. Typically it will pay for all the carpets and curtains in the new home.

The points to pay particular attention to are:

* If you use a package company, ask them for an itemised invoice in the form acceptable to the VAT authorities. Ensure that any last minute extras are included. The package companies know all about doing this, but as it involves a lot of typing they may wait to be asked.

* New buildings intended for occupation by the selfbuilder are covered by the scheme but if you are constructing the house with the intention to sell or let or for some other business reason you cannot use the scheme. That doesn't affect the selfbuilders right to work from home and it doesn't affect any subsequent sale or letting of the property – it is the first use that is the governing factor.

* Claims are eligible for conversions where existing buildings that do not have a residential use, or which have not been used as residential accommodation since 1st April 1973, are converted for residential use.

* Extensions to existing dwellings or the creation of additional self contained accommodation do not qualify.

* A VAT registered builder or sub-contractor will not charge you VAT for their work on the building, or for the materials which they supply. The size of your VAT claim will be dictated by the proportion of materials that you buy yourself.

* Beware paying VAT in error, as it cannot then be reclaimed. VAT is payable on materials. It is not payable on labour only or supply and fix contracts (apart from professional services). Nevertheless, I have seen bricklayers add the VAT to their bill. These were not even VAT registered and therefore the money would have gone into their pocket. If it had been paid then the only way of recovering it would have been to ask them nicely for its return, and how far do you think that would have got?

* You cannot reclaim the VAT on some quite unexpected materials and services. Amongst these are, architects and surveyors fees as well as any fees for management, consultancy, design and planning. The purchase or hire of tools and equipment, including skip hire are excluded, as are fuel and transport

costs and temporary fencing.

* In addition you cannot claim the VAT back on things like, carpets, underlay and carpet tiles, white goods such as cookers, hobs washing machines, refrigerators, dishwashers etc., even if they are built in. Fitted wardrobes bought in kit form or even the basic materials if you buy them yourself are excluded from any reclaim, as are doorbells and electrically operated doors or gates! Aerials and satellite dishes cannot be included in your VAT claim. There are others but these are perhaps the ones where their exclusion from the scheme might surprise you the most.

* With the shrinking of our world and the Chunnel there is an increasing incidence of cross border purchases for selfbuild projects. The VAT is reclaimable on these purchases, so long as they are eligible and it is reclaimable at the rate it was paid so long as you have all of the VAT appropriate invoices and proof, not only of purchase, but also of importation.

* You make one claim only, and it must be made within three months of receiving a certificate that the building is completed. It can include VAT paid in respect of boundary walls, drives, patios, a garage etc., etc. If you leave this ancillary work until after you move in, you may not find it convenient to delay the VAT claim while you wait for the bill from the tarmac contractor who is laying the drive. Take this into account when drawing up your programme.

* When you make your claim, package up all the precious invoices that you have collected so carefully, and either take them to the VAT office and get a receipt for them there and then, or send them off by registered post and make enquiries if you do not receive an acknowledgement within 14 days.

* Although not covered by the 719 notice, it is possible to avoid paying VAT on alterations to listed buildings so long as they fall within the criteria laid down in a questionnaire included in the 'Guide to VAT free works to your listed home', available from HM Customs & Excise. This relief is not by way of a refund and, instead, is given by allowing the builder to zero rate his services. You cannot claim relief if you carry out the works yourself or on materials that you purchase for a builder to do the work for you.

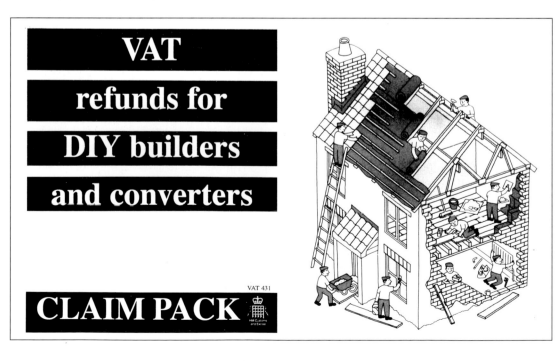

VAT refunds for DIY builders and converters

VAT 431

CLAIM PACK

HM Customs and Excise

19 Insurances and site safety

Appropriate insurances for a selfbuild operation are as essential as car insurance is to the motorist, and like car insurance they have to cover claims from others who are affected by an accident of some sort as well as taking care of any losses which you suffer yourself. The difference is that you have to arrange for car insurance before you can licence a vehicle at all, while selfbuild insurance is something you have to remember to do yourself. However, it probably will not cost you very much more to insure your selfbuild than it costs to insure your car, and the premiums are unlikely to total more than you will lay out on light fittings! However, you ignore insurances at your peril.

If you are placing a contract for the whole job with a builder, can you be confident of your builder's insurances? If you are placing the contract with a builder with an architect as an intermediary, and the architect confirms that he has established beyond all doubt that the builder has appropriate comprehensive cover, then you are all right. If you are placing a simple contract with a builder without an architect you must make sure the builder is fully insured in all the work he does on your site, with cover for your materials and all the risks of public and employers liability. If you are sure of this and it is noted in the contract then you are OK. You have to make a careful judgement here. If challenged to prove that he is insured your builder may produce the vehicle policy for his van! Do you feel like challenging him? If not, you may decide to take out your own insurances. Also, if you are covered via your builder's policy and then employ another firm to do any work in the house, like installing the kitchen, and there is a theft or an accident, then you have probably invalidated the cover via the builders policy and you will be left with all sorts of liabilities.

If you are arranging your own insurances you must consider three types of cover. The first is Public Liability Insurance, which is required to cover you against any claim made against you by a third party who suffers a loss as a result of your building operations. This includes injuries to either visitors or trespassers on your site, and also to anyone hurt outside the site because of your activities on the site. Typical claims concern incidents like traffic accidents caused by children moving building materials onto the road, and in 1995 there was a fatality for which a selfbuilder was held to be responsible. Fortunately he was insured.

Other public liability claims result from damage caused to other people's property, as happens when selfbuilders dig up electricity cables or water pipes by accident, even though the services were not where the electricity or water board showed them on their drawings. Other claims can arise from excavations on the selfbuilder's site affecting the stability of adjacent buildings belonging to a neighbour, and such claims can be very expensive indeed. More straightforward claims from neighbours relate to paint spilt by a painter working at first floor level blowing onto a car parked down wind, or to mortar splashes taking the same route.

Most householders have some form of public liability insurance as part of their normal householder's policy which covers them for accidents that happen in their home or garden. However, they do NOT apply to accidents stemming from building work, even if the new property is being constructed in their existing garden, and it is essential to have special cover. The law is definitely not on your side in this matter, and a child trespassing on your site who climbs a ladder left tied to your scaffolding and then falls off has grounds for a successful claim against you.

The next type of insurance is Employers Liability Cover. This is a legal requirement if you are employing anyone. Here it is important to understand what is meant by employment, as most selfbuilders use sub-contractors and do not employ anyone in the general sense of the word. They have no liability to collect PAYE from the people who are working for them, and their arrangements are generally outside the scope of the Employment Acts. However, as far as any accident to someone who is working for you is concerned, you certainly owe him a 'duty of care' to ensure that he does not get injured on your site, and if a sub-contractor is injured on your site his solicitor will try to establish that he has a 'deemed contract of employment'.

Many selfbuilders like to think that they are on such good terms with their sub-contractors that there is no risk of any unpleasantness. However, experience shows that when someone is hurt they tend to look for any advantage in the situation, and they are very quick to go to their solicitor. Remember that self-employed sub-contractors do not get unemployment or sick benefit if they are off work, and they will consider a case against you as a different route to the same financial benefit!

The third type of selfbuilders' insurance is Contract Works Insurance cover, sometimes called site risks insurance. This is the way in which you insure against the more usual problems, providing cover against theft, vandalism, storm damage, fire, flood, etc., etc. The most common claims are for thefts of materials, plant or tools. Timber, roof insulation and copper piping are always at risk, and concrete mixers that disappear in the middle of the night are

another common problem. Claims for this sort of loss are rarely at a figure that would jeopardise the success of the whole project, but fire and storm damage insurance is sometimes all that stands between the selfbuilder finishing his house and losing everything. In November 1987, in January and February 1991 and in February 1995 selfbuilders made hundreds of claims for gale damage, often involving both rebuilding costs and claims for damage to neighbouring property caused by falling brickwork, and the claimants were very glad they had remembered to get insured!

Vandalism is another problem giving rise to claims, and sadly it is growing. Graffiti on bus shelters is cleaned off by the council using special solvents: the same use of a spray can on your new brickwork will require the damaged bricks to be cut out and replaced, which is a horrendous job. Fortunately the more usual sort of claim involves a small boy with an air gun breaking your double glazing units.

The observant amongst you will have noticed that, several times within the main text of this book, but in particular when I am urging consultation over insurance matters, I have referred to DMS Services Ltd. Whilst I acknowledge the existence and the undoubted worth of many other companies it is, nevertheless, this company, with its unrivalled track record and its long association with both the selfbuild industry and this book, to which I am indebted for much of the information I am able to give on this subject. Copies of proposal forms are re-printed at the back of the book and these can be used to obtain cover or quotations but I would suggest that, perhaps, the best course of action would be to telephone them first, on *(01909) 591652)* to discuss your individual situation and obtain the best possible advice on how to proceed and, most importantly, who with. Always go for insurance that is underwritten by household insurance names with a proven track record of meeting claims and always make sure that you're dealing with people who understand all about the selfbuild market and the particular and peculiar circumstances of your needs.

A quick look at the main cover available from the two leading players in the market, Norwich Union and Guardian, will reveal why it's necessary to evaluate carefully just which policy is the one for you. Both policies provide Public Liability, Employers Liability and Contract Works cover, both base their premiums on the reinstatement value of the building, which is what it would cost to rebuild if it was destroyed just before you moved in, the value of the plot or the finished house being irrelevant. Both policies also involve a single premium to give cover until either the new home is finished or for a fixed period, whichever is the sooner and both can also be extended upon payment of an extra premium. Where they begin to differ is in the periods of cover and the ways in which cover can be extended to include plant and tools on site.

The Norwich Union policy automatically provides cover for up to £2000 worth of plant on site at any one time, whether owned or hired, whilst with the Guardian policy this is an extra which, if required, has the effect of making its premium more expensive. If, however, there is no requirement for cover for plant or tools then, certainly, at the lower to medium end of the scales of building costs, upon which the premiums are based, the Guardian policy becomes more attractive. Incidentally, claims for loss of plant with either policy involve £500 excess and so, unless you own plant to a significant value it might be better not to insure it and to take tools or mobile generators home each night. On the other hand, as I've already said in the section on building with subcontractors, if you're hiring plant then there may well be a more attractive option of paying a surcharge on the hire charge to provide cover for the plant or tools for the short periods they will be on site. Remember, you're insuring to protect yourself from some of the major disasters that can befall a building site, not to protect your favourite set of socket spanners and, in any case, the £500 excess may well make that notion as impracticable as it is inadvisable.

Again, with periods of cover. The Norwich Union policy is for a period of 24 months or until the building is finished, whichever is the sooner, whilst the Guardian policy is for 15 months or, again, until the building is finished, whichever is the soonest. Although on the face of it, the Norwich policy can look more expensive, at least at the lower to medium ends of the scales, the addition of a 6 months extension to the Guardian policy would make them more expensive. You can see, therefore, why I do urge you to talk to the people who know about these things and get the policy tailored to your own situation.

Some of the points to consider and discuss regarding insurance are:

Insurance when you move in

Your selfbuild insurance is not invalidated if you move in whilst the house is under construction and, indeed, recognition is given to the fact that everything is safer if you're on hand, by the Guardian policy offering a substantial discount on premiums for those either living on site or within 25 metres of the new building. However do have a care here as any selfbuild insurance policies will not give cover for personal possessions or furniture. When you do finish, you will need to change your selfbuild policy over to a normal household insurance policy and some selfbuild policies offer a cash voucher towards the first premium, if you take out this cover with their company. Others either offer discounts or rebates to those who have finished promptly and moved on to a normal householders policy, with special discounts for those who have made no claims on their selfbuild insurance policies.

Unoccupied property insurance

If a property is completed but for any reason it is unoccupied, you will need to arrange for special insurance. Your selfbuild policy will cease to give you cover upon completion and, in all probability, your existing householders insurance policy will not extend to the additional house.

Legal contingency insurance

I have discussed this at various points in the main text of this book under this heading and that of Single Premium Indemnity policies. They can be arranged to cover for things such as defective titles, disputes over access and anyone claiming rights over your land. They can also provide cover in the event of a possessory title being established by you over land upon which you will eventually seek an absolute title.

Restorations and conversions

Most selfbuilders policies are for new dwellings but there are special policies for conversions, renovations and extensions and, in much the same way as with new build, the premiums are based on the contract value of the intended works.

Caravans

Caravans on the site which are used as site huts are insured as plant. If the selfbuilder lives in a caravan on the site while the building work is in hand there may be no extra cost, although if the value of a residential caravan takes the total value of plant on the site at any one time over £2,000 a small additional premium is payable. Personal effects in a caravan on the site are not covered, although tools may be.

Life and health insurance

This is another category of risk for which you may consider insurance cover is appropriate. If you are using sub-contractors, or are doing any work yourself, you should consider the effect on the project if you step under a bus, or are taken ill, or are incapacitated due to an accident.

First of all, think about cover to meet additional costs if you are sick, injured or depart this life. If any of these sad circumstances would not affect the progress of the job at all, then you can meet them happily, but if not, you must consider health, accident and short term life insurances. The latter is probably the most important, and if you are managing the building work yourself you may consider it prudent to take out a simple short term life policy for a sum that would enable your executors to get it finished.

Security

Theft and vandalism on a selfbuild site involve financial loss, a setback to a carefully worked out programme and often a serious drain on enthusiasm. Sadly, it is a growing feature of society generally and building sites in particular, but although nothing can be done to guarantee it will not happen to you, it is possible to make it less likely.

First of all, don't lose any sleep worrying about it — the odds are it will never happen. Claims by policy holders who take out Norwich Union Selfbuilder's Insurance indicate that only a small proportion of those covered have any significant losses, about the same proportion of those who make claims on their car insurance every year. You have long ago come to terms with motoring risks, so accept the selfbuild risks in the same way. And, as with motoring, there is a lot that you can do to reduce the risk.

There are three basic rules for this: don't advertise, deter trespassers, and make your property difficulty to steal. They need considering separately.

Don't advertise. Potential thieves may be professional rogues who will use a vehicle, or children who may trespass on the site. The professionals are obviously less likely to take an interest in your property if it is not displayed for

Right: Keith Axelby was very careful to avoid an electricity board cable when digging a services trench for his selfbuilt bungalow. Unfortunately it was not where the plans showed it to be and his JCB cut off the power to the local betting shop, making the manager very cross. In law Keith was responsible. Norwich Union handled the claims for him and he is shown here with their local manager.

Below: Craig and Frances Jordan's selfbuilt home was badly damaged in an exceptional gale while under construction. Their insurers approved their estimate for rebuilding without delay and in six weeks the damage had all been made good.

Bottom right: Paul and Lorraine Doran had a series of thefts from their selfbuild home while they were building it. The losses totalled £4000. Their insurers covered the losses, but not the cost of the delays and the frustration.

their inspection. Keep tools and materials in a locked site hut if at all possible, and programme delivery of materials so that they arrive when they are required and not before. This is particularly true of high risk items like roof insulation, timber, copper pipe and plumbing and electrical fittings. If materials which are likely to be stolen must be stored in the open, stack them out of sight as far as possible and cover them up with a tarpaulin.

Secondly, deter trespassers. The first rule here is to keep a tidy site and not to give it the appearance of an interesting scrap yard. This is not always easy, particularly if you are building on a site where there are existing derelict out-buildings which you hope to renovate in due course. However, the tidier and more business like a building operation is seen to be, the less likely it is to be investigated by those with time on their hands.

Consider fencing the site, even with a single strand of wire, as a deterrent to trespassers. If it is already fenced it is likely that there was once a gate: you can buy a farm gate to hang on the old gate posts, and chain it up at night. It may even be worthwhile considering doing any fencing work included in your final plans for the site at a very early stage in order to make it more secure.

If you have electricity on site — and many selfbuilders arrange this so that they can use a electric mixer and electric power tools — con-sider putting up a floodlight with a proximity switch. If you are going to do this install a thousand watt light, as when this comes on suddenly in the dark it can be very startling. However, make sure that any such arrangement will not upset neighbours, as the detectors are sensitive to dogs and other animals. If it seems plausible put up a 'Beware of the Dog' notice.

Perhaps the most valuable thing of all is to contact neighbours when you first start work and to leave them your phone number so that they can call you if they see anything amiss. In some situations you may find someone prepared to 'keep an eye on things' for a small sum. If you are building in a built up area, cultivate the acquaint-ance of the local busybody and encourage him to come to chat to you while you are working. With

luck he will identify with you so that he or she will take action if they are suspicious about uninvited visitors to the site.

Make your tools and materials difficult to steal. First of all, take small tools home unless it is totally impracticable, and never leave the originals of planning documents, building regulation correspondence, quotations, invoices or any other paperwork in the site hut. The place for it is in an old case in the back of your car, or safely at your home. The site hut itself should be as secure as possible, with a sturdy locking bar to the door, a good quality lock, and a shutter to the window. Old steel shipping containers are becoming increasingly popular as site huts, although they suffer from not having windows. However, while they are probably secure against children, professional thieves with bolt croppers can gain access to them in a matter of seconds.

Concrete mixers are the tools most commonly stolen from sites. When the one which you have hired or bought is delivered, consider removing the tow bar and possibly one of the wheels, which will make it much more difficult to tow away. Ladders are also a prime target for thieves, and should be hidden away, chained up, or both. If you take all these precautions you are reducing the risks of direct losses very significantly.

You should also guard against indirect losses, the most common of which is damage from water due to theft of sanitary fittings, boilers, or other parts of your plumbing installation. Thieves will disconnect whatever they want with a hacksaw, and if you have not turned the water off, the damage caused by the resultant flooding can cost more than the value of the items stolen. Turn off water at the mains stop cock whenever you leave the site, and if the water board stop cock is not conveniently situated for this, make sure that you have one of your own installed for this purpose. Make sure it isolates the tap which is used for building water so that if small children leave it on it does not turn your site into a quagmire.

Pay particular attention to the site immedi-ately following delivery of high value items such as sanitaryware and kitchen units and appli-ances, the bulk of which often makes it necessary for them to be stored within the rooms they will eventually occupy. I don't know whether thieves keep a look out for their delivery or if there's a bush telegraph amongst villains that tells them when it's the best time to strike but I do know, from personal experience, that that's when they do so. Either way, it's as well to take some extra precautions in the days that follow, or at least until the units are unpacked and/or fitted to the walls when they become less attractive to flog on and less easy to manhandle.

If you do have losses, remember to collect all the evidence that you will require to support your insurance claim. Advise the police as soon as possible, asking for the name of the officer to whom you are making your report as this will be required to support the insurance claim. Take a whole series of photographs of any damage, and then contact the insurers with a coherent story. You will want to hear from them whether they are going to send an assessor along to visit your site, and whether you can start putting things right before he comes. The insurers can only help you if you give them appropriate information.

This can be in a phone call when you will:

* quote your policy number

* explain that it is a contractors risk loss, and that there are no others involved, or that it is an employers liability incident, or involves a third party.

* state simply the extent of your loss (vandals have broken my patio window or someone has stolen £2,000 worth of bathroom suites)

* tell them you are taking action to make the place secure again

* ask them if they are sending an assessor

* and confirm the address to which they should send the claim form.

Dealing with all of this in an efficient way will help to get you back on an even keel, although you will still be concerned to tell everyone about your new found enthusiasm for capital punishment.

Safety

In the chapter dealing with building with subcon-tractors, I dealt with aspects of Health and Safety legislation and its application to a selfbuild site but there is another side to all of this and that is your own personal safety and the safety of your family. To be a selfbuilder you have to be self confident, and this will lead to your belief that nothing nasty is ever going to happen to you personally. Let us examine this contention.

The building industry has a worse safety record than coal mining. Consider what will happen if you are injured and cannot deal with the work on your selfbuild site. Add to this the fact that amateurs are always more likely to be injured in any situation than professionals. Perhaps this will convince you that positive safety procedures should be part of your project planning.

First of all, who is covered by what sort of insurances?

Looking at the standard Norwich Union selfbuilders' policy, your employees whose misfortunes are covered by the employers liability section of the insurance are defined as:

* direct employees

* labour only sub-contractors, whether working directly for you or working for someone to whom you have given a sub-contract

* persons hired or borrowed from another employer.

This does not include members of your family who are working for you without any charge for their services, nor does it include friends who are giving you a hand. It is a nice legal point that it does not include other selfbuilders who are helping you in exchange for you helping them on their own job. However, these others who may be hurt on the site are covered under your public liability section of the policy, and this includes those who are on the site in connection with some sort of business arrangement made with you (the architect making a routine inspection), those invited to the site by you (your friends and family), and trespassers on your site (the child who climbs your scaffolding while you are not there). If you have children you will have to do some very careful thinking about the extent to

Selfbuild site safety

* Get into the habit of wearing a hard hat yourself on site and make sure that there a some spare hats in the site hut with a written notice, posted on the wall, that they should be worn at all times. When accepting subcontractor's quotations, slip a little paragraph in about expecting them to wear theirs on site.

* Wear protective footwear. Wellies and boots with steel toecaps are readily available - look under 'safety' in Yellow Pages.

* Buy two or three pairs of cheap plastic goggles and always use them with grinding tools, etc. Encourage others working on the site to use them, when appropriate, by hanging the spare pairs next to the hard hats with a suitable notice.

* Use specialist and bona fide scaffolding contractors only and make sure that when you accept their quotation, you confirm that the scaffold is to be erected in accordance with all of the Health and Safety legislation and by reference to best possible practice. If scaffold boards are, quite rightly, turned back at night by the bricklayers labourers or other trades, then make sure that they are properly replaced each day and that no 'traps' are formed by the boards failing to run to a putlock.

* With conventional scaffolding the short lengths of scaffold tube that carry the scaffold boards are called putlocks, and project beyond the scaffolding at head level. Building professionals know they are there by instinct: selfbuilders tend to bump into them and need a trip to hospital to get their scalps stitched. It is worthwhile collecting empty plastic bottles to tape these over the putlocks. This looks funny, but it is very effective.

* Whenever you hire equipment from a hire firm ask if instruction leaflets and particularly safety leaflets are available. You may feel rather self conscious about doing this, but most plant hire firms will welcome your enquiry, and will probably be pleased to give you the benefit of their own experience. They all have stories of the wife returning the tool that put the husband in hospital!

* Keep petrol for mixers in a locked hut, preferably in the type of can that is approved for carrying petrol in the boot of a car, and not in a cheap plastic container. Do not let anyone smoke in a site hut where you keep petrol. Better still use diesel equipment.

* Professional electric power tools from a plant hire company will normally be 110 volts and equipped with the appropriate safety cutouts, etc. If you are using 230 volt DIY power tools, or any other 230 volt equipment, including temporary lighting, take the supply via a RCD contact breaker. These are now readily available as plug in units, and should always be used, whether you have a site supply, a cable from a neighbour or a generator.

* If trenches for services or your foundation trenches are more than a metre deep treat them with respect, and go by the book with shoring. If they show any tendency to collapse, deal with them from above, in company with another person. Never ever work in a deep trench alone on site.

* Packs of bricks and blocks that are crane off-loaded with or without pallets, must always be stacked on a proper base, and never piled more than two high. Take great care when cutting the bands, and re-stack them by hand if packs are in any way unstable. If there is any risk of

children climbing on packs of bricks, particularly those which have been opened, it is good practice to sheet them before leaving the site. They will be all the better for protection from the weather anyway.

* Concrete burns are a selfbuild speciality. Bad ones can leave the bone visible and require skin grafts. Never handle concrete or mortar, and particularly do not let it get down your wellies or in your shoes. If it does get in your wellies or shoes, wash out the offending footwear at once and change your socks. Remember cement burns do not hurt until after the damage is done. If you get cement dust in your eyes, flood your face under the tap at once. **Do not let small children play with mortar or concrete, and if they are on the site with your permission warn them of the risk of cement burns.**

* Do not get involved with work on a roof unless you are well used to heights and positively like it. If you are uneasy up there you will not be able to do anything properly anyway. Do not be afraid to tell sub-contractors 'I am not a man for heights'. They will understand, and their probable reaction will be to show off by performing miracles of productivity while standing on one leg on your roof ridge.

* Selfbuilders regularly fall down stairwells. If they do not their visitors are likely to. Use scrap timber to form a rough balustrade until you fix the real one.

* There are still old type wooden ladders about without a wire under each rung, and these are often owned by selfbuilders. The only place for them is on a bonfire.

* Be obsessive about clearing away any loose boards or noggins with a nail sticking out of them, and in case you miss one, never ever wear shoes with a thin sole on the site.

* Put together a first aid box containing plasters and antiseptic and fasten it on the site hut wall or keep it in your car. You will suffer your fair share of cuts and abrasions, and a poisoned finger is a nuisance.

* Watch your back when unloading a very heavy item, or if you are unloading more weight than you normally handle in a day. This also applies to digging work. The risk of straining yourself is very real, even if you play rugger at the weekends and squash in your lunch hours. The most scrawny and unhealthy professionals can handle heavy weights, or unload and stack 16 tons of building blocks by hand, without any risk of injury. If you try it you are running the risk of putting yourself out of action for a week.

* Always be careful when walking on joists. Many inexperienced people fall through joists either because they are considerably less skilled at balancing than they supposed or because the joists may not yet be fixed. Use scaffold boards laid across the joists and make sure that the joists themselves are either built in firmly or held by battening nailed across and to each one.

* Cover up old or new drainage manholes and pay particular attention to the backfilling or covering over of disused septic tanks and the like. If dumper trucks or other site vehicles are likely to have to go near these then hire a metal plate rather than trust to a sheet of ply having to take the weight.

which you are going to let them visit the site. Having your kids help by clearing rubbish is happy family togetherness, and a good thing. The moment one of them is hurt it becomes irresponsible disregard of safety legislation to let them be on the site at all. There is no doubt at all about this: in law they should not be there. New European safety legislation emphasizes this. Unfortunately, in most family situations your children are likely to become involved with what you are doing. You will have to make your own careful decisions, decide what the rules are going to be, and see that everyone sticks to them. If you are living on the site in a caravan this will involve you deciding to fence off the caravan and family area from the building site. Remember that besides more obvious hazards, children are at risk from toxic materials on a building site. The worst of these, and certainly the one that gives most trouble, is cement. Cement dust, mixed concrete and wet mortar are very corrosive and lead to concrete burns.

As far as you are personally concerned, the selfbuilders' policy gives you no help at all if you are injured. For this you have to take out personal accident, death, and permanent injury insurances if you do not already have this insurance cover in some other way. This has been discussed on an earlier page.

Valuable as these insurances are, they should not encourage you to ignore common sense precautions. Not only is the food in a hospital unlikely to be up to the standard that you normally enjoy, your inability to manage the job while you are recovering from your injuries is going to be very expensive, and this loss is not covered by any sort of insurance.

Most of the precautions you should take are common sense matters but please do take serious note of all of this and use the checklist 'Selfbuild site safety' that is on the previous pages. Site safety is an aspect of site management that is every bit as important as any other and a well managed and tidy site is often the one that has the best safety record.

20 Group & Community selfbuild

In previous editions of this book great emphasis was placed on group selfbuild with a clear distinction drawn between ordinary group selfbuild and community selfbuild. Group selfbuild had, in many ways, been the pioneer and precursor to all selfbuild. Modern community selfbuild, in recognition of the social value of its enterprise, had followed on and taken the ideas and ideals which it espoused in order to bring a greater sense of belonging and worth to those who found themselves at the lower end of the market/social strata. I shall come on to community selfbuild in a moment, but first a brief history of, what I shall term, ordinary group selfbuild. This is where a group of individuals formed an association to work together to build as many houses as there were group members and when the houses were finished, and they'd all moved in, the association was then wound up. By working together they would all pool their skills and by forming an association they would obtain loan funds and help in finding the land. They didn't receive any grants or subsidies and when the houses were finished they all had to be paid for by the members at cost, usually through a Building Society mortgage. This cost was usually low in comparison with the market value and, by a pooling of labour and buying power, was also low in relation to other individual forms of selfbuild. Although there were many self managed groups set up by like minded individuals, usually with one particular member being the driving force, by far the most successful were those which were set up and managed by the commercial agencies. These organisations identified the land, advertised for suitable members who they then vetted, formed the association and arranged the necessary finance which had to be in place for both the initial purchase of the land and the building finance. This was done by registering the group under the Industrial and Provident Societies Act 1965 with a constitution based on the model rules of the National Federation of Housing Associations to whom it affiliated, thus enabling the group to act as a single entity. In the heady days of the middle to late eighties, much of this loan finance came from consortiums of building societies and banks, with the emphasis slipping, more and more, away from local authority and community based financial institutions. It all worked very well with members being able to live in their old home and then selling that when the time came to move into their brand new selfbuilt home.

In the second half of 1988, when the housing market crashed and interest rates practically doubled to over 15%, it all began to go horribly wrong. There were about 200 selfbuild associations working on sites throughout the land and all had difficulties with the interest on their association loans. Those in the South were faced with members who were, either completely unable to sell their homes or, if they did manage to get a buyer, were unable to sell at anything like the expected values. Over 70 associations failed and the members lost their initial loan funds, wasted all their hard work and had their hopes dashed. For some this led to serious personal problems but, sad as this was it can now be seen in perspective. Many other individuals had bought houses in the mad scramble of the late eighties to get on board the housing ladder. Many had taken on high mortgages to cover the inflated prices of their houses, in the expectation that prices would continue to rise and, with the crash, many lost considerably more than the group selfbuilders, with debts which follow many of them to this day.

The National & Provincial Building Society, which had financed a great many of the failed associations, had to make provision for debts in excess of £70 million, scuppering its ambitions to be the second building society to convert to bank status. More importantly for selfbuilders, the major financial institutions then took a long hard look at their whole attitude to selfbuild, turning their faces completely away from group selfbuild and looking askance even at individual selfbuild for a time. It is now impossible to obtain loan funds for group selfbuild from any of the banks or building societies without the involvement of the Housing Corporation which means that group selfbuild has slipped from the private sector into the social housing sector. Many of the professional management companies simply disappeared but a few of the more reputable ones, such as Wadsworth Landmark, remain and they have adapted to the new environment, working within the system to provide opportunities for people in housing need.

Which leads us on to the main consideration of this chapter – Community selfbuild is a term used of projects where those in housing need are enabled to build their own homes. It has a long history and over the years the definition of those in housing need has been changed. For 30 years to the end of the seventies, the phrase was used to describe those who, whilst invariably in employment, didn't have enough points to get to the top of the council house waiting list, or could not find an affordable home in an era of mortgage rationing. Those in housing need today are more often unemployed or suffer the other disadvantages we all associate with inner city deprivation or the breakdown of the rural economy.

The way in which selfbuild has been, and is, relevant to the needs of this changing 'housing need' scene is essential to a full understanding of the contribution which DIY construction can make to our society.

Group selfbuild in its modern form started in Brighton in 1948 with special schemes for ex servicemen to build their own homes on land provided by the Borough Council. They were a success, with 1194 homes being built by 58 associations over 20 years. As such schemes proliferated in an era of controls and nationalisation they attracted grudging recognition, limited support, and a concern that they should be fitted into the housing bureaucracy. By the 1970s a pattern had emerged where the building work was usually financed by the Housing Corporation and led to Local Authority mortgages. They used the National Building Agency as consultants, and were expected to register with the Federation of Housing Associations and to adopt its model rules. The land upon which they built was usually made available by a local authority, which often imposed pre-emption clauses in titles to prevent selfbuilders selling their homes to make a quick profit. There were other approaches too: in the 60s and 70s the West Midlands Council of Housing Associations financed 2,000 selfbuilt homes in Birmingham, often using funds from

Quaker charities. In time all of this became formalised, and so did the Housing Corporations view of selfbuild associations: they were specifically for those in housing need, defined as being those on a council housing list. Associations with a significant membership not on housing lists were ineligible for Housing Corporation finance. Selfbuild associations were ways of helping those in housing need to help themselves.

In the late 1970s all this started to change. Financial stringency had closed the NBA and severely limited the finance available through the Housing Corporation. The selfbuild management consultants arrived and found sources of private finance for the associations that they managed. Within a decade the typical selfbuild home was a four bedroom, detached unit instead of a three bedroom semi, and 'housing need' was rarely mentioned where selfbuild was at its strongest, in the outer suburbs and small towns. By the early 1980s group selfbuild had abandoned the inner cities where housing needs were still very real, and had become something for those who were using it as a way of jumping several rungs up the housing ladder at one bound. It had little relevance to those who wanted to get a foothold on the bottom rung unless, either they were exceptionally determined or able, or they could be found a place on a scheme which had made special provision for 'housing need' members. There were a few dozen such schemes in the 80s which built perhaps 500 homes in total, usually on the initiative of a local authority which would sell land to mainstream selfbuild groups on condition that they took a percentage of their members from council house waiting lists. This was a growing trend, but when the mainstream SBHA schemes crashed in 1989 these opportunities for selfbuilders in housing need disappeared as well.

Meanwhile, as the plight of the homeless became a national issue in the 80s, a number of charitable agencies and others of a like mind began to seek opportunities to promote selfbuild for those who could benefit from it most of all. One pioneer in this was a Dr. Barraclough, a consultant from St. Thomas' Hospital who, having built a striking house of his own from

reclaimed materials on the Isle of Dogs, decided to encourage East-Enders dispossessed by the Docklands Developments to do the same. Among a number of schemes with which he was concerned was the self managed Great Eastern project on the Thameside site where Brunel built his great steamship. Here 46 dockers and their friends built 46 homes with building society finance.

The photograph tells its story as effectively as any words can do and it helped get inner city selfbuild a great deal of publicity, as did a thirty minute TV programme featuring the members and their achievements. South of the river, Lewisham Council also became interested in selfbuild for people on their housing waiting list.

The architect, Walter Segal was asked to design simple form of building construction and to work with local residents to build homes for outright ownership. When Walter died, the Walter Segal Selfbuild Trust was set up and selfbuilders are still using Walter Segal designs in Lewisham to this day.

Another scheme at Bristol was to gain an even higher profile: it was called Zenzele, and was set up as an experiment in breaking the 'no job experience – no job opportunity' trap in the rundown St. Paul's area. This was approached by setting up a selfbuild housing association for twelve members who were described in the press as young, disadvantaged and unemployed, and this was made possible by some forceful management by a local J.P., Mrs Stella Clarke, and a very effective management team which she assembled.

Their first coup was to get the agreement of the D.H.S.S. that association members who were still unemployed when they finished building should have the interest on their mortgages paid by the department as if they had incurred the mortgage before they became unemployed. At that time the ceiling payment of this sort was £22.50 per week, which facilitated a mortgage of £10,800. The Bristol and West Building Society was persuaded to offer such mortgages. Building finance was arranged through the Housing Corporation. All that remained was to see if a scheme could be put together for new homes to be built for £10,800.

A site was found for £15,000, and architects Atkins and Walters designed a simple and cost effective one-bedroomed flats that could be built within the budget. The next stage was to form an association, and instead of the usual advertisements and public meetings the first four prospective members were assembled by Tana Adebiyo, another of Mrs Clarke's team who was a community worker in St. Paul's. Their first task was to find another eight members, all of them unemployed, who had some minimal building industry experience. The association was registered with the name Zenzele, which is Zulu for 'together'. The Federation's model rules were adopted and the association was in business.

Progress was at first quite fast, as members were on site for a full working day. The budget provided for the services of a working site foreman, and the first one appointed was a groundworks specialist as there were site problems with the cellars of old buildings. This involved some anxious moments as this sort of situation can never be costed with certainty, but after various worries everything worked out. The groundworks foreman handed over to another who was to take the building on to completion, and the walls started to rise.

Construction was entirely traditional, and the members handled all the trades themselves. The only contractors brought in were specialists to lay the concrete slab first floor, which, together with a 3" screed, had been designed to give the maximum sound insulation between flats. There were no building problems, but one very happy organisational problem … members started to get jobs. The whole scheme was based on the idea that people find it easier to find employment when they are already working and this is just what happened. The members were soon in two groups: those who were still unemployed and could put in a normal working day and those who worked on the flats in the evenings and at weekends like most other selfbuilders. At the end of the scheme eleven of the twelve members had found work, which was the original intention behind the whole project. By the time the block was completed costs had escalated by 11%. However the Building Society valuation of the individual flats had gone up to £18,500, and rises in the D.H.S.S. mortgage interest ceiling rates made mortgages of £12,000 possible. This not only covered building costs but also cookers, carpets and full interior decorations.

Zenzele provided the public housing establishment with a clear challenge to provide the opportunity for other selfbuild schemes for the disadvantaged and this led to the setting up of the *Community Selfbuild Agency* with Stella Clarke as its chairperson and representatives of a wide spectrum of bodies on its management committee. The agency has offices in London and the north of England, from which it offers impartial advice and information regarding the setting up and development of community selfbuild schemes. It promotes the sharing of experiences between groups and will act as an impartial broker in introducing them to possible partners, which are needed for these schemes to reach fruition. In recent years the agency has become involved in working with local organisations to set up more projects involving young, homeless, unemployed people, taking its inspiration from Zenzele. It provides a selfbuild presence at local authority housing conferences and its director, Anna McGettigan, is a regular speaker at these functions.

Unfortunately, whilst the challenge was met by this organisation and others, in government circles the reaction to it was woefully inadequate at the best and hopelessly obstructive at its

worst. The Benefits Agency adopted the practice of allowing each local office to make their own interpretation of the regulations concerning benefit payable to unemployed selfbuilders and, as officials didn't always understand that the selfbuilders weren't paid for working on a scheme this gave many would be selfbuilders the impression that they would lose benefits if they started working on the site. The CSBA has lobbied hard in an attempt to make the government agencies understand and encourage the efforts of unemployed people to employ their time usefully whilst continuing to search for work, arguing that involvement in selfbuild is not necessarily incompatible with continued benefit, so long as it doesn't preclude the claimants search for and availability for work. It has made considerable headway but there is a long way to go and mainstream community selfbuild schemes for the unemployed have really come down to those which offer rented schemes. The last Conservative governments decision (upheld by the new Labour Government), to withhold payments of the interest on a mortgage for the first nine months of any period of unemployment, effectively prevented any repetition of the Zenzele scheme and barred the unemployed from taking part in any of the shared or outright ownership schemes. Selfbuilders who become unemployed during a selfbuild project cannot claim any assistance with their mortgage payments for the first nine months and potential selfbuilders must make arrangements for insurance to cover this eventuality.

And all of this is against the known background that participation in a selfbuild scheme is demonstrably the most effficient way of getting the long term unemployed back into employment with the skills that they can undoubtedly acquire though membership. This was more than adequately demonstrated by another high profile scheme with different financial arrangements which started work in 1990 in Brighton. Behind this scheme lay two years of hard work by architect Kenneth Claxton and Brighton Housing Officer, Linda Beanland. Kenneth had been involved with innovative low cost housing initiatives since the seventies and Linda was responsible for packaging the bid to the then Department of the Environment for special funding. The project, known as the Hollingbury scheme, was built as part of the Brighton Council housing stock, with the selfbuilders getting tenancies at rents, which reflected their involvement in the construction of the houses.

John Tees was 16 years old and having to make his own way in the world when he read in the Brighton and Hove Herald of a proposed Council sponsored selfbuild scheme for teenagers in housing need, and he took himself down to the housing office to learn more about it. A fortnight later he found himself at the Aberdovey outward bound centre with 15 other selfbuild recruits of his own age, getting to know each other and discovering their potential via the challenges of the Welsh mountains and the Irish sea. This is believed to be the first time that this approach to team building had been linked with selfbuild. On their return they started work on a site at Hollingbury, a suburb on the downs above the town, which happily provided a convenient challenge by being littered with fallen trees which were victims of the 1987 gale. Clearing these was a splendid way to make a start, combining demanding physical work and the discipline of working in close proximity to heavy machinery. By then the selfbuilders were technically part of a TYS scheme involving TEC training to lead to National Vocational Qualifications (NVQs). (The proliferation of initials reminds an older generation of the army, a comparison worth making in the hearing of some concerned with community selfbuild just to witness the horrified reaction.)

Once the trees were cleared and the old iron fencing had been removed, contractors moved in to pour the plinths of 8 semi-detached timber framed homes while the trainees started their classroom training and paid a visit to the Meyers factory in Southampton to see the frames and walling panels of their new homes being made.

The timber frames were erected very quickly, walling panels complete with ready glazed windows were fitted into them, and the roof tiled by the trainees. This was arranged so that the selfbuilders worked in small teams, with two or more teams coming together for the heavy work of erecting the frames. Contractors were brought in to handle the plumbing and electrics, with trainees working with them like old fashioned apprentices. Site supervision, encouragement and firm direction was provided by Mile Bailey, a YTS supervisor who seems to have been an inspired appointment, and John Semple whose practical builders background was invaluable. They worked with a committee on which the trainees were represented.

The first selfbuilders moved into their new flats in July 1991, and all 16 were in their new homes by Christmas. However, there had been many changes in the group and only three of the original sixteen who went to Aberdovey finished the course and took up their leases. This was not surprising: 15 months is a very long time to a 17 year old, and a number of the most enthusiastic trainees were so inspired by their new lives as selfbuilders they went on to other things and moved away. Others moved on due to changed circumstances, and inevitably a few found the hard work through the winter was not to their liking and were expelled. The vacant places were quickly taken by others who took the scheme through to its successful conclusion, and there was a hard core of members for most of the programme.

The Hollingbury scheme and other similar schemes led to the formation of the Young Builders Trust which is a registered educational charity with its roots in actual projects, and campaigns for and promotes schemes with objectives to help disadvantaged unemployed youth in housing need. Vocational training is a key feature of all that it does and practise guides are published which draw on its unique experience. The YBT is currently involved in planning thirty future schemes, including one for the Inner London Probation Service. More widely it is part of a European network, and is already working in Bulgaria. It works closely with other agencies and is financed by D.E.T.R., special grants, charities and fees.

Meanwhile there were various other initiatives under way, of which the most important was the developing influence of the Community Selfbuild Agency, although almost immediately after it was founded, the housing market collapsed. The building societies withdrew their promised finance both for schemes and for the agencies direct costs, and the CSBA was left to promote community selfbuild without any guarantee that schemes could be funded. It took two years for it to become obvious that building society finance was not going to be available again, but during that time the agency and others lobbied the Government and the Housing Corporation to find a formula for making funds available for schemes involving those in housing need.

In 1990 the situation finally began to crystalise and ways forward were found to channel Housing Corporation funds into community selfbuild projects, utilising either, a Revolving Loan or subsidy in the form of Social Housing Grant (SHG), previously known as Housing Association Grant (HAG). Community selfbuild can now, therefore, be divided and discussed under three main headings with a further sub heading involving rural housing initiatives.

Outright Ownership Schemes, where members can be demonstrated to be in housing need and the scheme can initially be funded by a mixture of private loans and a Revolving Loan from the Housing Corporation. This Revolving Loan Fund helps fund up to 49% of the development costs – the criteria is that it must never be the largest source of funding and in practice it is usually about 40% of the costs. Members, the majority of whom must be first time buyers, must be able to demonstrate that they are in employment and each must be able to obtain a mortgage offer, in principle, before any development loans will be agreed. The initial funding usually allows for the purchase of the land and a start to be made on the building process; the Corporations loan acting as a pump primer with a private loan commencing later. The Revolving loan is just that   a loan. It is not a grant or a subsidy even though it is given at preferential rates. At the end of the building period it must be repaid allowing it to be lent out again on another project. In some cases the balance of the funding is insufficient for completion of the project and in these cases the members may have to draw down on their mortgages at an earlier time in order to

The Lord Mayor of Leeds, Councillor Peggy White D.B.E., with members of the Front Line Self Build Housing Association at the party to celebrate the successful completion of the new homes.

Maltby Association members with their new homes. The two women members qualified as carpenters and played their full part in all the work on the site.

271

finish the houses. The advice from the CSBA is that schemes such as this are managed by professional agencies and, in practice, it is those agencies that have the experience and the contacts to make things happen. Banks and building societies still run scared of group selfbuild, even with the involvement of the Housing Corporation, but their fears are allayed, somewhat, with the involvement of professionals.

In order to make each scheme a success a great deal of work needs to go into the preparation and management and perhaps the best way of explaining how the system works is to examine just how a Wadsworth Landmark scheme operates. The agency will, typically, identify the land and will then advertise for members who are then selected with almost as much rigour as the England football manager would use to select his World Cup team. Few employers would dare to admit to being so selective in their choice of personnel but this intrusive weeding out of prospective selfbuilders has one justification – it works! Building your own home, either individually or as part of a group, means working outside the system and it takes a very special type of person to be able to carry it off. The management agencies know that special kind of person and they can pick them, to the benefit of the group as a whole. The agency will then help with the setting up of a Corporate Body in the form of a Selfbuild Housing Association, registered under the 1965 Act, as above, and, again, registered and affiliated to the National Federation of Housing Associations, whose model rules they will adopt – these rules forming, in effect, the same function as the Memorandums and Articles of Association would for a normal limited company. All accepted members then make their initial contribution to the group in the form of a £1000 deposit and become shareholders and committee members with one member then elected as secretary and another as treasurer. All expenditure is paid by the treasurer on behalf of the association and all cheques have to have three signatories with all decisions taken by the members on a majority basis, such decisions being binding on all the members. The formation of such an association enables bank accounts to be opened, trade accounts to be set up and VAT to be reclaimed but, more importantly, it allows the, all important, overdraft facilities to be arranged which form the secondary funding after the Housing Corporation loan. Uniquely, the Housing Corporation allows the bank, or other financial institution giving this secondary funding, to have a first charge on the land.

The ideal membership of a group is between 12 and 20 members and, if at all possible, they look for the membership to be made up with at least 50% having some skills applicable to the building industry to give a professional feel to the operation. The requirement for couples to be married has largely fallen away but there is no doubt that the accepted members must be able to demonstrate a stable background. Balance is the key word here, in ages, skills and attitudes, backed up by established employment and demonstrable mortgage acceptability. Individual members contract to provide loan finance as agreed, arrange to buy the house when it's finished and contract to work for the association as set out in the working regulations. Typically this means a minimum of 14 hours per week in the winter, rising to 20 hours in the summer plus one full week of their annual holiday. Seventy five percent of the working hours must be worked at weekends but in practice, as the project becomes more and more of a lifestyle, the hours worked often exceed all of these minimums. Sometimes experienced bricklayers, joiners and plasterers receive an allowance of two free hours a week, recognising their higher productivity. Special arrangements cover sickness, otherwise absence or lateness results in an automatic fine, often £5 per hour. This is not paid in cash, but is built into the final cost of the member's house. These fines are rigorously imposed by most associations, who feel that, only in this way, can personal relationships survive resentment against the offender.

All members are expected to specialise in one aspect of the building work as decided by the committee, with everyone participating in tasks such as concreting, path laying and unloading materials. Experienced building tradesmen have their own role, the inexperienced quickly acquire

skills, and specialist work is put out to contract when necessary. This is particularly important where unprofessional work carries a risk – gas fitting, electrical work, scaffolding etc.

Occasionally members will need replacing for one reason or another, either at the behest of the group or as the result of unforeseen circumstances on the part of the individual. The work that any member puts into the project is charmingly referred to as their 'sweat equity' and it is this element that creates the typical savings of 25% on the value of their new home. If a member leaves a group then all he/she is formally entitled to is the return of their initial £1000 deposit. In practice this depends on the circumstances and it is open for the remaining members of the group to consider whether a greater amount is refunded. If a house is half finished and, through no real fault of their own, a member has to withdraw, or indeed becomes ill or dies, then the group will advertise for a new member, and when that new member joins the group they will be asked for a contribution which reflects the level the house has reached. The members can either keep that money within the group or they can elect to pay all or a proportion of it to the departing member or his family. The Federation also advises all associations to arrange life insurance for members so that the association can be paid for their lost labour should anybody die and their dependants can then take over the house.

In all of this the agency will want to be employed to manage the project for the group, negotiating with architects and planners, estimating and quantifying the costs for the whole project: materials, land, services, labour, fees, insurances and interest. They will keep the books for the group, organising the VAT, liaising with solicitors, warranty inspectors and those organisations funding the project. There are fees of course but the plain fact of the matter is that with the professionals on board the thing is likely to happen rather than just remaining a distant dream and the Housing Corporation, banks and building societies are usually only interested where a consultant is employed with the relevant experience in developing low cost selfbuild

housing projects. And, if despite these fees, you're still going to make a 25% saving, then what is there to winge about?

There is an interesting subheading to this sector known as *Village Selfbuild Schemes*. Wadsworth Landmark Ltd. pioneered these and their aim is to provide affordable rural village homes for local people. In essence they work in the same way as the schemes I've just described but they are a unique way of overcoming the problem caused by people moving from the towns and suburbs, raising the prices in the rural villages beyond the means of the local people. Approved by government, the Village schemes enable substantial savings to be made by making it possible for local authorities to grant planning permission on land for which it would otherwise never be available. This means that the land can be purchased for a fraction of the normal price of building land and that means that savings of 40% against the value of the finished houses can be achieved.

Now, that's all well and good but when these schemes were first mooted it became clear from the start that, if there was to be any gain in social terms from all of this, something had to be done to preserve the low cost nature of the new homes. Procedures had to be in place that would make sure that, as far as was possible, they started out and remained low cost in perpetuity and that they remained available for the very people they were envisaged for, local people. In order, therefore, to join the group in the first place a prospective member has to prove, in addition to the normal criteria, that they are local to the Parish or have lived or had strong connections there in the past and want to return. They also have to demonstrate, in much the same way, as do prospective members of an ordinary selfbuild scheme, that they have a housing need. They may wish to set up home for the first time. They may need to be close to dependant relatives or their present accommodation may be sub standard or unsuitable in some way.

The nature of the project is then ring fenced by calculating the 40% saving as being made up by two important elements. The first is the 'sweat equity' that is common to all forms of group selfbuild, but the second, comes about from the reduction in the land purchase costs. It is this second element that is 'saved' by the schemes, in perpetuity. Each member has to sign a Section 106 agreement covenanting them and their successors in title that, when they sell, they should a), sell to someone who also fulfils the original qualifying criteria and b), that they should sell at a price which is calculated as 80% of the agreed general market value. In other words when they come to sell, there is nothing to prevent them reaping a substantial profit but at the same time they will benefit future generations by continuing to provide affordable, high quality, low cost housing for their own village.

Shared Ownership Schemes are a way forward when potential selfbuilders are interested in ownership but the incomes are a bit on the low side. With these schemes the selfbuilder can part own and part rent the completed houses, normally starting off with a 50% ownership with an option to raise this to 100% after one year, should they so desire. A government subsidy is available in order to make these schemes affordable in the form of a Social Housing Grant (SHG) and this grant needs the active participation of a local Housing Association, who then become the landlord until such time as all the selfbuilders have purchased the full freeholds. Housing Associations do not have money of their own to spend and, instead, any association backing a selfbuild group has to apply for the SHG from the Housing Corporation and then top it up with private loans. The selfbuild group cannot apply for this funding, as it has to go through a Housing Association and, to qualify, a group must satisfy the criteria that its members are in housing need and that most or all of them come from the local area.

Increasingly, Housing Associations are required to help deliver priorities within the Housing Strategy drawn up by the local authority and thus a local authority would need to approve and prioritise any bid for grant funding. As grants are only normally made in September of each year, any bids must start to be negotiated early as there are limits on the number of shared ownership schemes that can be funded in any

one region. Not all local authorities and housing associations support shared ownership and if this kind of project is what appeals to you then the best bet is to contact the CSBA to find out what's going on in your locality and just how you can start off or join a suitable scheme.

The normal procedure is for shared owners to purchase a minimum of 50% equity, with their 'sweat equity' contributing up to half of this. The members are usually employed as, again, no benefits are available to cover any mortgage repayments for the first nine months of unemployment and the group is registered and affiliated with the National Housing Federation in exactly the same way as the outright ownership schemes are. The working arrangements do not differ significantly either and the only real difference is the involvement of the housing association and the fact that the finished articles are affordable for those on lower incomes, with building society and bank mortgages available to fund the part purchase of the finished houses.

Rented Schemes also rely on Social Housing Grants given via housing associations, or local authorities, to keep rents low and affordable for prospective selfbuilders on low incomes or in unemployment. In just the same way as with the shared ownership schemes, the bids can only be made annually, the exception being where local authorities have their own allocation of Social Housing Grant funding. For many years it was thought that people wouldn't be interested in joining schemes which only offered rented accommodation in return for all their hard work. The experiences gained from Hollingbury and similar projects proved, however, that if people were given the chance to become involved in worthwhile schemes they would return that opportunity by a demonstrable pride in their achievements which would reflect in the care and attention spent on the finished houses. It's a fine line to walk between 'workfare' and a useful and worthwhile opportunity for the disadvantaged but, in the main, these schemes seem to come down on the right side and, certainly, the CSBA is keen to make sure that the social benefits are maintained. Selfbuilders often come into their projects with limited skills in all fields. They usually leave them with their confidence raised, technical skill levels acquired and their communicative and social standing enhanced. The schemes themselves are expected to meet three important priorities in that, the finished houses should have 'added value', the rents are kept low and, if at all possible, they assist with the regeneration of disadvantaged areas. Housing associations have to bid competitively and the Housing Corporation has to evaluate each scheme on these criteria and make sure that the bids compare well in financial terms. Most rented schemes, therefore, end up offering the selfbuilders either a reduced rent, a capital repayment linked to a premium tenancy or a combination of the two. Some housing associations might suggest the setting up of a management co-op whilst others will require the group to register as a selfbuild association via the National Housing Federation in just the same way as the other forms of group selfbuild do. If this form of group selfbuild appeals to you then you should contact your local council, the CSBA or both and they'll point you in the right direction.

I've tried not to sound too gloomy about group selfbuild. Certainly, as a movement, it has gone through some pretty horrendous experiences and in the course of those experiences it has faltered at times and a lot of people have got their fingers burnt. But, equally as certainly, the movement has come out the other end in a healthy and socially important form. For a person whose experience has revolved around the market place and most of whose working life has been under the ethos and regime espoused by a Prime Minister who stated that there is no such thing as society, it is, indeed, a Damascene experience to meet and talk to people whose whole raison d'être is based on the good of the community. Such people, happily, do exist and there are four charities to help people in housing need to get started:

* The Community Selfbuild Agency, which I have mentioned a few times, offers impartial advice on all forms of selfbuild.

* The Walter Segal Selfbuild Trust promotes a particular form of timber frame construction

known as the Walter Segal Method.

* The Young Builders Trust targets its work at young people.

* Community Selfbuild (Scotland) which offers information and advice on developing schemes in Scotland.

These charities work together within limits, but inevitably they compete for funding. None of them has any long term security and all rely on sponsorship which has often to be sought by their staff in time which they would rather spend helping to launch a new scheme.

The political situation obviously has an enormous influence on group and community selfbuild, even more so, perhaps than it does on individual selfbuilding. At the time of writing, with the 'New Deal' arrangements and the emphasis on the useful employment of young people, there is an element of breath holding. Great hopes lie in many a breast but no-one is quite sure what is going to happen next – all the consensus does seem to be, is that something is going to happen and when it does it will be for the better.

Perhaps the best illustration of where most hopes lie and the best way of explaining just how the schemes described above can work, is demonstrated by two projects in Yorkshire which were completed within a few weeks of each other in late 1995. The Maltby Youth Selfbuild Association built nine houses in a mining village where the pit closure had led to very high unemployment and resultant social problems. As one of many initiatives to combat this, a church based community organisation, the Maltby Rainbow Project, arranged for land to be made available by a local authority with sponsorship from the Yorkshire Metropolitan Housing Association. The members, all young, all unemployed single people who didn't qualify for tenancies, were enrolled on a training for work package which enabled them to build the houses, leading to NVQ level 2 qualifications and leases on the new homes. The houses are part of the housing stock of the sponsoring association and the cost savings, resulting from the involvement of the

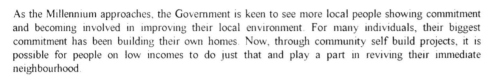

40 Bowling Green Lane   Tel 0171 415 7092   Fax 0171 415 7142
London EC1R 0NE

Northern Regional Office - York   Tel 01904 638 057   Fax 01904 610 985

South East Regional Office - Milton Keynes   Tel 01908 222 258   Fax 01908 226 759

— THE —
**COMMUNITY
SELFBUILD
A G E N C Y**

16 September 1998

Mr David Snell

Dear David

As the Millennium approaches, the Government is keen to see more local people showing commitment and becoming involved in improving their local environment. For many individuals, their biggest commitment has been building their own homes. Now, through community self build projects, it is possible for people on low incomes to do just that and play a part in reviving their immediate neighbourhood.

So far, 10% of local authorities have supported community self build projects. This means, for those families or single people living in their catchment areas, there is much more scope to form their own groups and receive support from the local authority. In the remaining local authority areas, anyone wanting to build or renovate a building to provide homes will need a helping hand. This is where our Agency can help.

Our Agency can offer advice on how to recruit other members to your group and how a case can be made to the local authority for support. It has to be stressed that community self builders must be registered on local authority or housing association waiting lists and their incomes must be insufficient to purchase housing in the normal way. That said, the next step is to explore ways of attracting funding and identifying a suitable site or building for conversion. In some areas of the country, land prices are extremely high and hence it is difficult to attract local authority support. So, before you spend too much time, think about how practical it will be to build in your locality.

Community self build is not for the faint-hearted - having a dogged approach helps. Many professional people choose to believe that because they cannot contemplate self build themselves that others will also experience difficulty building. Not so, it is really surprising just who makes it to the end. What is amazing, is the buzz that everyone experiences and also those who say, if they had to, they would do it again.

We would like to hear from those on low incomes, including the unemployed, who would like to form a local self build group. Remember though, that these projects do not provide instant solutions and members can be asked to hang-in for quite a long time before the wheels begin to turn. However, it is worth the investment of your time.

Sincerely,

Anna McGettigan
Director

Building Lives By Building Homes

CSBA is a charity committed to the promotion of self build housing initiatives, in particular by those in housing need. It is registered under the Industrial and Provident Societies Act 1965 Registration No. 26619R and is also recognised as a charity for taxation purposes by the Inland Revenue (Ref. XR 5019).

selfbuilders were passed on as cash payments to the members. Whilst not unique, this is unusual as normally the 'sweat equity' is reflected in lower rents. This time, however, it was recognised that, to young people just starting out in home life, money to enable them to furnish and equip their new homes was more important.

The impetus and arrangements for the Maltby scheme owed much to a local vicar David Walker and a lady called Christine Holman of the School of Urban and Regional Studies at Sheffield Hallam University. Christine had built her own home in the eighties and her own experience of the importance to the individual of a selfbuild opportunity led to her concern that the prospective Maltby selfbuilders should not be recruited, until it was certain that they would be able to start, with both land and finance in place. As a result, when the scheme was first advertised and the members enrolled, they were on a ten week training course almost at once and started digging the foundations a few weeks after that.

The experience of the Frontline Selfbuild Housing Association in Leeds was different, for the impetus came from within the local Afro-Caribbean community, from which it drew its members. First registered in 1988, the enthusiasm of all concerned was sorely tried while they considered six possible sites and a series of abortive financial arrangements. It took five long years to put together a package enabling work to eventually start in March 1994. Once under way, however, the twelve, two and three bedroomed, houses were built in a very creditable eighteen months. They are occupied on a shared ownership basis and, with the neighbourhood improving all around they have become first class investments. The members, who all gained NVQ qualifications, then put the tenacity and skills they had acquired, into forming a building company to handle Housing Association and other contracts and when I last heard of them were busily engaged on renovation work on houses in Chapletown.

Selfbuild Housing Association model rules

The National Association of Housing Associations publishes model legal documents for selfbuild associations. These are based on their 40 years of experience of registering associations and dealing with their legal and financial problems, and the whole of this experience is that the right legal framework for an association is essential. The draft rules that follow are part of this documentation, and are reproduced by permission of the Association as an example of appropriate rules only. Any new association should seek the current advice of the Association as a matter of course.

Note that selfbuild matters are dealt with by the Association at 175 Grays Inn Road, London WC1X 8UP. Telephone 0171 287 6571.

The regulations detailed below under 'Building Programme' have been designed to protect the interests of all members of the Group. It is obviously important that every member knows that he will not be called upon to 'subsidise' lack of effort by others.

These regulations are suggestions only and should be discussed in detail at an early meeting and ratified by the members of the association.

Membership

1 Nothing in these regulations shall apply, or be deemed to apply to any Local Authority or County Council holding a share in the Association.

2 For the purpose of filling vacancies, the committee shall cause to be kept a list of the names of persons desirous of becoming members of the Association. From this list all new members shall be elected by the Committee, who need not take the first on the list, but may take others matters into consideration.

3 The amount of Ordinary Loan Stock required under the rules of the Association to be taken up by members may be provided in instalments if necessary.

4 All payments made by members under the rules of the Association shall be made to the treasurer and to no other officer or person.

Building programme

1 With the exception of the building tradesmen referred to in Paragraph 2, all members will work 14 hours per week December, January and February, 16 hours per week March, October and November and 20 hours per week April to September inclusive, Breaks, when spent on site, are included in these figures. 75% of member working hours must be worked between the hours of 7.00 a.m. and 8.00 p.m. Saturdays and Sundays. Hours worked through the week between 8.30 a.m. and 5.00 p.m. will count as week-end hours.

2 Experienced bricklayers, house joiners and plasterers will receive an allowance of two hours per week, other fully experienced site tradesmen will receive an allowance of one hour per week. These allowances are at the discretion of the Managers and may only be altered by them.

3 All members will, when starting work, sign in at the exact time and sign off when they stop work. Details are to be recorded of the exact work if done at times other than at the week-end. Members must sign off when they leave the site, unless instructed to do so by the site foreman, and members are expected to sign off when they are not working. (Breaks accepted 10 mins morning, 30 mins lunch break, 20 mins tea - when part of the working day and spent on site.)

4 Each member's hours will be added at the end of each month, on the last Sunday in each month, and for each hour below minimum the member will be charged £xx, irrespective of any previous overtime worked, or sick hours granted. In the event of certified sickness during the last week-end of the month the members will be allowed to the end of the following month to make up the hours lost during that week-end. All fines are paid to the Association and are debited to the Members account.

5 Any time lost through site accident will not be subject to a fine unless the Association decide otherwise.

6 The Time-keeper will keep a cumulative total of each member's hours. Irrespective of any fines which may have been made, by the end of the scheme each member must be above an agreed minimum. In the event of certified sickness the fine will still apply but an allowance will be added to the member's total. The effect of this is that hours not worked on site will be fined and will also have to be made up, but although sickness hours are fined they do not have to be made up. The committee would also consider if necessary granting hours in respect of wife's illness. All fines accrue to the Association.

7 The Time-keeper will keep a list, up to date, showing the number of hours members have worked, sickness hours, penalty hours etc., and which members are above and which below the average.

8 Members will work 1 week of the annual holiday as well as their ordinary times, at a time to be agreed by the Committee and for this week the hours will be 8 hours per day. Members will also work one day extra at Spring Bank Holiday and Easter, the day to be decided by the Committee.

9 Extra Holiday Incentive Scheme - In order to help members have a longer holiday, a special bonus will operate as follows. 50% of extra hours worked between March and September (inclusive) may be used to offset extra holiday hours. The Time-keeper must be informed in advance as to when the member proposes to take this bonus.

10 All members will completely specialise in one aspect of the building work as decided by the Committee, and will be expected to become completely proficient in the craft.

11 Members will not do work of other trades unless specially instructed to do so by the site foreman.

12 The Association will insure its property against fire and also insure itself against claims made upon it by third parties or members in respect of accidents for which the Association may be held responsible.

13 A personal accident policy will be taken out by the Association to cover accident of the members. Any benefit from the policy belongs to the Association, but may be given to the injured member or to his dependants. In the event of the death of a member, his next of kin has the same right to occupy and purchase one of the houses. Due to the increase in insurance premiums and because of the earnings related benefits which now apply, there will be no weekly income accident insurance. However, the members are insured for major accidents, loss of life or limb.

14 The Managers shall, prior to the start of building operations, determine the order in which completed houses shall be allocated to the members. The order of building the houses may be varied by the committee. The committee may pass over the allocation of a house to a member who may be in default.

15 Members are requested to open a Building Society account with an approved Society at the beginning of the scheme and save regularly with that Society.

Equipment

1 The Association will purchase or hire certain items of equipment, and these will be maintained by the Association.

2 Members will be expected to completely equip themselves for the job they are required to do.

3 In certain cases, the Association will purchase certain items of equipment and put them into the care of various members, who will be responsible for them

Design

1 The basic design of the houses is as the approved drawings indicate and no other; standardisation is vital for economy. Certain minor internal modifications are permissible if approved by the Managers, the Association's Architects or otherwise, and will be charged to the individual. An additional 100% of the extras will be charged to compensate the Association for the losses which invariably arise when modifications are introduced.

2 If members choose to do personal work on their own houses before completion, this must not delay the main building programme; penalties may be imposed by the Committee if they do so.

3 The Managers reserve the right to amend the design in the interest of improved performance or general economy.

Amendment of regulations

1 In the event of there being any conflict between these regulations and the registered rules of the Association, the latter shall prevail.

2 Ignorance of the registered rules of the Association, and of these regulations, shall not be accepted as a valid reason for noncompliance herewith.

3 Amendment for these regulations may be made at a general meeting or a special general meeting providing two weeks notice of the resolution is sent in writing to the General Managers. A two thirds majority to amend the regulations is required.

Penalties

Any member who fails to observe the working conditions can be expelled from the Association upon a resolution carried by two thirds of the members, called for the specific purpose. If he should hold a licence to occupy, proceedings will be initiated to evict such a tenant.

Selfbuild stories

The problem, when relating stories of other people selfbuild projects, is that, with a book that has a shelf life as long as this book has, there is a danger that, by the very nature of the beast, they are out of date by the time they are read. Certainly the detailed case histories with their long lists of costs do not suit this forum and they do, perhaps, best belong in the monthly magazines recommended several times within this book where they are an undoubted source of up to date information.

I know, however, from talking to selfbuilders, that they love to read and hear about others who have done or are doing the same thing and I know that many readers would be disappointed if there were no true selfbuild stories in this book.

The selfbuild stories that follow are, quite deliberately, not written in the context of how one brick was placed on top of another or how such and such a timber frame was erected. Nor are they very detailed as far as costings go and, apart from a demonstration of the costs in relation to the market value, there is very little other information as far as prices are concerned.

Whether, by the time you read this book, there will have been changes in property values does nothing to devalue the ratios of cost to price that these figures illustrate and the undoubted achievement of all of the selfbuilders featured. As I have said in the main text, we can demonstrate the principles within this book but the detail will have to be checked out by you, by reference to the costs and values pertaining at the time of your selfbuild.

What these stories do seek to show is the human aspect of selfbuilding and what I hope they give to you is the knowledge that these people who have fulfilled their dream of building their own home, are ordinary mortals like you, from all walks of life and from all age groups. What they also serve to do is demonstrate, in the context of real life stories, some of the points, some of the warnings and some of the recommendations that are brought out within the main text of the book. The names are sometimes fictitious and the locations are not given, but I can assure you that they are all based on real life experiences and achievements and I look forward to the time when your selfbuild project can be similarly featured.

A traditional oak beamed house in Berkshire

As I drove into the exclusive private estate road, looking for the lane leading to Martin and Susan's new house, my heart dropped. This was familiar territory. Large detached houses in all kinds of modern styles ranging from mock Tudorbethan and Georgian, through to sixties kitsch, each one vying with its neighbour for importance, their clashing styles trumpeting their owners' aspirations and status. Had I come to do a story on one of these?

I turned left into a lane that wound down and then right again. Huge trees and a high, periwinkle covered bank, obscured the estate and I had immediately left suburbia and entered, once more, upon the Berkshire countryside. A gap in the bank came into view on the right leading down, past an outbuilding, to a house that nestled amidst the slope and the trees, proclaiming its place as part and parcel of this beautiful land. Surely this was the original house that had owned the land all around, before it was sold off for development?

I went to drive on past and then stopped as I noticed, out of the corner of my eye, the house name on the bank. This was the house I had come to see! I reversed and drove in past the open door of the garage outbuilding, inside which a gleaming blue 'E' type Jaguar crouched, greeting my own motorcar, its larger cousin, as I revved slightly and turned off the engine.

The thud of the knocker on the solid oak door sounded off down through the halls of the house and footsteps announced its opening. Martin and Susan stood there in greeting, joined by an exuberant wirehaired fox terrier, rejoicing, not unnaturally, in the name of Brillo. The door closed behind us with a comfortingly solid thump and we turned and went through the hall and into the kitchen where I could see the welcoming teapot and cups laid out for my arrival. Brillo scampered past us and out through the french doors, almost knocking Oscar the blue Persian cat over in his haste, as we sat down to talk. I looked around. Huge oak beams, delicately stencilled and flocked wallpaper, mellow brick and sturdy oak flooring. Was this really a new house? Of course it was but the entire ambience within it was that of tradition, of stability and permanence, in a way that I have very rarely experienced before, except in traditional farmhouses, the like of my late brothers 450 year old Essex home.

But enough of my first impressions, you want to read about how all of this happened. Well, it

happened through and because of the dream that Martin had always had of building his own home. A dream that had lain dormant for years before gradually enthusing Susan and culminating in the fabulous house that I was now sitting in. A dream that had found its perfect partnership with Border Oak Design & Construction Ltd., a company that has brought 15th century building technique into the modern world.

"What was the real motivation?" I asked. Martin looked sideways at Susan for a moment and then replied honestly that finance was probably his first spur but that it had been coupled with a wish to get just what he wanted in terms of design, privacy and materials. "Roots", said Susan quietly. "I wanted roots...to belong... to know that somewhere was really home".

It had taken nearly four years to get from the 'shall we?' stage to the beginnings of the realisa-

tion of their dreams. Martin is a self employed business transfer agent, working from home and Susan is a high flying accountant. They lived in a mock Georgian box in Wokingham that fulfilled its soulless purpose of being a house but not a home, and spent their free weekends together looking around for plots. By their own admission they were fussy but in the end that trait paid off and their very attention and insistence on detail runs through all they have subsequently achieved.

The plot came through the post one morning in April. The details didn't look particularly exciting and they just put them to one side. Then on the May Bank Holiday Monday, the two of them went out for a drive in the 'E' type and idly drove into the same estate I had driven though. They reached the lane and, if two people can sit bolt upright in an 'E' type Jaguar, then that's what they did as they approached the plot. Even before they fully saw it they had turned to each other and exclaimed that this was it.

It was heavily wooded with tall oak and wild cherry trees beneath which lay banks of Rhododendron, just coming into flower amid stands of shining holly. There was a huge slope and the whole place had an aura of untouched history. In fact that first impression was right, as the plot had once been part of the garden of the adjoining house, barely visible through the trees. The owners had found the garden too much to cope with and had just fenced it off years before and left it. Now new people had bought the house and, having got outline planning permission on it, they were selling the plot on.

The planning showed that the house was meant to go at the top of the bank with its access shared by the adjoining house. Straight away though, Martin and Susan felt that it should be built into the hill, further down the plot, and that the access should be an individual one from the lane they had driven in by. They would need the planners consent for that alteration but for now, come what may, this was the plot for them and they needed to secure it. An offer of £130,000 was made as quickly as they could and, when it was accepted, solicitors were instructed and their own house put on the market. They had some of the money from their own savings but the rest had to be borrowed in the form of a bridging loan which was to cost them dearly in the eighteen months that it took to sell their existing house. It was all worth it though and they used the time to good advantage by investigating everything and anything that they could about self building and the companies that worked within the industry.

They fancied the idea of building in timber frame, the incentive, for Martin at least, being that he understood that it would be cheaper. Further investigation proved that this was a misconception but, still, they both felt that this was the way to go and they arranged to visit the show houses of various companies throughout the country. They were completely disillusioned. Oh, there was nothing wrong with any of the houses they went in but, for them, they just didn't feel right. There wasn't that feeling of roots that was so very important now, to them both.

They changed tack completely and started to think in terms of a traditional brick and flint house and they had interviews with various architects in an effort to get to the bottom of what they really wanted. Still that all important spark wasn't there, besides which most of the architects, they spoke to, wanted fees of 12% or more. That wasn't really the problem, it was more that they just never met one that they felt comfortable with.

Budget was an important factor. They'd set a budget of £120,000 in the first instance and, despite their lack of any experience in the building industry, they had managed to glean from magazines and other sources, enough material to be able to cost out the various elements of their proposed self build. They approached the Nationwide Building Society and got approval in principle and then a firm offer of mortgage, based on this budget, with agreed stage payments. All now depended on and awaited the sale of their house in Wokingham.

At a self build show they'd picked up the brochures from Border Oak and, still casting about for the best way to move forward, they arranged to visit a house that had been built using this company and its system. As they walked into that house, it struck them like a thunderbolt. This was it! In just the same way as the plot had sung out to them, so this house did! This was what they wanted and, henceforth, all that they thought about in respect of their new home would be along these lines.

Very quickly, spurred on by the fact that the house at Wokingham had now, at last, been sold, they devised a plan of their own and together with the Border Oak architects, the initial drawings began to take shape. Martin even made a model of the house that took pride of place in his office, even as they moved out of their own home to live with Susan's father in his house in a nearby village.

Planning permission was applied for and, to their delight, there were no objections to the house being moved down the plot and the entrance coming in off the lane. Now Martin's management and communication skills really came into their own. He proved very adept at seeking out and getting prices from local subcontractors, something that some people, even so called professionals, find it terribly difficult to do. He made lists from the Yellow pages, looked up adverts in the local press and asked around at building sites and at local builders merchants. He hadn't done any building work before but he read up enough about it all to know that he could handle the project management of their new home. Of course, they were both becoming experts in the unique system employed by the Border Oak homes and the zeal with which they preach its worth, has to be seen to be believed. Their furniture, too, had to match what they were proposing and anything that didn't ring true to what they were trying to achieve had to go. A self confessed shopaholic, Susan threw herself with great gusto into the sourcing and acquisition of new and antique furniture and the choosing of materials and wallpaper to grace the walls of their new home.

The groundworkers were a local firm and their job was to carve out the level plinth for the new home and construct the foundations up to oversite. The subsoil was a mixture of clay and flint which meant that, with the levels and the presence of trees some of the foundations had to go down at least 3 metres and to prevent differential settlement, one end of the building, where the ground fell away had to employ a pot and beam floor.

It was then that disaster struck.

With barely 7 days to go before the Border Oak frame was delivered, a frame that had already been manufactured and pre-assembled as a test run, in the timber yard at the companies main depot, the groundworkers reported that the house wouldn't fit on the plot!

It fitted on alright as far as the plans were concerned – plans that had been drawn as the result of a levels, boundaries and tree survey that Martin and Susan had commissioned right at the start. But, it didn't fit on the ground and now that the levels had been changed and the land had been cleared, the builders were at a loss to explain just why.

The boundary to the adjoining house, the home of the vendors, was clearly marked with a line of pegs and, if the house was set out correctly, it would overlap this boundary by seven feet. It didn't look right to Susan and Martin. Something was wrong and they needed to get to the bottom of it very fast indeed. Solicitors were called out to the site, together with the surveyor who'd undertaken the original survey and they were joined on the site by the vendors and their solicitors for a crisis meeting.

It was with a heavy heart that Martin and Susan attended that meeting, fearing the worst, still struggling to come to terms with and understand just what had happened. For a while they all stood looking at the line of pegs and then it all began to dawn, first on their surveyor and then, on Martin, just what had happened. The pegs did not follow the line that they had originally taken. They came on their side of a large variegated holy bush and excluded several trees that had previously been marked down as being within their plot.

The vendor blamed the surveyor. The pegs had always been there and he must have got his survey wrong. As far as he was concerned the pegs marked the boundary of the plot he had sold, taking a straight line from an agreed point in the dog leg boundary to his retained property, to the fence at the bottom.

The argument got heated and Martin and Susan walked away and mooched around further on down the plot. Idly and half-heartedly, Martin pulled some branches aside from a stand of holly that was, on the strength of the other pegs, outside their boundary. There was a peg, hidden by the low foliage and in the position and the line that they had first recalled and as witnessed on the survey! At the bottom of the site, hidden in the nettles but in a straight line with the peg they had just found and the peg at the start of the dog leg, there was a clean square hole where once a peg had been.

Oh, there was some bluster and some protestation after that but the red faces gave the game away and the solicitors duly solemnised the agreement of the boundary along the original line, much to Martin and Susan's relief and joy.

The groundworks were completed and Border Oak arrived on site, first to do the brickwork for the plinth, and then for the all important bit of assembling and erecting the massive oak framework for the new house, after which they moved on to the fitting of their unique infill panels with their complex systems of trims, water bars, weather seals and drainage channels. The tilers came as a recommendation from the brick merchant, from whom Martin had bought both the bricks and the tiles and, pretty soon their new house really began to take shape. Susan talks fondly of how every time she arrived on site she could see the difference and the progress. She also talks about those times when, before the plasterers moved in to do their bit inside, she and Martin would be upstairs staining the beams and she would hear strangers just wandering in and around their new home as if it was some sort of show house or local theme park. Her feelings were a whole mixture of annoyance, amusement and pride, in roughly equal measure.

The plasterers, who came from near Border Oak's main yard in Herefordshire, actually camped out in the house whilst they did their job and the plumbers were from IPECC Systems Ltd., one of the countries leading companies dealing with underfloor central heating, something that they had become convinced of at one of their many visits to self build shows and something that they love to this day. The electricians were a local firm and Martin and Susan had great fun marking out just where they wanted everything to go.

Not as much fun as Susan was having looking for and choosing sanitaryware and fittings and fixtures. This was the shopping trip to beat all shopping trips and she admits to being, at times, almost overwhelmed by the enormity of it all, like a kid in a toy shop.

The costs had escalated wildly, rising £50,000 above their original estimates and budget, not that they had been caught out by too many unexpected things. No, this was a conscious choice on their part. They'd started off with the idea of building a normal timber framed house and instead they'd built themselves a

traditional oak framed manor house with everything in it that they could ever dream of. There were strains of course. Family and a separate loan from the bank filled the gap, but there were times when a little bit of panic stepped in, especially when the building society monies were due in and the inevitable delays in authorisation cropped up. With hindsight they realised that they would have been better off if they'd've not used their own capital in the early stages and saved it for the later ones, but at the time, they thought they would be saving on interest.

I've described my feelings as I entered the house and the photographs that you can see here, show, in better detail than I can muster, just what Martin and Susan have achieved. Including the cost of the land and the finance, the whole

project cost £300,000 to realise but when you set that against its value of approaching £580,000, you can see that Martin managed to achieve his first objective even if it did get subsumed by all the other ideals that they picked up along the way. It's taken the two of them all of the time since they finished until just before my visit to pay off the short term loans that covered the overspend but there are certainly no regrets on their part and the pride they display in their joint achievement is palpable.

As a final thought, I'll tell you about the kitchen. They ran out of money at the stage when the kitchen units would need to be ordered but there were plenty of bricks left over and quite a lot of oak from the flooring. Their kitchen is made up of brick built bases with the doors constructed and fitted by Martin under a maple wood worktop. With the exception of the sink unit, appliances and, of course, the worktop itself, the whole thing is made out of leftovers. But makeweight it ain't. It is the perfect answer to the whole feel of their new house and if they hadn't told me about it, I'd've thought that that was what they'd planned all along. What started off as necessity brought on by happenstance has ended up as one of the best features of their new home and, indeed, to imagine any modern kitchen fitting in quite so well, is difficult.

My visit over, we had time to talk Jaguars before I left, my last view in the mirror echoing my first impressions.

A rural bungalow in Kent

One of the most galling things for the prospective self builder, must be reading this book and seeing, after, perhaps years of looking, a story about someone who, without any prior planning, just stumbled on the idea and a plot at the same time. Galling it may be but the fact remains that for many people, self building, like life itself, is something that happens by accident.

So it was with Ray and Hazel, a delightful couple, full of life and laughter who, having remade their lives, with each other, then went on to self build their bungalow in a little corner of heaven in rural Kent.

Just to fill in the background. Ray had already retired way back in 1982, when a bad back forced him to give up working on the docks and, although he'd done bits and pieces here and there, including a spell as a high class chauffeur, he'd done very little since 1984. He was divorced, with two sons, one of whom has provided him with a lovely granddaughter, and, to get out of the house from time to time, he used to go to a singles club. There, one night, he met Hazel who, having been widowed two years earlier, had been persuaded by a friend to go out for the night. Hazel worked then, and still does, as the Finance Administrator for a local medical health centre, a fact that Ray will regale with pride at any and every given opportunity, trumpeting the virtues of his "young, clever and very important partner". Hazel just smiles as she listens to her "Jack the lad" singing her praises.

Well, before very long they had set up home together in a chalet bungalow in Welling. It was alright but they wanted a home that they could really call their own and they set about looking around for another house. They looked far and wide but there was nothing that really fitted the bill and they got fed up with constantly looking at houses where there was no outlook or where the kitchen was...well, where the kitchen was just someone else's. They even got as far as making an offer on a house in Somerset that would have meant completely uprooting their lives, taking them away from, not only Rays children but Hazel's doctor son, pharmacist daughter and, most importantly of all, her two granddaughters and four grandsons. I don't think anyone was too disappointed when they were gazumped.

Coming back from a visit to friends, one day, they saw the signs for a self build roadshow, run by 'Build It' magazine and popped in, more out of curiosity than any real interest. It didn't make them all fired up to go out and self build but it must have lit some sort of a slow fuse because when they went out looking again, they started to be a little more adventurous in their choice of what they looked at. They were offered and went to look at a partially finished house deep in the country up a long unmade up lane. It had been built as far as the weathertight shell but, unfortunately, it had all been very badly done. It sat in two thirds of an acre of land in the most glorious countryside but at £55,000, with countless problems clearly visible and goodness knows how many more covered up, they decided, quite wisely, to give it a miss.

There was a lovely bungalow next door and that too was for sale so they arranged to go back and have a look around it, leading up to them eventually making an offer of £95,000 subject to contract and subject also to a survey. The survey came in and from that it turned out that £20,000 of work would be needed just to make the bungalow habitable with lots more needed to get it to anything like they wanted. Reluctantly they pulled out but not before one last visit just to make sure that they were doing the right thing.

There was another house on the same lane and whilst they were nosing around, looking longingly but sadly at the bungalow they were rejecting, the owner came out and started to talk to them. "What about a plot?" he asked. "What about one?", was the reply, to which the answer came with the sweep of a hand, "There". Their new friend was pointing at the paddock adjoining his home.

Had it got planning permission? No it hadn't, "… but that shouldn't be a problem", said the owner. "They could have the plot for £42,000."

Ray and Hazel had picked up enough information at the self build show to know that the next thing they needed to do was visit the planning department of the local authority and find out just what the chances of planning on this plot were. And, that's just what they did. "Not a snowballs chance in hell", said the planner.

Of course they felt that they had to tell their prospective vendor that they wouldn't be going any further and it was in fairly sad heart that they, once again, drove down the lane that they were getting to know so well. They told the owner of the land what they'd found out and he, in turn told them that he'd only bought the land 6 weeks beforehand for £12,000, so they didn't feel all that bad about things. When I called, he'd still got the land up for sale, by the way.

What he said next, though, was the most important thing. "Why don't you try Hippy Ron, he might be selling his land and that's got planning permission?"

Hippy Ron had lived in a collection of motley caravans and sheds, on a corner plot, just down the hill, with his wife, two daughters and several dogs – that is before the council had evicted them. Nobody was ever quite sure how he'd acquired the land, whether he'd inherited it or just bought it for a song. He can't have been all that silly, because he did apply for planning permission and, remarkably for such a rural plot, he got it.

Where it had all gone wrong for him though, was, that having got planning permission and set himself up on the plot, he didn't have the where-withal to go any further. After nearly five years of a hippy encampment, the council took action and moved Hippy Ron off and into a house in Gravesend from where he returned from time to time to check on the dogs.

Ray and Hazel went down the lane to have a look and, if you consult the photograph of their partially finished bungalow and garage set amongst green fields and rolling hills, you'll see exactly why they decided, there and then, that, come what may, they wanted this plot. They tracked Hippy Ron to his home and offered him £40,000 on the spot. He wasn't that keen so they upped the offer to £45,000 and he said he'd consider it but that he really wanted more.

Things went quiet for a while but then, when Ray got home one day from an early morning stint of helping a friend out at a roadside trans-

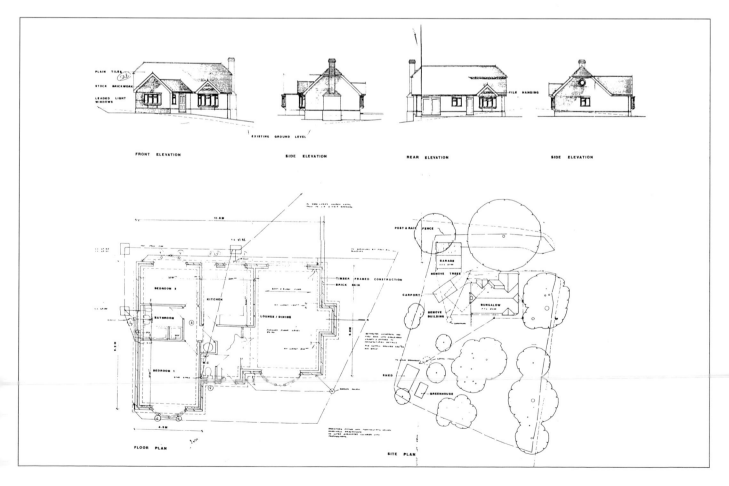

port café, there was a long and garbled message on the answerphone from Hippy Ron. If they upped their offer to £50,000 and paid very quickly in cash then the plot was theirs!

Ray and Hazel got round to Hippy Ron's house as quickly as they could that evening and duly upped their offer. They had a bit of trouble explaining why they hadn't got the money with them in a plastic bag and eventually Hippy Ron agreed that solicitors would be instructed and that it would all go ahead from there. But he still wanted cash and he still wanted it to go through very quickly. Of course he did. Ray and Hazel knew full well why he needed it all to go through quickly as they knew that the planning was due to expire in 3 months time, Given the planners attitude to the plot just up the hill, there was little doubt that if something wasn't done in connection with the existing planning permission very soon, the land would cease to be a plot.

Back to the plot went Ray and Hazel and it was then that they noticed, almost for the first time that the land across the way had a new bungalow on it that was nearing completion. They didn't dare to knock just then but when a little later that day, they mentioned it to the chap at the top of the road who'd originally tried to sell them his paddock, he took them back down and introduced them to the man who was, though they didn't know it just then, going to become their mentor. They looked around his new house and he explained that he was building in timber frame, using a company who were based not far away in Kent. That evening they sent off for that company's brochures and, from a borrowed 'Build It' magazine, for the brochures of a few other companies as well.

Hippy Ron's demands for cash were becoming ever more strident. Ray and Hazel had no qualms about giving him the money but the solicitors practically had the vapours at the thought, especially as Hippy Ron, seemed to have lost the deeds to the land and was having a little difficulty, having been outside the system for so long, proving just who he was! At one time he threatened to withdraw from the whole deal but Ray managed to mollify him and get him to sign a Statutory Declaration that allowed the solicitors

to proceed very quickly to an exchange of contracts. Only then did the plastic bag get used and the £5000 deposit was delivered to Hippy Ron in person.

While all this had been going on the sale of their own house in Welling had been proceeding quite normally and Christmas 1996 found them preparing to move out. A bright morning in January found them living in a newly positioned mobile home on the site, connected to the septic tank that Hippy Ron had installed for his caravans. Their furniture, or what they'd decided they wanted to keep, was stored in a wooden hut on the plot and evening found the two of them "as snug as bugs in a rug" in their new home. Well, nine of them really, because as well as their own 6 cats, it appeared that they'd inherited a large Alsation dog with a fearsome reputation! To this day the postman won't come through the gate although when I visited, she was an absolute softy and Hazel tells me that most people don't think it's the same dog.

Well, now they were on the plot, what should they do next? Sitting, the following evening, in their mobile home, they took a piece of paper each and drew out their ideal bungalows. When both of them had finished they swapped over and

were amazed that, without collusion, they had managed to come up with two practically identical plans. Their new next door neighbour arranged for the chap who'd done his plans and planning permissions to come and see them the following night and when he called they handed him their plans. He thought that he'd got some better ideas and he went away that night with their plans and a whole lot of notes, promising to come back to them very quickly with some sketch ideas.

When he came back they didn't like what he'd drawn at all and they told him so. He went away and came back again and, still the second lot failed to impress them. The third time, he came back with some plans that almost exactly followed their own original sketch designs and they professed themselves happy. Planning was applied for, just in time, in February 1997, for the exact self same bungalow that they have subsequently built, including the choice of materials, that they'd carefully thought about from all of the brochures that they'd been sending off for. They were told that they should expect trouble. They were told that the planning officer's legitimacy was in question, that he was a prominent member of the Third Reich. In fact nothing was further from the truth and there were no problems at all, in large part because they'd carefully thought about the bungalows design and, even more carefully, thought out the choices of external materials, especially bricks and tiles.

Things had to go through their various procedures, of course, and that gave Ray and Hazel time to gear up all of the materials and labour, with a lot of help and encouragement from their neighbour. The plans were sent off to three timber frame companies for a quotation and the one that they decided on was from a local manufacturer. A Maggie White came out to see them and "she was brilliant". No order could be placed until the planning permission was all settled but just as soon as it was they had no hesitation in ringing Maggie to give the go-ahead. They were going to build with subcontractors, not for any particular reason but, more because that's how their new friend next door had done it and he was already supplying them with the names of the guys he'd used.

The chap who'd drawn their plans also provided them with a full bill of quantities, which obviously helped a great deal when it came to the ordering of materials and he organised, and recommended that the building would be inspected by Zurich 'Custombuild' so that a warranty could be issued on completion.

The first quotations came in from the groundworkers and they were all well beyond that which they'd budgeted for. Ray happened to mention this to Maggie when he was on the phone to her one day and she told him of another firm and arranged for the plans to be sent off to them. When that quotation came in it was 42% lower than the highest of the original quotations!

In early May 1997, planning permission and Building Regulations approval having all been granted, a start was made on site, with the digger clearing in a matter of minutes, an area of ground that had taken Ray and Hazel ages to hack down. The subsoil was chalk, natures concrete, and the footings were dug and concreted in next to no time.

Then came what proved to be their only real mistake, in that, as the groundworker was so good, they decided to accept his offer of going on from the oversite and taking on responsibility for the brickwork to the superstructure. The manufacturers delivered and erected the frame, including the roof, and the fitting of the window and door frames. The tile representative arranged for the felt and battening to be carried out as quickly as possible to take advantage of the weather.

When the bricklayers first started everything seemed fine, if a bit slow at times, but nobody worried too much as by now the bungalow was dry and secure, even if one did have to duck down under the scaffolding to get in. A total of 17 different bricklayers came and went at various times, with 'went' being the operative word for days on end. Perhaps it's testament to the bricks, perhaps it's because the bricklayers, one and all, weren't that bad, but today, when one looks at the finished bungalow you wouldn't know the history of their laying. One day the chaps who were on

the last leg of the bricklaying happened to mention to Ray, that they would be away that evening and would come back, in a few days, when he'd got hold of the lintels for the last bit of their work. "I've already got them!" Ray announced proudly. "They're in the shed and if you don't come back tomorrow and stay 'till it's done then there's no more money". They were back the next day.

They sourced all of their materials through adverts in the magazine and from a subsequent visit to the self build show at Alexandra Palace. The plumber, who worked on a labour only basis, was Hazel's late husband's business partner, the electrician who did things on a supply and fix basis was introduced to them by their neighbour and the plasterer came as another introduction. From their visit to the show they came away convinced that, for them, underfloor central heating was the answer and, whilst they could, they also installed a central vacuum system.

One of their only undoings was the contact they made at the show with a kitchen company. They were bombarded with calls until they agreed to a visit and the representative came to see them in their mobile home, when the bungalow was still only a shell. He got there in the early evening and he was still there at 1 o'clock in the morning, trying to get them to sign an order! In the end, more out of desperation and tiredness, than anything else, they signed the order and paid a £575 deposit. The bungalow wasn't even built. The measurements the man had taken took no account of the fact that the walls were yet to be plastered. They knew they'd done the wrong thing and eventually they managed, after strings of telephone calls to the managing director, to get their deposit back and cancel the order.

As I sat talking to them in their lounge, staring enviously out of the window at the glorious view of the Kent countryside, I asked Ray whether there had been any really bad moments. "I don't think so", he said. Then he thought for a moment. "Maybe the time Steve, one of the groundworkers drove the dumper down and into the old septic tank. That was a bit hairy".

I turned to Hazel and asked the same question. She too thought for a moment and as she thought, I turned back to see Ray sitting in his chair, staring through a pair of binoculars at the corner of the brick fireplace. I looked back at Hazel. "It's his pet spider" she whispered. "It lives in a hole in the bricks and he feeds it on flies that he catches by the window. I smiled back in sympathy before the two of us, joined then by Ray, rocked with laughter, the tears streaming down our faces.

As she recovered, Hazel raised her hand and said that she'd remembered her worst bit. It was when she'd come home from work one evening, just after they'd received a letter from the council telling them to remove the mobile home, to find two old age pensioners, one of them Ray of course, trying hard to stop the mobile home they'd been trying to move, from slipping down the bank. One of the wheels had buckled and it was perched and balanced precariously above their new bungalow.

The neighbours were summoned. Order was restored to chaos and the mobile home that they'd originally paid £1050 for was duly dispatched on the low loader, sold for £750. Not bad really. If you work that out, they'd housed themselves in complete comfort for £25 per month!

Today their lovely bungalow with its large double garage, all of which cost them around £150,000, is valued at above £200,000. That was never the motivation, though.

That was always to get what they wanted, where they wanted it, for what they had. And all of that, they achieved, whilst still managing to laugh their way through life.

A country home in Herefordshire

It all really began long before the beginning of this self build story when, back in 1951, Tony, then aged 15, and his brother, on their summer holidays, took a train from London to Oxford and went cycling, for a fortnight, around Herefordshire, Wales and Shropshire. Then, as now, there were vast stretches of open countryside and roads with little or no traffic to disturb the tranquillity. Then, as now, there were peaceful wooded valleys and rural life moved in its slow and gentle way from season to season. It all made a lasting impression on the young Tony and the image of where it would be nice to live one day was imprinted on his mind.

The young boy grew to a man in London and ended up as an international banker spending many years living abroad in, amongst other countries, Holland where he met his wife Luva, and America, where the two of them bought a home and raised a family. But not before Tony had taken Luva on honeymoon in England to shew her the country. And where did he take her? Well, he took her to the very same places that he's visited as a boy all those years before and she was equally as impressed. To Luva England, and especially Herefordshire, seemed like one big park after the dreariness and uniformity of the Dutch countryside.

At 53 Tony took early retirement and they returned to England to live, where he took on a less demanding job as an Insurance Administrative Consultant. Their house in America remained unsold and so they rented various large to medium sized black and white houses in rural Kent, which they loved despite the fact that they were so cold and draughty. "Gorgeous in summer but hell in winter", Luva told me, as she shivered at the memory.

After three moves, Tony retired once more and, as the house in America had now sold, they resolved to buy one in England, looking, first of all, around where they lived in Kent. Nothing was suitable and, as time went on, they began to look further and further afield. They were really looking for the same sort of house that they'd been living in, having been spoilt by the accommodation and the surroundings they were now so used to. Their horizons widened ever further until they encompassed and alighted on Herefordshire where they continued their search for an existing older house. They were torn now. New houses, as they'd known from their home in America and as they'd discovered from the relatively modern extension on one of the old houses they'd rented, could be so much warmer. Yet the thought of living in an estate situation, as most of the modern homes they came across were, was horrid. Even their home in America had been set in 2.5 acres. What they really wanted was an old house looking as if it could grace the front of a chocolate box, set in its own grounds and with all the modern conveniences and warmth that they craved for. Deep down they knew that they weren't ever going to find it and that feeling was only ever increased when they received details and went trotting out, yet again, to see what always proved to be a disappointment. Even the houses that were halfway decent needed £50k spent on them just to bring them up to the standard they wanted.

All new houses are ugly, Luva convinced herself, even as she realised that by setting her face firmly against the idea, she was condemning them both to a life of cold and draughts.

Then somewhere and somehow, he can't remember where or how, Tony got hold of *Build It* magazine and from that, he quite naturally picked up on the idea of self building. Luva wasn't at all interested but Tony saw from the magazine that the Self Build Homes Show at London's Alexandra Palace was coming up shortly and he arranged to go. Luva point blank refused to go, so, in the end, Tony went without her and had an exhausting but happy day from which he came back with carrier bags full of brochures amongst which was the one from Potton. This was the company he'd been most impressed with, not least because their designs echoed his own ideals of what the house he'd been searching for, for so long, should look like. On top of that the Potton houses were timber framed and from their experiences in America he knew that, if they ever were to self build, this was the way he'd want to go.

Still, Luva was unimpressed, even as Tony argued that this was possibly the way out of their dilemma and pleaded with her to just go with him to see the show houses. Another round of useless details from the estate agents may have made the difference but in the end Luva agreed to go with Tony to see the show homes and attend the seminars. "It was a horrid journey and a very long day", Luva told me, "but when we got there everything changed and the long trek proved worthwhile". Once there she was delighted by the seminar, and then completely bowled over by the show homes that finally swung her around to Tony's way of thinking. She loved the light and the sense of distance in the houses and they were both impressed by the speed of build that they were told was possible and the thought of underfloor central heating and all that lovely warmth. Now they were both on board the self build train.

They still needed to find a plot though and Tony went back to the Yellow Pages and telephoned every estate agent listed. They hadn't completely abandoned the idea of buying a house but, instead, they increased their list of requirements to plots and, in amongst the piles of details that now came through, one or two bits of land began to appear. One day, another lot arrived from an agent in Ross-on-Wye and in with the usual dross were the details of a plot on the edge of the Forest of Dean, in a valley half remembered by Tony. It was February and they'd already arranged to go and stay at the Green Dragon in Hereford so, when they went, they took these details with them and put the plot on the list of all of the other things they'd gone to see. They arrived at the plot on a cold and damp day and were singularly unimpressed. The plot was forty metres square and in fact there were two plots, the same size, one of which appeared to have been sold, side by side on a narrow lane opposite a church with farmland and wooded hills, concealed by the mist, to the rear. It was a possibility but they weren't that enthusiastic and they put it in the 'Perhaps' file and drove on to the next viewing.

A month later Tony had to go to a reunion meeting in Newport, South Wales, and, as he was going virtually right past the site and as it was also a lovely sunny day, he arranged to drop in and see it again. He was very impressed this time, so much so that, on the way back, he stopped off again and this time he went next door and chatted to the occupant of the cottage. Then he went over and into the church and talked to someone sitting quietly in the pews and later he

spoke to three ladies visiting the tiny graveyard. His question to them all was the same. "What's it like living around here?" To each question the answer was the same, it was lovely. Tony got home truly enthused and two days later he was back there with Luva who, this time, was equally as enthusiastic. They knew exactly what house they wanted, it was the Milchester from the Potton range with a few alterations that Tony had drawn up already, enough to know that, to make the plot truly what they were looking for, it would be so much better if they could also acquire the land at the rear. They met the vendor who explained that the land to the immediate rear of the plots, which if included would have the effect of doubling their size, was the subject of a legal agreement with the local authority, forbidding any development taking place on it. Did that mean that the land couldn't even be used as garden land, Tony wondered? The vendor didn't know but he did say that if they could get the council to agree to that, they could have it with the land at the same price of £40,000, as it was no use to him without the front land anyway.

Straightway, Tony wrote to the local authority and it wasn't long before he had agreement from them that the land could be included as garden land and that, therefore, he could site the house right to the back of the original plot. They lifted the restriction on the land at the rear of the other plot as well and although that had been sold when Tony and Luva had first seen it, that sale had since fallen through. Needless to say with its area practically doubled it wasn't long before that plot was sold again and this time the sale went through quite quickly, as indeed, did Tony and Luva's purchase.

Planning permission wasn't a problem either, with Potton's help, and in late September they moved across from Kent, having put all of their furniture in store, to live in a rented holiday cottage in the next village.

Right from the very first moment that he'd decided to self build, Tony had planned to do so using subcontract labour that he intended to find and manage himself. As far as he was concerned, he'd spent his whole working life managing various diverse projects around the world and

this was going to be just one more project. All he needed to do was to apply those management skills that he undoubtedly possessed and add to them a little knowledge, or as much as he could possibly get. He started his research with a copy of an earlier edition of this book and he expanded it by subscriptions to *Build It* and *Homebuilding & Renovating* magazines. "Tony was single minded in his pursuit of knowledge", Luva told me, as she poured the coffee in their lovely lounge. "He read everything that he could get hold of and learnt all he needed to know". "Well I tried", interrupted Tony, "but I didn't get everything right. I learnt words and terminology like soffit and facia, but I still got muddled up from time to time".

They knew nobody , of course, as they were new to the area and so they had to really start from scratch in finding subcontractors. They asked around and they visited any building sites that they saw going on in the area. Gradually they built up a list of names and from that list they got other names. A carpenter working in the forest who eventually did all of their second fix work and built them their lovely kitchen gave them some of the best names and prices started to come in.

There was no way Tony, with his new found and scant knowledge, was going to interfere with the main and first fix trades but there was no doubt, at all, that he was going to want to influence the second fix trades and, in particular, the plumbers and electricians. They hadn't lived in the States for all those years not to appreciate the benefits of a sealed water system and their visit to the exhibitions had further convinced them that plastic plumbing and underfloor central heating were a must. The subcontractors were dyed in their own ways, the ways of their fathers and grandfathers before them, and they hadn't really moved with the times. There was scepticism at first but when Tony explained everything to one young plumber, that soon changed to enthusiasm and, although Tony found that he was always way ahead of the chap in his knowledge they managed to create a working relationship.

The groundwork costs came in very high, as

indeed, so did the prices from the stonemasons. At the exhibition, Tony had met one of the chaps who was speaking at the seminars and he'd got his card, even though he worked for another package deal company. He lived in South Wales and, during their chat, he'd said that, if he could be of any help, he'd be pleased to do what he could. That may sound strange to some of you but the facts are that, in this industry, especially if one is asked to speak at the seminars, one does so in a non partisan capacity and it's a legacy of and a testament to the comradeship within the industry that, sometimes, commercial interests can be set aside for the common good. Anyway, this man knew of a gang of groundworkers who would be prepared to do the job and pretty soon there was a price in that Tony had no hesitation in accepting. Work started on site in November and proceeded as far as oversite without incident.

At this point, Tony decided to stop until February, not just to wait out the winter snows but also, to give himself time to gear up and sort out the following trades. He knew that with the major groundworks out of the way the rest of the build programme could easily be calculated as far as timing was concerned and, even with the break in the building process, they were going to be on time to get things finished before the lease ran out on the cottage. The biggest problem was getting prices for the stonework and at one stage they even considered taking it off and dropping the whole idea of having the front elevation in stone – after all it was only cosmetic. Then they met a chap doing some stonework nearby and they were impressed by the work and even more pleased when he readily agreed to give them a price for their job which, when it arrived was just about right. Now they could really get going.

The erection of the frame by Potton's erection

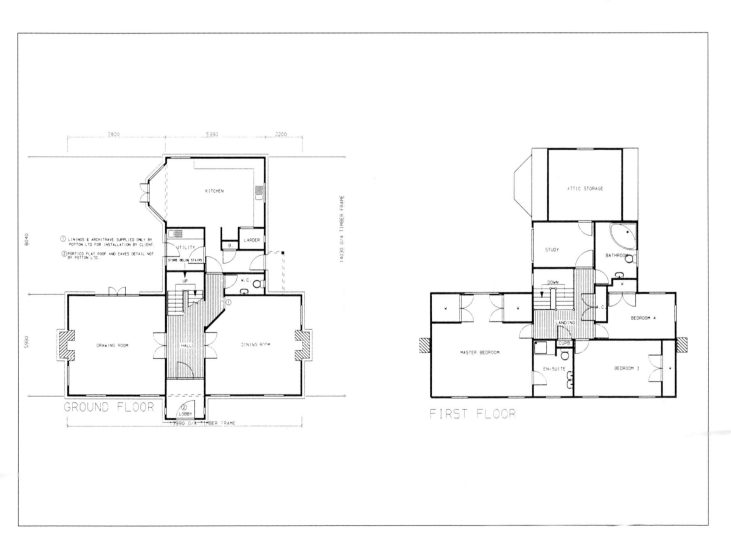

team went like a dream and, as Luva walked the dogs over to the site, she was amazed just how fast everything went and just how much progress was made in a few short days. Every time she looked, the metamorphosis, from a pile of panels and lumber, to a new home, seemed to have proceeded apace. With the frame up, it wasn't long before the roof tilers, again recommended to them by the seminar speaker, were hard at work, felting and battening the roof and fixing the natural Spanish slates. With that done, the property was dry and the work could start inside with the fitting out and second fix trades just as soon as Tony had finished putting in the insulation, a job he had very bravely elected to do himself.

The stonemasons started and, as they turned up, Tony was horrified to learn that the chap he'd engaged to do the job had subbed it out to another stonemason. Happily the fellow doing the work seemed to be, if anything, better than the chap they'd originally given the job to, so with a few reservations, and a careful eye kept on things, Tony decided to leave things as they were. Things went fine until one day the stonemason just packed up his tools, whilst Tony was away from the site, and walked off the job. Tony went

looking for him and when he found him he found out that the problem was that the first chap hadn't paid him, even though Tony had been paying his invoices on time. A stage had been reached in the work and another payment was going to be due, in any event, so Tony arranged for both men to be on site the next day. At that meeting, he handed over the relevant payment in cash and stood and watched as the first man counted out and handed over the money to the chap doing the work. There were no more problems with that trade although there was a little bit of a scare on another one, namely the plumber.

It turned out that the young and enthusiastic plumber from the forest who had so eagerly gone along with their plans and successfully installed the system to include a Combi boiler, plastic plumbing and underfloor central heating from Nu-Heat, wasn't, after all, 'Corgi' registered. For a moment the thought was heartstopping but, in the event, another plumber that the chap knew, came and tested out and fired up the system, which worked beautifully then as it does now. Tony, however, made a mental note to make sure, that if he ever built again, he'd check up to see that the plumber was suitably qualified and registered.

I asked, as I ask all the self builders, what their warmest thoughts were about the whole self build. Luva looked across at Tony and smiled "I was impressed most of all by Tony's skills at management. His tenacity and dedication to the task...and his firmness in the face of my...at times...harsh criticism".

Tony beamed with pride. And his thoughts? "I think the fulfilment...the fact of having built your own home to your own specification is very rewarding".

We sat and talked as the light from the sun that had just broken through the morning fog, streamed though the windows of the lounge, lighting up the leaves of the house plants that thrive in the spacious airiness of their new home. We talked about management and then, Tony came out with something that, up until then I'd thought I was the only one to recognise. Sometimes the subcontractors would come up to him and ask a question of him, seeking his opinion as to how they should do something. As I've said before Tony doesn't pretend to be an expert on building, even though he's now built his own home, but he soon learnt a trick that I'd learnt nearly three decades ago when I built the first house that my wife and I got married into. "What would you normally do?" he would ask, furrowing his brow and pretending to be thinking about the problem. The chap would then explain in detail, just how he would normally get out of the problem. "Sounds fine to me", Tony would reply, "do that then".

And the costs? Well, a lot of hard work went into this project, not least a full landscaping and planting scheme that Tony and Luva followed to the letter but, now with everything done, they can add up the total costs to around £200,000. It hasn't been valued as such but similar properties in the area would fetch over £280,000 and those figures add up to a very worthwhile investment of time and energy.

A woodland home in Kent

How many of us have a game plan in life and how many of us are able to stick to it? Fifteen and a bit years ago Michael and Patricia bought a Residential Care Home business in Dartford in Kent and moved into accommodation on the premises, from where they knew that they would not only be able to run their business efficiently but that they would become slaves to it as well. Well not slaves in any bad sense of the word but certainly, in the sense of living on top of the job.

The plan was that they would give it fifteen years and then Michael would seek early retirement, from his job as a surveyor for a large insurance company, prior to a big lifestyle change. Quite what form that change would take, they weren't really sure of at the time but in the meantime they divided what free time they had between their holiday home in Florida and their beloved touring caravan. It was on one such trip in the caravan that they first of all saw a television programme about a barn that was being converted and then, secondly they dropped in at the Alexandra Palace Self Build Exhibition. It certainly helped to crystallise their thoughts and, when the fifteen year mark came up and Michael, sure enough, got his early retirement package, they put the business on the market and went out looking for plots.

Not that it was as easy as all that. Oh, the business sold alright, maybe too quickly really, but that, as you've guessed it, wasn't the problem. That was finding the plot! They wanted to stay in the Dartford area to be close to family and friends but there was nothing even remotely suitable. Fed up with looking at grotty little plots, they visited the Homebuilding & Renovation show at Birmingham's NEC and attended some seminars for pointers about how to find land. There really wasn't anything new, no magic formulae that would give them what they wanted. Perseverance was the thing they needed, that and, maybe, to widen their horizons a little. They did pick up one thing though and that was that Estate Agents sell land but that it's awfully difficult for the self builder to get them to sell it to them. On their return and by their own admission, Patricia and Michael made themselves a thorough nuisance to every estate agent

that they contacted, keeping up an almost unrelenting pressure in their renewed determination to find a plot. And it paid off!

One day an estate agent gave them details of a small bungalow in rural Kent, a bit further out than they'd originally thought in terms of but, certainly not the end of the world. "It either needs upgrading or it could be a plot", he said. They were out there like a shot, wandering around the narrow country lanes that link the villages around Ashford, down though the village and out the other side again until they found it - a small brick built and rendered bungalow that had been built in the early fifties. No central heating. No insulation. Draughty single glazed metal windows. Subsidence with a bill estimated at £35,000 to put it right. And all for sale at £120,000! Well, that's the minus points but there were a few plus points, or rather one huge plus point and that was its setting of two and a half acres of glorious woodland in an area of Outstanding Natural Beauty with views over countryside most of us would die for.

There was no quibling. The business had sold and they had to get out of the accommodation, so, as it was late summer, they put their furniture in store and decamped into their caravan with the intention of spending a few weeks visiting friends and family on an extended touring holiday. Four months later they were still touring, only by now it was winter and there were a few worries that their constant 'dropping in' on friends and family was wearing a bit thin. The problem was that the vendors, an old couple who had lived in the bungalow since they first built it in the fifties, couldn't find anywhere to go. In the end, it was in January, six months, practically to the day, since they had first made their offer, that they were finally to claim the property as their own.

They moved into the old bungalow, glad in some ways to be out of the caravan, even if it was only to be a brief respite. It was alright really. They confined themselves to living and sleeping in what had been the dining room and the kitchen and bathrooms were just about manageable. Some rooms, especially the bedrooms they simply left alone, the doors firmly shut, pretending they didn't exist. The greatest bonus was the large garage and shed out the back, which allowed them to get their furniture and effects out of expensive storage. That building really has been a boon, even if, now that they're approaching finishing, they realise that it's in exactly the wrong place. Still, for the time being it'll have to stay where it is, even if it does pinch the best of the sunlight and partially obscure the view of their woodland at the back.

And it's that woodland that's the governing factor in the rest of the story of their self build and the principal determiner in many of the costs and of the design. Carpeted in wood anemones in spring time, darkened by countless green oak leaves in summer and blanketed by their rusting stillness in winter, the woodland is the joy of the plot, disturbed only by the green clearing that made room for the old bungalow. Any design would have to occupy that same clearing and would have to reflect the limits of that open space so as to preserve each and every one of the trees. Michael knew enough about building from his previous job to know immediately that, trees plus clay equals special foundations. Even if he hadn't of done the subsidence in the existing bungalow would surely have flagged that one up. Strangely enough there wasn't an individual Tree Preservation Order on any of the trees but that wasn't the point. From a building point of view, removal of the trees would cause more problems than leaving them. Anyway, why buy a woodland plot and then proceed to cut down the very assets that attracted you to it in the first place?

There was another reason why the trees were safe, in that the local authority, in common with many rural authorities, had a policy that, in the event of houses being demolished and replaced with new ones, they would insist that the new dwelling did not exceed the floor area of the original by more than 35%. Authorities who adopt this policy are usually fairly strict in its interpretation, although the percentage increase allowed varies from council to council and ranges between 20% and 50%. Anyway, Michael and Patricia were left in no doubt at all that 35% bigger was all they were going to get and they adapted all of their subsequent design ideas to this premiss.

At the last big show they'd been to, Michael and Patricia had gone onto the stand and met the chaps from Custom Homes. Now that they were in the bungalow, they arranged for Shaun Powers, the local representative, to come down and see them, and the plot, and explain in greater detail, just what the company had to offer them. It was timber frame of course, they knew that but they still wanted to hear about costs and the level of service that the company could offer them. Shaun explained that all of their business started with a feasibility study and that this study would include the plans, a quotation for the timber frame and erection and an idea of the probable completion costs. They liked what they heard and it wasn't many days later that Shaun returned, only this time in company with their architect, Kit Vincent who spent four or five hours with them discussing what they wanted and plotting the positions of the relevant trees. They certainly clicked with Kit. They'd prepared a wish list of their requirements, to include a preference for which rooms faced which way, but they hadn't done a plan of their own. Never mind, Kit took away their list, his own notes and plans from their conversations and he came back with a bungalow design that almost exactly fitted their bill. They'd wanted a big family room, kitchen living area and that's what they got. They'd wanted a separate lounge with an attractive fireplace and cathedral ceilings and that's what they got. Add that to three good sized bedrooms downstairs, spacious bathrooms and an upper part that could be converted at a later date and they were more than just pleased.

Only what would the planners say? The upper part was perhaps a bit cheeky. It was down on the plans as storage area, even if it did have a turned staircase leading up to it. Would the planners consider it as being living accommodation and strike it out. Permitted Development Rights were almost certainly going to be curtailed, given where they were building and the known restriction on increase in size over the original.

The costs were all right. Custom Homes' quotation came in just about as expected, including provision for the upper part and the staircase and Shaun was able to confirm that the ancillary costs would mean that, if they kept a careful rein on things, they could build it within their budget. There was nothing else for it. The planners had already told them that they would accept a Full application and now was the time to take the plunge, accept the Custom Homes quotation, and go for planning.

The planners said nothing about the upper part. They did work out the ground floor area and they discovered that it was six square feet over the 35% limit. A redraw was demanded and the bungalow was duly shrunk by six square feet! Then it was, that the planning officer noticed that part of the roof was shewn overhanging, providing a covered patio area. This could be filled in at some future date and that would mean that there would be extra space in the bungalow. Patiently Kit explained that there was no such intention and that this should be considered as being outside the floor area. Happily his argument was accepted. Still there was nothing about the upper part and two months after they had moved in, planning was received and they prepared, once more, to decamp to the caravan, as the first job in their building programme was the demolition of the existing bungalow, their temporary home.

That meant that early April found them taking advantage of some unusually fine weather and a long dry spell, to start the groundworks. As they were using a pot and beam ground floor, they hadn't needed to grub up the foundations of the old bungalow and, on two sides at least, the lines of the trenches hugged the outside of the old building's foundations. There all similarity ended. Their foundations were going to have to go down to 3 metres in depth and the sides would have to be lined, on the inside, with a compressible material and, on the outside, with a slip membrane.

Everything was hunky dory for that first day and one of the photographs shews the neat line and smart sides to one of the first trenches to be dug. That night, after half of the dig was completed, the heavens opened. It chucked it down for a full 36 hours, during which, Michael and Patricia, in their caravan close by, could hear the

sides of the trenches peeling away and crashing down like claps of thunder. When it was all over and they crept from their caravan like drowned rats, when their groundworkers ventured back onto site to survey the damage, their 3 metre deep foundations were all but backfilled with mud and water.

They'd have to be dug out again of course but not, their groundworker explained, before they'd got hold of some sheet piling and strutting to shore up the sides of the trenches, a job that wasn't going to be all that easy, considering that they also had to get the claymaster down the sides. By the time it was all dug out again, the trenches were over 2 metres wide in places and resembled something from the Battle of the

Somme. 100 cubic metres of concrete was needed to fill them, poured over two days with the sheet piling carefully pulled out as the concrete went in, so as not to disturb the claymaster or the membranes. It had taken a total of seven weeks but they were out of the ground and the first of every self builders three goals had been achieved, but at a cost.

I asked where the old bungalow had gone and Michael pointed to the drive. I nodded and asked where on earth they'd sent all of the spoil from their extensive foundations. Patricia took my arm and led me round and behind the new bungalow and into the shade of the woods behind. "There it all is", announced Michael, sweeping his arm around. And there, indeed it all was. Not the mounds you'd expect but, instead, after time and weather had reduced its bulk, just gentle rises between the trees and a slightly higher one in what had been a hollow. In years to come, when the bluebells and wood anemones push though this year's covering leaf litter, all trace will have gone.

But I've jumped ahead a little, carried away, no doubt, by the sheer scale of the problem that this charming couple managed to overcome. Oh, they always knew that the ground was going to cost them more than if they'd built somewhere else but nothing had quite prepared them for what they eventually faced and yet, they'd still succeeded, as indeed most self builders do. They'd always known, as well, that they were going to build with subcontractors. Not for any other reason than that was the way they always thought about going about it and, with them both now free, they knew that they'd have the time to manage things. In the months of camping out, they'd spent time going into builders merchants, asking around at other self build sites and generally finding out as much as they could about local subcontractors. Every one they used came with a recommendation and every one, bar one, proved worthy of that recommendation and even the odd one out, in hindsight, wasn't that bad.

The planning officer reared his head again when they were nearing the point at which the frame was up and erected and the roof was felt and battened, thus achieving the second goal of a self builder, namely a weathertight shell. There'd been a condition on the planning consent that all external materials had to be approved by the officers before their use and although the bricks had been accepted, it now appeared that they weren't too happy about Michael and Patricia's choice of an interlocking pantile. Shaun reported to them that the planners were indicating that they wanted them to use a hand made Kent peg tile and the cost implications of that were in the order of £8,500!

They didn't buckle under and instead they held firm that they wanted to use the pantile and that they saw nothing wrong with it. The planner couldn't agree but he did consent to come out to site and discuss it with them in person. In the event, and on the day, a different planning officer came out, a young lady. She stood at the bottom of the driveway with a sample pantile in her hand. "What seems to be the problem here? she asked, holding it up to gauge it against the brickwork. "We don't have one", Michael and Patricia chorused. "Neither do I", announced the planning officer.

Well, work proceeded apace after that with the second fix trades inside even as the last of the external brickwork and tiling was going on. They'd decided on underfloor heating and a

central vacuum, right from the word go and Nu-heat, the underfloor heating and hot water specialists, had recommended them to a plumber who also undertook to do the domestic plumbing and fitting out of the bathrooms. Custom Homes had, as I've said, included all of the materials for the upper part in their supply and erection package and when it came to it they adapted that package to fit in with an on site alteration that removed one of the walls by the staircase and turned the top landing into an open gallery. Now, although, there's no natural light, as they'd need express planning consent for the necessary Velux windows, they've got the potential for a large bedroom, the sitting gallery, a bathroom and a storage room. It's all plastered out ready and, who knows, maybe they'll approach the planners very soon for three rooflights on the rear slope of the roof but, then again, maybe they won't just yet.

All in all, with two days to go before moving in, the third big goal of every self builder, Michael and Patricia have spent £220,000 on their new home in the woods, with £120,000 of that taken up by the cost of the plot. It was an expensive buy as far as the land was concerned but it was all worth it when you take into account the acreage and its position. And it was especially worth it when you consider the most recent

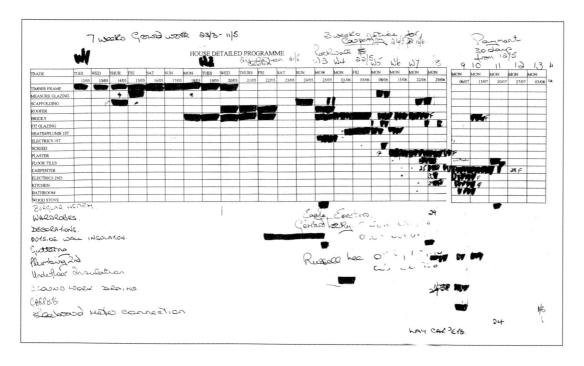

valuation of the completed bungalow of just over £275,000.

All the while I was with them, I kept wanting to ask about a fairly big shiner that Patricia was sporting, but I hadn't dared to. "You'd better ask about the black eye", laughed Michael finally. I laughed and told them that I'd been dying to and Patricia smiled as she told me what had happened. Well, they'd decided the week before that they really didn't need it anymore and, more out of curiosity that anything else, they'd advertised it 'for sale' in the local paper. A couple had immediately rung up for it and agreed to buy it but they had no means of transporting it the short distance down the lanes to their house, where they planned to turn it into a kids playroom. Not to worry, Michael had a four wheel drive motor car and he agreed to tow it round for them. They turned up the next evening and the four of them

hitched the mobile up to the vehicle and pulled and manhandled it down past the new bungalow and onto the drive. At the last bit, when they'd almost cleared the bridge over the stream at the front, Patricia, guiding Michael as he gently eased it past the pond, slipped and tumbled onto the 'A' frame blacking her eye and bruising her arm. Patricia told me that she was glad to see the back of the mobile and that she'd be equally as glad to see the back of the touring van when they finally moved out in two days time. Michael nodded in agreement. Neither ever want to set foot through the portals of a caravan again and the loss of their previous hobby, and sanity mainstay when they ran the Care Home, is one thing that they're going to have to live with. Still, with what they've achieved to replace it, I somehow think they'll manage.

LOUNGE	15'-8" x 17'-0"
DINING	12'-3" x 12'-3"
KITCHEN	12'-3" x 12'-3"
STUDY	9'-0" x 12'-0"
BED 1	19'-0" x 17'-2"
BED 2	11'-0" x 10'-0"
BED 3	10'-0" x 12'-6"

A house in the centre of town

My overriding and abiding impression of this new self built home, is one of colour and form. Colour from the masses of heeled in plants waiting patiently in their beds and pots for the completion of the garden. Colour from the primary colours of the walls with their boldly framed modern pictures. Colour from the potato prints that marched around the dado in the cloakroom and the utility room, and form from the high vaulted ceilings of the central hallway and the circular windows that streamed light down on me from all angles. Everything proclaimed a joy and an exuberance that was matched and mirrored by the sense of fulfilment displayed by Adrian and Andrea.

When they first met, they both had houses of their own. Adrian's was, in his own words, nothing to write home about, a modern chalet bungalow on an estate. Andrea, on the other hand, had already created something wonderful from a three storey Edwardian semi, into which she'd put her own inimitable style and character. They were happy there for a while, but in the end, as with so many couples I have met, they wanted to do something together that was a reflection of both their individuality and their partnership. The idea was to find a cottage to renovate and for ages they looked and looked, but nothing seemed suitable and they became more and more frustrated with what was on offer. In part, the problem was that their dream of a cottage had to fit in with their other requirement, that they wanted to stay in the city, within walking distance of the shops and an easy bus ride from various amenities. As you can imagine, dream and requirement were largely incompatible. In equal measure, they came to realise that, even if they did spend the £125- £150,000 that most of the likely prospects seemed to fetch, by the time they'd spent the bare minimum to bring the properties up to scratch, they probably wouldn't be worth as much as they'd spent. If you took into account the fact that the VAT was non-recoverable on extensions and refurbishments, the figures got even worse.

Still, they kept on looking, until, one day, they saw an advert for a lecture by Julian Owen, a local Nottingham architect, and they went along,

quite frankly, more for an evening out that for any other reason. Julian talked about self building and they suddenly realised that maybe, just maybe, they could achieve what they were looking for by building a new home, rather than by trying to change an existing format. The tack changed after that and they switched the search to plots. But plots in the city are even more difficult to come by than in the country and those that they did come across always seemed to have problems. Either they were at the bottom of someone's garden with an attendant lack of privacy or they had to be approached by either shared driveways or by long tunnels of drive that squeezed past and between other houses. Anything that was any good was snapped up by builders, almost before they knew of its existence and the only one they came across that nearly fitted their bill, a plot for sale by another local architect, had so many restrictions placed on it, that they pretty soon had to pull out. The idea of self building began to look just as hopeless as their original idea of renovation.

That is until, one day, Adrian noticed a little house up for sale at the end of a cul-de-sac quite near their home, set on a relatively large corner site. It had previously been occupied by a brewery retainer who'd lived there for ages at a rent of £1 a week and at that rent, the brewery had done little or nothing to it over the years.

306

Never mind that, for all the fact that no modernisation had taken place it was still in pretty good nick and, perhaps because of its lack of facilities, the estate agent had only valued it at £60,000. Neither he, nor anyone else, for that matter, seemed to realise what Adrian and Andrea twigged from the moment they saw it. This was a plot!

Julian came out to see it and, although like many who are interested in buildings and architecture, there was an initial reluctance to demolish, he pretty soon saw that they were right and that, especially at the price being asked, it did make sense to think of it as a plot. The important thing that Julian identified, however, was that, if they were going to buy it, they needed to move quickly, before the estate agent realised that it was a plot and arranged to sell it to one of his builder clients. That was it. They went straight around to the estate agents, put the offer

in at the full asking price and waited while it was accepted. With solicitors instructed, the next thing was to have detailed discussions about just what they were going to build. Julian came to see them at their home and they spent a long time discussing every aspect of their lifestyles, about what they wanted to achieve, about their budget and, of course his fees. £90,000 was what they allocated, to take them to a plastered out liveable shell that they could then decorate and finish off in their own time and in their own unique style.

A little while later Julian came back to see them with some sketch plans that he'd drawn up. To be honest they weren't what they wanted, but that didn't deter them and they sat down to talk it all through again, feeling then, as now, that this was a partnership that they had entered into and that Julian was, quite properly, "feeling his way to what they really wanted". They'd done their own plans in the meantime and that may have had something to do with why they rejected Julian's first attempt. In any event they showed them to him and impressed though he was, he couldn't help commenting that what they'd drawn was really two houses. In fact, in many ways, that really was their intention. Oh, not in the sense of any physical separation but more in the sense of a division of family activities. They'd thought about grandchildren, and a good job too as, when I went to see them they were about to be presented with their first. They thought about a united household only with all members able to achieve their own personal space. They thought about an internal hall with all rooms radiating off it, even if that meant a separate entrance hall. Circulation between the lounge, kitchen and dining room was important, as was the conservatory that they definitely wanted to be part of their normal living environment rather than as some scarcely used adjunct. They would be building in brick and block throughout and, for cost reasons the plan form would have to be simple with all walls lined up top and bottom, but that didn't mean that they wanted to sacrifice any visual interest as far as the outside was concerned. The list went on and on. Disabled access for friends and relatives. A double garage with access to the house and with a pit so that Adrian could indulge his hobby of classic motor cars. A utility/laundry room that was separate from the kitchen with access to the hallway, something I have long championed, arguing that the activities associated with kitchens and utility/laundry rooms are not, in any way associated.

Julian wasn't at all daunted or put out by all of this. Why should he be, after all the very thought processes that had led to all of these considerations, had been sparked off by his own questions and by his own insistence that they should examine just how their lifestyle should dictate the eventual design. As a founder member of Associated Self Build Architects, the whole point of the exercise, as far as Julian was concerned, was for Adrian and Andrea to get what they wanted, not what he or anybody else, for that matter, thought they should have. He took away their sketches and came back with exactly what they wanted, translating their rough ideas into a buildable plan into which he fitted so many more exciting features, the piece de resistance of which, was undoubtedly the cathedral ceiling and circular window to the central hallway and landing.

They were delighted. Everything seemed to be going well. The plot was now theirs and they now had a plan that they really felt comfortable with but there was one more thing to do before Julian made the planning application, and that was to go through the costs and the budget once more. Julian came to see them again and they had a long talk about costs and he confirmed that, in his opinion, they were still on course to achieve their original budget. They took his advice and made the decision to instruct him to get on and get the planning permission.

At no stage was there any thought of self managing the site. That had never been on the cards as far as Adrian and Andrea were concerned and Julian agreed that the best course of action would be to seek a builder to take on the complete job, at least up to the plastered out and liveable stage. He arranged for a Quantity Surveyor to do a budget estimate and when that was ready, and with the planners seeming perfectly amenable to all that they proposed, he arranged for various builders to provide a

quotation. "Never run it like a romantic adventure", Julian warned them as the hefty tenders went out, "Tie it down".

The first quotations came in and the romance, if there was any, was quickly replaced by a slight feeling of panic as all of the prices, except one, were way higher that they'd envisaged and the one that wasn't, was very quickly withdrawn.

Planning was alright though and that came through at about the same time that all this was happening, even if its arrival was muted by their concerns. For Adrian and Andrea this was a worrying time. Julian though, didn't seem that worried and expressed well founded confidence in his own predictions. He'd seen all this before and he knew that one of the advantages of city life is that, unlike many rural areas, there are so many more builders to choose from. He calmly prepared a new set of tender documents and sent them out to another batch of builders and, this time, when they came back, the prices were much more in line with what they were aiming at and there was one that was acceptable. A meeting was arranged and Julian sorted out the final details of the contract and negotiated the stage payments.

As far as Adrian and Andrea were concerned that was the last real problem solved and they could now concentrate on selling their old home and look forward to moving in day. The old house was demolished for £1800 and all the spoil taken away and the builders started work. The huge larch tree that they have retained just outside their lounge window, meant that the foundations had to go deeper than they otherwise would but, even that, failed to push the project beyond their budget. They got on awfully well with the builders and built up an excellent relationship with all of the labour on site. There was no noise, no bad language and precious few risqué jokes. "We really like working here", the bricklayer said.

Of course there were things for Adrian and Andrea to do and the, almost unrelenting pace, or so it seemed, of having to make the choices was exhilarating. Roof tiles and bricks had to be chosen, then wall tiles, floor tiles, kitchen units, bathroom suites…the choices seemed almost endless but they all led up to one thing and that

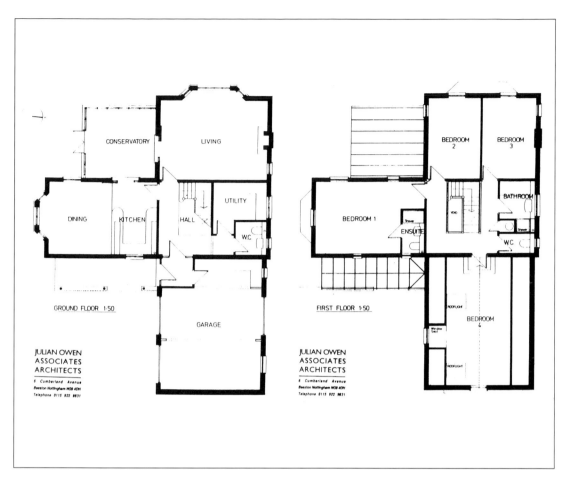

was their own new home. Including the land, it ended up costing almost exactly what they had planned which meant a total cost for the project of around £150,000. "What do you think it's worth now?" I asked. The reply, which I'd been half expecting anyway, was that they didn't know and they didn't really care. That wasn't why they'd done it.

I asked around afterwards and was told that the house was worth at least £200,000. I shan't tell Adrian and Andrea, as they really didn't want to know, so it'll just have to be our little secret.

A family enclave in Wiltshire

The thing that strikes you when you visit self builders in their new home is the obvious pride they take, not only in their own achievements but also in the choices they have made. Nowhere was this more palpable than when I visited this site in rural Wiltshire where David and Glenys, and her brother Alan, have built two Scandia-Hus bungalows side by side. As my motor car scrunched to a halt on the immaculate gravel driveway, Alan bustled happily out of his front door to greet me and after a very brief whirlwind tour of his bungalow, I was ushered out and across to the front door of the other bungalow. Obviously we were expected because before we even had time to push the bell, the door opened to reveal David and Glenys beaming broadly as they guided the two of us though the hall and into their open plan dining area where coffee was already set out on the table.

We all sat down as I cast my eyes around the place noting the wide open spaces of the superbly fitted kitchen, the solid sliding patio doors leading out to the raised timber decking. Even my palate, jaded by decades of looking at other people's homes, received a lift as I noted the superb quality of everything I saw. "Where would you like to start?" David asked. "Would you like to look around first...or what's your pro-gramme?" They were used to this, I could tell. So they should be, so delighted were they with their new homes that they'd held a couple of open days a little while before, that close on 150 people had attended. "Let's just have coffee first", I suggested, "and you can tell me how all of this came about...what brought you to this point".

Glenys and Alan both looked at David. Ah, here was the culprit, here was the main instiga-tor. I Looked at David and he began the story. He'd wanted to self build for about seven years before anything concrete happened. On the train commuting every day of his working life between their home in Northamptonshire to the West End of London, he'd dreamt of early retirement, whiling away the hours harbouring thoughts, that he shared with Glenys, of moving to a bungalow in Devon, and thoughts of self building, that he more or less kept to himself. I glanced up at Alan who shook his head at my unspoken question.

"No not me", he said, "I was happily living in London in a semi detached house that I loved but they came to see me quite often, especially as mother lived with me". "We've always all been pals", Glenys interrupted. David carried on with the story. They'd moved three times within a small area in Northamptonshire, always to better themselves, always in a small village. They'd ended up in a very nice bungalow, but somehow it never seemed as if it was the ideal and there was always a feeling that there was something much better just around the corner. Glenys interrupted again. "He's always had itchy feet...always been a doer".

They'd had a hobby, still have for that matter, and that was caravanning and most weekends found them out and about, keeping a look out for property and a look out for plots. Glenys was beginning to be half convinced of the benefits of self building now and, just the two of them went to some seminars and some show houses that they thought were very nice, but they did nothing more about it. They told Alan about their idea of self building and, though extremely sceptical, he wished them well in their endeavours.

Homeworld was next, an exhibition in Milton Keynes where various companies had built show houses. It was there, that they first came across, and went into, a home built by Scandia-Hus. To say that they were excited would be an understatement and the following weekend found them on their way to view the show homes at the Scandia-Hus headquarters in East Grinstead, stopping off on the way back to tell Alan all about it.

The next weekend they were back down in East Grinstead, only this time Alan and their mother accompanied them, more out of curiosity then anything else. They had to see for themselves just what David and Glenys had got so excited about for the past few weekends. There was no real thought of self building in Alan's mind at that time, he was perfectly happy in his home and, in any event, it was near his work as a teacher of Latin and English at a private school. What he was prepared to concede though, was, that if ever David and his sister were to self build, this was the way they should go. There was a feeling of solidity, a marvellous transference of light, and the spacious and luxurious quality of all that he saw, impressed. If ever, and the thought must have been entering his mind, even as he denied it to himself, he was to move, then this too would be his choice. Buoyed up by family approval and their own new convictions, David and Glenys renewed their attempts to find a plot. As often as they could, they travelled to the West Country and the southern counties, touring around the towns and villages keeping an eye open for boards and dropping in to see estate agents, some of whom they got to know quite well.

Then Glenys and Alan's mother fell ill and their search for land came to a halt as, instead, she and David travelled each and every weekend to see her. Alan retired to be able to devote all his time to her care but, sadly, she died not long afterwards. Brother and sister were naturally distraught but their grief had taught them one very important thing, and that was their own mortality. One day, if the distances between them remained as they were, then they too would be alone and they might not be able to get to each other when they were needed. Northampton was far enough away as it was, but, if David and Glenys found a plot and moved west, then it would be ever more difficult for them to remain in touch and, now, more than ever, family was important. They needed to be closer not further from each other and the seed that had been planted in Alan's mind, that weekend in East Grinstead, germinated. Now the search was on for two plots, preferably next door to each other but at least in the same village.

They tried all the usual sources and widened their scope by contacting various builders, especially those with a linkage to the main package deal companies. Nothing was suitable until they found a plot in Ferndown in Dorset. They spent ages trying to buy this but, in the end, after negotiations that just dragged on and on they had to give up and the land was sold to a builder. Disappointed but undaunted, Glenys gathered up the papers in the caravan as they prepared to head home to Northamptonshire. "That's the end of that", she said, "we'd better get cracking looking for something else".

Another weekend found them in Devises, a town they hadn't actually concentrated on before. There was a sign on the side of the road as they entered the town, reading 'Superior Building plots For Sale' and underneath, it expanded on its claim, announcing that the site had planning permission for two bungalows. Nothing much could be seen and it was difficult to make out just where any boundaries were. It was eight o'clock in the morning, so they parked up and waited outside for the estate agents to open. When they did, they were disappointed to find out that the site was far too small for anything like what they had in mind. Nevertheless, they "did the rounds" as they were in the town anyway and visited every estate agent. In one, they asked at the front desk and the chap dealing with them told them gravely that, "no, they hadn't got anything but that they'd let them know", a phrase they were, by now, used to hearing. They turned to go and as they did so, a chap sitting at a desk further back in the office put down the telephone he'd been talking at and called out for them to "wait a minute". He then told them of two plots

near Melksham and gave them directions as to how to get there.

Within the hour they were staring at a rather unprepossessing site, covered in old concrete block sheds, all overgrown with weeds and with notices warning against entry. To coin the words of Glenys, "it was a right heap, but it had potential". The farmhouse, behind which the land lay, had sold off most of its land some time previously and a developer had built an estate of new houses. The area of land they had come to see had been retained from the original sale, together with a tongue of land leading up to the access roadway of the estate, although the farm had separate access to the main road. Apparently the owners had tried to get planning permission for a further six houses and when that was unsuccessful they'd reduced the numbers down to four and then finally, and successfully, to two.

There wasn't that much for David and Glenys to negotiate about. The land was, or soon would be when it was cleared, everything that they'd been looking for and at £90,000 for the two plots it was also well within their price range. Within days they'd taken Alan to see it and, when he gave his approval, they put the offer in. That's when it all started to drag and for a while they feared that it would go the same way as the Ferndown land but they had one enormous advantage in that now, with money David had inherited, they had the money available to buy just as soon as the legalities could be sorted out. The problem proved to be the tongue of land, through to the estate road. Yes, the vendors had retained the strip of land in the hope of future planning permission but, equally as anticipatory, the estate developers had foreseen the possibility and retained a small strip of land between the end of the tongue and the estate road. It was a ransom strip and, if access to the two plots was going to come off the estate road, something the planning permission insisted on, then the ransom would have to be paid. It cost a further £3000 and when they told me of it I couldn't help but remark that they'd got off lightly – a third of the value of the land is far more usual.

One 'benefit' of the long drawn out legal arrangements was that it gave David and Glenys

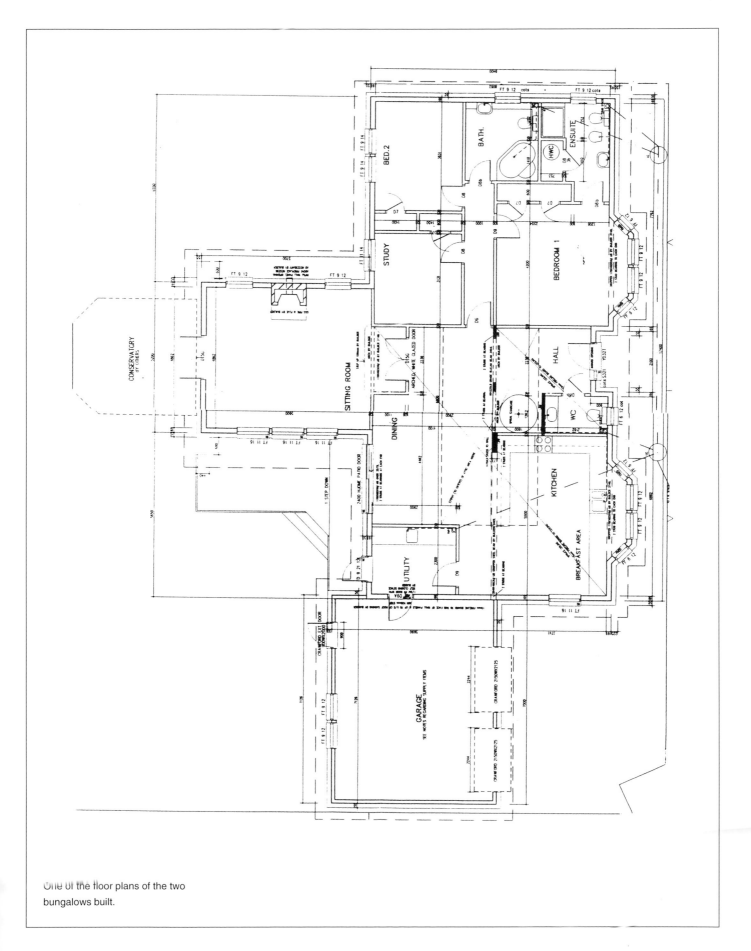

One of the floor plans of the two bungalows built.

time to sell their home and, by prior arrangement, they moved down to live with Alan. Now that they were all together they could plan their next moves and talk meaningfully about what they were going to build and just how they were going to go about it. Alan chose a standard design from the Scandia-Hus catalogue, albeit with a few modifications, whilst David and Glenys, drew out their own layout on graph paper. The sketches were sent off to Scandia-Hus and the next thing they knew they were in touch with their own project manager, Derek Dawson, who arranged to meet them on the land. The meeting went well and before very long, Derek had arranged for them to receive a quotation for the Scandia-Hus kit, together with the erection costs. Now, comprehensive as that was, he also explained that, on top of the quoted price they would have to think about the builders prices and that, basically there were two ways of doing things. Either they could approach one of the builders that the company knew for a complete price for all of the work, or they could go to a builder on a project management basis, whereby the builder would undertake the project upon payment of the demonstrable costs of labour and materials plus an agreed fee of £6000. Alan, David and Glenys thought about things for a bit and then decided that they'd choose this second, project management route, as any savings that could then be realised would be passed onto them.

They were advised that they should choose from two or three builders and Scandia-Hus suggested some names and then arranged for plans and specifications to be sent off to each one for budget figures. In the event, however, they arranged to meet one of them, Steve Peake, for lunch one day and, so impressed were they with him, that they decided there and then that this was the person they wished to entrust their joint project to.

Planning permission was the next hurdle but it proved to be an easy one. At Alan's house the three of them had cut out scale outlines of each of the bungalows and carefully moved them about on a scale plan of the site, to determine just where and how they would fit on. Scandia-

Hus had taken this into account on the submitted drawings and it showed the corner of Alan's bungalow, about two metres from one of the boundaries. There was an objection from a neighbour and the planners asked for the bungalow to be moved so as to increase the distance to the boundary to six metres. In the end a balance was reached at four metres but that, meant that the bungalows were now much closer together at the front and, in turn, that created a pinch point on the driveway. The solution was fairly simple, in that the garage of Glenys and David's bungalow, which had been drawn in line with the main front elevation, could be slid back to create a step in the frontage. To every action there is a reaction and the consequence of this was that the planned staircase from the garage to the upper part roof space of the bungalow was compromised. For a while there was despair until Derek suggested a spiral staircase from the hallway, something, that with hindsight, has proven to be much more useful and certainly much more attractive.

When work started on site, David and Glenys moved onto site in their caravan, and although Alan didn't go very often, they videoed each days proceedings and re-lived the week with him when they arrived back at his place every weekend for a bath and the laundry. The plan always was to get their house done, after which Alan would sell his London home and move in with them until his bungalow was finished, and really, that's just what happened. I asked about budgets and values and they all clammed up, laughing my question off. "We're really not interested" was all I could get out of them. "We set aside a budget for building and we built the bungalows for and within that budget and as for market value…". "I really don't have a clue", said Alan laughing, "I've never even thought about it". "This is where we stay…we're going out of here feet first in a wooden box", David laughed and the three of them looked at each other and rolled on their seats with mirth. They went for the best of everything. Steel up and over roller doors to the garages with electric operation. Underfloor central heating. The kitchens, though not from Scandia-Hus direct were from a nominated

supplier. "Whole house ventilation and heat recovery", I asked. No, they hadn't gone for that, even though the people at Scandia-Hus had recommended it, as they were all fresh air fiends anyway and liked open windows and 'proper' fireplaces.

I asked my usual question about the worst and the best bits of the whole thing. And the thoughts tumbled out of the three of them. David – "The builder stuck to his timetable...he was excellent and there were no moments of anxiety throughout the whole build". "Did you become friendly with the labour?" I asked. David misheard me. "They weren't labourers, they were craftsmen, each and every one of them!" Glenys – "The most exciting bit was seeing the lorries arriving with our houses on them and the worst bit was one week in the caravan in the rain, when it just wouldn't stop and everything was drenched including us". Alan – "For me the best bit is my beloved courtyard...you must come over and see it". David – "I was very pleased with the organisation and quality of the Scandia-Hus kits. Nothing was skimped...we made some very good friends...the digger driver...to see him, you wouldn't like to meet him on a dark night but appearances were deceptive...he was a gentle giant and a really nice bloke".

I struggled to write down their impressions and then looked up as Alan dreamily said, "I still get a thrill every morning when I open my curtains". And the last word to Glenys. "Nothing ever felt strange or new. We'd watched everything and every stage and when we came to move in, it was all so familiar. It was as if...as if we'd been dreaming for a long time about the house and then one day we woke up and the dream was all true".

A replacement house in Hertfordshire

Throughout the Kingdom, but particularly in the south-eastern corner of England, there are countless unmade up private roads. If one takes a trip down them, you enter a world of large plots, often housing small, but beautifully kept bungalows built of wood and asbestos, their gardens frequently given over to row upon row of neat vegetables.

In the main, these small developments, hark back to the years immediately following the 2nd World War, when men returned to find their homes in the towns and cities razed to the ground. In the countryside the post-war need to be self sufficient in agriculture was being threatened by the gradual dissolution of the Land Army, as the women and girls left to rejoin husbands and lovers. Labour was needed to replace them and a ready supply was found amongst the disillusioned and dispossessed men and women of the towns. Annual working holidays picking fruit or hops were an established feature for many inner London families and there were 'camps' of wooden hoppers homes on many a farm. Here was a marvellous meeting of two needs. The farmers had land but no labour. The refugees from the cities had their demob pay and money from the sale of their ruined possessions and, most importantly, they were prepared to work to make a new life. There were no planning laws and so, fields were set aside and plots sold off for the construction of what really amounted to shanty towns, many of which exist to this day with local names like 'Tintown' or 'Hopper Town'. Even when the planning laws came into force in 1948, recognition had to be given to these existing settlements with the codifying of what were known as unexpired development rights and the prescription of 8th Schedule Development giving owners the right to replace or repair with suitable materials, any existing dwelling.

Now after nearly half a century of disparagement these settlements are beginning to take on a new and distinctive character as the old bungalows come down, to be replaced by smart new homes. For now, the old wooden and asbestos bungalows with their corrugated iron roofs have to cower alongside their new neighbours but

their nemesis approaches and, before very long, these second class outposts will become exclusive precincts of modern middle class country life.

For the self builder these developments are a bountiful source of plots despite the inherent problems of indeterminate titles, the unmade up roads and the frequent lack of mains drainage, all of which I have spoken about within the main text of the book. I am told, by reliable sources, that many of the self build projects happening in the south-eastern counties fall into the category of replacement dwellings and, having done just that thing myself, I can well believe it.

John & Ann lived in a bungalow that had been built in the seventies on a small triangular plot, hived off a larger plot, on just such a lane in the heart of the Hertfordshire countryside. By the time they lived there the lane was a mixture of small post war cottages and their replacements, mostly set on large, well screened, plots. They were very happy in their bungalow, but for the fact that their garden was so small. When they acquired three chickens, almost by accident, and there was literally nowhere for them to construct a proper run, without depriving themselves, their dog and three cats of any garden, they decided to try and look for something else. Well, they looked all around but there was never anything that they liked and whenever, after a trip out to see properties, they returned to the lane, they realised just what they'd be missing. Then, by chance one day, they heard that the old man living in the cottage just five doors up the lane wanted to sell up and move away to be nearer his family in Norfolk.

The cottage was tiny and was built of timber and asbestos sheeting with an asbestos tiled roof. A small extension was the only major change that had been undertaken since it was first built, apart from the fact that the roof had been occupied by the insertion of windows to each gable end. Otherwise, its front facade bore a remarkable similarity to the old photograph that now adorns the kitchen wall of John and Ann's new home. It was habitable but it needed a lot doing to it and it stood in a large mature plot about 95 feet wide and around 260 feet deep.

Estate agents had already valued the cottage at £140,000 and John and Ann had no hesitation in offering £137,500, which was accepted almost immediately.

The following day, the old man arrived at their bungalow on his bicycle with a plastic Sainsbury's bag full of all of the deeds to the cottage. "You keep these", he said, "and give me the money as soon as you can".

John had the greatest difficulty explaining that he really shouldn't take them and it took a lot of persuading to get the old man to remount his bicycle and take them to a solicitor. Unfortunately he cycled straight to John and Ann's solicitor to try to leave them with her and, again, it took a great deal more persuasion to get him to finally pedal off to another solicitor, who gratefully accepted his business and the plastic bag full of documents.

The purchase of the cottage relied on John and Ann selling their existing bungalow but that went through fairly quickly and in October they moved into their new home. It was comfortable and warm but it really, only then, hit them that they needed to decide what to do next. Should they think about extending? They had lots of experience of extensions from previous homes and, certainly, there was plenty of space around the cottage for further development. John talked to architects and builders around the town and at work about prices and gradually built up a picture of the likely costs. The two of them started to doodle on pieces of paper, trying to work out just how they could add to the building. It was where they wanted it to be. The garden was lovely and they were very happy there but, try as they might, every drawing just didn't seem to work out and, when they costed their ideas up and added on the VAT, none of them seemed to make economic sense.

Then John read somewhere that VAT was zero rated for new buildings and, almost for the first time, he began to think in terms of a complete new build. He rang several of the largest builders and developers in the area, asking if they would consider a one off house. Not surprisingly, as he was talking to entirely the wrong sort of people, they told him that this wasn't their forte but, one of them did suggest that he try the magazine 'Build It'.

He got the magazine from the local newsagents and took it home the next evening to read. This was it! This was the answer! They would demolish the existing cottage and self build a new home of their own. The magazine was scanned from cover to cover and they sent off for as many of the brochures as they could, as well as for a copy of a previous edition of the book you are now reading.

John's a BT training manager, used to evaluating people and projects. He knew that budgets had to be set and that everything would need careful evaluation before any start buttons were pushed and he knew that if this was to be their home they needed to move carefully and methodically through the minefields of conflicting advice. The impression gained, from the majority of articles they read, was that the best way forward, was to build in timber frame yet, that never really appealed to them. They could never put a finger on just why but, that's what they felt and both of them knew, from past experiences, that they should always trust their gut feelings.

Amongst the various company brochures that came back from their initial enquiries was one from a company called Design & Materials Ltd.. This is a package deal company that specialises in brick and block construction and, as part and parcel of their brochure, there was a book of plans. They poured over this book until they came across a design that they liked a lot, called by the rather unprepossessing name of the 'Swillbrook', a name that they later discovered was supposed to have been 'Swalebrook', were it not for a printing error! Be that as it may, this was the design they liked, albeit with a few alterations and the addition of a double garage. It was then that John noticed the clinching factor. The house was described in the brochure as being typical of, and inspired by, a railway cottage. Well, as a model railway enthusiast did he really have to look further?

Now it was, that John's management skills and training came to the fore. He knew that it was no good planning to build this house unless it all stacked up and it could be done within their budget. From the information contained in most of the 'case histories' in the magazines and the guidelines contained in the brochure it seemed that they were on the right lines. He knew also that the opinion of the planning officer would have to be sought as to whether or not the authority would accept the principle of a replacement dwelling. They didn't expect any trouble and, indeed, when they went to the local planning office and consulted the officer, he told them as much and told them also that they should apply for 'Full' planning permission, rolling up the 'outline' and 'detailed' stages into one application.

They fixed up an appointment for Richard Coles, D&M's Regional Manager in the south of England, to come and see them at their home and then, before he arrived, they went through the company's brochure line by line with a fine tooth comb, ticking off each aspect of their service and their materials supply. From this they compiled a long list of questions that they then faxed off to him so that, when he came, he'd have all of the answers.

As John told me about this, Ann looked at me and I noticed a very slight raising of her eyebrows. I picked up the unspoken question in her eyes and assured them that any company representative, coming a long way to see them, would have welcomed this. Even if you don't send off a list of questions as John and Ann did, it's as well to make a list of all of your queries. I can assure you that what's worse for any representative is if, having got back home and prepared a full brief for their architects department and sent it off, he then receives a phone call with a series of questions that seek to undermine or negate what he has just prepared. In similar vein, I can imagine the frustration of the self builder if, when the representative has just left, they finally remember the question they had needed to ask.

Anyway, Richard came to see them, armed with the answers to their list of questions, only to be faced with yet another list that the three of them worked their way through over copious cups of tea. What Richard didn't know, and what wasn't discussed, is that John had already got hold of a financial profile of the company to make sure that, if and when he did do business with

them, he was putting his trust in the right place.

Richard explained to them that most of his company's clients chose to have a bespoke design prepared for them, rather than choose one of the examples in the brochure. Nevertheless, as John and Ann were adamant that what they wanted was a variation of one of the designs featured, they would do a feasibility study based on that design, with a large attached double garage. They also discussed external materials and decided upon stock bricks with feature panels in flint, under a plain clay tiled roof with PVCu casement windows, double glazed with Jacobean lights.

A feasibility study starts off with the prepara-

tion of the initial drawings and then moves on to the production of a quotation for the company's complete services, including the preparation and submission of plans for Planning and Building Regulations approval, and the supply of a kit of materials. The plans arrived a couple of weeks later and were just as they'd envisaged they would be and then, a few days after that, the quotation came in and, yes, you've guessed it, produced yet another long list of questions!

The quotation referred to a pot and beam floor for both the house and the garage but John had another hobby, his TVR motor car, and he wanted a solid floor with a pit in it. As well as that there were some other bits and pieces that

needed changing but, no matter, the changes were duly noted and a revised quotation shortly followed. Still, John didn't want to give the go-ahead for D&M to proceed beyond the initial drawing stage until he was comfortable with all the costs, and that meant getting prices from builders.

Most companies working within the self build industry, and D&M are no exception, know of builders that they can safely introduce to their clients. Plans and specifications were duly sent off to three builders for prices to construct the house and garage to the stage of a weathertight shell, using the package deal materials supply service from D&M that John and Ann would pay for. In the meantime, John busied himself with getting prices in from the second fix tradesmen, and as well as for the odd bits and pieces that he would need to buy for them and, for the jobs that he and Ann had decided to undertake.

With all the prices in they were, at last, able to set a fixed budget, rather than the estimated one they had been working on up to now and they set that budget at £93,000 for the entire project, *including* a contingency fund of 10%.

The builders price was from a chap called John King, now sadly deceased. Right from the very moment they first met him, they knew they were going to get along and, in hindsight, it was his cheerful, yet calming presence that made the whole project work. He came to see them one Sunday afternoon and his obvious knowledge and gravitas made them comfortable with what they were planning and helped them make the decision to take the next big step of formally accepting D&M's quotation and instructing them to get on with a submission to the planning authorities.

The planning application shewed the new house set back on the plot, behind the existing cottage as they were hoping to live in it whilst their new home was built. There were some immediate objections from neighbours but these were soon smoothed out by a visit and a chat and it wasn't long before Richard was able to ring them with the glad tidings that planning permission had been granted and that it had been given with a condition that the existing cottage was

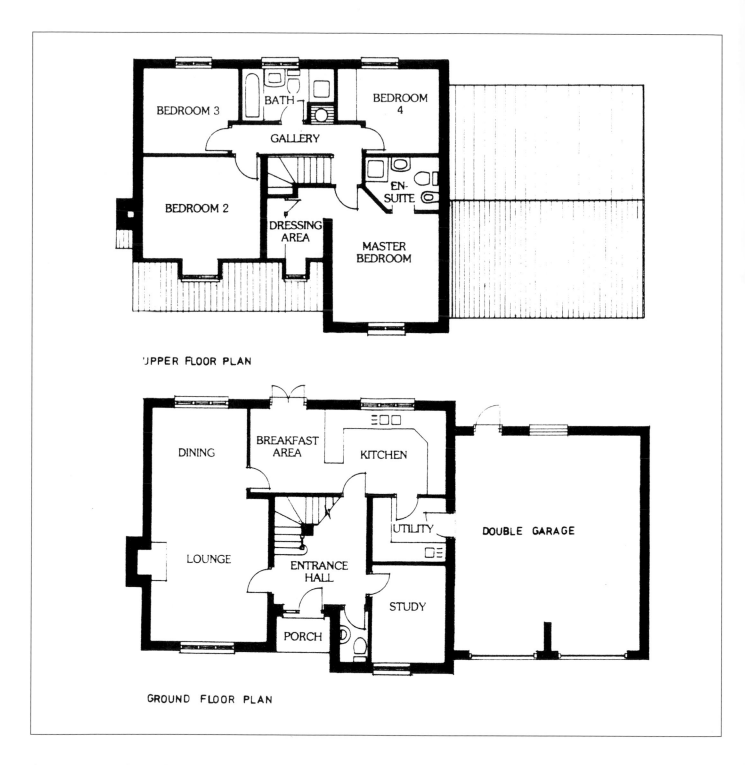

UPPER FLOOR PLAN

GROUND FLOOR PLAN

demolished once the new house was finished. This was truly great news and an enormous weight off their minds. They wouldn't have to move into temporary accommodation during the build.

Site insurance was arranged through DMS Services Ltd. and John King was able to make a start on site in the middle of April. The foundations had to go down to 2.5 metres in depth, due to the presence of trees and clay but they'd already been warned of that possibility and taken the extra costs into account. What they weren't fully prepared for was the sudden transformation of their peaceful rural idyll into a very busy building site and, with the new building taking shape, barely yards from the wall of the cottage, all privacy vanished. They soon got used to it, of course, and the daily start up of work, with the inevitable badly tuned radio only partially drowned out by the chugging of the mixer, became a welcome part of their routine. From the moment that she first saw the trenches and could envisage the rooms of her new home, Ann was excited.

Most of the planned for problems failed to materialise, not that anyone was too distressed about that. They'd thought, right at the beginning, that there'd be a problem with the drainage but, in the end, it turned out that, not only did the main sewer run across the bottom of their garden but that, the connection from the existing cottage could be utilised with the very minimum of disturbance. The narrow winding unmade up lane was a problem of course, but it was one that the builder had taken into account when he first quoted. Long vehicles couldn't get down it and that meant that things like the floor beams had to be off loaded at the junction with the main road and brought down to the site on a dumper or a digger. John went to work one morning and had to carefully negotiate and drive past one such delivery but, quite rightly, left it. After all he'd devolved responsibility for that particular headache to John King and, sure enough, when he got home, everything was cleared.

The builder's responsibility ended at the weathertight shell, although John continued to be a fabulous source of help and inspiration right up until his sad death. He put them onto a plasterer for the dry lining, skim coating and artexing, something that they had, quite sensibly decided that they couldn't or shouldn't try their hand at. Much of the second fix work was, however, undertaken by John and Ann, either by helping out a labour only tradesman or doing the work themselves. They took on complete responsibility for the fitting of the kitchen units and the decoration, both inside and outside and Ann did the ceramic flooring to the kitchen and utility room all by herself. As she told me this, I looked down at a very professional job and then looked up at John. "And the electrician who came to test out said that I'd done a very professional job", he boasted. Why not? They, like all self builders have a lot to blow their own trumpet about.

Not without the odd twinge of sadness, the old cottage had been taken down and cleared away in the week before my visit. It had cost a bit more than they had originally hoped for, due to the presence of asbestos but that still meant that the final cost of the entire project, including the driveway and all of the service connections, was £82,250 after the VAT had been recovered. They hadn't needed their contingency fund and they were over £10,000 inside their original budget for a house that's now worth around £350,000!

As I left, the last bits of the double entrance gravel driveway were being laid and the final rubble was being cleared so that I could take a photograph of the two of them standing by their front door, pleased as punch and just as proud.

A bungalow by the sea

Within the main text of this book, there are warnings about the effects that self building can have on a shaky marriage and how many who try to use a self build project to reinvigorate a dying relationship, actually succeed in finally breaking it. The other side of that coin is that the act of self building can also firmly cement, if you'll pardon the metaphor, an enduring partnership or, indeed endow a new one with a particular sense of worth.

I didn't ask, or even really want to know, what had preceded Gordon and Jenny getting together but, together they have been for the last few years and the joy and determination with which the two of them proclaim their new life through their self build is palpable. Just like many others I have met in their situation, although they met in circumstances where they had two homes, either one of which would have been suitable for them, there was a strong desire that they should set up a new home and an equally strong desire that any new home should be self built. "We wanted it to be really *ours*", said Jenny.

In Gordon and Jenny's case, they took this striving for independence and individuality, several stages further by eschewing many of the normal channels and creating a few of their own. I wouldn't even have heard of their self build were it not for the fact that Jenny works with my daughter, Naomi.

In the chapter 'Making the choices' I talked about 'going it alone' and, in the section dealing with package deal companies, I discussed the fact that, of those who choose not to avail themselves of the professional companies, a large proportion are people who are connected with or have some knowledge of the building industry. Gordon is one such chap, in that, his job is fitting garage doors and during the course of his work he found himself, not unnaturally, working on new homes. For years he looked and he listened, he watched and he waited, whilst he evaluated the differing methods of building. For years he dreamt of building his own home and studied all of the innovations and ideas that it would be possible to incorporate.

Underfloor central heating? That would be a must. Plenty of insulation? That too would be paramount. Timber frame? Yes, that too would be how he would go when he started. Why? So that he could get a weathertight shell up quickly and be able to get in and do the work of fitting it out as soon as it was dry.

So where did they start? Well they didn't completely strike out alone in that they did subscribe to 'Build It' magazine and they did visit the Alexandra Place show on every possible occasion, picking up even more information to add to the stock of opinions that Gordon had formed over the years.

They ventured onto some of the stands and the various package deal companies tried very hard to interest them in their services but that wasn't the way they wanted to go. Gordon and Jenny really wanted to paddle their own canoe and, as Jenny put it, "We wanted to make all our own choices". But they still had to think about design. They didn't want anything too big, there was, after all only the two of them. Still, there was time enough to keep on looking for their ideal, as the main thing was to find the land.

In the event that didn't prove to be as hard as they had originally feared as they received details of a plot on the Kent coast that was occupied by an old tram coach that had been converted into a holiday home. It was only 45 feet wide by just about 100 feet deep, there were no visible boundaries except the dike at the back and the view to the sea was obscured by the high sea wall defences that protect this low lying area. It was for sale at £27,000, though and its situation was perfect for both of them to be able to get to work, so they had no hesitation in putting in an offer that was accepted almost immediately. It's not the swishest of plots. It's not very big and it's close to the coast road that runs along behind the sea defences. But the price was right and, when all's said and done, there's the sea itself. High sea wall there may be but popular seaside it still is, as is evidenced by the holiday parks all along the coast. It was a hot day when I visited and when I'd finished talking to Jenny and Gordon, I left her painting the outside render as he tacked plasterboard inside, and walked across the road and up the steps to where my wife was waiting. We'd come prepared, of course, and the two of us

enjoyed a glorious swim followed by a long lie in the sun before we set off home.

At about the time they found the land, they also received a brochure from a timber frame manufacturer in Cornwall known as Frame Homes Ltd. and in there was a design that suited Jenny and Gordon right down to the ground. It showed a chalet bungalow with a lounge and separate dining room downstairs, as well as a good sized kitchen, a utility room and a bedroom come study. Upstairs there were three bedrooms and a bathroom and from the master suite a door led onto a cantilevered balcony that was underneath the roof overhang. It was perfect and it was just what they wanted. Gordon telephoned Frame Homes and asked if he could use the design and they told him that, yes he could, but that he'd have to buy the frame from them. Fair enough, thought Gordon, they'd decided against stickbuilding due to the time factor and he'd got to get the frame from somewhere, so why not them?

I spoke to Keith Lowe, of Frames Homes, a couple of days after I got back home and he remembered Gordon and Jenny straight off. "They're the ones near Folkestone who just wanted the frame delivered and that's all", he said. "That's them", I agreed. Keith went on to explain that his company doesn't have standard designs as such as they usually either provide a service for people who've already got their design sorted out or else they take the thing all the way through, including getting a special design drawn up. The design that Gordon and Jenny had picked from their brochure wasn't anything other than an illustration of something that they'd done before. But, with the exception of a requirement for the kitchen to be 3 inches wider, that's what they wanted and that was that. He sounded almost sad that he hadn't been able to give more help and even remembered that, during the erection stages, all they'd received was a couple of telephone calls asking for specific information. "We really do a lot more than that for our normal clients", he lamented, "but they simply didn't want anything else except the right to use the design and the supply only of the frame".

Anyway, going back a little, Gordon and

Jenny now knew what they wanted to build and they needed to get planning permission and Building Regulations approval. Now they did a sensible thing in that they engaged an architect to draw up the plans to the design, basically already formulated by Frame Homes, and submit the drawings for approval. There weren't any problems. It's not that kind of area and whilst it's not a case of anything goes, what they were proposing wasn't out of keeping with all of the other redevelopments and rebuilds that have gone on over the years. Pretty soon they had planning permission, the land, with the sale of their own houses, was legally theirs and they were ready to start building.

Now it was that Gordon's long planning came to full fruition. Now it was that he called in the favours and engaged the tradesmen that he would need and who he had identified as being the best over the long years of waiting. Groundworker first, and here was a big surprise. They'd expected that as they were barely 100 yards from the high water mark, they'd be building on sand or gravel. In fact it was clay but, still the Building inspector said that they'd only need to go down the bare minimum of one metre and that 225 mm of concrete in the bottom of the trench would suffice. The day after they'd dug, his reasoning became apparent. This clay wasn't going to shrink. Every time the tide came in the trenches filled with water and when it went out, they dried out. If ever proof was needed of the necessity of the sea wall on this low lying land, then this was it.

The garage walls were the first to go up and this is, perhaps, the first site I have come across where the plan to build the garage first actually came off. Gordon planned it that way and when the bricklayers had finished on the groundworks to the house they went straight on to the garage walls. He had to plan it that way because they were now in rented accommodation and they needed somewhere to store the mass of materials that they were already accumulating. You remember the three inch increase that was necessary for the kitchen? Well, that was needed because they'd already bought the kitchen units for half their original price, as ex display units from

Homebase. And then there was their other little 'hobby'.

For many people living near the channel ports, going to France has become almost a way of life and, with the Chunnel, nipping of to the off licence means driving onto a train and coming back loaded with cheap booze. Gordon and Jenny are not really that different and an evening out may well be in France just as much as in Folkestone. But, whilst they do, of course, bring back the odd few cases of libation, their shopping trips are a little different to many others, in that their van is not groaning on its return from the weight of bottles, but from the building materials they have bought.

Building materials, especially second fix or ancillary items, in France and Belgium are often of superior quality to those available in this country and, most importantly they are often a lot cheaper. If you buy materials or fittings from within the European Community, you can claim back the VAT paid, at the rate it was paid, so long as you have proof of importation, a VAT receipt and so long as the materials were definitely used in the construction of your new home. Even with VAT at 20.6% in France, at the time of writing, the savings are staggering and as Jenny and Gordon recited them to me, I tumbled over myself to write them down. Roof lights were 60% cheaper in France. 12 volt lighting systems, wall lights and many other electrical fittings cost about half what they would in England. The ceramic floor and wall tiles that they needed for the kitchens, bathrooms and utility room cost exactly one quarter the price in France, as did the outside roller blind that they needed to shield the lounge window from the southern sun. Where do I stop? Sanitaryware one third of the price you'd pay in England, shower and bath mixer taps 20% of the price...if only the people driving the Transit vans filled with booze, poured it all out and filled up instead with building materials, then they'd make more money - and they'd not be liable to arrest.

But back to the self build. When the frame arrived Gordon engaged a couple of carpenter chums of his and worked with them over the next ten days to get the shell erected. It rained of course, that's a feature of every self build story.

But they had a roofer on standby and it was a blessed relief to get covered in and weatherproof, especially as they had discovered that the concrete oversite was a little low, in one corner, and that end of the building often resembled a swimming pool. It doesn't matter now and it has no structural implications apart from the fact that the screed, at that point, is now a little thicker.

With the frame up and roofed, Jenny and Gordon took on the bulk of the remaining work with the exception of the supply and fix electrician. As I've already said, they had opted for underfloor central heating and for this they'd chosen to use a company called Nu-heat who supplied them with all of the materials and a layout of where everything had to go. Jenny proudly showed me the plans of the loops and coils that I could still see in the floor zones where they were yet to be covered up and Gordon, equally as proudly, displayed the mass of differently coloured pipes and terminations in the downstairs cupboard. I looked up and remarked that they had also chosen to have underfloor central heating to the upstairs as well as to the ground floor. Yes, they had read about it not being quite as efficient upstairs as down but, nevertheless, that's what they chosen and the difference, with their lifestyle and in the maritime environment wasn't going to break the bank. They had also installed the central vacuum and the pipework hung loose in the studs that they had not yet tacked as did some other, larger corrugated pipes that I remarked on. These turned out to be the pipes for the ventilation and extraction system, also bought in France, that were worked by a series of hydrostats, something that they simply didn't find in England.

They're doing the entire second fix and tacking themselves although they're employing a plasterer for the outside render and the internal skim coat. I looked around as they told me this and my eyes lighted on the hardwood double opening casement windows. Were those from France? No, they weren't but they had bought them themselves, from a local manufacturer and the frame company hadn't supplied them. Gordon turned and indicated the internal doors.

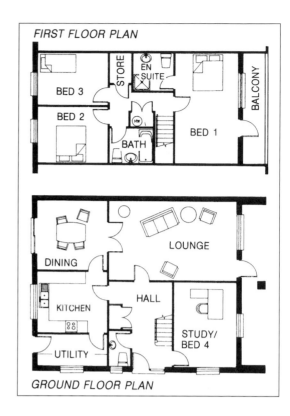

FIRST FLOOR PLAN

BED 3, STORE, EN SUITE, BALCONY, BED 2, BED 1, BATH, HW

GROUND FLOOR PLAN

DINING, LOUNGE, KITCHEN, HALL, STUDY/BED 4, UTILITY

These had been brought from France, as pre-hung door sets. They were super. Solid wood with stylish mouldings and timber and brass furniture. Expensive? No not really, about the same but of superior quality and the fact that they were pre-hung meant that the job of second fix carpentry could be completely carried out by Gordon.

With two weeks to go before the moving in date when I visited, they were able to estimate the costs fairly accurately, especially as most of the stuff they needed was already on site and it was only really their own labour that had yet to be added to the equation. With the land costing £27,000, it looked as if their total costs would be around the £85,000 mark to set against a market value of about £120,000.

Did they have any problems? No not really. The only trade that was difficult to get hold of sometimes, due to the mass of work available in the area was the bricklayer but even that didn't hold them up too much. Any funny bits, I asked. Jenny smiled. Yes, when it was her 50th birthday and Gordon had taken her out for the evening. At work the next day, all her friends asked where he'd taken her and she replied that she'd had a real treat. He'd taken her to a DIY store in France!

A new home in Oxfordshire

There's an old saying about the cobbler's shoes. The cobbler apparently always had holes in his shoes because he was so busy mending other people's that he didn't have time for his own.

You'd have thought that Michael, being the editor of 'Homebuilding & Renovating' magazine, would have been the best placed person in the country to self build successfully, and to a large extent you'd be right, because, in common with most self build projects, in the end everything turned out alright. What that statement hides, however, is the fact that, by his own admission, Michael's made more than his fair share of mistakes, many of which have even flown in the face of advice I have heard him giving other people when I've shared a seminar platform with him. To be fair to him, he has catalogued those mistakes in a self build diary, published in his magazine, within which he has agonised at his own failings.

So where did it all go wrong? Well, let's leave the wrong out for the moment because, as I've said, for all the mistakes, this is, nevertheless, a success story by any measure, especially when you consider that the end result is a property with a value that's 70% higher than the costs!

The success started and, in large part is founded upon, a literally brilliant piece of foresight by Michael and his wife, Emma. They lived in a flat in Maida Vale, London but with Michael's offices being just south of Birmingham, they were aware for some time that, sooner or later, they'd have to think about moving and that when they did, self building would be the only real option. Then Emma became pregnant and the search for that all elusive plot became much more urgent. They concentrated on Oxfordshire for two reasons, one, Emma's parents lived there and that meant that, if the land was nearby, they could live with them during the build and two, it was equidistant between Birmingham and London, where they still had many connections.

The plot was advertised in the local newspaper, for sale by sealed bid tender, a way of selling land or houses that's a bit like an auction, only with the added uncertainty caused by not knowing what all the other bids are. Emma saw it first and she very quickly told Michael about it

and the two of them went out to see it. It was a small plot, on a narrow lane just off a picturesque village, overlooking open countryside with a paddock beside it that was also for sale. The estate agents had given a guide price for the plot of £70,000 with a further £15,000 being asked for the paddock and Michael and Emma's immediate thought was that, if the paddock could be included in the plot, then the plot size would very nearly quadruple and the whole thing would take on a completely different hue. Of course, they weren't the first ones to think that way and they very soon discovered that the vendors and others had previously tried, in vain, to enlarge the plot in this way. The planners, though, were having none of that; the paddock was in the green belt and they would not countenance any building encroaching upon it. That meant that the planning that had been granted, and then only at the second appeal, was for a pretty small house, fronting the lane with its access within its frontage. The fact that the plot narrowed towards its rear meant that, in turn it would then have a very small garden and that this would be further encroached upon by any requirement for parking or turning area.

All of this pointed to the guideline price of the plot being at the higher end of the scale when compared to the probable market value of the

small house that could be built upon it. If one considered that, in this particular area, the probability was that the planners would insist on fairly expensive external materials and a design that was sympathetic to the local vernacular, then the squeeze on profitability, as things stood, threatened the viability of any project.

Many people would have walked away at that point and, indeed, luckily, as it proved for Michael and Emma, quite a few probably did, reasoning that the sums just didn't add up. But, right from the start Michael had seen a possibility that nobody else seems to have thought of. If the house was turned around to face north south with its gable end towards the road, then it could be designed so that all of its major windows looked over the open countryside to the south and, whilst the house could then be considerably bigger, it still wouldn't need to encroach on the green belt land of the paddock. Oh, that would mean that they'd need to get planning permission for change of use on the paddock, in order for it to become garden land, but it certainly wouldn't be built on.

Bright ideas and theory is fine but Michael realised that, if they were going to take the matter any further, then he really needed to test the water with the planners. He felt too that they really needed to have some ideas about what sort of house they could build, both for their own sake and in order to show the planners. Time was of the essence in all of this. What would be the point of doing anything if, in the end they lost the plot because the tender date had come and gone. An old friend, Beverley Pemberton, who is chief designer for Design & Materials Ltd, agreed to do some sketches for them and they rushed up the A1 to see her on a Friday evening and by the following Monday she'd faxed back a design that just staggered them with how close it got to all their aspirations. It showed a traditional Cotswold stone house with a modest footprint, on three floors with all major rooms overlooking the proposed open ground and with the highly chauvinistic master suite, dressing room and en suite arrangement that they'd asked for, plus plenty of space for their expected and anticipated future family.

Now all they needed to do was convince the planners that they were on the right lines and Michael fixed up a meeting with them just as soon as he could. If, in the euphoria of seeing their new home illustrated to them, he had imagined that the planning stages were going to

be easy, then Michael was in for a rude awakening when he visited the local authority a few days later. Although the planning officer seemed amenable to many of the ideas that he was putting forward, most importantly the concept of the paddock becoming garden land, he realised, with a heavy heart, that the plans that resided in the envelope in his briefcase, would have to stay right there. Any house that they built would have to be no higher than the Grade 2 listed farmhouse to the north of the plot and that meant that the three storey house they'd hoped for was out of the question. Michael left the meeting pretty down hearted but consoled himself with the one important 'victory', that the major hurdle of the inclusion of the paddock seemed to have been largely cleared. So they had moved forward, even if they were going to have to do some serious thinking about the design.

They'd cleared another big hurdle whilst all of this had been going on, in that they'd also managed to agree the mortgage finance. Although based on the plans that they now knew they would have to amend, the valuations, nevertheless, confirmed the value of the plot and the projected market value of the completed house. That meant that they could now put together a firm figure for the tender, and they sat down to work things out based on Michael's knowledge and experience of the likely costs they would build for. They made up their minds that, as they really wanted this plot, and in the belief that they would get planning for more or less what they wanted, including the change of use on the paddock, they should put the offer in at £90,000, which was £5000 over the original guideline price. On the morning of the tender date though, they upped the offer to £91,000, just to make sure and, as it turned out, a good job too because, even so, they only just won. Win they did, however, and solicitors were instructed, although Michael asked theirs to delay contracts as long as possible so as to give them time to get along with the planning and hopefully get it all through beforehand.

A few years before all this Michael had tried to deal with a tax problem, on his own, without the aid of an expert, and the experience had

taught him a lesson. He had made up his mind that the next time he had to deal with authority, where he wasn't completely au fait with procedures and laws, he would employ a professional. He realised now that, in the sensitive planning environment of their plot, they really needed to engage an architect to handle their application and, more and more he was coming to the opinion that, if at all possible, the architect should be reasonably local, and possibly known to the local authority. By asking around the obvious contacts Michael had in the industry, they heard of a chap called Ian Whittaker of 'Four Square Design', and the two of them arranged to see him. They clicked with him immediately, so much so that they very quickly engaged him and it wasn't long before he'd made a planning application. This was a full application rather than an approval of reserved matters in view of the fact that the house and orientation had changed significantly from the original outline approval and in order to incorporate the change of use on the paddock. The house drawn con-

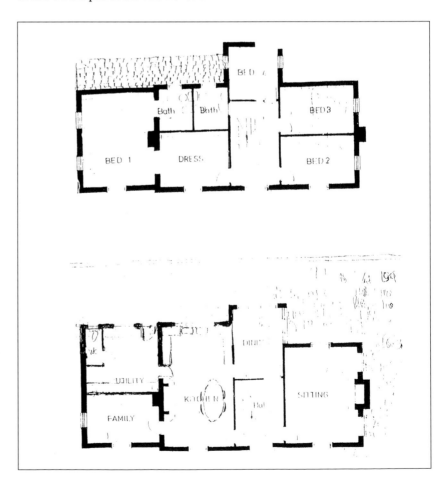

tained many of the features of the original house drawn by Beverley, but it was two storey only with low ceiling heights to bring the ridge height down and it included an annex that had the effect of pushing its probable costs beyond their anticipated budget. That wasn't really the point, for when it was discovered that the planners had recommended refusal on the grounds that the house was too big, they were able to chop off the annex and reduce the overall scale of the building by reverting to a two storey house that bore a remarkable similarity to their original proposal.

Still this failed to satisfy the planners entirely. They were still worried about the ridge height, even though they now seemed happy with the overall footprint of the proposed house. Michael and Emma worried over what to do next. The vendors were now pushing them to contract on the land and a refusal would set them right back. There had to be some way forward.

And then Michael remembered a chap that he'd featured in the magazine some time before, who'd had a similar problem. That guy had got around the ridge height by reducing the level of the land, so why not them? Ian thought it was a good idea and, more to the point, so did the planners. Planning permission was granted, albeit with 15 conditions, most of which referred to external materials and the proposed ridge height and the rest of which related to the treatment and landscaping of the gardens. Most importantly the consent included the change of use for the paddock.

As you can imagine Michael and Emma wasted no time in contracting on the land. They had got more or less what they wanted in design terms. The house was only two storeys but there was scope for extension into the roof void under permitted development rights, which hadn't been curtailed. Most importantly, instead of a £70,000 plot being capable of supporting a house with a ceiling value of £180,000 they had now, by quadrupling the size of the plot got the capability of building a house that would have a market value of at least £300,000! Foresight, imagination and nerves of steel had brought them to this pitch and, when he told me that at this point they'd decided to take a breather before actually

starting work, I wasn't in the least bit surprised. I was even less surprised when Michael explained that by this time, they were living at his in-laws house and, when I raised the customary eyebrow, he also explained that her parents were super people that he got on very well with and, in any event, they were away during the week only returning at weekends. Oh, and by the way, Emma also took advantage of the lull in activities to have a lovely baby boy called Freddie.

So now we get to the building bit and here's where, as he told me all about it, the hairs on the back of my neck stood up from time to time. Michael's job means that he is an 'expert' in the self build industry and from time to time he is called upon to pontificate on all aspects of self building. But he soon realised that he was subject to the same fears, the same insecurities and liable to make the same mistakes as any of his readers. Oh, he did have an enormous advantage, in that he had access to a huge pool of advice and, although much of that advice is available to most self builders, for him it was, literally at his fingertips. Still self building can be a nerve wracking procedure at times and he began to understand some of the feelings of his audiences at the seminars. It all came home to him with a big bang on the day work started on site when he suddenly realised that he'd jumped off the top board and that there was no going back. A phone call confirmed that a digger was on its way to site on a low loader and that the price was £120 each way plus £100 per day. If the digger had to go back then he'd still have to pay. Had he done everything he needed to have done? No, he hadn't! The Highways Authority needed two weeks prior notification of the creation of a new access and he'd forgotten. A grovelling telephone call and the man at the Highways Authority's realisation that, as it was a dead end lane, they needn't be as strict got him out of that problem but it was a foretaste of things to come.

The architect had advised them to use a builder but Michael and Emma realised that they really couldn't afford to build by that route. They also realised that they didn't have the time to manage subcontractors. Instead, and I felt a distinct tingling in my neck region as he told me of it, they'd made an arrangement with a local builder whereby he'd project manage the job on a cost plus basis. Now that's not that unusual, many of the package deal companies can offer a similar arrangement, but what was different was that the 'plus' basis, in their case, was a percentage of the cost rather than a fixed fee. If you're going to make that sort of arrangement then you need to know the builder pretty well, you need to be very good at evaluating men, you need to know, every day, that you're getting the right amount of work done and you need to know that all of the prices for labour and materials are right. Michael got away with it, in the main, and his builder turned out to be a pretty good guy but the thought of most self builders going down that road gives me the jiggers.

What convinced Michael of the worth of his choice, and I have to admit once more that his trust paid off, was his fear of hidden extras. At least this way, he figured, the only extras would be elective ones and he wouldn't have to pay out any VAT, thus easing his cash flow. On top of that it would leave Michael free to source the majority of the materials, most of which he got at trade prices, due in whole or in part to his position within the industry. The first bad moment and an illustration of the difficulties of trying to manage a self build project in concert with a busy job that took him away a lot, was a telephone call to say that the building wouldn't fit. In the event, this turned out to be nothing and the truth was that when the digger came to excavate the trenches, they found out that they hadn't stripped and reduced the oversite for a large enough area. 'Chinese whispers' magnified that one into how it had been reported but, at the time, it was pretty scary, at least until Michael got home and found out the truth. Then came the phone call that made Michael's blood run cold as a tearful and frightened Emma told him that she'd been to the site and that the Building Inspector had condemned it and that it all had to come down. As they'd nearly reached first floor joist height, you can understand why Michael had the vapours. The walls were 400mm thick as they'd decided, in spite of the extra costs involved, to use

random coursed traditional stone, that came from the quarry as dug rather than dressed and cut. They were using Durox big blocks for the inside leaf with urethane insulation sandwiched between this internal leaf and the external stonework. There was no cavity as such and in recognition of that the outside face of the blockwork had been given three coats of damp proofing material. It all sounds as reasonable as it is unconventional, although what persuaded Michael and Emma to step so far outside the norm, one is only left to wonder at. The Building Inspector was equally as puzzled and he had indeed said that unless they could prove the efficacy and compliance of such a system of walling, he would have no option but to condemn it. He was worried about whether urethane was suitable for full filled walls and whether it would provide the necessary waterproofing and 'U' values especially as the company providing the material didn't have a BBA certificate for its use in a solid walling situation.

It sounds like a horror story, doesn't it, and indeed, as Michael told me all about it over lunch in a pub, some months later, it was still easy to detect the fear that he had gone through over those few days. In the event everything was sorted out. The manufacturers were able to prove a 'U' value of .26, way better than the required .45 and the Building Inspector accepted their contentions that "if the world sank, the urethane would remain afloat". By stepping outside convention, by using a material designed for one purpose, for another, they had brought this unhappiness upon themselves and, even though it all turned out right in the end, the memory of it will stay with them.

Perhaps Michael and Emma will take up bungy jumping for a hobby one day. They certainly seem to live on the edge. They decided that they wanted to extend the building to make the kitchen larger, something they could have done anyway, when they'd finished, under permitted development rights. When the planners said that they couldn't approve it as a minor amendment to the consent, they made a planning application but then carried on with its construction. They changed the roof slates, to a different and much more expensive reformed stone slate and then went ahead and fixed them whilst still awaiting the approval of the planners. All of it

paid off but they must have nerves of steel and I have to warn self builders not to emulate them.

I say that knowing that many of you will admire their courage and determination– that's the kind of people self builders are. Michael and Emma refused to compromise. They went over budget but they knew, even as they did so, that they could raise the extra finance and they knew, also, that by their foresight at the planning stages they had created a cushion of equity to fall back upon. What they finish up with is a very valuable house that, in spite of the fact that they'll probably sell it on one day, they'll always be proud of and which, as you can see from the photographs, looks every bit as, if not more, in keeping with its surroundings than many of its neighbours.

If anything, many of the ills that befell Michael came about because of his position in the industry. As such he was forever the target of single interest advice or advice given within a narrow perspective that was often linked to a desire to promote a product. Much of this was useful but some of it, like the advice he received to use a concrete pump to get the screed up to the first floor, which in the event was very expensive and totally useless, was simply wrong. On the other hand, the IPECC underfloor central heating, the plastic plumbing, the beautiful oak vaulted ceilings in their bedroom, the stone flagged floors and the breathtaking view from their windows, especially the first floor landing, bear testament to a successful self build as do the host of other innovations that I just don't have room to mention here.

And if I sound smug about their 'mistakes'? Well, I was that cobbler.

Further information

Books

Plans for a Dream Home, Murray Armor, Ebury Press, Ryton Books 01909 591652

The Home Plans Book, David Snell & Murray Armor, Ebury Press, Ryton Books 01909 591652

Practical Housebuilding, Bob Matthews, J.M.Dent, Ryton Books 01909 591652

The Housebuilders Bible, Mark Brinkley, Ryton Books 01909 591652

How to find a Building Plot, Speer & Dade, Stonepound Books, Ryton Books 01909 591652

How to get Planning Permission, Speer & Dade, Stonepound Books, Ryton Books 01909591652

Magazines

Homebuilding & Renovating, 01527 834400
Build It 0171 837 8727
Self Build 01283 742950

Useful Agencies and Associations

The Association of Selfbuilders 01604 493757 & 0116 270 8843
Royal Institute of British Architects (RIBA) 0171 580 5533
Associated Self Build Architects (ASBA) 0800 387310
Royal Town Planning Institute 0171636 9107
Planning Inspectorate: England 0117 987 8754, Wales 0122 282 3308, Scotland 0131 244 5649, N. Ireland 01232 244710
The Building Research Establishment (and BRECSU) 01983 664000
National Radiological Protection Board 01235 831600
Commission for New Towns 01908 692692
Timber & Brick Information Council 01923 778136
Disabled Living Foundation 0171 289 6111

Companies and Agencies assisting in Land Finding

Plotfinder 01527 834444
Landbank Services 0118 961 8002
Commission for New Towns 01908 692692
HM Land Registry 0171 917 8888

Agencies involved in Group and Community Self Build

The Community Self Build Association 0171 415 7092
Landmark Services 0117 940 9800
The National Federation of Housing Associations 0171 278 6571
The Housing Corporation 0171 393 2000
The Young Builders Trust 01730 266766
The Walter Segal Trust 0171 388 9582

Exhibitions

The Homebuilding and Renovating Show, run by Homebuilding & Renovating magazine. Every spring at the NEC and in early summer at Sandown Park, Surrey 01527 834400

The Self Build Homes Show, run by Build It magazine. Every autumn at Alexandra Palace, London with another major show in Scotland, plus at least 5 regional shows. 0171 837 8727

Ideal Homes Exhibition, every spring at Earls Court, London.

The Building Centre, 26 Store Street, London, Nr.Goodge Street underground. The Building Bookshop is in the same building.

Self Build Insurances

DMS Services Ltd. 01909 591652 Offering Norwich Union and Guardian insurance policies to selfbuilders and individual builders.

Vulcan Insurance Insurances for conversions and renovations 01909 591652

Warranties

NHBC 'Buildmark' and 'Solo' 01494 434477
Zurich 'Custombuild' 01252 522000
Project Builder
Trenwick Willis Coroon (Forest of Dean Scheme) 0151 625 3883

Package Deal Companies, Timber Frame Manufacturers and Architectural Practices

Alpha Timber Frame Ltd. 01483 427733
Associated Self Build Architects 0800 387310
Border Oak Design & Construction Ltd.. 01568 708752
The Bungalow Company. 01767 263300
Custom Homes Ltd. 01293 822898
Design & Materials Ltd. 01909 730333
Frame Homes (South West) Ltd. 01872 572882
Kingpost Design Company Ltd. 01684 566494
Juliam Owen Associates, Architects. 0115 922 9831
Potton Homes Ltd. 01767 263300
Scandia-Hus Ltd. 01342 327977
The Swedish House Company Ltd. 01892 665007

ACKNOWLEDGEMENTS

Jeanne, Charles & Katie Armor
Keith Bishop RIBA, Andrew Smith RIBA – Kingpost Design Ltd.
Phil Brain – Gloucestershire CC
John & Ann Carter
Joe Chetcuti – Forest of Dean DC
Richard Coles, Bruce Macdonald, Dante Mutti, Beverley Pemberton, Tom Somerville ARIBA – Design & Materials Ltd.
Richard Crisp, Alasdair Dando, Jeffery Emms ARIBA, Mick Jewel, Terry Mahoney – Potton Ltd.
Fred Entwistle – Thorpe & Thorpe Solicitors
John Figeira – Alpha Timber Frame Ltd.
Anne Galloway – Scandia-Hus Ltd.
Jenny Gannaway & Gordon Carmichael
Myra Giles
David & Glenys Gilbert & Alan Jones
John Greene – Border Oak Design & Construction Ltd.
Simon & Jane Hayes – The Swedish House Company Ltd.
Christopher Heath – Custom Homes Ltd.
Adrian Hirst & Andrea MacPherson
Michael Holmes – Homebuilding & Renovating Magazine
Emma & Freddie Holmes
Ray Holmes & Hazel Elmes
Nick Jones – BRECSU
Reginald Jordan – Zurich Building Guarantees
Michael & Patricia Jupp
Michael Kilcommon – NHBC 'Solo'
Brian Lovell
Keith Lowe – Frame Homes (South West) Ltd.
Roy Magro
Kevin & Drucilla Maizey
Anna McGettigan – Community Self Build Association
Julian Owen – Associated Self Build Architects
Janet Parker – DMS Services Ltd.
Robert & Ruth Pennicott – Landbank Services Ltd.
David Ransley Accountancy Services
David Scott – Timber & Brick Information Council
Naomi Snell
Adrian Spawforth RIBA – Associated Self Build Architects
Colin & Pearl Spooner
Derek Spence
Jim Stewart – Forest of Dean DC
Jenny de Villiers – DMS Services Ltd.
Colin Wadsworth – Landmark Services Ltd.
Tony & Luva Washington
Gunnel Westley – Scandia-Hus Ltd.
Nick Whittle – Alpha Timber Frame Ltd.
Sue Woodward – Build It magazine

Index

Also by the same authors, **Murray Armor & David Snell**

THE HOME PLANS BOOK
and PLANS FOR A DREAM HOME

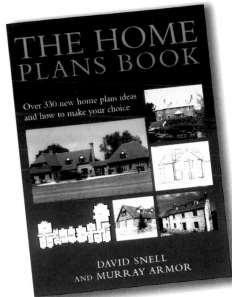

The essential companion books to *'Building Your Own Home'*, featuring over 700 plans and design ideas to whet the appetite of any self-builder.

THE HOME PLANS BOOK
David Snell & Murray Armor

The Home Plans Book carefully guides the prospective self-builder through the choices that have to be made and helps select the right design for your lifestyle, budget and site. It is packed full of information and contains over 300 breathtaking and innovative plans drawn from a cross section of the major players in the self-build world. The designs are categorised in clearly marked chapters and range from simple bungalows and houses through to large and more complicated family homes. You will marvel at the clever ways that the various designers have overcome the many problems associated with modern living to present a truly wonderful display of ideas for you to incorporate in your own new home.

PLANS FOR A DREAM HOME
Murray Armor

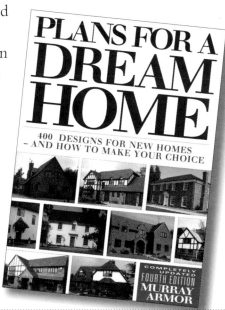

Now in its fourth edition, this is a blockbuster of a book with over 400 plans of homes created for the clients of five of the leading companies working within the self-build field. They vary from five- and six-bedroom houses to small retirement bungalows.

ORDERS BY POST
Ryton Books, Orchard House, Blyth, Worksop, Notts S81 8HF

Please supply books as indicated

Name ....

Address ....

....

The Home Plans Book   £25 ☐
Plans for a Dream Home   £20 ☐   (Both books deduct £2)

p&p free for delivery within the UK. Books despatched within 24 hours

Card No. ☐☐☐☐ ☐☐☐☐ ☐☐☐☐ ☐☐☐☐ ☐☐☐☐   expiry ☐☐ ☐☐

MASTERCARD/VISA/CHEQUE ORDER
PHONE 01909 591652
FAX 01909 591031
E.Mail.insurance@selfbuild.demon.co.uk

Both of these books are published by Ebury Press Ltd. and are available from all good booksellers or by post from Ryton Books, Orchard House, Blyth, Worksop, S81 8HF. Telephone 01909 591652 for credit card orders. Books despatched within 24 hours together with details of other books and services of interest to would-be self-builders.

INSURANCE

CHOOSE THE RIGHT POLICY TO COVER EVERY ASPECT OF YOUR SELFBUILD PROJECT.

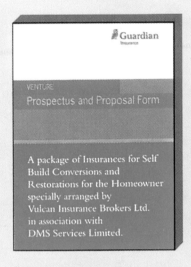
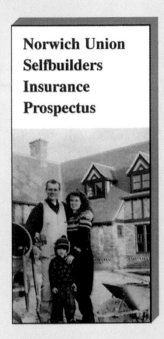

FOR PROSPECTUSES AND ADVICE FROM AN EXPERT – RING D.M.S. SERVICES LTD.
01909 591652

UNDERWRITTEN BY
NORWICH UNION AND GUARDIAN INSURANCE

DMS Services Ltd., Orchard House, Blyth, Nr. Worksop, Notts. S81 8HF.
Website – http://www.selfbuild.demon.co.uk
Fax: 01909 591031

BUILDERS RISKS INSURANCES
FOR THOSE BUILDING ON THEIR OWN LAND

NORWICH UNION

The Norwich Union is able to offer an insurance package for those who are building for their own occupation private dwellings of traditional construction with or without the help of builders or sub-contractors. It does not apply to the extension, alteration, repair or renovation of existing buildings. This affords Contract Works, Public Liability and Employers' Liability cover and automatically includes the interest of any Mortgagee. Cover is provided in one policy document, summarised as follows. This description of insurance must be regarded only as an outline. The policy is a legal document and as such defines the insurance in precise terms. A specimen copy of the policy form is available on request.

CONTRACT WORKS

Cover   "All Risks" of loss or damage to:
  (a) the new building whilst under construction and materials for incorporation therein
  (b) plant, tools, equipment, temporary buildings and caravans.

Sum insured   The full rebuilding cost of the property, excluding the value of the land.

Including
  (a) your own and hired plant, tools and equipment used in connection with the work up to a total sum insured of £2000 (can be increased if required).
  (b) Employees personal effects and tools whilst on the site up to a sum insured of £330 any one employee in accordance with standard Building Industry/Union agreements.
  (c) Architects, Surveyors and other fees necessarily incurred in rebuilding following loss or damage.
  (d) the cost of removing debris following any claim.

Excluding
  (a) The first £50 of each and every claim for loss or damage to employees personal effects or tools.
  (b) The first £500 of each and every other loss.

EMPLOYERS LIABILITY (compulsory by law)

Cover   Your legal liability for death or bodily injury to employees, including labour only sub-contractors, arising out of the building work.

Limit   £10,000,000 each occurrence.

Including   Legal costs and expenses in defending any claim.

Note   A Certificate of Insurance will be provided, and must by law be displayed on site.

PUBLIC LIABILITY

Cover   Your legal liability to members of the public, (including sub-contractors working on the site not classed as employees) for death, bodily injury or damage to property, arising out of the building work.

Limit   £1,000,000 any one loss. (Can be increased if required)

Including   Legal costs and expenses in defending any claim

Excluding   The first £250 of any claim for damage to property.

PERIOD   From the commencement date you specify (which should be no earlier than the date you complete the proposal form) up to completion of the building work, subject to a maximum of 24 months. Extensions to this period may be available on payment of an additional premium. There is no refund for early completion.

THE POLICY   Will be sent direct to you by DMS Services Ltd. on behalf of the Insurance Company.

THE PREMIUM   £5.95 per 1,000 on the rebuilding cost of the property. (Minimum £80,000). This is a total rate for all the cover set out above, subject to submission of the completed proposal form overleaf, and includes insurance premium tax at 4%. Proposal forms should be accompanied by cheques for the relevant premium made out to DMS Services Ltd. or credit card details should be provided

Rebuilding Cost Up to £	Premium £	Rebuilding Cost Up to £	Premium £	Rebuilding Cost Up to £	Premium £
80,000	476.00	100,000	595.00	140,000	833.00
85,000	505.75	110,000	654.50	150,000	892.50
90,000	535.50	120,000	714.00		
95,000	565.25	130,000	773.50	Over 150,000 @ £5.95 per £1000	

TAX   The scale of premiums shown in this prospectus and proposal are inclusive of Insurance Premium Tax at 4% and are only valid while the rate of tax remains at this level. DMS Services Ltd. will advise on revised premiums should the rate of tax change.

REBATE VOUCHER

If you complete within 6 months without any claims you will be entitled to use the Discount Voucher of £40 towards a Norwich Union Home Plus Policy

IMPORTANT The above terms only apply:
(a) up to 31st December 1998. Amended terms may be necessary for proposal forms completed after that date.
(b) to risks in Mainland Great Britain only. Proposals from N. Ireland are quoted individually and special excesses may apply. Phone 01909 591652 or fax 01909 591031 for a quotation. Proposals cannot be accepted from Eire.
(c) Where there is no abnormal exposure to risk of floods, storm damage or vandalism.

THE AGENCY

The Agency is DMS Services Ltd., a company which provides specialised insurance services to those building on their own. The proposal form overleaf should be completed and sent to the agency with a cheque or Credit Card details for the premium payable to DMS Services Ltd.

D.M.S. Services Ltd., Orchard House, Blyth, Worksop, Notts. S81 8HF.
Phone 01909 591652   Fax 01909 591031

Agency: DMS Services Ltd   Agency Reference: 50GA59   Policy No.

Proposal – BUILDING OWN PRIVATE DWELLING
The Insurer: Norwich Union Insurance Limited

NORWICH UNION

Name of Proposer	Phone No.
MR/MRS/MISS	

Full Postal Address

....

.... Postcode ....

Address of property to be erected

....

....

Name and address of any interested party – eg Bank or Building Society	Commencing date of insurance
....	....

Important – Please give a definite answer to each question (block letters) or tick appropriate boxes

	Yes	No	If "Yes" please give details
1. Have you made any other proposal for insurance in respect of the risk proposed?	☐	☐	
2. Has any company or underwriter declined your proposal?	☐	☐	
3. Have you ever been convicted of (or charged but not yet tried with) arson or any offence involving dishonesty of any kind (eg fraud, theft, handling stolen goods)?	☐	☐	

4. Will the property be

(a) a completely new structure and not an extension, conversion or restoration of an existing building?   ☐ ☐   (If "No" please refer to DMS Services Ltd.) Phone 01909 591652

(b) of conventional construction, either in loadbearing masonry, or with a timber frame, and built to drawings approved under the requirements of the Building Regulations as meeting the requirements of the regulations in full?   ☐ ☐

(c) occupied as your permanent residence on completion?   ☐ ☐   (If "No" please refer to DMS Services Ltd.) Phone 01909 591652

5. (a) Will the total value of plant, tools, equipment and temporary buildings, whether hired or owned on site at any one time exceed £2,000. If so see overleaf for the additional premium required (cover for plant on site can be altered at any time while the policy is in force). Phone 01909 591652 if in doubt.   ☐ ☐   Contractors plant hired in with operators, such as excavators, need not be included if proposers are wholly satisfied the hirers insurances cover all risks. However if cover is required on such machines phone DMS Services on 01909 591652

6. Is there any abnormal exposure to risk of flooding, storm damage or vandalism?   ☐ ☐

7. State estimated value of building work on completion at builder price for reinstatement.   £ _____   It is important that this sum is the cost of a professional building firm rebuilding the entire dwelling should it be completely destroyed just prior to completion. This will be the limit of indemnity for item (A) of the Contract Works section, and payments of premium on a lesser figure will result in any contracts works claim being proportionately reduced. Please discuss with DMS Services Ltd if in any doubt

8. Material facts – state any other material facts here. Failure to do so could invalidate the policy. A material fact is one which is likely to influence an insurer in the assessment and acceptance of the proposal. If you are in any doubt as to whether a fact is material it should be disclosed to the insurer.   If work on site has started certify here that there have been no incidents on site which would have given rise to a claim

Note:
1. You should keep a record (including copies of letters) of all information supplied to the insurer for the purpose of entering into the contract.
2. A copy of this proposal form will be supplied by the Insurer on request.
3. Please note that the details you are asked to supply may be used to provide you with information about other products and services which the Norwich Union Group can offer.

Declaration To be completed in all cases
I desire to insure with the Insurer in the terms of the Policy used in this class of Insurance. I declare that the above statements and particulars are true to the best of my knowledge and belief and that I have not withheld any material information. I agree to give immediate notice to the insurer of any alteration to the circumstances described herein and that this proposal shall form the basis of the contract between us.

Proposer's signature	Date

Send completed form to DMS Services Ltd. Orchard House, Blyth, Worksop, Notts, S81 8HF, together with a cheque made payable to DMS Services Ltd. or provide credit card details. Any queries to DMS Services. Phone 01909 591652

Norwich Union Insurance Limited. Registered in England No. 99122. Registered Office: Surrey Street, Norwich NR1 3NS. Member of the Association of British Insurers. Member of the Insurance Ombudsman Bureau.

HOME PLUS COVER
Quotations will be provided for household insurances when the building approaches completion. If this is not required please tick box – ☐

SELFBUILDERS INSURANCES
ASSESSING YOUR INSURANCE REQUIREMENTS

Guardian
Insurance

STANDARD COVER

LIABILITIES	Limit of Liability
A. Employers Liability – *no excess*	£10,000,000
B. Public Liability	£2,000,000

in respect of the site, the natural features on it including trees and the work proposed – *excess of £250 for property damage*

CONTRACT WORKS

C. Contract Works insurance to the value declared in respect of the works and materials for use in the works, with a standard excess of £500

OPTIONAL COVER

PLANT

D. Plant and tools owned by the proposer, cover on the site only with a standard excess of £500

E. Employees tools or plant, cover effective on the site only with a standard excess of £50. (Maximum 2 employees)

F. Plant and tools hired in by the proposer and NOT covered by Hiresafe or other hirers scheme, cover for the whole term of the policy with the standard excess of £500

G. Plant and tools hired in by the proposer and NOT covered by Hiresafe or other hirers scheme, short term cover for a 14 day period. (Phone 01909 591652 to arrange)

CARAVAN

H. Caravan on the site, used as a site hut or temporary dwelling, excess £250

value £

INCREASED PUBLIC LIABILITY LIMITS

J. Increase Public Liability cover for a 14 day period if required by an authority to facilitate a drain connection or similar purpose

K. Public Liability to £1,000,000 and Fire Cover to an agreed value on existing buildings, walls and other structures on the site which are not part of the construction project.

The above cover extends for the duration of the building work or 15 months whichever is the sooner. It applies to mainland UK, C. Isles, IoM, and Shetlands. Rates for N. Ireland exactly double the mainland rates above.

TERRORISM – cover only applies for sum insured on works and plant up to £100,000 total sum insured. If additional cover is required premiums will be quoted.

REBATES

A rebate of the premium will be made as a credit towards the cost of a Buildings and Contents policy for the finished homes arranged by DMS Services Ltd. or its associates if the building work is finished and the new policy arranged

| within 6 months | 10% of the premium paid for basic selfbuild cover |
| within 9 months | 5% of the premium paid for basic selfbuild cover |

Basic selfbuild cover on a home with a £80,000 rebuilding value completed in six months by a selfbuilder living on the site and opting for the increased excess on contract works cover would thus cost only £299 after crediting the rebate.

Public Liability and Employers Liability premiums account for £100 in the premiums below:

INCLUSIVE PREMIUMS

Rebuild Cost Up to £	Premium £	Rebuild Cost Up to £	Premium £
80,000 *(min)*	395	90,000	432
100,000	469	110,000	506
120,000	543	130,000	580
140,000	617	150,000	654

Premiums for larger sums on application
Premiums INCLUDE Insurance Premium Tax

£2 per £100 of value

value £

Cover for £330 each employee, premium £30

£2.50 per £100 of value

value £

Premiums will be quoted after consultation

£52 per £1,000 value of caravan. (Does not include cover for personal possessions)

REVISED LIMIT OF INDEMNITY
£2,500,000   *fixed premium £25*
£5,000,000   *fixed premium £45*
Premiums will be quoted after consultation

If living within 25 metres of the new building deduct 10% from the contract works premium. Refer to 01909 591652 for advice of discounted premium.

If excesses on Sections C, D & F are to be increased to £1000 deduct 10% from contract works premiums. Refer to 01909 591652 for advice of discounted premium.

PREMIUM PAYABLE
(Premiums above are inclusive of Insurance Premium Tax at 4%)

PAYMENT – Please tick as appropriate
☐ Cheque for payment enclosed
☐ Payment to be made by credit card
Card No. ☐☐☐☐ ☐☐☐☐ ☐☐☐☐ ☐☐☐☐ expiry ☐☐ ☐☐

*The **minimum** total premium for Section D, E & F is £250. It is recommended that proposers requiring this cover telephone 01909 591652 to discuss their requirements*

COMPLETED FORMS AND PREMIUMS SHOULD BE SENT TO DMS SERVICES LTD, ORCHARD HOUSE, BLYTH, WORKSOP, NOTTS. S81 8HF
TEL. 01909 591652 FAX. 01909 591031

SELFBUILDERS INSURANCES
PROPOSAL

Guardian
Insurance

Name of proposer: Mr/Mrs/Ms .... Phone number: ....

Full postal address: ....

.... Post Code: ....

Address of property to be insured: ....

....

Name, address and any reference number of any interested party, e.g. Building Society: ....

....

YOUR PROPOSAL

1. Have you made any other proposal for insurance in respect of the risk proposed? **YES/NO**
   If "yes" give details at 10 below.

2. Has any company or underwriter declined your proposal? *If "yes" give details at 10 below.* **YES/NO**

3. Have you been convicted of (or charged but not yet tried with) arson or any offence involving dishonesty of any kind (e.g. fraud, theft, handling stolen goods etc.) *If "yes" give details at 10 below.* **YES/NO**

YOUR PROGRAMME

4(a). Commencing date of insurance ..../........../..........

4(b). Date work commenced if a start has been made on the site? ..../........../..........

4(c). Have there been any incidents on the site which could have given rise to a claim? **YES/NO**
   If "yes" give details at 10 below.

4(d). Target completion date ..../........../..........
   Standard policy is for 15 months.

THE BUILDING

5(a). Is the building a completely new structure? **YES/NO**
   If "no" refer to DMS Services on 01909 591652 or provide details at 10 below.

5(b). State the value of the new building at builders reinstatement cost.
   (The minimum premium is for the value up to £80,000) **£**

5(c). Will the new dwelling have brick or masonry walls with or without a timber frame under a tile or slate roof? **YES/NO**
   If "no" refer to DMS Services on 01909 591652 or provide details at 10 below.

5(d). Will the building qualify for N.H.B.C., Zurich Custombuild or surveyors or architects progress certificates **YES/NO**
   If "no" refer to DMS Services on 01909 591652 or provide details at 10 below.

THE SITE

6. Is the site and any existing building on it subject to any special hazard such as flooding, subsidence or other ground conditions **YES/NO**
   If "yes" give details at 10 below.

7. Do the Planning Consent or Building Regulation Approvals indicate any special requirements or special precautions to be taken in the construction of the building? *If "yes" give details at 10 below.* **YES/NO**

SECURITY

8. Does the proposer intend to live within 25 metres of the new work during the construction period? **YES/NO**
   If "yes" a discount can be claimed on the proposal form opposite

9. Will security arrangements on site be to good standard practice on building sites in the local area? **YES/NO**
   (A limit of £20,000 will apply to unfixed electrical, plumbing, heating, kitchen and bathroom fitments which must be contained in a locked building, hut or steel container whenever left unattended)

SPECIAL CIRCUMSTANCES

10. State the circumstances of any unusual circumstances or other facts which might influence the decision of the insurer when considering this proposal.
   If insufficient space please continue on a separate sheet.

I/we declare that all the work to which this proposal relates will be carried out in accordance with the Building Regulations, and that arrangements for the approval or certification of the works under the regulations will be made before any works are carried out.

I/we declare that to the best of my/our knowledge and belief all the statements and particulars made with regard to this proposal are true and I/we agree that this proposal shall be the basis of the contract of insurance between me/us and Guardian Insurance Ltd. I/we consent to the seeking of information from other insurers to check the answers I/we have provided, and I/we authorise the giving of information for such purposes.

Signature _____ Date _____

COMPLETED FORMS AND PREMIUMS SHOULD BE SENT TO DMS SERVICES, ORCHARD HOUSE, BLYTH, WORKSOP, NOTTS. S81 8HF TEL. 01909 591652 FAX. 01909 591031